The Case-or-Controversy Provision

The Case-or-Controversy Provision

James E. Radcliffe

The Pennsylvania State University Press
University Park and London

41493

Library of Congress Cataloging in Publication Data

Radcliffe, James E
 The case-or-controversy provision.

 Includes bibliography and index.
 1. Judicial power—United States. 2. Political
questions and judicial power—United States. 3. Locus
standi—United States. I. Title.
KF5130.R27 347'.73'1 77-1683
ISBN 0-271-00509-2

Portions of this book copyright 1973 James Edward Radcliffe under the title
*The Case-or-Controversy Provision—How Limited Is the Political Role of the Federal
Courts?*

Designed by Glenn Ruby

Printed in the United States of America

Contents

41493

Preface

According to Article III Section 2 of the United States Constitution, federal judicial power is limited to "cases" or "controversies." This book explores the United States Supreme Court's application of the case-or-controversy provision. The methodology is limited to what the Supreme Court has said or done. The focus is on the case-or-controversy provision's evolution and the federal courts' discretion in determining the presence of a "case" or "controversy."

To date, political scientists have shown little or no interest in the case-or-controversy provision although this provision, assuming that the courts have jurisdiction, controls the inputs into the federal courts. While it is true that the case-or-controversy provision has a legal derivation, it has come to have tremendous political implications. This provision's application determines who may bring what political issue before the federal courts and when judicial power may be invoked. Thus the disciplines of law and political science share an interest in the case-or-controversy provision.

The case-or-controversy provision is analyzed from the perspective of the constitutional context, the intent of the Constitution's framers, the Supreme Court's general application, and commentators' analyses. Each component of a "case" or "controversy" is also analyzed. These include: (1) adversity, (2) sources of legal rights and remedies, (3) the existence of sufficient interest by the parties, (4) the presence of an actual justiciable controversy, and (5) the finality of the federal court's judgment. The relationship between the judicially created doctrines of advisory opinions, standing, ripeness, mootness, and political questions and the case-or-controversy provision is also analyzed. Supreme Court decisions through the 1975–76 term are analyzed.

I wish to express my gratitude to those who assisted me in completing this book. The library staffs at Dickinson Law School, The Pennsylvania State University, and Shippensburg State College were all very helpful and cooperative. Professor Ruth C. Silva provided substantive, editorial, and moral assistance without which this book would never have been completed. Elsa J. Radcliffe provided valuable typing and editorial assistance as well as great patience. Mrs. Nancy Frantz assisted by typing the original manuscript. Mr. John M. Pickering of The Pennsylvania State University Press provided valuable editorial advice. All errors are, of course, the author's responsibility.

A Note Concerning Case Citations

Because of the many Supreme Court cases cited in this book, it has been necessary to alter the usual format for case citations. The only complete citations for cases will be found in the Table of Cases. Page citations for quotations from, or references to, *cases only* are found in parentheses throughout the text. While most case citations are to the *United States Reports,* recent case citations are to the *Supreme Court Reporter* as indicated by the Table of Cases. Sources other than cases are fully cited in the notes.

1 Introduction

Alexis de Tocqueville observed that "[s]carcely any political question arises in the United States that is not resolved, sooner or later, into a judicial question."[1] Although this quotation is justly famous, de Tocqueville's explanation that the judicial power is limited has been virtually ignored.

> [T]he American judge is brought into the political arena independently of his own will. He only judges the law because he is obliged to judge a case. The political question which he is called upon to resolve is connected with the interest of the parties, and he cannot refuse to decide it without abdicating the duties of his post. . . . It is true that upon this system the judicial censureship which is exercised by the courts of justice over legislation cannot extend equally to all laws, in as much as some of them can never give rise to that precise species of contestation which is termed a lawsuit; and even when such a contestation is possible, it may happen that no one cares to bring it before a court of justice.[2]

Over a century later, Professor Bernard Schwartz stated the same thoughts in constitutional terms.

> As a practical matter, the "case" or "controversy" requirement, as it has been construed by the highest bench, has resulted in government by lawsuit as the outstanding characteristic of the American constitutional system. Fundamental constitutional issues are ultimately determined through the technical forms of the lawsuit. . . . It is only when a constitutional issue is presented to it in the form of an action at law or in equity between two adverse parties that a federal court may attempt to dispose of it. No matter how important the issue may be, or how pressing its resolution may be for the nation, its decision by the courts—and ultimately the highest court—must await presentation to them of an actual suit for settlement.[3]

The federal judiciary plays as important a political role today as it did in the nineteenth century. Yet the federal judiciary's political role results from its primarily legal function of deciding "cases" and "controversies." To become a political actor, the federal judiciary must be presented with a "case" or "controversy." This book will attempt to delineate the limitation that the case-or-controversy requirement imposes on the federal judiciary's political role.

The Problem—A Case or Controversy as the Vehicle for Exercising Judicial Power

The United States Constitution establishes separation of powers by granting legislative, executive, and judicial power to the three branches of government. The specificity with which these powers are granted varies greatly. Article I limits Congress to "[a]ll legislative power herein granted." Article III does not place a similar limitation on judicial power: "The judicial power of the United States shall be vested in one Supreme Court, and in such inferior courts as the Congress may from time to time ordain and establish." In *Kansas* v. *Colorado,** the Supreme Court indicated that there are few, if any, limitations on the judicial power.

> By this is granted the entire judicial power of the nation. Section 2, which provides that "the judicial power shall extend to all cases in law and equity, arising under this Constitution, the laws of the United States," etc., is not a limitation nor an enumeration. It is a definite declaration,—a provision that the judicial power shall extend to—that is, shall include—the several matters particularly mentioned, leaving unrestricted the general grant of the entire judicial power. There may be, of course, limitations on that grant of powers, but, if there are any, they must be expressed; for otherwise the general grant would vest in the courts all the judicial power which the new nation was capable of exercising.(82)

Since judicial power is not defined in the Constitution, the Court, as the Constitution's sovereign definer, has assumed this responsibility.

While Article III does not define judicial power, Section 2 does specify that judicial power shall extend to certain classes of "cases" and "controversies." In *Muskrat* v. *United States* the Court defined this grant of power as a limitation:

> [T]he exercise of the judicial power is limited to "cases" and "controversies." Beyond this it does not extend, and unless it is asserted in a case or controversy within the meaning of the

*The number and date of each case discussed in the text can be found in the Table of Cases preceding the index. Page citations for direct quotations from cases will be found in parentheses.

Constitution, the power to exercise it is nowhere conferred. (356)

As Professor Edward S. Corwin suggested, "[t]he meaning attached to the terms 'cases' or 'controversies' determines the extent of the judicial power."[4] Like the term "judicial power," the Constitution does not offer any definition of the terms "cases" or "controversies." The Court has assumed the duty of defining all these terms.

The existence of a "case" or "controversy" is, therefore, a prerequisite to the exercise of the judicial power (see exceptions in text accompanying notes 10–20 *infra*). The role that federal courts play in the American political system is predicated primarily on their exercising judicial power in a "case" or "controversy." The disciplines of law and political science necessarily overlap concerning this significant question. Judicial power is the legal power to determine the rights of individual litigants in a lawsuit. Today, however, few would accept the statement that the federal courts' functions "do not go one step beyond the administration of justice to individual litigants."[5] The federal courts', and particularly the Supreme Court's, role as a political policy maker is well recognized by lawyers as well as by political scientists.[6] The determination of what constitutes a "case" or "controversy" activates judicial power not only to determine the litigants' rights but also to establish public policy. The existence of a "case" or "controversy" is a central question in the field of public law.[7] This is where the disciplines of law and political science merge.

> [T]he generation of public law provides an input for the legal system of which the courts are the major portion. Not all public law matters reach the court as an input, but those which produce resistance and disputation will be fed into the legal system at some time. The overlap of the legal and political systems is often apparent, but nowhere more evident than in the area of public law.[8]

In other words, the same factors determine the inputs into the legal and political systems, since the federal courts perform both legal and political functions.

Although the terms "judicial activism" and "judicial self-restraint" are often applied to the courts' substantive decisions, they are just as applicable to the procedural question of what constitutes a "case" or "controversy."[9] The Supreme Court determines the federal courts' political role to a large extent by how it defines and applies the terms "cases" or "controversies." The extent to which the judicial doors are open to individual litigants will determine, at least partially, the federal courts' political role.

Limitations

Other Aspects of Judicial Power

As the enactment of legislation is central to the exercise of legislative power, the decisions in "cases" or "controversies" are central to the exercise of judicial power. In order to perform their major function, however, both Congress and the federal courts must exercise auxiliary powers. Thus Congress may conduct investigations precedent to enacting legislative power. While the existence of a "case" or "controversy" is central to the exercise of judicial power, the federal courts must also exercise auxiliary judicial powers.[10] That is, the federal courts exercise judicial power precedent and subsequent to deciding a "case" or "controversy." Since no court may decide a case unless it possesses jurisdiction, the judicial power must include the power to determine whether the court has jurisdiction. Also, prior to exercising judicial power in a "case" or "controversy," a federal court must determine whether an actual justiciable "case" or "controversy" exists. For instance, in determining that an actual justiciable "case" or "controversy" did not exist in *Luther* v. *Borden* and *Muskrat* v. *United States,* the Court was exercising judicial power. The Court uses judicial power to define the extent and limitations of judicial power.

The Court has developed rules for judicial self-restraint that are not directly related to the existence of a "case" or "controversy" but relate to the exercise of judicial power in a "case" or "controversy." For example, as Justice Louis D. Brandeis stated in a concurring opinion in *Ashwander* v. *Tennessee Valley Authority*: "The Court will not pass upon a constitutional question although properly presented by the record, if there is also present some other ground upon which the case may be disposed of" (347). Judicial parsimony in deciding a case properly before a federal court is beyond the scope of this study.

The federal courts do not exercise judicial power only in "cases" or "controversies," but the judicial power revolves around the existence of a "case" or "controversy." Yet it remains true that "the most significant and least comprehended limitation upon the judicial power is that this power extends to only 'cases' and 'controversies.' "[11] This study will attempt to partially fill this void, since "procedure is instrumental, it is the means of effectuating policy. Particularly is this true of the federal courts."[12]

Jurisdiction

This study is limited to an analysis of the case-or-controversy provision, but a federal court, like any other judicial tribunal, must possess jurisdiction before it may act. "The proceedings in any court are void if it wants jurisdiction of the case in which it has assumed to act. Jurisdiction is, *first* of the subject-matter; and, *second,* of the persons whose rights are to be passed upon."[13] Thus jurisdiction is a prerequisite to the exercise of judicial power in a "case" or "controversy." Unless otherwise specified, this study will assume that the federal courts possess jurisdiction and will concentrate on the second threshold question, the existence of a "case" or "controversy" (see discussion of federal courts' discretionary jurisdiction in text accompanying notes 4–20 in Chapter 6 *infra*).

Article III, Section 2, establishes the maximum jurisdiction of the federal courts. As to subject matter, the federal courts' jurisdiction extends to cases involving the Constitution, laws of the United States, treaties, admiralty and maritime jurisdiction, and lands granted by one state to citizens of different states. As to parties, the federal courts' jurisdiction is limited to cases affecting ambassadors, public ministers, and consuls; controversies involving the United States; controversies between two or more states or a state and citizens of another state,[14] between citizens of different states and between a state or citizens thereof and foreign states, citizens, or subjects. The federal courts are courts of limited jurisdiction, and before they may exercise judicial power, they must have jurisdiction over one of the subject matters or parties listed by the Constitution.[15]

With the exception of the original jurisdiction granted the Supreme Court by the Constitution, however, the lower federal courts' complete jurisdiction and the Supreme Court's appellate jurisdiction are subject to congressional regulation.[16] With the exception of the Supreme Court's original jurisdiction, a federal court has jurisdiction only if the Constitution specifies the subject matter and parties and if a congressional statute grants jurisdiction within the constitutional limitations. Without jurisdiction, a federal court is powerless to act.

Since the federal courts are courts of limited jurisdiction, they must exercise judicial power to determine whether they may properly entertain a legal action. That is, the federal courts must entertain "jurisdiction to determine jurisdiction."[17] In determining jurisdictional questions, the federal courts may exercise judicial power to declare a congressional enactment void. In *Marbury* v. *Madison,* for example, the Court struck down an attempt to enlarge its original jurisdiction.[18] The Supreme Court may also have to interpret the United States Constitution to determine whether a federal question is involved so that an action may be appealed from a state court. In *Barron* v. *Baltimore,* for example, the Court held that the Fifth Amendment's due process clause did not apply to the states, and therefore the Court did not have jurisdiction since no federal question was involved. A federal court exercises judicial power in determining whether an action is within its limited jurisdiction.

Unfortunately, the distinction between jurisdiction and judicial power has been unnecessarily confused. One leading commentator suggests that "[t]he terms 'judicial power' and 'jurisdiction' are often used synonymously."[19] The Supreme Court increased the confusion in two recent cases, *Baker* v. *Carr* and *Powell* v. *McCormack*. In both cases, the Court suggested that jurisdiction is predicated on the subject matter and parties enumerated in Article III, Section 2, the presence of a "case" or "controversy," and a jurisdictional statute. The first and third requirements are indisputable, but a federal court must possess jurisdiction before it may determine whether a "case" or "controversy" is present. The Court stated the situation succinctly in *Bell* v. *Hood*. "[T]he court must assume jurisdiction to decide whether the allegations state a cause of action on which the court can grant relief as well as to determine issues of facts arising in the controversy" (682).

While it is true that a federal court may not exercise its jurisdiction if a "case" or "controversy" is not present, this does not make the existence of a "case" or "controversy" a jurisdictional question. If a "case" or "controversy" is a jurisdictional question, Congress would have complete control over what constitutes a "case" or "controversy" under its power to determine the lower federal courts' jurisdiction and the Supreme Court's appellate jurisdiction. The Court hardly intended such a conclusion in *Baker* or *Powell*.[20]

Two separate threshold barriers must be surmounted before the full judicial power may be exercised. First, a federal court must determine if it has jurisdiction over the subject matter or parties. Second, the court must determine if a "case" or "controversy" is present. The present study is limited to the second question.

Limited to Federal Courts Created under the Authority of Article III

The case-or-controversy provision applies only to federal courts created under the authority of Article III. Previously, the Court held that certain courts were legislative courts and not constitutional courts, or, more properly, not courts created under Article III but under other congressional authority.[21] Legislative courts are not limited to exercising judicial power under Article III, and therefore the case-or-controversy provision does not apply to them.[22] In *Glidden* v. *Zdanok*, the Supreme Court questioned the entire concept of legislative courts and decided definitely that the Court of Claims and the Court of Patent Appeals are constitutional courts rather than legislative courts. To the extent that legislative courts still exist, they are not limited by the case-or-controversy provision.[23]

Under our federal system, the case-or-controversy provision is not a limitation on the state courts' judicial power. That is, state courts are not limited to deciding "cases" or "controversies" and therefore may give advisory opinions. Although the state judicial systems are beyond the scope of this study, one important and relevant problem does arise. A state court may decide an issue involving a federal question in an action that is not a "case" or "controversy." Beyond this specific problem, the state judicial systems are outside the scope of this study.

Treatment of Cases Discussed

Since this study is concerned only with the input of issues into the federal judicial system, no attempt is made to discuss court decisions *in toto*. That is, the emphasis is only on those factors that determine whether a "case" or "controversy" is present. Since a single opinion may cover several aspects of the case-or-controversy provision, some opinions are discussed under several different topics to illustrate different points.

Cases are discussed from the perspective of the minimum requirements of a "case" or "controversy." For instance, more than two parties are often involved in legal actions, but since the minimum requirement is two adverse parties, cases are discussed in terms of this minimum requirement.[24]

Questions and Hypotheses

The basic question of this book is: What constitutes a "case" or "controversy"? This basic question automatically raises subsidiary questions. Who may institute a "case" or "controversy"? When may a "case" or "controversy" be instituted? Have the necessary prerequisites for a "case" or "controversy" been substantially altered since 1789? What is the relationship between judicially created doctrines of justiciability, such as standing, ripeness, mootness, advisory opinions, and political questions, and the case-or-controversy provision, if any?

The major hypothesis is that the Supreme Court has expanded the concept of "case" or "controversy" since 1789. This is predicated on the fact that, as federal legislative and executive power has grown, the only way anything approaching equilibrium among the three branches of government could be maintained necessitated the growth of judicial power. Since the primary source of judicial power is deciding "cases" or "controversies," one could logically assume that the Court would expand its perception of a "case" or "controversy." As the legislative and executive branches increased the exercise of their power, those who felt deprived by these actions often turned to the judiciary. Also, with the growth of the federal bureaucracy, the federal courts were bound to be presented with issues that did not exist in 1789. As the role of public law has increased in other sectors of the American political system, it would be quite surprising if this did not increase the concept of what constitutes a "case" or "controversy."

As Alexander Hamilton suggested, the federal courts possess neither the power of the purse nor the sword.[25] Consequently, if the federal courts become too involved in the political process, they may lose or lessen their influence.[26] A second basic question is: What discretion do the federal courts exercise in determining whether judicial power shall be exercised in a "case" or "controversy"? The Supreme Court determines the basic scope of judicial power by defining and applying the terms "case" or "controversy." If the Court did this with great specificity, assuming this could be done, the federal courts might be forced to become involved in a political issue that could vitiate their prestige. A subsidiary hypothesis is that the Court has developed malleable rules concerning the existence of a "case" or "controversy" so that the federal courts possess great discretion in determining whether to intervene or to avoid a political issue. In terms of the initial input of a "case" or "controversy," the federal courts exercise significant discretion in determining whether to exercise judicial activism or judicial self-restraint.

Methodology

The methodology employed in this book is dictated by the status of knowledge concerning the case-or-controversy provision. Since this study is exploratory in scope, in the sense of attempting to delineate the application of the case-or-controversy provision and the discretion exercised by the Supreme Court in applying this provision, the emphasis is primarily on what the Court has said. This is not a rejection of any other methodologies but simply an attempt to apply the proper methodology to the subject to be studied. E.g., one could concentrate on specific justices or the Court during a specific time period. These are relevant studies but beyond the present endeavor. As Walter F. Murphy and Joseph Tanenhaus have recently stated:

> We think the value of any research method or mode of analysis lies in its capacity to help provide answers to interesting questions; and it is on this basis that we look at the writings of traditionalists, behavioralists, and those who identify with neither faction.[27]

Since the Supreme Court has the ultimate power to define the United States Constitution, the Court's opinions must be examined to determine the metes and bounds of the case-or-controversy provision. Technically, every time the Supreme Court acts, with the exceptions already noted, it is determining that a "case" or "controversy" exists. One could not conceivably examine every case the Court has decided to determine what the elements of a "case" or "controversy" are. This study is limited, therefore, primarily to what the Supreme Court has said rather than what it has done.

For the same practical reasons, this study does not encompass the lower federal courts' opinions. This does not imply that they are not important, since they too are limited to deciding "cases" or "controversies." In fact, in one instance they have been very instrumental in altering the concept of a "case" or "controversy" (see text accompanying notes 19–22 in Chapter 5 *infra*).

While the major source materials are United States Supreme Court opinions, other sources, both primary and secondary, will be used.[28] In attempting to analyze the case-or-controversy provision, the United States Constitution will be examined first to see what intrinsic aids the Constitution provides. Second, the debates of the Constitutional Convention will be reviewed to see if the framers intended a specific meaning for the case-or-controversy provision. The United States Supreme Court's general interpretation of the case-or-controversy provision will then be reviewed. The secondary sources and their treatment of the case-or-controversy provision will also be examined.

The heart of the study will examine the Supreme Court's treatment of each component of the case-or-controversy provision. This will include examinations of adversity, a sufficient interest in a legal right, the existence of a justiciable controversy, and the court's ability to render a final and binding judgment.

The third portion of the analysis will concentrate on judicially created doctrines of justiciability. In recent years, the Court has often eschewed any discussion of the case-or-controversy provision and has relied on doctrines such as standing, ripeness, mootness, and political questions in order to determine justiciability.

The conclusion will analyze the meaning and application of the case-or-controversy provision and the federal courts' discretion in determining whether a political issue may be presented in the form of a "case" or "controversy." Finally, the relationship between the case-or-controversy provision and the role of the federal courts in the American political system will be analyzed.

2 The Case-or-Controversy Provision

The federal judiciary's role in the American political system is circumscribed by the constitutional provision commonly referred to as the case-or-controversy clause. This provision, Article III, Section 2, sets boundaries for the federal government's judicial power in basically legalistic terms:

> The judicial power shall extend to all cases, in law and equity, arising under this Constitution, the laws of the United States, and treaties made, or which shall be made, under their authority; to all cases affecting ambassadors, other public ministers, and consuls; to all cases of admiralty and maritime jurisdiction; to controversies to which the United States shall be a party; to controversies between two or more states; between a state and citizens of another state; between citizens of different states; between citizens of the same state claiming lands under grants of different states, and between a state or the citizens thereof, and foreign states, citizens or subjects.

Federal judicial power is limited to instances in which a "case" or "controversy" exists. This chapter will pursue the question of what constitutes a "case" or "controversy." If one assumes that jurisdiction exists, what other factors or elements are required before the federal judicial power may be exercised?

The Constitution should first be examined to determine what meaning (if any) the Constitution's phrases may give to "case" or "controversy," since intrinsic aids to interpretation are to be preferred to extrinsic ones.[1] The judicial article's evolution in the Constitutional Convention should then be traced in an attempt to ascertain the intent of the Constitution's framers. The third task will be to study the Supreme Court's interpretation of the case-or-controversy clause. Finally, the commentators' perceptions of the requirement will be reviewed.

Intrinsic Meaning

Looking at the Constitution, one should note first that the judicial power is granted in the Third Article. Although this obvious fact does not help to provide a definition for the case-or-controversy provision, it does place the provision in perspective and indicates certain limitations upon the judicial power. Any power that had been granted in Article I or Article II as part of the legislative or the executive power could not logically also have been granted as part of the judicial power. Although analysis of the legislative or executive power is beyond this study's scope, two examples should show how these may implicitly limit judicial power. Such limitation exists when power that is judicial in nature has been granted in Article I or II. The most obvious example, in Article I, Sections 2 and 3, is congressional power relating to impeachment. If this power had not been specifically granted to Congress and if this power were still assumed to exist, the logical conclusion would be that this power is part of the judicial power as a case arising under the Constitution. (This is supported by Article III, Section 2, wherein the third clause excepts "cases of impeachment" from the guarantee of trial by jury in criminal cases.) The other type of limitation is less obvious but more important. This is the type of limitation that has led, at least partially, to the formulation of the political questions doctrine. All of the factors necessary to create a "case" or "controversy" may be present, but since the Constitution has explicitly or implicitly granted a coordinate branch of the federal government the power to decide the issue on which the dispute before the Court turns, the Court will refrain from hearing the issue. The determination of when or whether a war has ended is one illustration. These two examples show that the case-or-controversy provision must be read in the context of the entire Constitution, and that judicial power may be limited by the Constitution's granting power to the legislative or executive branch.

If one examines the wording of the first clause in Article III's second section, no clue to the specific meaning of either "case" or "controversy" is found, although the different ways that the terms are used should be noted. The three times that "cases" are mentioned, the word is preceded by the adjective "all," but this adjective is not used to modify "controversies." This clause suggests that the federal judicial power may be all-inclusive in respect to the three categories of cases, but extends only to some (but not necessarily all) of the controversies listed. When the clause is examined in context, however, this conclusion becomes questionable. Before any court may try a "case" or "controversy," it must possess jurisdiction over the parties or subject matter. Since the only jurisdiction that the Constitution directly vests is the Supreme Court's original jurisdiction, in Article III, over "all cases affecting ambassadors, other public ministers and consuls, and those in which a state shall be a party," Congress was left with the power of determining when and to what extent the other instances of "cases" or "controversies" could be brought within the reach of federal judicial power.[2] No "case" or "controversy" may be heard under the Supreme Court's appellate jurisdiction or by the lower federal courts until Congess has granted jurisdiction. Theoretically, Congress could refrain from granting any federal court jurisdiction in admiralty and maritime cases. If it did so, the term "all" would be a nullity. Conversely, there is no limitation on congressional power to grant jurisdiction in the controversies enumerated. Congress could grant the federal courts jurisdiction in all controversies between citizens of different states. The conclusion must be that the inclusion of the word "all" before "cases" and not before "controversies" is not significant.

The first time that the term "cases" is mentioned, it is modified by the terms "in law and equity." This is obviously not an attempt to distinguish between "cases" and "controversies" but to describe the federal court's jurisdiction. It would be difficult to contend that the extension of the judicial power to controversies between states was to be in actions at law but not in equity, since such disputes would usually entail the exercise of equity power. The only logical conclusion is that the equitable power of the federal courts extends to all of the "cases" and "controversies" enumerated.

The final question that arises is whether there is any evident intrinsic difference between "cases" and "controversies." The term "controversy" is used only to describe the extension of the judicial power to disputes in which jurisdiction is predicated upon the parties, while the term "cases" is used to describe the invocation of such power when jurisdiction results either from the issues or from the parties. The term "cases" is, therefore, used in a more comprehensive sense than is "controversies." It could be suggested that "controversies" is used as a less technical term since it relates only to the parties involved. But the second section's second clause, in Article III, vitiates any such thesis.

> In all cases affecting ambassadors, other public ministers and consuls, and those in which a state shall be a party, the Supreme Court shall have original jurisdiction. In all the other cases before mentioned, the Supreme Court shall have appellate jurisdiction both as to law and fact, with such exceptions, and under such regulations as the Congress shall make.

In describing the Supreme Court's original and appellate jurisdiction, the Constitution does not use the term "controversies," but uses the term "cases" to refer to all the situations described in the preceding clause. More specifically, in describing the Supreme Court's original jurisdiction, "those in which a state shall be a party" refers back to "cases" and possibly even to "all cases." One might argue that appellate jurisdiction was intended to be limited only to the other two classes of cases mentioned in the preceding clause, but this interpretation would exclude appellate jurisdiction in controversies to which the United States is a party. Since the term "cases" is used to include situations previously described as "controversies" in the provision for the Supreme Court's original jurisdiction, however, it would follow that the term is used in the same comprehensive sense in the provision for the Supreme Court's appellate jurisdiction. Therefore, there seems to be no intrinsic difference between the terms, other than that "cases" is used in a more comprehensive sense than is the term "controversies."

The Constitution itself provides no real definition of "cases" or "controversies." Therefore, it is necessary to examine the debates in the Constitutional Convention to see what the framers may have meant by "cases" and "controversies."

The Framers' Intent

One caveat should be mentioned before commencing a discussion of the case-or-controversy clause's genesis. As the previous chapter emphasizes, this analysis is concerned with judicial power. Federal judicial power may be exercised only when a "case" or "controversy" exists. But before a court may take any action it must possess jurisdiction over the parties and/or subject matter. Jurisdiction must exist before judicial power may be exercised. The Constitution's framers used the terms "jurisdiction" and "judicial power" almost interchangeably.[3] Thus many quotations cited in this section use the word "jurisdiction."

The case-or-controversy provision's evolution during the Convention of 1787 reveals little about the meaning of this important phrase. Edmund Randolph's plan, submitted on the third day of the Convention, described the power to be exercised by the judiciary:

> That the jurisdiction of the inferior tribunals shall be to hear and determine, in the first instance, and of the supreme tribunal to hear and determine, in the *dernier resort,* all piracies and felonies on the high seas; captures from an enemy; cases in which foreigners, or citizens of other states, applying to such jurisdiction, may be interested, or which respect the collection of the national revenue, impeachments of any national officers, and questions which may involve the national peace and harmony.[4]

The term "cases" is used only in the instances of foreigners or citizens of other states attempting to invoke the proposed national judiciary's power. It could be assumed that "cases" was implied in all instances except the last, i.e., "questions which may involve the national peace and harmony." This last phrase was consistent with the broad grant of powers that the Virginia Plan would have conferred upon the national government. Exactly how judicial power would have been exercised in "questions [involving] . . . national peace and harmony" is purely an academic question, since the Convention deleted provision for such jurisdiction. Nevertheless, it would be difficult to argue that such language was intended to greatly restrict the national judiciary's power or jurisdiction, or that it necessarily limited the judicial branch to traditional cases at law.

On June 13, during the Committee of the Whole's consideration of Randolph's proposal, the Committee unanimously agreed to eliminate the entire definition of jurisdiction and to concentrate on the federal judiciary's organization. Randolph and James Madison then moved to reinsert the latter part of the deleted sentence in the following words:

"[T]hat the jurisdiction of the national judiciary shall extend to cases which respect the collection of the national revenue, impeachments of any national officers, and questions which involve the national peace and harmony."[5]

The Committee of the Whole accepted this. Again, the phrase "questions which involve the national peace and harmony" would seem to imply a broad grant of jurisdiction. There is evidence, however, that the phrase "questions which involve the national peace and harmony" was used for tactical purposes only. Robert Yates's *Notes* indicate that on June 13:

Gov. Randolph observed the difficulty in establishing the power of the judiciary—the object however at present is to establish this principle, to wit, the security of foreigners where treaties are in their favor, and to preserve the harmony of states and of the citizens thereof. This being once established, it will be the business of a sub-committee to detail it.[6]

Relying on a letter written by Madison in 1833, Charles Warren makes the same inference.[7] In any event, the proposal adopted on June 13 became the thirteenth resolution reported to the Convention by the Committee of the Whole.

When the Convention took up the Committee's report and after unreported criticisms of the thirteenth resolution had been made, Madison proposed and the Convention unanimously agreed to the following description of the national courts: "That the jurisdiction shall extend to all cases arising under the national laws, and to such other questions as may involve the national peace and harmony."[8] The jurisdiction was thus extended to "all cases" arising under the national laws and still referred to "questions," but "jurisdiction in cases of impeachments" was deleted. Madison's proposal was contained in the sixteenth resolution submitted to the Committee of Detail. The only significant difference was that the word "all" had been removed for some inexplicable reason not shown in the debates.[9]

The Convention referred its twenty-one resolutions, along with Charles Pinckney's and William Patterson's proposals, to the Committee of Detail although these latter proposals had not been discussed either by the Convention or by its Committee of the Whole. The portion of each proposal dealing with judicial power is important because the final report of the Committee of Detail relied more heavily on these than on the Convention's thirteenth resolution. On May 29, Pinckney had proposed:

> The legislature of the United States shall have the power, and it shall be their duty, to establish such courts of law, equity, and admiralty, as shall be necessary.
>
> One of these courts shall be termed the supreme court; whose jurisdiction shall extend to all cases arising under the laws of the United States, or affecting ambassadors, other public ministers and consuls; to the trial or impeachment of officers of the United States' to all cases of admiralty and maritime jurisdiction. In other cases of impeachment[,] affecting ambassadors, and other public ministers this jurisdiction shall be original; and in all other cases appellate.[10]

Pinckney would have given the Senate power to settle certain disputes between states. "They [the Senate] shall have the exclusive power to regulate the manner of deciding all disputes and controversies now existing, or which may arise, between states, respecting jurisdiction or territory."[11]

Patterson presented his plan to the Convention on June 15 after the Committee of the Whole had presented its twenty-one resolutions, and proposed in part:

> That a federal judiciary be established, to consist of a supreme tribunal. . . . That the judiciary so established shall have authority to hear and determine, in the first instance, on all impeachments of federal officers, and, by way of appeal, in the dernier resort, in all cases touching the rights of ambassadors; in all cases of captures from an enemy; in all cases of piracies and felonies on the high seas; in all cases in which foreigners may be interested; in the construction of any treaty or treaties, or which may arise on any of the acts for regulation of trade, or the collection of the federal revenue.[12]

Patterson's plan appended to the official journal also provided: "Resolved, that Provision ought to be made for hearing and deciding upon all disputes arising between the United States and Individual States respecting Territory.""[13] This proposal, however, was not part of Patterson's plan for the judiciary but was a completely separate resolution.[14]

This was the raw material with which the Committee of Detail had to work. This committee consisted of John Rutledge of South Carolina, Edmund Randolph of Virginia, Nathaniel Gorham of Massachusetts, Oliver Ellsworth of Connecticut, and James Wilson of Pennsylvania. Little is known or reported of its actual work. Max Farrand does, however, reproduce two undated documents relating to the Committee's operation. The first, allegedly written by Randolph with insertions by John Rutledge, spelled out the federal judicial power in these terms:

7. The jurisdiction of the supreme tribunal shall extend:

1. to all cases arising under laws passed by the general [legislature].

2. to impeachments of officers, and

3. to *such* other cases, as the national legislature may assign, as involving the national peace and harmony.

in the collection of the revenue

in the disputes between citizens of different states

[in disputes between a State and a Citizen or Citizens of another State]

in disputes between different states; and

in disputes, in which subjects or citizens of other countries are concerned [and in Cases of Admiralty Jurisdn]

But this supreme jurisdiction shall be appellate only except in [Cases of Impeachment and (in)] those instances, in which the Legislature shall make it original. and the legislature shall organize it.

8. The whole or part of the jurisdiction aforesaid according to the discretion of the legislature may be assigned to the inferior tribunals, as original tribunals.[15]

Farrand also reproduces a draft in James Wilson's handwriting with Rutledge's emendations. This draft appears to be the result of the Committee's deliberations. The only material difference between Wilson's draft and the proposed jurisdictional section submitted to the Convention was that Wilson's did not include "controversies between two or more states."[16]

The proposal submitted by the Committee of Detail read:

The jurisdiction of the supreme court shall extend to all cases arising under the laws passed by the legislature of the United States; to all cases affecting ambassadors, other public ministers and consuls; to the trial of impeachments of officers of the United States; to all cases of admiralty and maritime jurisdiction; to controversies between two or more states, (except such as shall regard territory or jurisdiction;) between a state and citizens of another state; between citizens of different states; and between a state, or the citizens thereof, and foreign states, citizens, or subjects. In cases of impeachment, cases affecting ambassadors, other public ministers and consuls, and those in which a state shall be party, this jurisdiction shall be original. In all other cases before mentioned, it shall be appellate, with such exceptions, and under such regulations, as the legislature shall make. The legislature may assign any part of the jurisdiction above mentioned, (except the trial of the President of the United States,) in the manner and under the limitations which it shall think proper, to inferior courts as it shall constitute from time to time.[17]

The derivation of most of this proposal is not difficult to ascertain. With only insignificant changes, the first portion, with its reference to controversies, was borrowed from Pinckney's plan submitted on May 29. The substance of the remainder can be traced directly to Randolph's memorandum with Rutledge's emendations that was submitted to the Committee of Detail. More indirectly, this can be traced to Randolph's original plan.[18]

What is not clear is why the term "cases" was used in the proposal's first portion but "controversies" was used in the second. In Randolph's memorandum to the Committee of Detail, he had used the terminology "disputes." The only previous reference to controversies was in Pinckney's proposal, quoted in text accompanying note 10 *supra*, to permit the Senate to settle "disputes and controversies" between states "respecting jurisdiction or territory." Acceptance of this recommendation by the Committee of Detail explains the reason for the exception noted concerning controversies between two or more states.[19] Why the Committee adopted this terminology for part of the judiciary article and why they omitted the word "all" before controversies seems inexplicable. The latter could be explained by the Committee's reliance on Pinckney's proposal, which did use the word "all" before cases, but even here the Committee inserted "all" before "cases affecting ambassadors," although Pinckney had not.

After the Committee of Detail's original report, Pinckney submitted several proposals that were in turn submitted to the Committee without debate or consideration in the Convention. Among these proposals was one that stated: "The jurisdiction of the Supreme Court shall be extended to all controversies between the United States and an individual state."[20] With the exception of the word "all," the Committee accepted Pinckney's proposal and amended their original report to include it, but failed to explain the deletion of "all."[21]

Dr. William S. Johnson suggested the next change in the proposal concerning the federal courts' jurisdiction when he moved that "both in law and equity" be inserted in the proposed judicial article's first section. By a vote of six to two, Johnson's motion was accepted.[22]

This change occurred on August 27, the only day when the entire Convention really discussed the judiciary article. Madison moved, Gouverneur Morris seconded, and the Convention unanimously voted to replace Pinckney's language with the phrase "to which the United States shall be a party."[23] The next change was important:

> Dr. JOHNSON moved to insert the words "this Constitution and the" before the word "laws."
>
> Mr. MADISON doubted whether it was not going too far, to extend the jurisdiction of the court generally to cases arising under the Constitution, and whether it ought not to be limited to cases of a judiciary nature. The right of expounding the Constitution, in cases not of this nature, ought not to be given to that department.
>
> The motion of Dr. Johnson was agreed to, *nem. con.*, it being generally supposed that the jurisdiction given was constructively limited to cases of a judiciary nature.[24]

This is the closest the Convention came to an actual discussion of the meaning of "case" or "controversy." Just what would be a "case of a judiciary nature" arising under the Constitution was not explained. Two other changes that were proposed shortly after Dr. Johnson's altered the first six words of the jurisdictional paragraph. The term "the judicial power" was substituted for "the jurisdiction of the supreme court," the phrase "passed by the legislature" was dropped, and "and treaties made or which shall be made under their authority" was added after "United States." The only other pertinent change made on August 27 was that controversies should include those "between citizens of the same state claiming land under grants of different states."[25]

On August 27, the Convention voted to postpone the question of whether impeachment should be within the Supreme Court's jurisdiction. A special committee on postponed matters later recommended that this power be given to the Senate.[26] Despite Madison's objection, the Convention accepted this change so that impeachment trials were excluded from the Supreme Court's jurisdiction.[27] The Convention also decided that territorial controversies between states should be decided by the judiciary, and this overruled the Committee of Detail, which would have exempted such from the Court's jurisdiction in controversies between two or more states.[28]

These were the provisions submitted to the Committee on Style, and the Committee's only important change was that the phrase "in law and equity" was more properly placed in the section describing the federal courts' jurisdiction than in the section describing the judiciary's structure, tenure, and compensation.[29]

The Constitutional Convention's debates throw little light on the meaning of the case-or-controversy provision. They do indicate, however, what was not to be included in the federal court's jurisdiction. The Randolph Plan proposed a Council of Revision composed of "a convenient number of national judiciary"[30] and the executive. This council was to examine every federal statute before the statute became operative. On June 4, 1787, the Convention eliminated the judiciary's participation in the exercise of this power.[31] Despite several attempts to reinstate the provision, it was rejected.[32] Although various reasons were given for excluding the judiciary from participating in the exercise of this power, the basic reason was that the power of revision was thought to be an executive rather than a judicial power. Thus the federal judiciary was not to have a general power of revision over the legislature.

But exactly what did the framers have in mind when they used the terms "case" or "controversy"? The closest the Convention came to answering this question was the general response to Madison's inquiry about whether the judicial power would be limited to cases of a judicial nature. It might be suggested that the Convention had in mind such cases as had been considered properly "judicial" in the states, the colonies, and in England, as Justice Felix Frankfurter has suggested.[33] If this were true, the federal courts could hand down advisory opinions, but they cannot.[34] Moreover, the legal issues raised by a written constitution were unknown in England and had existed in the states for only a short time. Furthermore, the federal system raised questions for which there were no precedents. Pinckney originally proposed that controversies between states be considered part of the legislative rather than judicial power. The courts have generally adopted the legalistic view, however, that what constituted a case in law or equity in 1787 was what the framers intended to include in the case-or-controversy provision. It may have been that the framers thought the legalistic view to be self-evident, or on the other hand, that they never realized the judiciary's future political importance.

Judicial Interpretation of the Case-or-Controversy Provision

The federal judiciary, here meaning only those courts created under Article III, may exercise judicial power only when a "case" or "controversy" is before the court. Therefore, each time a federal court renders a decision, it is helping to determine the meaning of "case" or "controversy." Courts' opinions tend to emphasize the resolution of the substantive question, however, and usually assume the existence of a "case" or "controversy" *sub silentio*. The United States Supreme Court has come to grips with these terms in only a few instances. This paucity of judicial explication has led one observer to conclude: "Under the Federal Constitution, the courts of the U.S. can render decisions only in 'cases' and 'controversies.' However, these terms inherently are capable of many varying interpretations and have never been defined authoritatively."[35] Justice Felix Frankfurter asserted that the presence of a "case" or "controversy" could be ascertained only by "the expert feel of lawyers" (see note 33 *supra*). Although these statements carry an element of truth, the Court has indicated certain factors that must be present before a "case" or "controversy" exists. The Court's interpretation of what constitutes a "case" or "controversy" will be examined in this section.

It should be mentioned first that the omission of "all" before "controversies" has not been significant (see text accompanying note 2 *supra*). One opinion suggests that under the rule that every word in the Constitution must be given its full force and effect, the inclusion of "all" before "cases" must have some relevance. The example given was that the judicial power obviously does not extend to "all controversies" involving the United States (*Williams* v. *United States* 572–73), since the sovereign cannot be sued without its consent. Another opinion suggests that the omission of "all" before "controversies" gives Congress greater control in defining the controversies to which the judicial power of Article III courts may extend (*Stevenson* v. *Fain* 197). Other than these two suggestions that jurisdiction over "cases" is more extensive than over "controversies," the omission of "all" before "controversies" has had no real impact on the exercise of judicial power. These two instances appear to be aberrations, since the Court otherwise has ignored the distinction.

The Court has also treated the terms "cases" and "controversies" as synonymous. In *Chisholm* v. *Georgia,* Justice James Iredell suggested that "controversies" is more restrictive than "cases."

> The act of Congress more particularly mentions civil controversies, a qualification of the general word in the constitution, which I do not doubt every reasonable man will think well warranted, for it cannot be presumed that the general word, "controversies" was intended to include any proceedings that relate to criminal cases, which in all instances that respect the same government only, are uniformly considered of a local

nature, and to be decided by its particular laws. The word "controversy" indeed, would not naturally justify any such construction.[36] (431–32)

Justice Stephen J. Field cited Iredell's statement as authority in a circuit court opinion when he suggested: "The term 'controversies' if distinguishable at all from 'cases,' is so in that it is less comprehensive than the latter and includes only suits of a civil nature" (In re *Pacific Railway Commission* 255). Chief Justice Charles Evans Hughes quoted Field's suggested distinction without comment in a 1937 opinion (*Aetna Life Insurance Co. v. Haworth* 239). The Court has made no other attempts to distinguish between the two terms. If the distinction is valid, and this is questionable, since the framers of the Constitution did not indicate any such intention, it has had no real impact on the Court's interpretation of these terms. Therefore the ensuing discussion will treat the terms "cases" and "controversies" as synonymous.

The case-or-controversy provision was not discussed *in toto* in *Marbury* v. *Madison*. One particular element was stressed, however, as was the concept's importance to judicial review. Chief Justice John Marshall emphasized the direct nexus between the existence of a "case" and the judiciary's exercise of constitutional review:

> So if a law be in opposition to the Constitution; if both the law and the Constitution apply to a particular case, so that the court must either decide the case comfortably to the law, disregarding the Constitution; or comfortably to the Constitution, disregarding the law; the Court must determine which of these conflicting rules governs the case. This is of the very essence of judicial duty. (177)

The opinion stressed that judicial power is exercised in "cases."

> The judicial power of the United States is extended to all cases arising under the Constitution.

> Could it be the intention of those who gave this power, to say that in using it the Constitution should not be looked into? That a case arising under the Constitution should be decided without examining the instrument under which it arises? (178–79)

Marshall's major argument for judicial review concerned exercising judicial power in "cases."

Since the Court decided that it lacked jurisdiction in *Marbury*, it is technically true that Marshall's discussion of the existence of a "case" is *obiter dicta*. If the Court lacked jurisdiction, the question of justiciability was not properly before it. Marshall's discussion is worth noting, however, since one element of a "case" was analyzed in detail. After arguing that Marbury had a right to his commission as a justice of the peace in the District of Columbia, Marshall asked the rhetorical question: "If he has a right and that right has been violated, do the laws of this country afford him a remedy?"(162). Marshall then quoted Blackstone: "that when there is a legal right, there is also a legal remedy." The opinion suggests that the United States could hardly be considered a "government of law, and not of men . . . if the laws furnish no remedy for this violation of a vested legal right"(163). Marshall noted exceptions, however, to the general rule of no legal right without a legal remedy. One involves a loss without a legal injury or *damnum absque injuria*. An appointment to an office of trust, honor, or profit could never fall into this category according to Marshall's opinion. The other exception involves separation of powers. Executive action may invade a legal right, but if the act is constitutionally within the President's discretion, he cannot be held accountable before a judicial tribunal. However, this did not apply to Marbury, Marshall contended, since the commission's delivery was a ministerial act and did not involve discretion. The Court concluded that Marbury's claim was the proper basis for a "case." "This [judicial] power is expressly extended to all cases arising under the laws of the U.S., and consequently, in some form, may be exercised over the present case; because the right claimed is given by a law of the U.S."(173–74). A case arises when a legal right has been violated unless there is a loss without legal injury or the loss results from discretionary action within the executive's power. *Marbury* discloses two necessary but complementary elements of a "case"—a violation of a legal right and the existence of a remedy—the latter to be assumed unless proven otherwise (see discussion of legal rights and legal remedies in Chapter 4 *infra*).

Marshall's opinion suggests one other problem. A "case" exists if a legal right has been violated. This appears to be purely a procedural question, i.e., a federal court has no power to act unless a legal right has been violated. Yet the substantive question, at least in part, was whether Marbury had a legal right to the commission. The existence of a "case" is a necessary prerequisite in order to exercise judicial power, but it is possible that this threshold question cannot be answered without adjudicating, at least partially, the substantive issue.

According to Marshall, a "case" is the traditional lawsuit. One party has been legally injured and is attempting to gain redress against the person directly responsible. The only new aspect added by the Constitution is whether separation of powers makes the executive immune from suit in certain instances.

Chief Justice Marshall again discussed the case-or-controversy provision in *Cohens* v. *Virginia*. This case was concerned primarily with the Supreme Court's jurisdiction over appeals of criminal convictions from a state court. Virginia argued that a "case" could arise under the Constitution or a federal law only when a plaintiff demanded something conferred on him by the Constitution or a federal statute. In other words, the United States Supreme Court could not hear an appeal by a defendant convicted in a state criminal action because no "case" arose under the Constitution or a federal statute. The Court held: "A case in law or equity consists of the right of the one party, as well as of the other and may truly be said to arise under the Constitution or a law of the U.S., whenever its correct decision depends on the construction of either"(379).

More importantly, Marshall accepted the contention that there might be violations of the United States Constitution that would not lend themselves to judicial scrutiny, e.g., a state's violation of Article I Section 9's prohibition against granting a patent of nobility. Marshall suggested that such instances would result only when a "case" is not present:

> Although they [Virginia] show that there may be violations of the Constitution of which the courts can take no cognizance, they do not show that an interpretation more restrictive than the words themselves import ought to be given to this article. They do not show that there can be "a case in law or equity" arising under the Constitution, to which the judicial power does not extend.(405)

In *Osborn* v. *Bank of the United States,* in which the major issue was the federal court's jurisdiction over actions of state officials, Chief Justice Marshall again emphasized the necessity of a "case." He did not add anything, however, to his previous descriptions except the manner of instituting a "case."

> The [judicial] power is capable of acting only when the subject is submitted to it by a party who asserts his rights in the form prescribed by law. It then becomes a case, and the Constitution declares that the judicial power shall extend to all cases arising under the Constitution, laws, and treaties of the U.S.(819)

A decision handed down in 1842 illustrates how the case-or-controversy provision's interpretation may involve current social controversies. *Prigg* v. *Pennsylvania* concerned extradition proceedings in which Pennsylvania had refused to extradite a fugitive slave under the Federal Fugitive Slave Act. Justice Joseph Story delivered the Court's opinion holding that the extradition proceeding included the necessary elements of a "case."

> It is plain then, that where a claim is made by the owner, out of possession, for the delivery of a slave, it must be made, if at all, against some other person; and inasmuch as the right is a right of property capable of being recognized and asserted by

proceedings before a court of justice, between parties adverse to each other, it constitutes in the strictest sense a controversy between the parties, and a case "arising under the Constitution" of the U.S., within the express delegation of judicial power given by that instrument. (616)

Story stressed the existence of a legal right as Marshall had done, but added the emphasis of a "right of property." Story made explicit what Marshall seems to have implied—the parties must be adverse.

These early decisions show how the Court discussed the concept of a "case" without offering any concrete definition. Marshall emphasized the importance of legal rights and legal remedies in *Marbury*. Story stressed property rights and adversity in *Prigg*. *Cohens* indicated that some constitutional violations might not constitute a "case." This was the extent, however, of the Court's pronouncements on what constitutes a "case" or "controversy" during the Court's first ninety years. The Court emerged as an important participant in the political process, yet at the time, there seems to have been little question that the Court was exercising traditional judicial functions and that its political impact was an incidental result of deciding *bona fide* "cases" or "controversies." The major exception was *Marbury*, and even here the basic dispute was over Marshall's *dictum*.[37]

We find greater emphasis on what constitutes a "case" or "controversy" beginning in the late nineteenth century. In 1880, in *Tennessee v. Davis*, the Court reiterated Marshall's definition in *Cohens* and stressed that Article III Section 2 covers criminal as well as civil cases. The first instance of the justices' disagreeing about the existence of a justiciable case occurred two years later, in *United States v. Lee*. In an ejectment action against federal officials, a federal jury returned a verdict for the plaintiffs who were contesting the confiscation of the Lee estate, and the Supreme Court upheld the judgment in a 5–4 decision. Justice Samuel F. Miller declared in the majority opinion:

> In the *case* supposed the court has before it a plaintiff capable of suing, a defendant who has no personal exemption from suit and a cause of action cognizable in the Court—a *case* within the meaning of that term as employed in the Constitution and defined by the decisions of this court.(219)

For the minority, Justice Horace Gray contended "that the Court had no authority to proceed to trial and judgment." Gray did not phrase his opinion in "case" or "controversy" terms, but his arguments partially involved this provision. He contended that the Court could not take judicial cognizance of the action because it has "no authority to render a judgment on which it has no power to issue execution." Gray asserted that the federal agents were only temporarily in possession of the property and could be replaced at any time. Thus the judgment's execution would have to be against the United States. The Government's agents are not immune from suit, but the sovereign is. In "case" or "controversy" terms, Gray is saying two things: as instituted, the action was not a proper "case" because the Court could not execute its judgment. Secondly, the agents were not, but the United States itself was, the proper adverse party. Since the United States is immune from suit, a "case" did not exist. Thus ideas of proper parties and execution of judgment were added to the earlier concepts of adverse parties and protection of a legal right, albeit by a dissenting opinion.

In 1885 the Supreme Court held that a factual situation before it did not constitute a "case." A Virginia bondholder obtained a federal circuit court injunction restraining Virginia's tax collectors from refusing to receive the coupons on his bonds for tax payments. The complainant did not allege and it did not appear that he was a Virginia taxpayer. Justice Stanley Matthews stated for the Court:

> The bill as framed, therefore, calls for a declaration of an abstract character, that the contract set out requiring coupons to be received in payment of taxes and debts due to the state is valid. . . . But no court sits to determine questions of law *in thesi*. There must be a litigation upon actual transactions between real parties, growing out of a controversy affecting legal or equitable rights as to person or property. All questions of law arising in such cases are judicially determinable. The present is not a case of that description. (*Marye* v. *Parsons* 329–30)

No one had presented the coupons nor was the bondholder in a position to present them, so that the litigation presented a hypothetical situation. Although the Court ruled that a "case" did not exist, its definition of "case" was the most comprehensive offered up to that time.

Two years later, in a circuit court opinion, Justice Stephen J. Field examined the case-or-controversy provision. After suggesting a possible distinction between the two terms, he stated:

> By cases and controversies are intended the claims of litigants brought before the courts for determination by such regular proceedings as are established by law or custom for the protection or enforcement of rights, or the prevention, redress, or punishment of wrongs. Whenever a claim of a party under the constitution, laws, or treaties, of the U.S. takes such a form that the judicial power is capable of acting upon it, then it has become a case. The term implies the existence of present or possible adverse parties whose contentions are submitted to the court for adjudication. (In re *Pacific Railway Commission* 255)

Field offered a fairly comprehensive definition of "cases" or "controversies." The allusion to "possible" adversity is, however, an aberration. The Supreme Court has consistently insisted upon present adversity (see *contra, Tutun* v. *United States*). Field later inferred a distinction between a "case" and an action for a writ of habeas corpus.[38] This, however, has not been accepted by the Supreme Court either. An action for a writ of habeas corpus has consistently been treated as a "case" within the requirements of Article III (see text accompanying note 1 in Chapter 4 *infra*).

In 1889, Justice Field repeated his previously quoted definition, this time in a Supreme Court opinion.[39] Significantly, he did not repeat his suggestion of "possible" adversity. Nor did he make any distinction between a "case" and an action for a writ of habeas corpus.

Chicago & Grand Trunk Railway v. *Wellman* is an interesting decision from the perspective of a "case" or "controversy." The Michigan courts had entertained a suit challenging the constitutionality of legislatively enacted railroad rates. The Michigan Supreme Court had affirmed a judgment holding the United States Constitution had not been violated by the statute. For a unanimous United States Supreme Court, Justice David J. Brewer asserted that no "case" or "controversy" was present because the suit was collusive, i.e., both parties desired the statute to be declared unconstitutional, and this was the only reason for the action's being instituted. The Court held that "an honest and actual antagonistic assertion of rights by one individual against another" was not present. Courts can exercise judicial power only "as a necessity in the determination of [a] real, earnest, and vital controversy between individuals"(344–45). Brewer portrayed the Court's role by proclaiming: "It never was thought that by means of a friendly suit a party beaten in the legislature could transfer to the courts an inquiry as to the constitutionality of the legislative Act"(345).

The most interesting aspect concerning *Wellman* is that the lower court's decision was affirmed. The United States Supreme Court did not attempt to explain how it could render a decision when a "case" did not exist. Brewer had emphasized that the sole issue before the Court was whether the trial court had erred in refusing to declare the Act unconstitutional as a matter of law. Nevertheless, the question remains how the Court could render a decision if there was no "case" present.

Interstate Commerce Commission v. *Brimson* illustrates the expansion of governmental activity and the resulting expansion of the case-or-controversy concept in the late nineteenth century. The ICC appealed a federal circuit court's decision dismissing a petition that had sought the court's aid in requiring testimony of witnesses and the production of documents, books, and papers at a hearing before the Commission.

The Supreme Court held the action had been improperly dismissed, since a "controversy" involving federal statutes existed (the Act of 1887 creating the ICC as amended) and the courts could render a conclusive judgment. The first Justice John Marshall Harlan explained the situation:

> Is it not clear that there are here parties on each side of a dispute involving given questions of legal rights, that their respective positions are defined by pleadings, and that the customary forms of judicial procedure have been pursued? The performance of the duty which according to the contention of the government, rests upon the defendant cannot be enforced except by judicial process.(487)

This was not the business of the courts at Westminster, so that it does not seem possible that the framers envisioned such a "case." It was inevitable, however, as independent regulatory commissions emerged, that judicial power would be invoked to assist them in performing their functions.

In 1911 the Court handed down an opinion that partially summarizes its previous discussion of the case-or-controversy provision. In *Muskrat* v. *United States,* a statute, enacted in 1907 and granting the Court of Claims original jurisdiction and the Supreme Court appellate jurisdiction, was held to be unconstitutional. Congress had enacted legislation in 1902 allocating lands and funds belonging to certain Cherokee Indians, but altered this original allocation by laws passed in 1904 and 1906. In 1907, Congress enacted a law giving certain grantees under the Act of 1902 the right to test the validity of the subsequent enactments. The opinion is a landmark in the area of justiciability but a controversial one.[40] For present purposes, one should note that Justice William R. Day's opinion, for a unanimous Court, is an example of judicial overkill. He goes to great length to show that every element of a "case" is absent, although the absence of any one element would have been sufficient to decide the action. The opinion does provide, therefore, a detailed analysis of the case-or-controversy requirement.

After reviewing earlier opinions concerning jurisdiction and judicial power, Day emphasized:

> [B]y the express terms of the Constitution, the exercise of the judicial power is limited to "cases" and "controversies." Beyond this it does not extend, and unless it is asserted in a case or controversy within the meaning of the Constitution, the power to exercise it is nowhere conferred.(356)

Judicial power "is the right to determine actual controversies arising between adverse litigants, duly instituted in courts of proper jurisdiction"(361).

Justice Day contended that the suit before the Court lacked every conceivable element of a "case" or "controversy."

This attempt to obtain a judicial declaration of the validity of the act of Congress is not presented in a "case" or "controversy," to which, under the Constitution of the United States, the judicial power alone extends. It is true the United States is made a defendant to this action, but it has no interest adverse to the claimants. The object is not to assert a property right as against the government, or to demand compensation for alleged wrongs because of action upon its part. The whole purpose of the law is to determine the constitutional validity of this class of legislation, in a suit not arising between parties concerning a property right necessarily involved in the decision in question, but in a proceeding against the government in its sovereign capacity, and concerning which the only judgment required is to settle the doubtful character of the legislation in question. Such judgment will not conclude private parties, when actual litigation brings to the court the question of the constitutionality of such legislation. In a legal sense the judgment could not be executed, and amounts in fact to no more than an expression of opinion upon the validity of the acts in question. Confining the jurisdiction of this court within the limitations conferred by the Constitution, which the Court has hitherto been careful to observe, and whose boundaries it has refused to transcend, we think the Congress, in the act of March 1, 1907, exceeded the limitations of legislative authority, so far as it required of this Court action not judicial in its nature within the meaning of the Constitution.(361–62)

The Court held, therefore, that the action was tantamount to a request for an advisory opinion.

If such actions as are here attempted, to determine the validity of legislation, are sustained, the result will be that this court, instead of keeping within the limits of judicial power, and deciding cases or controversies arising between opposing parties, as the Constitution intended it should, will be required to give opinions in the nature of advice concerning legislative action,— a function never conferred upon it by the Constitution, and against the exercise of which this court has steadily set its face from the beginning.(362)

Not leaving out any possible objections, the Court also suggested that collusion might have existed.

If *Muskrat* is viewed from the perspective of the elements of a "case" or "controversy," one finds that four factors are stressed. These are: (1) the existence of an actual controversy (2) between adverse litigants (3) involving a property (legal) right (4) concerning which the court may render and carry out a final judgment.[41] The Court found all four elements lacking.

Since *Muskrat,* the Court has struggled to apply these basic requirements to factual situations. One of the Court's biggest problems has been the question of execution when a dispute is presented in the form of a declaratory judgment. A declaratory judgment's purpose is to establish the parties' rights and make a binding declaration concerning such rights, but not to grant any immediate relief; therefore, no execution of the judgment is required. The Court's dilemma is illustrated by its apparent vacillation in three cases decided in 1927 and 1928. In *Liberty Warehouse Co.* v. *Grannis,* the petitioner attempted to obtain a declaratory judgment against the constitutional validity of a Kentucky statute. There was no evidence of prosecution, although it was alleged prosecution was about to be initiated. A federal district court had sustained a demur, and the Supreme Court upheld this ruling. Justice Edward T. Sanford summarized, for the Court, the necessary elements of a "case." He then emphasized that judicial power "does not extend to the determination of abstract questions or issues framed for the purpose of invoking the advice of the Court without real parties or a real case"(74). Sanford concluded that federal courts have no jurisdiction to entertain a declaratory judgment petition.[42]

In 1927 the Court spoke approvingly, however, of declaratory actions in *Fidelity National Bank & Trust Co. of Kansas City* v. *Swope.* Kansas City had brought an action against property owners in a district that was deemed to be benefited by the construction of a boulevard and therefore subject to a special assessment. The district's boundaries had been determined by the city council, and a county court upheld the ordinance as valid in a declaratory judgment action. Later the Bank became the holder of tax bills, and appellees brought a new action to have the tax bills canceled. For a unanimous Court, Justice Harlan F. Stone held that all the elements of a "case" were present in the original declaratory judgment action.

> The issues presented and the subject matter are such that the judicial power is capable of acting upon them. There is no want of adverse parties necessary to the creation of a controversy. . . . The judgment is not merely advisory. . . . It operates to determine judicially the legal limits of the benefit district and to define rights of the parties in lands specifically described in the pleadings. . . .
>
> That the judgment is binding on the parties and their

privies and hence not open to collateral attack would seem to be the only reasonable construction of the statute.(134)

A year later, however, in *Willing* v. *Chicago Auditorium Association,* the Court declared: "What the plaintiff seeks is simply a declaratory judgment. To grant that relief is beyond the power conferred upon the Federal judiciary"(288). The declaratory judgment procedure was rejected not because of lack of execution but because: "No defendant has wronged the plaintiff or has threatened to do so"(290). The plaintiff was the lessee of property on which he wished to raze an auditorium and construct an office building. The lessor asserted that this action would violate the lease, so that the lessee had brought the action to determine his rights under the lease. For the Court, Justice Louis D. Brandeis indicated that every element of a "case" was present except injury to a legal right.

> It is true that this is not a moot case, . . . the matter which it is here sought to have determined is not an administrative question; that the bill presents a case, which if it were the subject of judicial cognizance would in form come under a familiar head of equity jurisdiction; . . . a final judgment might be given; . . . the parties are adverse in interest; . . . there is no lack of a substantive interest of the plaintiff in the question which it seeks to have adjudicated; . . . the alleged interest of the plaintiff is here definite and specific; and that here there is no attempt to secure an abstract determination by the Court of the validity of a statute. . . . But still the proceeding is not a case or controversy within the meaning of Article 3 of the Constitution. The fact that the plaintiff's desires are thwarted by his own doubts, or by the fears of others, does not confer a cause of action.(289–90)

Justice Stone concurred in the result but rejected Brandeis's contention that a declaratory judgment action did not constitute a "case."

In 1933 the Supreme Court upheld a state declaratory judgment statute in *Nashville, Chattanooga & St. Louis Railway Co.* v. *Wallace.* Justice Harlan F. Stone asserted, for a unanimous Court, that the real question is "the nature of the proceedings which the statute authorizes, and the effect of the judgment rendered upon the rights which the appellant asserts" and not mere form or the labels that may be attached to the proceeding (259). The Railway Company had sought a declaratory judgment against an excise tax on the storage of gasoline and appealed the Tennessee Supreme Court's adverse decision. Stone emphasized that all the necessary elements of a "case" or "controversy" were present: adverse parties, a legal right which was threatened with imminent invasion, and the fact that the Court's decision would be final and not subject to revision by another governmental branch. The Court concluded that if an injunction had been sought, there would be no question of justiciability, and therefore the action should not be considered nonjusticiable simply because it was commenced as a declaratory judgment. The "case" or "controversy" element that appeared to be missing was execution of judgment. Stone argued that "such relief is not an indispensable adjunct to the exercise of the judicial function"(262). He noted that the Court had entertained actions involving border disputes between states, naturalization appeals, determination of matrimonial status, instructions to trustees or executors, and bills of interpleader by stakeholders, none of which required execution of judgment. Stone concluded:

> The issues raised here are the same as those which under old forms of procedure could be raised only in a suit for an injunction or one to recover the tax after its payment. But the Constitution does not require that the case or controversy should be presented by traditional forms of procedure, invoking only traditional remedies. The judicial clause of the Constitution defined and limited judicial power, not the particular method by which that power might be invoked. It did not crystallize into changeless form the procedure of 1789 as the only possible means for presenting a case or controversy otherwise cognizable by the federal courts. Whenever the judicial power is invoked to review a judgment of a state court, the ultimate constitutional purpose is the protection, by the exercise of the judicial function, of rights arising under the Constitution and laws of the United States. The states are left free to regulate their own judicial procedure. Hence changes merely in the form or method of procedure by which federal rights are brought to final adjudication in the state courts are not enough to preclude review of the adjudication by this Court, so long as the case retains the essentials of an adversary proceeding, involving a real, not a hypothetical controversy, which is finally determined by the judgment below.(264)

The *Nashville Railway* case did not determine, however, the federal judiciary's original jurisdiction over declaratory judgments. In 1934 Alabama attempted to invoke the Supreme Court's original jurisdiction to prevent Arizona from enforcing a statute prohibiting the sale of convict-made goods. In *Alabama* v. *Arizona,* Justice Pierce Butler announced, for the Court, that: "This court may not be called on to give advisory opinions or to pronounce declaratory judgments"(291). This decision also illustrates how case-or-controversy requirements may be applied differently in various factual situations. The Court indicated that its jurisdiction over controversies between states could be invoked only in instances of "absolute necessity."

> [N]ot every matter of sufficient moment to resort to equity by one person against another would justify an interference by this Court with the action of a state. . . . The burden upon the plaintiff state fully and clearly to establish all essential elements of its case is greater than that generally required to be borne by one seeking an injunction in a suit between private parties.(291)

The federal judiciary's original jurisdiction over declaratory judgment actions was established by *Aetna Life Insurance Co.* v. *Haworth* in 1937, when the Court upheld the Federal Declaratory Judgment Act.[43] Haworth had discontinued payment on four Aetna life insurance policies, alleging that he had become totally and permanently disabled, and therefore, under the policies' terms, he was no longer required to pay premiums. The company countered that Haworth was not totally and permanently disabled, and therefore the policies had lapsed. The insurance company desired to know whether it would be required to make payments under the policies sometime in the future. A unanimous Court found all the necessary elements of a "case" present: "There is here a dispute between parties who face each other in an adversary proceeding. The dispute relates to legal rights and obligations arising from the contracts of insurance. The dispute is definite and concrete, not hypothetical or abstract"(242).

Chief Justice Charles Evans Hughes discussed the Declaratory Judgment Act and the case-or-controversy provision. He stressed that the Act was specifically limited to "cases of actual controversy," and held that Congress had used this terminology to refer to the case-or-controversy provision (239–40). He concluded that the Act is limited to controversies in the constitutional sense, since Congress had used the word "actual" as one of emphasis only. The Court held that the declaratory judgment is procedural and therefore within congressional power to control the federal courts' jurisdiction. As in *Nashville Railway*, the Court declared the federal judiciary is not limited to procedures known in 1789. The Court did admit, *sub silentio*, that the declaratory judgment might be related more directly to the case-or-controversy doctrine than it suggested explicitly. Hughes held that Congress is limited to neither traditional forms nor traditional remedies in granting jurisdiction. However, legal remedies help determine the existence of a legal right, which is a basic element of a "case." The Court was saying, albeit implicitly, that Congress may have an impact on the case-or-controversy concept by creating new remedies.

Hughes gave the following summation of the case-or-controversy doctrine.

A "controversy" in this sense must be one that is appropriate for judicial determination. . . . A justiciable controversy is thus distinguished from a difference or dispute of a hypothetical or abstract character; from one that is academic or moot. . . . The controversy must be definite and concrete touching the legal relations of parties having adverse legal interests. . . . It must be a real and substantial controversy admitting of specific relief through a decree of a conclusive character, as distinguished from an opinion advising what the law would be upon a hypothetical state of facts. . . . Where there is such a concrete case admitting of an immediate and definitive determination of the legal rights of the parties in adversary proceedings upon the facts alleged, the judicial function may be appropriately exercised although the adjudication of the rights of the litigants may not require the award of process or the payment of damages. . . . And as it is not essential to the exercise of the judicial power that an injunction be sought, allegations that irreparable injury is threatened are not required.(240–41)

Although this description has been criticized for using "elastic labels,"[44] Hughes did add slightly to the definition proferred in *Muskrat*. In *Aetna*, the Court found (1) a legal right—the liability of the insurance company; (2) in dispute in an actual controversy—whether the policies were still in force; (3) which affected the legal relations of adverse parties; (4) and that the Court was capable of making a definite determination of legal rights. *Aetna* altered the case-or-controversy concept, as discussed in *Muskrat*, by eliminating the necessity of execution of judgment. *Muskrat* emphasized that a court's decision must result in some type of enforcement action. "In a legal sense the judgment could not be executed, and amounts in fact to no more than an expression of opinion upon the validity of acts in question"(362). The *Aetna* Court held: "[T]he judicial function may be appropriately exercised although the adjudication of the rights of the litigants may not require the award of process or payment of damages"(241). The earlier action involved the constitutionality of statutes while *Aetna* involved the determination of private rights, but one can hardly assert that the definition of a "case" varies with the issue involved.

Since *Aetna*, the Court has not offered a comprehensive analysis of the case-or-controversy provision. This is not to suggest that the requirement has become less important. Actually, the opposite is true. Since *Aetna*, however, the Court has concentrated primarily on the provision's specific elements.

Other than Justice Frankfurter's subjective definition offered in three concurring opinions, i.e., a "case's" existence can be known only to the expert feel of a lawyer (see note 33 *supra*), only four recent decisions are worth noting for their discussion of the case-or-controversy concept. In 1945 the Court held that Illinois' refusal to admit an individual to practice law constituted a "case."

> A case arises within the meaning of the Constitution, when any question respecting the Constitution, treaties or laws of the United States have assumed "such a form that the judicial power is capable of acting on it" *Osborn* v. *Bank of the United States*, 9 Wheat. 738. . . . A declaration on rights as they stand must be sought not on rights which may arise in the future . . . and there must be an actual controversy over an issue, not a desire for an abstract declaration of the law. . . . The form of the proceeding is not significant. It is the nature and effect which is controlling. (In re *Summers* 566)

The issue presented for adjudication was an alleged present legal right to admission to the bar. The Court held that a denial of that right was a "controversy" within the meaning of Article III.

Since immediacy has become a question of paramount concern, a decision involving a New York civil rights statute is significant (*Railway Mail Assoc.* v. *Corsi*). The statute prohibited any labor organization from denying any person membership because of race, color, or creed. The labor union involved had an article in its constitution restricting membership to Caucasians and native American Indians. Justice Stanley Reed argued for the court that the plaintiff was "faced with the threat of enforcement of the statute" although it apparently had not yet been enforced. The Court held that this constituted a "case."

> Prior to the consideration of the issues, it is necessary to determine whether appeal from this state court declaratory judgment proceeding presents a justiciable "case or controversy" under sections 1 and 2 of Article III of the federal Constitution. We are of the opinion that it does. The conflicting contentions of the parties in this case as to the validity of the state statute presents a real substantial controversy between parties having adverse legal interests, a dispute definite and concrete, not hypothetical or abstract. Legal rights asserted by appellant are threatened with imminent invasion by appellees and will be directly affected to a specific and substantial degree by decision of the question of law.(93)

As the Court indicated, all the prerequisites established by *Muskrat* and *Aetna* were present. This case is illustrative, however, of the additional issue that is created by declaratory judgments. The petitioner's legal rights had not yet been invaded, but a statute existed that threatened invasion. If the judiciary exercises its discretionary power to grant a declaratory judgment, the legal right concept is expanded to include threatened as well as actual invasions.

Poe v. *Ullman,* one in a series of Supreme Court actions involving the Connecticut anticontraception statute, also concerned the problem of immediacy. Justice Frankfurter's plurality opinion came to the conclusion that the issue was not "ripe" for judicial determination. In a dissenting opinion, however, the second Justice John Marshall Harlan summarized much that had been said about the case-or-controversy provision. In discussing the need for "exigent adversity" and "a policy against premature constitutional decision," he said:

> The policy referred to is one to which I unreservedly subscribe. Without undertaking to be definitive, I would suppose it is a policy the wisdom of which is woven of several strands: (1) Due regard for the fact that the source of the Court's power lies ultimately in its duty to decide, in conformity with the Constitution, the particular controversies which come to it, and does not arise from some generalized power of supervision over state and national legislatures; (2) therefore it should insist that litigants bring to the Court interests and rights which require present recognition and controversies demanding immediate resolution; (3) also it follows that the controversy must be one which is in truth and fact the litigants' own, so that the clash of adversary contest which is needed to sharpen and illuminate issues is present and gives that aid on which our adjudicatory system has come to rely; (4) finally, it is required that other means of redress for that particular right claimed be unavailable, so that the process of the Court may not become overburdened and conflicts with other courts or departments of government may not needlessly be created, which might come about if either those truly affected are not the ones demanding relief, or if the relief we can give is not truly needed.(525)

Justice Harlan's four points are significant because they articulate the principles that have generally been applied in order to determine whether a "case" exists. Harlan's statement makes explicit what must be assumed in any discussion of the case-or-controversy provision. The requirement cannot be considered a mere legal technicality, since it partially determines the role that the federal judiciary is to play in the American political system. How the Court defines and applies the terms "cases" and "controversies" affects the scope of that role.

The terms "case" and "controversy" were also discussed by Chief Justice Earl Warren in *Flast* v. *Cohen,* which provides an apt quotation with which to close this study of the Court's attempts to define these elusive terms.

The jurisdiction of the federal courts is defined and limited by Article III of the Constitution. In terms relevant to the question for decision in this case, the judicial power of federal courts is constitutionally restricted to "cases" and "controversies." As is so often the situation in constitutional adjudication, those two words have an iceberg quality, containing beneath their surface simplicity submerged complexities which go to the very heart of our constitutional form of government. Embodied in the words "cases" and "controversies" are two complementary but somewhat different limitations. In part those words limit the business of federal courts to questions presented in an adversary context and in a form historically viewed as capable of resolution through the judicial process. And in part those words define the role assigned to the judiciary in the tripartite allocation of power to assure that the federal courts will not intrude into areas committed to the other branches of government. Justiciability is the term of art employed to give expression to this dual limitation placed upon federal courts by the case and controversy doctrine.(94–95)

The case-or-controversy provision's evolution is indicated by the Harlan and Warren quotations. In the nineteenth century, the phrase was viewed in almost purely legalistic terms. As the political role of the federal courts, and especially that of the United States Supreme Court, has increased, the phrase's definition and application has come to have tremendous implications. Whether the Court is pursuing a policy of judicial activism or self-restraint may be apparent from the manner in which the Court is defining or applying the terms "case" or "controversy."

A "case" or "controversy" must exist before judicial power may be exercised. Therefore, the federal judiciary may exercise its most important power, constitutional review, only when a "case" or "controversy" exists. In fact, the federal courts cannot rule on a patent violation of the United States Constitution unless the issue is presented in such a "case."

The preceding discussion also indicates the elements the Supreme Court has held are necessary to create a "case" or "controversy." An actual dispute must exist when the action is initiated and the dispute must be between adverse parties. The adverse parties must be contesting a legal right (or attempting to prevent a legal wrong) and the federal court must be able to render a final and binding decision concerning the disputed legal right. If these four elements are present, a

"case" or "controversy" is before the court. It is easier to determine the
necessary elements, however, than it is to apply them. The succeeding
chapters will examine each element's application.

This analysis has also suggested important trends in the Court's
treatment of the case-or-controversy provision. Until late in the nineteenth century, the Court discussed the doctrine in only a few opinions,
while from 1880 to 1937 there was extensive discussion of this requirement. Since 1937 the Court has been preoccupied with applying the
provision and has shied away from any extensive discussion of "case" or
"controversy." In this latter period, the Court has been more concerned with judicially created doctrines than with the constitutional
requirement, although these doctrines are all directly related to the
case-or-controversy provision.

The adaptation of the case-or-controversy doctrine is shown by the
eventual acceptance of the declaratory judgment action. Although the
Court refers to this action as a "mere form of procedure," it has altered
the case-or-controversy concept by eliminating the necessity of execut-
ing a judgment. The declaratory judgment action also permits a "case"
to be commenced earlier, since potential and not actual injury is all that
need be shown. Despite the Court's inference, it is not tantamount to
an action seeking an injunction, since one seeking a declaratory judgment need not show irreparable harm. The case-or-controversy concept has not been a static one but a dynamic one.

One final observation should be made concerning the Court's interpretation of the case-or-controversy provision. Since the Court usually discusses the issue when some doubt is raised about the existence of
a "case" or "controversy," the phrase is ordinarily perceived as a limitation on the federal judiciary's role in the American political system. As
Chief Justice Marshall suggested in *Cohens* v. *Virginia,* however, it is also
a positive grant of power.

> It is most true that this Court will not take jurisdiction if it
> should not; but it is equally true, that it must take jurisdiction if
> it should. The judiciary cannot, as the legislature may, avoid a
> measure because it approaches the confines of the Constitution.
> We cannot pass it by because it is doubtful. With whatever
> doubts, with whatever difficulties, a case may be attended, we
> must decide it, if it be brought before us. We have no more
> right to decline the exercise of jurisdiction which is given, than
> to usurp that which is not given. The one or the other would be
> treason to the Constitution.[45](404)

One must bear in mind, therefore, that once a federal court is properly
presented with a "case" or "controversy," theoretically it must act no
matter what the political implications may be. (Marshall's conclusion is,

however, stated too absolutely. See discussion of discretionary power over jurisdiction in Chapter 6 *infra*.) The Court emphasized this point in *Baker* v. *Carr*.

> The doctrine of which we treat is one of "political questions," not one of "political cases." The courts cannot reject as "no law suit" a bona fide controversy as to whether some action denominated "political" exceeds constitutional authority.(217)

Marshall did not use the terminology "political cases," but by 1962 Justice William J. Brennan apparently had no qualms about readily admitting that the terms "case" and "controversy" might be categorized as political as well as legal in nature. The judiciary may be "the least dangerous branch," but technically it is the only branch of the federal government that may not be able to ignore a political issue.

Commentators' Perception of the Case-or-Controversy Provision

As one reviews the literature concerning the case-or-controversy provision, one finds the same trend as in the Court's opinions—a movement from the assumption that the meaning is self-evident to a realization that the provision does have the iceberg effect Chief Justice Warren suggested in *Flast* v. *Cohen*. The assumption that the terms are self-explanatory was indicated as early as the debate on the Constitution's adoption. Although Alexander Hamilton frequently used the term "case" in four Federalist Papers discussing the proposed judiciary's jurisdiction and authority, he never proffered a definition.[46] At one point, he did infer the possibility that the federal judiciary might not be limited to the traditional legal case. In *Federalist* No. 80, Hamilton asserted "that there ought always to be a constitutional method of giving efficacy to constitutional provisions."[47] He emphasized the limitations placed on the states and argued that these limitations had to be enforced. Hamilton pointed out that the Constitutional Convention chose judicial enforcement rather than a direct congressional negative on state laws.

> What, for instance, would avail restrictions on the authority of the State legislatures, without some constitutional mode of enforcing the observance of them? The States, by the plan of the convention, are prohibited from doing a variety of things, some of which are incompatible with the interests of the Union, and others with the principles of good government. The imposition

of duties on imported articles, and the emission of paper money, are specimens of each kind. No man of sense will believe, that such prohibitions would be scrupulously regarded, without some effectual power in the government to restrain or correct the infractions of them. This power must either be a direct negative on the State laws, or an authority in the federal courts to overrule such as might be in manifest contravention of the articles of Union. There is no third course that I can imagine. The latter appears to have been thought by the convention preferable to the former, and, I presume, will be most agreeable to the States.[48]

Later Hamilton returned to this topic when he discussed the extension of the judicial power to all cases arising under the Constitution and the laws of the United States.

It has been asked, what is meant by "cases arising under the Constitution," in contradistinction from those "arising under the laws of the United States?" The difference has been already explained. All the restrictions upon the authority of the State legislatures furnish examples of it. They are not, for instance, to emit paper money; but the interdiction results from the Constitution, and will have no connection with any law of the United States. Should paper money, notwithstanding, be emitted, the controversies concerning it would be cases arising under the Constitution and not the laws of the United States, in the ordinary signification of the terms. This may serve as a sample of the whole.[49]

Hamilton suggested that every constitutional provision should be enforced—especially restrictions on state power. Exactly what he meant by the term "controversies" in the above quotation is difficult to ascertain. Read in conjunction with the earlier quotations, it could mean any dispute or question, since the federal courts rather than Congress were by implication given power to overrule state actions manifestly in contravention of the Constitution. Read in conjunction with his further discussion of judicial authority, the term "controversies" could be used synonymously with cases. Since Hamilton did not go into detail on how such a "case" might arise, it is impossible to draw any definite conclusion.

Otherwise, Hamilton discussed "cases" as the traditional lawsuit. For instance, in discussing equitable actions he said:

What equitable causes can grow out of the Constitution and laws of the United States? There is hardly a subject of litigation between individuals, which may not involve those ingredients of *fraud, accident, trust,* or *hardship,* which would render the matter an object of equitable rather than of legal jurisdiction, as the distinction is known and established in several of the States.[50]

He was obviously referring to the traditional private law action. With the exception previously noted, Hamilton used the terms "case" or "controversy" as though everyone should know their meaning. Exactly what new "cases" or "controversies" might be created by the existence of a written constitution and the establishment of a federal system were not explained.

Commentators showed little interest in the case-or-controversy provision during the nineteenth century. Two Supreme Court justices, however, did discuss the terms in extrajudicial writings. The views Justice Joseph Story expressed in *Prigg* v. *Pennsylvania* were echoed in his writings on the case-or-controversy provision.

Another inquiry may be, what constitutes a *case* within the meaning of this clause? It is clear that the judicial department is authorized to exercise jurisdiction to the full extent of the Constitution, laws, and treaties of the United States, whenever any question respecting them shall assume such a form that the judicial power is capable of acting upon it. When it has assumed such a form, it then becomes a case; and then, and not till then, the judicial power attaches to it. A case, then, in the sense of this clause of the Constitution arises when some subject touching the Constitution, law, or treaties of the United States is submitted to the courts by a party who asserts his rights in the form prescribed by law. In other words, a case is a suit in law or equity, instituted according to the regular course of judicial proceedings; and when it involves any question arising under the Constitution, laws, or treaties of the United States, it is within the judicial power confided to the Union.[51]

In his *Lectures on the Constitution,* Justice Samuel F. Miller examined judicial power in detail. "Before there can be any proper exercise of it [judicial power] a 'case' must be presented in the court for its action. A case implies parties, an assertion of rights, or a wrong to be remedied."[52] In discussing the public's apparent misunderstanding of judicial power, particularly as it is related to the United States Supreme Court's determination of a statute's constitutionality, Miller continued his definition of a "case."

But it has been over and again held by that court [United States Supreme Court], that all it can do in that regard is to decide such questions as involve a construction of its provisions, and only those when they are brought before it in a suit between proper parties. In some cases these parties have been very dignified ones. The United States and great States have appeared before its bar, but in the great majority of cases, where it has been called upon to construe the Constitution of the United States, it has been a conflict between individuals, where-in the validity of some law, or the determination of some right asserted by one party and denied by the other, must be settled by the authority of this great fundamental charter. So this court only does, in its higher position as the last court to which such cases can be brought, what every other court in the United States has to do, whether it be a State or Federal court. It only decides such cases as arise in the progress of ordinary litigation.[53]

Miller asserted that proper parties must be before the court, that there must be a conflict over a legal right, and that the court must be able to settle the conflict on the basis of legal authority. He assumed that judicial power would be exercised only in cases that "arise in the progress of ordinary litigation."

Miller continued with a unique argument.

This extension of power over all cases is, however, qualified by the words immediately following: "in law and equity." These cases must be in law or in equity, with the exception of admiralty, as to which there is a separate clause further on in the section. Under this provision an attempt has been made to exclude a very large class of cases arising in the state and other courts, which were of an anomalous character. Some actions where remedies were given by peculiar modes of proceedings, by summary proceedings, by attachment, and others at variance with the common law, were said not to be suits at law, and yet did not come under any head of equity jurisprudence. But the decisions of the Supreme Court of the United States are abundant to the effect that, with the exception of admiralty, all modes of procedure for the assertion of rights must be arranged under the one class or the other, either law or equity, within the meaning of this clause.[54]

The quotation is interesting because Miller seemed to be arguing, in the late nineteenth century, that it is not the procedure that produces a case but the assertion of a right. If what he said was true, it is impossible to comprehend why the Supreme Court refused to accept the declaratory judgment procedure until 1933. Furthermore, a literal reading of Miller's argument would mean that the United States Supreme Court would have to accept whatever a state determines to be a "case" or "controversy." If a state gave a remedy to a state taxpayer and permitted him to assert a constitutional right, the Supreme Court could not rule that a "case" or "controversy" did not exist. This is not the situation, however.

Present-day commentators place less emphasis on what constitutes a "case" or "controversy" than on what results in their absence. Since the purpose of this chapter is to examine attempts to define the case-or-controversy provision, discussion concerning the nonexistence of a "case" will be reserved for the following chapters. One example of this negative approach should suffice for the present. A *Harvard Law Review* description in 1927 declared:

> The Supreme and inferior courts of our federal system have with rigidity refused to act unless a case or controversy in which the judicial power could be exercised was presented. Collusive suits, moot cases, advisory functions and political questions are all without the scope of the judicial power. Beyond these situations the principles are not so clearly defined.[55]

Despite this trend, a few contemporary studies do discuss the necessary elements of a "case" or "controversy." The *Harvard Law Review* article cited above did suggest that the criteria for determining a "case" or "controversy" included interested parties, adverse claims, rights of the litigants, and the necessity that the finding be final.[56] In commenting on *Muskrat* v. *United States,* Professor Edwin Borchard suggested: "The case . . . lacked every element of a justiciable controversy, adversary parties, a plaintiff or defendant adequately interested, and personal or property rights, private or public, which would be definitely affected."[57]

Justice Robert H. Jackson and Professor Bernard Schwartz have suggested legally oriented interpretations of the case-or-controversy provision. Jackson commented: "The result of the limitation is that the Court's only power is to decide lawsuits between adversary litigants with real interests at stake, and its only method of proceeding is by the conventional judicial, as distinguished from legislative or administrative process."[58] Schwartz contended:

> The result of the constitutional restriction is that the federal bench's sole power is to decide lawsuits between opposing litigants with real interests at stake, and its only method of proceeding is by the conventional, judicial process. . . . The nature of the action challenged, the kind of injury inflicted, and the relationship between the parties must be such that judicial determination is consonant with traditional exercise of the judicial function.[59]

Three other scholars have offered fourfold criteria for determining the existence of a "case" or "controversy." Professor Louis L. Jaffe's criteria were:

(1) the presence before the court of two or more adverse parties, (2) a contest as to their respective rights or duties or both, (3) an adjudication by the application of relatively firm principles characteristically presumed to exclude the exercise of broad discretion and (4) a decision not subject to subsequent revision by the executive or legislature.[60]

Professor C. Herman Pritchett has indicated that for a dispute to take the form of a "case" or "controversy," "(1) it must involve *adverse parties,* (2) who have a substantial *legal interest* (3) in a controversy growing out of a *real set of facts* (4) which admits of an *enforceable determination* of the legal rights of the parties."[61] In analyzing *Muskrat,* Professor Edward S. Corwin found that the Court emphasized four necessary elements: (1) adverse litigants, (2) adverse interests, (3) actual controversies, and (4) conclusiveness or finality of judgment.[62] It is interesting to note, however, that Corwin subdivided his ensuing discussion into adverse litigants, substantial interests, and abstract, contingent and hypothetical questions, advisory opinions, and declaratory judgments.

Commentators have added little to our knowledge of the case-or-controversy provision. Until the twentieth century, practically no interest was shown in this important provision. In the present century the interest has seldom gone beyond a cursory examination and this has usually been limited to an examination of *Muskrat* v. *United States* and *Aetna Life Insurance Co.* v. *Haworth*.

Summary—The Case-or-Controversy Provision

The federal judicial power extends to "cases" or "controversies," but one has difficulty ascertaining the meaning of these terms by use of intrinsic aids to interpretation. The United States Constitution provides no definition. The most that one can determine from the Constitution is that limitations on what constitutes a "case" or "controversy" may result from Articles I and II. One can also deduce from the Constitution that the use of the word "all" before "cases" and not before "controversies" is not significant and the terms "case" and "controversy" are used synonymously.

The Constitutional Convention provides even less help in determining the meaning of "case" or "controversy" in Article III Section 2. The wording of the section was predicated upon proposals that were not discussed in the Committee of the Whole or on the Convention floor. The Committee of Detail, about whose proceedings there is no record, played the largest role in formulating the case-or-controversy provision. The closest the Convention came to discussing the provision was on August 27, 1787, when Madison raised doubts about extending jurisdiction to cases arising under the Constitution, but the general consensus was "that the jurisdiction given was constructively limited to cases of a judiciary nature." Exactly what would be "cases of a judiciary nature" under a written constitution that established a division of power between a central government and the states was not explained.

Since neither the Constitution nor the Constitutional Convention defined the terms "case" or "controversy," it is not surprising that the task has been assumed by the sovereign definer of the Constitution, the United States Supreme Court. Throughout most of the nineteenth century, the Court was only tangentially concerned with these terms. As attempted access to the courts grew, the Court was forced to elaborate on the terms. This culminated in two cases, *Muskrat* v. *United States* and *Aetna Life Insurance Co.* v. *Haworth,* which have come to stand for the basic definition of these terms. Commentators have added little to our knowledge since they have been forced to rely almost wholly on the Court's elaboration of the provision.

The established requirements include adversity, parties with an interest in a disputed legal right, the existence of an actual justiciable controversy, and a federal court's ability to render a final and binding judgment. Although there may be differences of opinion concerning the exact appellation of these four requirements, the preceding discussion of the Court's interpretation of the case-or-controversy provision makes it evident that these are the general requirements. The fact remains that these four elements are merely the tip of the suggested iceberg. The elements do not suggest anything more than the traditional private common law action.[63] Yet few can deny that the federal courts, and particularly the United States Supreme Court, have come to play a vital political as well as legal role within the American political system. This role can be ascertained only by exploring the underwater portion of the iceberg and examining the way in which these four elements have been applied.

If the facts presented to a federal court indicate the presence of adversity, parties with an interest in a disputed legal right, an issue susceptible to adjudication at the present time, and if the court's decision will be final, a case theoretically exists. Both the Court and the commentators have often treated these requirements as mechanical provisions.[64] The implication is that the courts simply insert the facts into the four necessary slots, and if each criterion is met, a "case" is present. In fact, however, the federal courts exercise a great deal of discretion in determining whether each element is present. Just as a "case" or "controversy" is what the Supreme Court says is a "case" or "controversy," each of the elements may or may not be found present depending on how stringently a federal court applies the requirement in that particular instance. When a federal court wishes to avoid an issue, it may apply the criteria rigorously, but when a federal court wishes to decide an action, it may adjust the slots so that the requirements are met. The United States Supreme Court has never defined the terms "case" or "controversy"; it has simply established four criteria that must be met before a "case" or "controversy" is present. In applying these criteria, the federal courts may indicate whether they are pursuing a policy of judicial activism or judicial self-restraint.

Although the specific requirements of a "case" or "controversy" will be analyzed separately, one should not assume that the components are in any way mutually exclusive. The absence of one element may automatically result in the absence of other elements. If adverse parties are not present, an issue susceptible to adjudication at the present time may not be present.[65] All four elements—adversity, parties with an interest in a disputed legal right, an issue susceptible to adjudication at the present time, and finality—are interrelated. They should be analyzed separately, however, to show their respective relationship to the existence of a "case" or "controversy" and the federal courts' discretion in determining the existence of each element.

3 Adversity

One may use the term "adversity" in many different contexts. In 1927, a commentator stated that "[t]he first essential of a case or controversy is that there be interested parties asserting adverse claims."[1] Justice Felix Frankfurter, in a concurring opinion in *Joint Anti-Fascist Refugee Committee* v. *McGrath,* used the concept in several different contexts.

> The simplest application of the concept of "standing" is to situations in which there is no real controversy between the parties. Regard for the separation of powers . . . and for the importance to correct decision of adequate presentation of issues by clashing interests . . . restricts the courts of the United States to issues presented in an adversary manner. A petitioner does not have standing to sue unless he is "interested in and affected adversely by the decision" of which he seeks review. . . . *Braxton County Court* v. *West Virginia,* 208 U.S. 192, 197.(151)

Thus one finds the terms "adverse claims," "issues presented in an adversary manner," and "affected adversely by the decision." Adversity has therefore been used to describe the issues, the parties, and the impact of the decision. This study will use adversity to describe the relationship between the parties. For a "case" or "controversy" to exist, adverse parties must be present before the court.

Adversity is the most obvious and accepted element of a "case" or "controversy." Since Anglo-American jurisprudence is based upon the adversary system, this is almost a natural development.[2] The requirement of adversity also seems to be a natural development in American constitutional law. The term "controversy" implies adversity, and if, as previously discussed, "case" was meant to include "controversy," the same conclusion would follow. If both parties desire the same result, no controversy is present. It is worth noting that Justice Louis D. Brandeis in his famous Ashwander rules, although not directly discussing the case-or-controversy provision, placed adversity at the head of the list.[3]

The rationale requiring adversity is logically sound. The probability that a court will be presented with all the pertinent data necessary for an authoritative decision is more likely when adversity exists. One commentator has suggested that adversity also aids the courts by presenting fairly narrow and manageable issues.[4] As the Supreme Court has indicated, adversity is a "safeguard essential to the integrity of the judicial process, and one which we have held to be indispensable to adjudication of constitutional questions by this Court" (*United States* v. *Johnson* 305).

Two commentators have argued that adversity as a means of presenting a court, especially the Supreme Court, "with the data relevant and necessary to [a] decision is an obvious fiction."[5] While it is true that liberalized procedures for intervention, for presenting *amicus curiae* briefs, and reliance upon judicial self-information have increased in recent years, these factors are not directly related to the existence of a "case" or "controversy."[6] It may be a myth that adversity is necessary to present the courts with the relevant facts upon which to predicate their decision, but adversity is an element that must be present before any of the other avenues may be opened. If adversity is absent, no "case" or "controversy" exists, and other means of supplying the judiciary with data become irrelevant.

The fact that adversity is a relative factor is best illustrated by examining the generic term "test case." This study will use the terminology "test case" to describe the situation that exists when both parties cooperate to get an issue before the courts.[7] A test case may or may not involve adverse parties.[8] The parties may agree completely on the facts and the issue but disagree on the decision the court should render. In this situation the necessary adversity exists because the parties are in an adverse position concerning the interpretation of a law, an order, or their constitutionality. When the parties also seek the same result, however, adversity is absent. The pertinent question is: When does a test case cease to be merely a friendly adversary action and become a collusive suit without any real adversity?[9]

Lord v. *Veazie* is a prime example of a collusive suit. In dismissing the action, the Court stressed the lack of adversity.

> The court is satisfied upon examining the record in this case, and affidavits filed in the motion to dismiss, that the contract set out in the pleadings was made for the purpose of instituting this suit, and there is no real dispute between the plaintiff and defendant. On the contrary, it is evident that their interest in the question brought here for decision is one and the same, and not adverse, and that in these proceedings the plaintiff and defendant are attempting to procure the opinion of the court upon a question of law, in the decision of which they have a common interest opposed to that of other persons, who are not parties to the suit, who had no knowledge of it while it was pending in the Circuit Court, and no opportunity of it being heard there in defense of their rights. And their conduct is more objectionable because they have brought up

the question upon a statement of facts agreed upon between themselves without the knowledge of the parties with whom they were in truth in dispute, and upon a judgment pro forma entered by their mutual consent, without any actual judicial decision by the court.(254)

One would have difficulty in finding a factual situation that could be characterized as more collusive than the one presented here. The parties were brothers-in-law and on the basis of a contract between them, they were attempting to quiet title to rights claimed by a third party. This is a classic example of a collusive action.

The Court made a clear distinction, however, between a collusive suit and an amicable action.

> The suit is spoken of, in the affidavits filed in support of it, as an amicable action, and the proceeding defended on that ground. But an amicable action, in the sense in which these words are used in courts of justice, presupposes that there is a real dispute between the parties concerning some matter of right. . . . But there must be an actual controversy, and adverse interests. The amity consists in the manner in which it is brought to issue before the court. . . . The objection in the case before us is not that the proceedings were amicable, but that there is no real conflict of interest between them; that the plaintiff and defendant have the same interest and that interest [is] adverse and in conflict with the interest of third persons.(255)

Total adversity is not required, but adversity must be present to some degree. The judicial door is left open for a test case wherein the parties disagree only on the judgment to be rendered. The parties may agree on the factual situation and even cooperate in instituting the action, as long as their interests are adverse concerning the final judgment to be rendered.

The Court held that *Chicago & Grand Trunk Railway Co.* v. *Wellman* was an action that fell into the collusive rather than the amicable classification. It was a test case in the sense that the parties were attempting to test the validity of a Michigan rate-making statute. It appeared, however, that the parties had cooperated in creating the factual situation with Wellman's only pretending to desire to purchase a railroad ticket under the old rates. The Michigan Supreme Court had permitted the Michigan attorney general to intervene "to represent the public interest" since the record indicated that the suit was collusive. The United States Supreme Court rejected the Railway Company's contention that the parties' cooperation in creating the factual situation was immaterial. "This may be conceded, but what of it?" the Railway Company asked. "There is no ground for the claim that any fraud or trickery has been practiced in presenting the testimony"(344). The Court's opinion did not mention collusion, but accented the necessary relationship between the parties. There must be "an honest and actual antagonistic assertion of rights by one individual against another" before a court may act. Constitutional questions may be decided only if necessary for the "determination of [a] real, earnest, and vital controversy between individuals." The Court concluded: "It never was thought that by means of a friendly suit a party beaten in the Legislature could transfer to the courts an inquiry as to the constitutionality of the legislative Act"(344–45). One should note, however, that the term "friendly suit" as used in *Wellman* must be distinguished from the "amicable action" suggested in *Lord* v. *Veazie*. In *Wellman*, the Court used the term "friendly suit" as analogous to a collusive action.

In *Muskrat* v. *United States*, the Court found a lack of adversity and hinted at the possibility of collusion. "It is true the United States is made a defendant to this action, but it has no interest adverse to the claimants"(361). One may certainly question the accuracy of this statement. The federal government had no property or pecuniary interest in the land and funds involved, but the Government does have a vital interest in upholding federal statutes. Muskrat claimed the disputed laws were unconstitutional, while the Government took the position that they were constitutional. This was not a feigned issue—there was every indication that adversity existed, although the adversity did not directly involve traditional property rights. The presence of adversity in *Muskrat* is substantiated by the fact that the Court handed down a unanimous opinion the following year in an action seeking an injunction against the Secretary of the Interior and the Secretary of the Treasury commenced by one of the other plaintiffs in *Muskrat*. In *Gritts* v. *Fisher*, the Court upheld the constitutionality of the Acts passed in 1906 that had enlarged the number of grantees provided for in the Act of 1902. The Court never raised the issue of adversity in *Gritts*, however, and made no reference to *Muskrat*. From the perspective of adversity, the only distinction between the two cases is that *Muskrat* was commenced against the United States government and *Gritts* was an action against agents of the government (it should be stressed that this discussion is limited solely to the presence of adversity).

In *Muskrat*, the statute permitting the action provided that the compensation paid to the plaintiffs' attorneys would be reimbursed from the Treasury of the United States if the disputed statutes of 1904 and 1906 were declared unconstitutional. This, however, did not create the type of collusive action that existed in *Lord* v. *Veazie* or *Chicago & Grand Trunk Railway* v. *Wellman*. The Court did not claim that the plaintiffs' attorneys in *Muskrat* would be under the control of the United States Government. The statute of 1907 provided that plaintiffs' attorney fees would be paid out of Treasury funds, but from money that constructively belonged to the plaintiffs. In applying its "kitchen sink" approach, the Court apparently felt that it was necessary to show that all elements of a "case" were absent. The Court declared that adversity did not exist, but the facts do not support the declaration.

The Court ordinarily discusses adversity when adversity is found to be absent. One notable exception, however, is *Old Colony Trust Co. v. Commissioner of Internal Revenue*.[10] Chief Justice William Howard Taft emphasized the relationship between adversity and a "case" or "controversy."

> In the case we have here, there are adverse parties. The United States or its authorized official asserts its rights to the payment by a taxpayer of a tax due from him to the government, and the taxpayer is resisting that payment or is seeking to recover what he has already paid as taxes when by law they were not properly due. That makes a case or controversy.(724)

United States v. *Johnson* is an important example of a collusive suit. The original action was brought in a federal district court in the name of Edward Roach against Johnson. The United States intervened, and when the district court refused to dismiss the action as collusive, the Government appealed to the Supreme Court. In a *per curiam* opinion, the Court explained why the suit should be dismissed as a classic example of collusion.

> The affidavit of the plaintiff [Roach], submitted by the Government on its motion to dismiss the suit as collusive, shows without contradiction that he brought the present proceeding in a fictitious name; that it was instituted as a "friendly suit" at appellee's [Johnson's] request; that the plaintiff did not employ, pay, or even meet, the attorney who appeared of record in his behalf; that he had no knowledge who paid the $15 filing fee in the district court, but was assured by appellee that as plaintiff he would incur no expense in bringing the suit; that he did not read the complaint which was filed in his name as plaintiff; that in his conferences with the appellee and appellee's attorney of record, nothing was said of treble damages and he had no knowledge of the amount of the judgment until he read of it in a local newspaper.(303–4)

One would have great difficulty in devising a situation that would more obviously display the lack of any real adversity. If one party completely controls the action, adversity is obviously absent.

Poe v. *Ullman* is an action in which the question of the presence of adversity was fully disputed by two members of the Court. Justices Felix Frankfurter and John M. Harlan expressed diametrically opposite views on the existence of adversity. In delivering the Court's plurality opinion, Frankfurter emphasized the necessity of adversity.

> This principle was given early application and has been recurringly enforced in the Court's refusal to entertain cases which disclosed a want of a truly adversary contest, of a collision of activity asserted and differing claims. . . . Such cases may not be "collusive" in the derogatory sense of *Lord* v. *Veazie*, 8 How. 251—in the sense of merely colorable disputes got up to secure an advantageous ruling from the Court. . . . The Court has found unfit for adjudication any cause that "is not in any real sense adversary."(505)

Poe sought an injunction and a declaratory judgment against enforcement of Connecticut's anticontraception law. Frankfurter concluded that since the State had not been enforcing the statute, an adversary contest did not exist. "If the prosecutor expressly agrees not to prosecute, a suit against him for declaratory and injunctive relief is not such an adversary case as will be reviewed here"(507–8). Although there was no express agreement, Frankfurter declared that eighty years of nonenforcement was tantamount to a "tacit agreement" not to prosecute.

In his dissenting opinion, Harlan agreed that adversity is necessary to create a "case" or "controversy." "[A]lso it follows that the controversy must be one which is in truth and fact the litigant's own, so that the clash of adversary contest which is needed to sharpen and illuminate issues is present and gives the aid on which our adjudicatory system has come to rely"(525). Harlan vehemently disagreed, however, with Frankfurter's contention that adversity was not present.

> This is not a feigned, hypothetical, friendly or colorable suit such as discloses "a want of a truly adversary contest." Clearly these cases are not analogous to *American Wood-Paper Co.* v. *Heft*, 8 Wall. 333 or *South Spring Hill Gold Min. Co.* v. *Amador Median Gold Min. Co.*, 145 U.S. 300 where prior to consideration the controversy in effect became moot by the merger of the two contesting interests. Nor is there any question of collusion as in *Lord* v. *Veazie*, 8 How. 251 or in *United States* v. *Johnson*, 319 U.S. 302. And there is nothing to suggest that the parties by their conduct of this litigation have cooperated to force an adjudication of a Constitutional issue which—were the parties interested solely in winning their cases rather than obtaining a constitutional decision—might not arise in an arm's-length contested proceeding.(528–29)

Harlan contended that the majority was distorting the factual situation in order to avoid a decision.

> Indeed . . . I think both the plurality and concurring opinions confuse on this score the predictive likelihood that, had they not brought themselves to appellee's attention, he would not enforce the statute against them, with some entirely suppositious "tacit agreement" not to prosecute, thereby ignoring the prosecutor's claim, asserted in these very proceedings, of a right, at his unbounded prosecutorial discretion, to enforce the statute.(529–30)

Although the two Justices viewed the factual situation differently, they both emphasized the necessity of adversity as an element of a "case" or "controversy."

Poe v. *Ullman* does indicate the extent of the Court's discretion in determining whether adversity exists. Adversity was only one of the elements of justiciability involved in *Poe*, but the Court was able to avoid rendering a decision, at least partially, on the basis that the facts implied that adversity did not exist. There was no evidence of collusion, and the litigation was not controlled by one party. An intervenor had not brought any facts to the Court's attention that substantiated a lack of adversity. If adversity is not present, it is, of course, the Supreme Court's or any federal court's duty to dismiss the action as not presenting a "case" or "controversy." *Poe* indicates, however, that this discretion may be used in order to avoid rendering a decision on a very controversial issue. (The Court only delayed rendering a decision on Connecticut's anticontraception statute. See *Griswold* v. *Connecticut*.)

Moore v. *Charlotte-Mecklenburg Board of Education* emphasized the Court's overt insistence on adversity as an element of a "case" or "controversy." A unanimous Court dismissed an action because it was apparent that both parties desired the same result.

> At the hearings both parties argued to the three-judge court that the anti-busing law was constitutional and urged that the order of the District Court adopting the Finger plan should be set aside. We are thus confronted with the anomaly that both litigants desire precisely the same result, namely a holding that the anti-busing statute is constitutional. There is, therefore, no case or controversy within the meaning of Article III of the Constitution.(47–48)

A "case" or "controversy" is no longer present if adversity ceases to exist while the issue is being litigated. In two cases decided in the 1860s, the Supreme Court dismissed the appeal in each instance because the adversity had been resolved since the lower courts' decisions.[11] Although a "case" or "controversy" had originally existed, when the litigation reached the Supreme Court, one party controlled both sides of the action. The Court dismissed each suit on the basis of *Lord* v. *Veazie*.

Modern class actions raise some difficult questions concerning the existence of adversity throughout the appellate process. Adversity may exist between the named plaintiff and named defendant when the action is instituted, but that adversity may cease to exist before the case reaches the appellate court. In *Sosna* v. *Iowa* the Court held that if adversity continued to exist between the plaintiff's class and the named defendant, Article III requirements were met. Sosna was challenging the Iowa residency requirements to obtain a divorce on her own behalf and that of all those similarly situated. By the time the action reached the United States Supreme Court, she not only met the residency requirements but she had also obtained her divorce. (The question whether the action was moot was also involved. See discussion of mootness in Chapter 9 *infra*.) Only Justice Byron White objected to the Court's recognition of continuing adversity. "For all practical purposes, this case has become one-sided and has lost the adversary quality necessary to satisfy the constitutional 'case or controversy' requirement. A real issue unquestionably remains, but the necessary adverse party to press it has disappeared"(564).

As the preceding opinions disclose, the Court has continuously insisted on the existence of adversity as a necessary element of a "case" or "controversy." The decisions reveal, however, that the determination of the existence of adversity is not a mechanical process, because adversity is a relative factor. While actions at the two extremes, when either complete adversity exists or where collusion is present, are not difficult to discern if the facts are brought to a court's attention, the area between these two extreme positions does permit the federal courts to exercise a great deal of discretion.

Adversity's tenuous nature is indicated by the Court's unanimous decision in *Kentucky* v. *Indiana*. The two states had entered into a contract to construct a bridge across the Ohio River between Evansville, Indiana and Henderson, Kentucky. Certain Indiana taxpayers and citizens instituted an equity action in a state court seeking an injunction against the construction of the bridge. Indiana refused to proceed with the construction until the state court action was settled. Kentucky then brought an original action in the United States Supreme Court to require specific performance of the contract. (Kentucky also brought the action against the citizens and taxpayers who had instituted the state action, but the Court dismissed the State's action against them.) Indiana admitted all the allegations made by Kentucky, including the validity of the contract and its willingness to perform, but pleaded that it was not willing to perform until the state courts rendered a final decision. In accepting jurisdiction and deciding for specific performance, the Supreme Court stated: "There is thus a controversy between the States, although a limited one"(173).

The Court confirmed the relative nature of adversity in *Pope* v. *United States* in 1944. The Court of Claims had ruled that a congressional enactment admitting the government's liability and requiring the Court of Claims to determine only the amount due was administrative action and not the exercise of judicial power. In a unanimous opinion, the Supreme Court reversed this decision. "When a plaintiff brings suit to enforce a legal obligation it is not any the less a case or controversy upon which a court possessing the federal judicial power may rightly give judgment, because the plaintiff's claim is uncontested or incontestable"(11). The necessary adversity existed over the exact amount due, and this was all that was required.

Despite the Court's insistence on adversity, commentators have pointed out that it has decided cases, in fact some of the most significant cases in American constitutional history, when adversity was either absent or at least questionable.[12] The Supreme Court did not reject the necessity of adversity in these cases. It was either not aware of the questionable situation, or it desired to decide the cases and simply ignored the factors surrounding adversity.

Three early landmark decisions fall into this category. In *Hylton* v. *United States,* which upheld the constitutionality of a federal tax on carriages, the Government paid all attorneys' fees for the argument before the Supreme Court. The Government had also entered into a fictitious stipulation that Hylton owned 125 carriages strictly for his own personal use.[13] The Court may not have been aware of the first fact and apparently chose to ignore the second.

The Court for the first time held a state law unconstitutional in *Fletcher* v. *Peck* in 1810. Evidence indicates that the parties arranged the suit in order to test the validity of Georgia's revocation, in 1796, of grants of land made by the state legislature. Chief Justice John Marshall and Justice H. B. Livingston apparently suspected this to be the situation, but they chose to ignore the possibility.[14] Justice William Johnson suggested the possibility of collusion in his dissenting opinion, but felt this was disproved because of the stature of counsel (115–16). Other than the allusion by Johnson, the Court decided the case without raising the question of adversity.

The third decision is the *Dred Scott Case*. There is every indication that the federal circuit court action was collusive. Scott's original owner's widow, who had married an abolitionist Congressman, sold Scott to her brother so that a federal court would have diversity jurisdiction. Although the Court must have been aware of this situation, it proceeded to judgment without raising the question of adversity.[15]

These three cases further demonstrate the tenuous nature of adversity. The Court may ignore patent or circumstantial facts that tend to suggest the absence of adversity. In cases similar to the above, the Court may, and theoretically should, probe further into the facts in order to determine whether adversity actually exists. If the Court desires to render a decision, however, it may see or hear no evil. As Professor Edwin Borchard stated:

> The made case or test case is a familiar institution in American jurisprudence, it may or may not involve a legitimate controversy and both parties may possibly want the same judgment. But if the court wishes to render judgment it will close its eyes to the realities and perceive only the ostensible conflict of interests.[16]

Commentators have also alleged that the federal courts, and specifically the Supreme Court, have decided nonadversary proceedings in stockholders' suits. A corporation may comply with a statute solely because the sanctions imposed for noncompliance are quite onerous. The board of directors may actually desire that the statute be declared unconstitutional but may decide that the potential loss in directly violating the statute to create a test case is too great. A stockholder may then bring a suit against the corporation alleging that compliance with the statute is detrimental to his interest, illegal, and/or *ultra vires*. Famous cases, such as *Pollock* v. *Farmers' Loan & Trust Co.*[17] and *Carter* v. *Carter Coal Co.*,[18] have resulted in decisions on significant constitutional issues when the real adversity of the parties was questionable, because both the stockholder and the corporation undoubtedly desired a decision against the constitutionality of a statute.

Does adversity exist in these situations? The Court has usually answered "yes" on the basis of the record before it.[19] The corporation has taken action, and one or more stockholders are challenging this action. If one looks beyond the record, adversity may be lacking, but the federal courts will generally accept the record as evidence of the necessary adversity to create a "case" or "controversy."[20] Stockholders' suits, therefore, may result in actions like *Carter Coal* in which a stockholder was suing a family corporation.[21] One must conclude that the Court desired to hear and settle the issue in these stockholders' suits.

The Court has adapted its application of the adversity requirement to include suits involving the United States, or one of its agencies, as both plaintiff and defendant. One would assume that, if the same party was both plaintiff and defendant, the requisite adversity would be lacking. In *United States* v. *Interstate Commerce Commission,* a three-judge district court dismissed an action by the United States against the Interstate Commerce Commission and pointed out that representatives of the Department of Justice were arguing both sides of the case. In a 6–3 decision, the Supreme Court reversed this holding. The United States was not only the plaintiff but the United States was required by statute to be a defendant in addition to the ICC. Justice Hugo Black, for the Court, suggested that one must examine more than the title of the case.

> There is much argument with citation of many cases to establish the long recognized general principle that no person may sue himself. Properly understood the general principle is sound, for courts only adjudicate justiciable controversies. They do not engage in the academic pastime of rendering judgments in favor of persons against themselves. Thus a suit filed by John Smith against John Smith might present no case or controversy which courts could determine. But one person named John Smith might have a justiciable controversy with another John Smith. This illustrates that courts must look behind names that symbolize the parties to determine whether a justiciable case or controversy is present.(430)

The United States was attempting to recover railroad charges for services that the Government claimed had not been performed. The Government had first filed its complaint with the ICC, which upheld the charges by the railroads. The Court concluded that the actual controversy was between the United States and the railroads, although the latter were not parties of record. "Consequently, the established principle that a person cannot create a justiciable controversy against himself has no application here"(430).

Justice Black indicated that all the necessary prerequisites of an adversary contest were actually present despite their apparent absence.

> Although the formal appearance of the Attorney General for the Government as statutory defendant does create a surface anomaly, his representation of the Government as a shipper does not in any way prevent a full defense of the Commission's order. The Interstate Commerce Act contains adequate provisions for protection of Commission orders by the Commission and by railroads when, as here, they are the real parties in interest. For whether the Attorney General defends or not, the Commission and the railroads are authorized to interpose all defenses to the Government's charges and claims. . . . In this case the Commission and the railroads have availed themselves of this statutory authorization. They have vigorously defended the legality of the allowances and the validity of the Commission order at every stage of the litigation.(432)

Justice Felix Frankfurter, joined by Justices Robert H. Jackson and Harold Burton, dissented on the ground that the ICC determination was not subject to judicial review and did not discuss the issue of adversity.

If one analyzes Justice Black's opinion, his conclusions are difficult to accept from the perspective of the case-or-controversy provision. One cannot deny that there may be two John Smiths who are parties to a "case" or "controversy." In the present case, however, there were not two United States Governments but only one, and the Interstate Commerce Commission is an integral part of the United States Government. The railroads were not original defendants but were permitted to intervene. The railroads could intervene, however, only if a "case" or "controversy" was already present before the court, and this latter situation existed only if the United States were permitted to sue itself and/or one of its agencies. The fact that the railroads could and did intervene is irrelevant to the existence of a "case" or "controversy" in the first instance. Subsequent cases have indicated that *United States* v. *Interstate Commerce Commission* established the principle that adversity is not to be applied stringently when the United States Government, or one of its agencies, is both plaintiff and defendant.[22]

The Court has established the general rule that an official performing ministerial duties does not possess an adverse relationship to his governmental employer, and therefore he is not entitled to test the constitutionality of a statute under which he is required to act. This situation existed in *Tregea* v. *Board of Directors of the Modesto Irrigation District* in 1896 when the board of directors of an irrigation district brought an action to determine the validity of a proposed bond issue. The size of the district had been reduced subsequent to voter approval, but the California courts upheld the validity of the bonds. The Supreme Court dismissed the appeal because of the absence of a "case" or "controversy." Among other reasons, the Court found a lack of adversity.

> The directors of an irrigation district occupy no position antagonistic to the district. They are the agents, and the district is the principal. The interests are identical, and it is practically an ex parte application on behalf of the district. . . .
>
> This is not the mere reverse of an injunction suit brought by an inhabitant of the district to restrain a board from issuing bonds, for in such case there is an adversary proceeding.[23](186)

Although the Court has never explicitly reversed this general rule, it has ignored the rule in at least one recent case. In *Board of Education* v. *Allen,* the Court heard an action by a local school board against the Commissioner of Education of the State of New York. The Court did not discuss the issue of adversity, but a note indicating that the school board had standing inferred that adversity was present.

Appellants have taken an oath to support the United States Constitution. Believing § 701 [of the Education Law of the State of New York] to be unconstitutional, they are in the position of having to choose between violating their oath and taking a step—refusal to comply with § 701—that would be likely to bring their expulsion from office and also a reduction in state funds for their school districts.(241)

The same statement could have been made concerning the directors of the irrigation district in the action discussed above. Quite obviously, the Court does exercise great discretion in determining the existence of adversity in such a situation.

The rule that one who takes advantage of a statute will not be permitted to question its validity is partially related to adversity. Justice Brandeis included this point in his famous Ashwander rules. "The Court will not pass upon the Constitutionality of a statute at the instance of one who has availed himself of its benefits"(348). A party may have waived his legal rights, but the question of adversity is at least indirectly present. In *Buck* v. *Kuykendall,* Buck was denied a certificate by the State of Washington to operate an "auto state line" to the city of Seattle from Portland, Oregon. The Court discussed this problem in terms of the legal doctrine of estoppel,[24] but implied that adversity was at least indirectly involved.

> By motion to dismiss filed in this court, the state makes the further contention that Buck is estopped from seeking relief against the provisions of section 4. The argument is this: Buck's claim is not that the department action is unconstitutional because arbitrary or unreasonable. It is that section 4 is unconstitutional because use of the highways for interstate commerce is denied unless the prescribed certificate shall have been secured. Buck applied for a certificate. Thus he invoked the exercise of the power which he now assails. One who invokes the provisions of a law may not thereafter question its constitutionality. The argument is unsound. It is true that one cannot in the same proceeding both assail a statute and rely upon it. . . . Nor can one who avails himself of the benefits conferred by a statute deny its validity. . . . But in the case at bar Buck does not rely upon any provision of the statute assailed; and he has received no benefit under it. He was willing, if permitted to use the highways, to comply with all laws relating to common carriers. But the permission sought was denied. The case presents no element of estoppel. (316–17)

While it is true the Court does not mention adversity, it seems clear that one of the elements that would not have been present if Buck had been granted his certificate was real adversity.

Adversity has been discussed to this point as an isolated element of the case-or-controversy requirement. All four elements are interrelated, however, as indicated earlier. The exigent adversity must be related to the legal right that gives the litigation life and allows the court to make some type of final determination. A court's perception of the legal right being litigated may determine whether adversity is present.

One can make an interesting comparison in this respect between *Muskrat* v. *United States* and the more recent decision in *Flast* v. *Cohen*. In *Flast,* the major issue was a federal taxpayer's standing to challenge a congressional enactment that allegedly violated the First Amendment's establishment clause. The Court upheld the taxpayer's standing to institute the action. The question, therefore, arises: What was the basis of adversity? Although the Court did not directly answer the question, it obviously assumed adversity existed once it found the other three elements present.[25] The Court decided that the taxpayer had a sufficient interest in a legal right and that a final determination could be rendered in an actual controversy—the constitutionality of the Elementary and Secondary Education Act of 1965. The necessary adversity was apparently assumed to exist between the plaintiff and the Government as represented by the Secretary of Health, Education and Welfare.[26] The point is not that *Muskrat* and *Flast* are in any way analogous, but whether a court perceives adversity as present depends on what it determines are the interests involved and the actual controversy that it is asked to resolve. In *Muskrat,* adversity was absent, according to the Court, because the dispute was over property rights in which the Government had no interest. In *Flast,* adversity was present because both parties had a legal interest in the constitutionality of the Elementary and Secondary Education Act. If the Court, in *Muskrat,* had perceived the action as involving the constitutionality of the statutes involved, Justice Day could not have come to the conclusion that adversity was absent.

Most commentators agree that adversity is a necessary element of a "case" or "controversy," but one leading authority, Professor Kenneth Culp Davis, has rather categorically denied that adversity is required. While discussing ripeness, Davis declared: "The Constitution nowhere says so, but the idea has grown up in some quarters that federal courts have no power under the Constitution unless issues have crystallized between two parties who are opposing each other."[27] Davis does not substantiate his argument, however. He cites consent decrees and pleas of guilty as indicating adversity's absence, but these are examples of the resolution of the adversity—one can hardly argue that the defendant comes into court of his own volition in either instance. Davis asserts that adversity may not exist in requests for an eighty-day injunction under the Taft-Hartley Act, and that appeals to enforce orders of the National Labor Relations Board may not involve adversity. If a union has voluntarily agreed to a cooling-off period, or if a party is willing to comply with the NLRB's order, there would be no issue for a federal court to adjudicate. It is significant that in the latter two instances Davis does not cite one case in which the federal courts actually acted in a nonadversary proceeding.

Davis suggests that the federal courts "issue orders enforcing subpena whether or not the party subpenaed denies the validity of the subpena."[28] In most instances this power is ancillary to the federal judicial power. In other words, a "case" or "controversy" is already before the court, and the issuance of the subpoena is simply ancillary to the basic power of deciding a justiciable issue in a "case" or "controversy." In other situations, another governmental entity may ask the courts to issue a subpoena in order to obtain testimony and documents from recalcitrant witnesses. *Interstate Commerce Commission* v. *Brimson,* the only case cited by Davis, was an adversary proceeding since it was alleged that under an Act of Congress, the Interstate Commerce Act as amended, the Commission had no right to gather certain information, while the Commission claimed that it did. The courts were being asked to settle this adversary controversy and to issue a subpoena to help the Commission gain information from a recalcitrant witness.

Davis does present two examples that are exceptions to the general rule. Neither situation ordinarily involves any question of public law. Federal courts do handle voluntary proceedings in bankruptcy and do not lose their power to proceed in such actions if all parties are in agreement. This exception is not the result of the Court's interpretation of the case-or-controversy provision but is, rather, a direct result of the power granted to Congress to make "uniform laws on the subject of bankruptcies throughout the United States"(U.S. Constitution, Article I, Section 8. That is, a nonadversary bankruptcy proceeding is a result of congressional action and not of the Court's interpretation of the case-or-controversy provision. Like naturalization proceedings, nonadversary bankruptcy proceedings are an accepted exception to the general rule). Davis also points out that the federal courts act in naturalization proceedings even though adverse parties may not exist *ab initio* or at any other time. The federal courts have performed this function since the institution of our present constitutional system, but the Supreme Court was not faced with the question of whether Article III courts were properly exercising judicial power in naturalization proceedings until 1926. In *Tutun* v. *United States,* the Court finessed the issue by alleging that the Government is always a possible adverse party. One can only ask what other decision could have been reached in 1926? What must be admitted is that, by custom, the federal courts have come to perform a ceremonial function, which is really neither a "case" nor "controversy," although the Supreme Court in *Tutun* did find all the necessary elements present.[29]

In all fairness, it must be stressed that Davis is not discussing the case-or-controversy requirement but ripeness. He does, however, reject the idea of adversity without proving his point. The two valid exceptions are just that—exceptions. Like most rules relating to the case-or-controversy provision, adversity is not an ironclad requirement. But two exceptions that practically never involve important questions of public law hardly disprove that adversity has come to be an accepted requirement of a "case" or "controversy."

Of the four elements comprising the case-or-controversy provision, adversity is the one that has been altered the least throughout American constitutional history. The Court has continually insisted on the presence of adversity as a necessary element of a "case" or "controversy." Although minor exceptions, such as naturalization proceedings and voluntary bankruptcy proceedings, may result in the exercise of judicial power in nonadversary proceedings, the general rule is that judicial power may be exercised only when adverse parties are before a federal court.

What the Court says about adversity and the way the requirement has been applied are not necessarily congruous. This results from the relative and tenuous nature of adversity, which permits the federal courts to exercise a great deal of discretion in determining whether adversity is present or not. When the Court has desired to rule on an issue, it has simply closed its eyes to evidence that might disclose the absence of adversity. On the other hand, the Court has held that lack of adversity was implied by the record even though there was no evidence of any type of agreement or cooperation between the parties. There are undoubtedly those actions at the two extreme ends of the continuum where the existence or nonexistence of adversity is indisputable. Many actions, however, fall between these two extremes. In these latter instances, federal courts may determine the presence or absence of adversity on the basis of whether they wish to decide the substantive issue.

Adversity is the case-or-controversy provision's requirement that parties may most easily evade. Since the courts depend primarily on the parties for the presentation of the factual situation, the parties may fictitiously present the appearance of adversity although they are actually in collusion. Unless the record gives some hint of collusion or an intervenor brings the collusion to the court's attention, a court may obviously proceed to judgment in a collusive case without any suspicion of the actual situation.[30]

Adversity is the most generally accepted element of a "case" or "controversy" and is one the Court has always overtly required. When it comes to examining the factual application of the requirement, the situation is much more complex. The federal courts exercise a great amount of discretion in determining whether adversity exists, and parties have the greatest chance of evading this requirement, since the court may have to depend entirely on the evidence presented by the parties.

4 Sources of Legal Rights and Remedies

If federal courts act only in adversary situations, the courts also act only to protect legal rights. That is, federal judicial power may be invoked only to protect a legal right or to prevent a legal wrong. (A legal wrong results when a legal right is violated. Since the present chapter is concerned with the existence of a legal right, the terminology "legal right" will be emphasized throughout this chapter. Thus, in an equity action, a federal court may act to prevent a legal wrong, but the threatened legal wrong must be a violation of a legal right. That is, a federal court acts only to protect legal rights, although the court may exercise its equity jurisdiction before the legal right is invaded.) The very heart of the judicial function is to settle disputes over legal rights, and the existence of a legal right is an undisputed element of a "case" or "controversy." The existence of a legal right is an important factor, therefore, in determining whether the courts will play an active role in the political process.

A legal right is a complex and complicated factor. For instance, the existence of a legal remedy is a necessary corollary to the existence of a legal right. That is, the courts must be able to provide redress before any loss or injury can be considered a violation of a legal right. (The legal term *"damnum absque injuria"* describes an injury or loss that is not the result of a violation of a legal right. The Court's refusal to decide "political questions" is partially predicated on the fact that federal courts would not be able to afford any redress.) The federal courts may derive the existence of a legal remedy from one source, however—e.g., statutory law—and derive the existence of a legal right from another source, e.g., the Constitution. If a federal court provides a remedy, it is acting to protect a legal right. If a federal court decides that no remedy exists, however, it is determining that the party does not have a legally protected right.

The concept of a legal right is further complicated by the multiplicity of sources available to federal courts. The Constitution, statutes, treaties, state law, common law, and equity are potential sources of legal rights. The federal courts may use any of these sources to determine the presence of this element of a "case" or "controversy," and they have great discretion in making this determination. So many potential sources also indicate the dynamic nature of this element. The Constitution's framers would have little difficulty recognizing adversity as it is applied today, but they would undoubtedly be completely bewildered by the multiplicity of legal rights. Judicial interpretations as well as statutory enactments have greatly increased enforceable legal rights.

The problem is complicated further by Supreme Court opinions in which the legal right that gives rise to the "case" or "controversy" is not clear. The Court may decide a case on the basis of a legal right other than the right on which the "case" or "controversy" was based. For instance, a stockholder may be permitted to bring an action against a corporation, but the Court may dispose of the case on the basis of a constitutional provision that did not give the stockholder any right against his corporation. Or, in issuing an injunction, the Court may exercise its equitable power without clearly stating the legal right that is being protected. If a "case" or "controversy" is present, the Court is acting to protect a legal right. Yet the legal right that originally gave life to the "case" or "controversy" may be ignored in deciding a more important substantive issue.

The sources that the federal courts use to find the existence of a legal right and a legal remedy will be examined in this chapter. No attempt will be made to be definitive concerning each source, but illustrations of each source will be given.

The United States Constitution as a Source of Legal Rights and Remedies

The United States Constitution is one source that the federal courts may use to determine the existence of a legally protected right. The courts' power to interpret the Constitution gives them great latitude in discerning what rights are protected by the Constitution. The Supreme Court has used three means of determining the legal rights protected by the Constitution. (1) Certain legal rights are self-evident or made explicit by the Constitution. The right of an individual to a writ of habeas corpus or the right of a state not to be deprived of its territory without its consent are examples. (2) The Court may find that legal rights are logically implied by the Constitution. Although no one is guaranteed the right to vote for members of the House of Representatives by Article I Section 2, the Court has held that one who meets the requirements to vote for the most numerous branch of the state legislature has a right to vote protected by the Constitution. (3) Legal rights may be derived from two or more provisions of the Constitution. The Court has held that a taxpayer has a legally protected right to challenge congressional power to tax and spend for the general welfare if there is a valid claim that Congress has simultaneously violated the establishment clause of the First Amendment.

Although the Constitution creates legal rights, it does not provide any remedies. (The writ of habeas corpus may be considered both a right and a remedy guaranteed by the Constitution.) The Supreme Court has not encountered any problems concerning its original jurisdiction because of this situation. (The Supreme Court's original jurisdiction is specified in the U.S. Constitution, Article III Section 2: "In all cases affecting ambassadors, other public ministers and consuls, and those in which a state shall be party, the Supreme Court shall have original jurisdiction. In all the other cases before mentioned, the Supreme Court shall have appellate jurisdiction, both as to law and fact, with such exceptions, and under such regulations as the Congress shall make.") The Court has had no reservations about adopting common law to settle both substantive and procedural questions in disputes between states. Chief Justice Charles Evans Hughes wrote for the Court in *Massachusetts* v. *Missouri:*

> The proposed bill of complaint does not present a justiciable controversy between the States. To constitute such a controversy, it must appear that the complaining State has suffered a wrong through the action of the other State, furnishing ground for judicial redress, or is asserting a right against the other State which is susceptible of judicial enforcement according to the accepted principles of the common law or equity systems of jurisprudence.(15)

Where the Constitution directly vests original jurisdiction in the Supreme Court, the Court has complete discretion in determining the existence of legal rights as well as remedies.[1] The remedies available in the lower federal courts and under the Supreme Court's appellate jurisdiction raises a more difficult question. In these instances, the Constitution leaves the question of jurisdiction to Congress, and the courts may not enforce any constitutional right until Congress confers jurisdiction. Even when jurisdiction has been conferred, must Congress also provide a specific remedy? Once the federal courts have been granted jurisdiction, they may supply a remedy to protect a constitutional right even in absence of a statutory remedy. This is illustrated by the following discussion of the issuance of the writ of habeas corpus.

Legal Rights Explicitly Protected by the Constitution

The Constitution, in Article I Section 9, states that: "The privilege of the writ of habeas corpus shall not be suspended, unless when in cases of rebellion or invasion the public safety may require it." In Ex parte *Bollman* the Court held, however, "that for the meaning of the term habeas corpus, resort must unquestionably be had to the common law; but the power to award the writ by any of the courts of the United States, must be given by the written law"(93–94). Before the federal courts may enforce this right, Congress must grant jurisdiction. Congress has granted such jurisdiction to all federal courts since 1789, and the Court has generally given a liberal interpretation to this power.[2]

Two cases indicate the federal courts' ability to issue the writ once jurisdiction has been conferred. In *Wong Yang Sung* v. *McGrath,* the Supreme Court issued a writ of habeas corpus on behalf of an alien who was being held for deportation. Immigration officials had determined that he had illegally entered the country, and the lower federal courts had denied the writ on the basis that no law, specifically the Administrative Procedure Act, had been violated. Congress had provided that:

> The writ of habeas corpus shall not extend to a prisoner unless—(4) He, being a citizen of a foreign state and domiciled therein is in custody for an act done or omitted under any alleged right, title, authority, privilege, protection, or exemption claimed under the commission, order or sanction of any foreign state, or under color thereof, the validity and effect of which depend upon the law of nations . . .[3]

Wong Yang Sung was a native-born citizen of China and was in the United States as a result of "having overstayed shore leave as one of a shipping crew"(35). The Supreme Court ignored the statutory limitation and did not discuss its power to issue the writ. It determined that the Administrative Procedure Act applied to deportation proceedings and, since the proceedings had not conformed to that Act, the "prisoner" was entitled to be released.[4] The Court apparently relied on the general grant of jurisdiction to the federal courts and ignored the limitations on that power.[5]

The Court has also upheld the federal courts' right to issue the writ of habeas corpus when one has been illegally inducted into the armed forces. In *Eagles* v. *United States,* Justice William O. Douglas did not discuss why one inducted into the armed forces in violation of the Selective Service Act could bring an action for a writ of habeas corpus in the federal courts, but the Court apparently relied on the general grant of jurisdiction. Although the Court denied the release of the inductee, Douglas left no doubt that it did so on substantive grounds.

The function of habeas corpus is not to correct a practice, but only to ascertain whether the procedure complained of has resulted in an unlawful detention. It is the impact of the procedure on the person seeking the writ that is crucial. Whatever potentialities of abuse a particular proceeding may have, the case is at an end if the challenged proceeding cannot be said to have been so corrupted as to have made it unfair.(315)

These two cases indicate that, once Congress has granted jurisdiction, the federal judiciary has great discretion in determining whether a legal remedy is available. The Court has relied on the general grant of jurisdiction and has applied the legal right to a writ of habeas corpus to individuals held for deportation on the basis of administrative determinations as well as to those inducted into the armed forces on the basis of administrative determination. If one concludes that such persons are "prisoners," the legal remedy was granted by statute.[6] In neither instance cited above did the Court deem it significant to examine this question. Once jurisdiction has been granted, the federal courts, and ultimately the Supreme Court, determine the availability of remedies to protect rights explicitly guaranteed by the Constitution.

When legal rights are specifically guaranteed by the Constitution, the only relevant question is whether the federal courts have been granted jurisdiction. If jurisdiction has been granted, federal judicial power may be invoked to protect a right that is specifically guaranteed by the Constitution. Although the "privilege" of the writ of habeas corpus may be viewed as a constitutionally guaranteed right to a specific remedy, its enforcement indicates the federal judiciary's power to enforce any right guaranteed by the Constitution. A more difficult problem arises when the right in question is not expressly guaranteed by the Constitution.

Legal Rights Implied by the Constitution

The Constitution does not guarantee a right to vote for members of the United State House of Representatives, since according to Article I Section 2 this was to be determined by the states in defining suffrage for the "most numerous branch of the state legislature." The Supreme Court has held, however, that this provision does create a constitutionally protected right to vote. The Court declared in Ex parte *Yarbrough:*

But it is not correct to say that the right to vote for a member of Congress does not depend on the Constitution of the United States. . . . They [the states] define who are to vote for the popular branch of their own legislature, and the Constitution of the United States says the same persons shall vote for members of Congress in that state. It adopts the qualifications thus furnished as the qualifications of its own electors for members of Congress. It is not true, therefore, that electors for members of Congress owe their right to vote to the state law in any sense which makes the exercise of the right to depend exclusively on the law of the state.(663–64)

The Constitution does not guarantee the right to vote, but once the states have acted, anyone permitted to vote for the most numerous branch of the state legislature has a constitutionally protected right to vote for a member of the House. In *United States* v. *Classic,* the Court indicated that one of the questions to be decided was "whether the right of qualified voters to vote in the Louisiana primary and to have their ballots counted is a right 'secured by the Constitution' "(307). The Court answered the question in the affirmative.

> The right to participate in the choice of representatives for Congress includes, as we have said, the right to cast a ballot and to have it counted at the general election whether for the successful candidate or not. Where the state law has made the primary an integral part of the procedure of choice, or where in fact the primary effectively controls the choice, the right of the elector to have his ballot counted at the primary, is likewise included in the right protected by Article I, § 2.(318)

Although these cases were criminal actions, these same rules concerning legal rights have followed in civil actions.[7]

The Court's power to determine that constitutionally protected rights may be implied by the Constitution is even more vividly illustrated by *Baker* v. *Carr.* While the right to vote for members of the House could logically be implied from Article I Section 2, the Fourteenth Amendment's equal protection clause hardly suggests the right to vote. One could argue, in fact, that the Fourteenth and Fifteenth Amendments read together would imply that the Fourteenth was not intended to apply to voting (Amendment XV, adopted in 1870, reads: "The right of citizens of the United States to vote shall not be denied or abridged by the United States or by any state on account of race, color, or previous condition of servitude"). In the landmark reapportionment case, however, the Court held that the equal protection clause does create a legally enforceable right to vote.

> Their constitutional claim is, in substance, that the 1901 statute constitutes arbitrary and capricious state action, offensive to the Fourteenth Amendment in its irrational disregard of the standard of apportionment prescribed by the State's Constitution or of any standard, effecting a gross disproportion of representation to voting population. The injury which appellants assert

is that this classification disfavors the voters in the counties in which they reside, placing them in a position of constitutionally unjustifiable inequality *vis-a-vis* voters in irrationally favored counties. A citizen's right to vote free of arbitrary impairment by state action has been judicially recognized as a right secured by the Constitution, when such impairment resulted from dilution by a false tally, *cf. United States* v. *Classic,* 313 U.S. 299; or by a refusal to count votes from arbitrarily selected precincts, *cf. United States* v. *Mosley,* 238 U.S. 383, or by a stuffing of the ballot box, *cf.* Ex parte *Siebold,* 100 U.S. 371; *United States* v. *Saylor,* 322 U.S. 385.(207–8)

The Court found that a citizen's right to vote is protected against dilution by malapportionment. The equal protection clause establishes a constitutionally protected right to vote, but only because the Court has found the right implied by the language of the Fourteenth Amendment.

To what extent may constitutional provisions that are apparently designed as defenses to a criminal prosecution be used as a basis for commencing a civil action? (See Article I, Sections 9 and 10, and the Fourth, Fifth, Sixth, and Eighth Amendments.) As a defense, the constitutional provision does not form the basis of a "case" or "controversy," but is interposed against an action instituted under a criminal statute. In the case of civil actions, the constitutional provision is the legal right on which the "case" or "controversy" is predicated.

In *Bell* v. *Hood* the Court held that the petitioners had a right to bring an action for damages against agents of the Federal Bureau of Investigation. Bell and others alleged that their Fourth Amendment rights to be free from unreasonable searches and seizures and their Fifth Amendment right to be free from the deprivation of liberty and property without due process of law had been violated. The lower federal courts had dismissed the action since it did not arise under the Constitution or laws of the United States.

Justice Hugo Black delivered the Court's opinion and rejected the FBI agents' contention "that the petitioners could not recover under the Constitution or laws of the United States since the Constitution does not expressly provide for recovery in money damages for violations of the Fourth and Fifth Amendments and Congress has not enacted a statute that does so provide"(681). The Court clearly indicated that a legal right could be predicated on the Fourth and Fifth Amendment claims. The Court held that jurisdiction could not be denied solely because the petitioners might not be entitled to recover damages, since this was a question to be determined on the merits. A federal court may deny jurisdiction only if the "alleged claim under the Constitution or federal statutes clearly appears to be immaterial and made solely for the purpose of obtaining jurisdiction or where such a claim is wholly insubstantial and frivolous" (682–83). The Court found that neither was true in the present case.

Black agreed that "[t]he Circuit Court of Appeals correctly stated that 'the complaint states strong cases, and if the allegations have any foundation in truth, the plaintiffs' legal rights have been ruthlessly violated' "(683). Black suggested that the real issue was whether the petitioners could recover money damages under the remedial statute on which they relied. This was a question that had not been decided and that should have been adjudicated in the district court.

Black pointed out that it was not unusual for the federal courts to entertain suits based on guarantees such as those found in the Fourth Amendment and in the Fifth Amendment's due process clause. "And it is established practice for this Court to sustain the jurisdiction of the federal courts to issue injunctions to protect rights safeguarded by the Constitution and to restrain individual state officers from doing what the Fourteenth Amendment forbids the state to do"(684). Black suggested that, when a legal right exists, a remedy should be available if the federal courts have been granted jurisdiction.

> Moreover, where federally protected rights have been invaded, it has been the rule from the beginning that courts will be alert to adjust their remedies so as to grant the necessary relief. And it is also well settled that where legal rights have been invaded, and a federal statute provides for a general right to sue for such invasion, federal courts may use any available remedy to make good the wrong done.(684)

Chief Justice Harlan F. Stone dissented primarily on the basis of the absence of remedy. Stone alleged that neither the Constitution nor any statute provided a remedy, and therefore the lower courts had properly dismissed the action for lack of jurisdiction. He did not discuss the existence of a legal right under the Constitution but proffered that, if any legal action existed, it should be one under state law in trespass to person and property.

Legal Rights Derived from Provisions of the Constitution

The Court's discretion in finding legally protected rights in the Constitution is illustrated by its decision in *Flast* v. *Cohen*. The Court did not discuss traditional legal rights but relied upon the petitioner's "stake as a taxpayer" to permit her to challenge the constitutionality of federal expenditures. The "stake as a taxpayer" was derived from the combination of two constitutional provisions, neither of which guaranteed any legal right to an individual.

> [O]ur point of reference in this case is the standing of
> individuals who assert only the status of federal taxpayers and
> who challenge the constitutionality of a federal spending pro-
> gram. Whether such individuals have standing to maintain that
> form of action turns on whether they can demonstrate the nec-
> essary stake as taxpayers in the outcome of the litigation to
> satisfy Article III requirements.
>
> The nexus demanded of federal taxpayers has two aspects
> to it. First, the taxpayer must establish a logical link between
> that status and the type of legislative enactment attacked. Thus,
> a taxpayer will be a proper party to allege the unconstitutional-
> ity only of exercises of congressional power under the taxing
> and spending clause of Art. 1 § 8, of the Constitution. . . . Sec-
> ondly the taxpayer must establish a nexus between that status
> and the precise nature of the constitutional infringement al-
> leged. Under the requirement, the taxpayer must show that the
> challenged enactment exceeds specific constitutional limitations
> imposed upon the exercise of the congressional taxing and
> spending power and not simply that the enactment is generally
> beyond the powers delegated to Congress by Art. I § 8.(102–3)

While the Court did not use the term "legal right," it did go to great
lengths to explain the existence of a "legally protected right" that resulted from a combination of two specific provisions of the Constitution.
Flast did not reject the necessity of a legal right's existence but expanded
the means of discerning a legal right from the Constitution. The demon-
stration "of the necessary stake as taxpayer" is tantamount to the traditional legal right.[8] One could argue that *Flast* is merely an aberration,
but the precedent does exist for the Court to find a legally protected
right derived from two or more provisions of the Constitution.

The Constitution is a major source of legally protected rights that
may be the basis of a "case" or "controversy." In the final analysis, the
Supreme Court determines the extent to which the federal judiciary
may become an active participant in the political process predicated on
protecting rights guaranteed by the Constitution. If the Constitution
means what the Supreme Court says it means, the Constitution protects
those rights that the Court says it protects.

Statutory Law—Legal Rights and Remedies

The general rule is that, when a legal right has been violated, the
courts will afford a remedy. One commentator has suggested, however,

that this is a mere tautology. If the courts provide a remedy, a legal right exists, but if no remedy is available, no legal right exists.[9] When one examines statutory law, the relationship between rights and remedies becomes very complex. Three potential situations exist. (1) Congress may simultaneously establish a legal right and provide a remedy. (2) A statute may establish a legal right with the assumption that a remedy will be available under general jurisdiction or remedial statutes. (3) Congress may establish a remedy for someone who otherwise would not possess a legal right. The last situation is the most difficult to square with the general axiom that no right exists without a remedy. Has Congress by implication created a legal right or, as Professor Kenneth Culp Davis has suggested, has Congress created the anomalous situation where one has a legal remedy but no legal right?[10]

Congress May Simultaneously Establish a Legal Right and Provide a Remedy

Congressional power to simultaneously create legal rights and provide judicially enforceable remedies follows naturally from powers granted by Article I Section 8 and Article III Section 2. Congress may establish legal rights and provide legal remedies as long as it does not exceed its constitutionally delegated powers. But Congress may not exceed its constitutional powers in creating new legal rights nor in providing a remedy.[11]

In the Open Housing Section of the Civil Rights Act of 1968 Congress not only created legal rights for minorities in the sale, lease, or renting of real estate handled by a broker but also provided remedies for any infringement of these rights.[12] Congress relied on its power to control interstate commerce and its enforcement power under the Fourteenth Amendment's Fifth Section as the basis for the creation of legal rights.[13] Congress ensured the protection of those rights by both administrative and judicial remedies. The statute provided that a "person aggrieved," that is, one who claims to have been injured or believes he is about to be irrevocably injured by discriminatory housing practices, may file a complaint with the Secretary of Housing and Urban Development. Unless there is comparable state or local administrative machinery for handling the complaint, the Secretary will attempt to resolve the dispute. If, within thirty days of filing such a complaint, the Secretary or a state or local agency has not resolved the matter, then a civil action may be commenced. The action may be brought in the proper federal district court unless a state or local fair housing law "provides rights and remedies for alleged discriminatory housing practices which are substantially equivalent to the rights and remedies provided in this subchapter."[14]

A general remedial section specified the remedies that the courts could enforce.

> The rights granted by section 3603, 3604, 3605 and 3606 may be enforced by civil actions in appropriate United States district courts without regard to the amount in controversy and in appropriate State or local courts of general jurisdiction. . . .
>
> (c) The court may grant as relief, as it deems appropriate, any permanent or temporary injunction, temporary restraining order, or other order, and may award to the plaintiff actual damages and not more than $1,000 punitive damages, together with court costs and reasonable attorney fees in the case of a prevailing plaintiff: *Provided,* That the said plaintiff in the opinion of the court is not financially able to assume said attorney's fees.[15]

Thus Congress created legal rights and simultaneously provided both administrative and judicial remedies.

In *Trafficante* v. *Metropolitan Life Insurance Company,* the Court unanimously upheld this simultaneous creation of legal rights and legal remedies by Congress. The Court accepted a determination by a Department of Housing and Urban Development assistant regional administrator that the petitioners were "aggrieved persons" covered by the statute. Trafficante and the other petitioners were whites who alleged that they were aggrieved because their landlord discriminated against nonwhites. Although the Court's decision was unanimous, three Justices apparently felt that it was necessary to emphasize the role Congress had played in creating a "case" or "controversy."

> Absent the Civil Rights Act of 1968, I would have great difficulty in concluding that petitioners complaints in this case presented a case or controversy within the jurisdiction of the District Court under Art. III of the Constitution. But with the statute purporting to give all those who are authorized to complain to the agency the right also to sue in court, I would sustain the statute insofar as it extends standing to those in the position of the petitioners in this case.(212)

Congress May Establish a Legal Right with the Assumption That a Remedy Will Be Available under General Jurisdictional or Remedial Statutes

The second situation arises when Congress enacts a statute creating a legal right but does not indicate any specific remedy. The Civil Rights Act of 1968 also illustrates this situation:

It shall be unlawful to coerce, intimidate, threaten, or interfere with any person in the exercise or enjoyment of, or on
account of his having exercised or enjoyed, or on account of his
having aided or encouraged any other person in the exercise or
enjoyment of, any right granted or protected by Section 3603,
3604, 3605 or 3606 of this title. This section may be enforced
by appropriate civil actions.[16]

A legal right was established to remain free from interference in exercising the rights guaranteed by the Act or in aiding someone else in the
exercise of these rights. The courts could supply a remedy under the
provisions of general remedial and jurisdictional statutes.

Two recent Supreme Court decisions are illustrative of this point.
The decisions concerned open housing but were predicated on the
Civil Rights Act of 1866. In the Act of 1866, Congress provided: "All
citizens of the United States shall have the same right, in every State
and Territory, as is enjoyed by white citizens thereof to inherit, purchase, lease, sell, hold, and convey real and personal property."[17] The
Act provided only for criminal penalties against any person denying
such rights under color of law.

In *Jones* v. *Alfred H. Mayer Co.*, Jones brought a civil action under
the Act of 1866 alleging damages and seeking injunctive and other
relief. Jones alleged that the realty company had refused to sell him a
house solely because he was black. The lower federal courts had dismissed the action on the basis that the Act of 1866 had created rights
only against state action. The Supreme Court reversed and held that
the Act had created a right against private invasions as well as state
action under the power granted to Congress by the Thirteenth
Amendment.

For the Court, Justice Potter Stewart upheld Jones's right to seek
an injunction, but denied any right to damages. "And, although it can
be enforced by injunction, it contains no provision expressly authorizing a federal court to order the payment of damages"(414). Stewart did
not deny that damages might be awarded, but indicated that the question was not properly pleaded and that the issue could be settled by
equitable means. Stewart also indicated in a note that the absence of
any specific provision for equitable relief in the Act was immaterial.
"The fact that 42 U.S.C. 1982 is couched in declaratory terms and
provides no explicit method of enforcement does not, of course, prevent a federal court from fashioning an effective equitable remedy"(414). The Court held, therefore, that Jones had a legal right
under the 1866 Act to purchase the home involved and that the federal
courts could provide a remedy in the form of an injunction.

Justice John Marshall Harlan dissented on the basis that the 1866

Act did not apply to private actions, as well as on the basis that the issue lacked "public importance" since the 1968 Civil Rights Act had been enacted, although the latter was not in effect at the time of the decision. Since Harlan contended that the Act of 1866 did not create a legally protected right, he did not reach the question of whether a remedy could be implied.

The Court also examined the question of whether remedies were available for allegedly private discrimination under the Act of 1866 in *Sullivan* v. *Little Hunting Park, Inc.* The action originated in a state court, but both the majority and minority opinions analyzed the availability of implied remedies. As a member of Little Hunting Park, Inc., Sullivan had been entitled to the use of the corporation's recreational facilities. Sullivan built a new house in the neighborhood and attempted to transfer his original membership share to the lessee of his original home, a black named Freeman. Freeman was refused membership by the board, and when Sullivan objected, he was expelled from the corporation. Sullivan brought an action for injunctive relief and damages, while Freeman joined in the action seeking only damages since he had moved out of the area. Both parties predicated their actions on the same section of the Act that was involved in *Jones*.

The Court held that damages might be recovered in a state court as well as in a federal court. In delivering the opinion of the Court, Justice William O. Douglas relied on a general principle enunciated in *Bell* v. *Hood*.

> [W]here federally protected rights have been invaded, it has been the rule from the beginning that courts will be alert to adjust their remedies so as to grant the necessary relief. And it is also well settled that where legal rights have been invaded, and a federal statute provides for a general right to sue for such invasion, federal courts may use any available remedy to make good the wrong done.(238)

Douglas concluded: "The existence of a statutory right implies the existence of all necessary and appropriate remedies." He also asserted that it was possible for either federal or state courts to grant relief in the form of damages on the basis of 42 U.S.C. 1988, which Douglas quoted.

> "The jurisdiction in civil *** matters conferred on the district courts by the provisions of this chapter and Title 18, for the protection of all persons in the United States in their civil rights, and for their vindication, shall be exercised and enforced in conformity with the laws of the United States, so far as such laws are suitable to carry the same into effect; but in all cases were they are not adopted to the object, or are deficient in

the provisions necesary to furnish suitable remedies and punish offenses against law, the common law, as modified and changed by the constitution and statutes of the state wherein the court having jurisdiction of such civil or criminal cause is held, so far as the same is not inconsistent with the Constitution and laws of the United States, shall be extended to and govern the said courts in the trial and disposition of the cause."(239–40)

Douglas interpreted the statute to mean that either federal or state remedies could be invoked. He concluded that a remedy in the form of damages was available: "The rule of damages, whether drawn from federal or state sources, is a federal rule responsive to the need whenever a federal right is impaired"(240).

In a dissenting opinion, Justice Harlan argued that the majority was attempting to simplify a complex situation in relation to the question of remedies.

In deciding that there is a right to recover damages in this case, the majority overlooks the complications involved by dint of the fact that a state court is being asked to provide a remedy for a federal right bottomed on a federal statute which itself has no remedial provisions.

Implied remedies for federal rights are sometimes solely a matter of federal law and other times dependent, either wholly or partially, upon state law. Difficult and complex questions are involved in determining what remedies a state court must or must not provide in cases involving federal rights.(255–56)

Harlan argued that Section 1988 of Title 42 did not apply to remedial powers to be exercised by state courts but only by federal courts.

Jones and *Sullivan* illustrate that, once Congress creates a legally protected right and, as *Jones* indicates, the courts really define the extent of such legal right, a remedy may be found in jurisdictional and remedial statutes, in equity, or in some instances, as Section 1988 of Title 42 makes explicit, under the common law. Although Congress creates the legal rights and provides the remedies, the courts interpret them and collate them.

Congress May Establish a Remedy for Someone Who Otherwise Would Not Possess a Legal Right

The most controversial situation arises when Congress provides a remedy and thereby provides access to the federal courts for a party who without the specific remedial statute would be denied access to the courts on the ground that he did not possess a legally protected right.

These statutes may be classified either as general, where "any person aggrieved" by stipulated action may commence a "case" or "controversy," or specific, where the Attorney General is granted the right to commence a legal action.

The latter situation is found in the Open Housing Title of the Civil Rights Act of 1968.

> Whenever the Attorney General has reasonable cause to believe that any person or group of persons is engaged in a pattern or practice of resistance to the full enjoyment of any of the rights granted by this subchapter, or that any group of persons has been denied any of the rights granted by this subchapter and such denial raises an issue of general public importance, he may bring a civil action in any appropriate United States district court by filing with it a complaint setting forth the facts and requesting such preventive relief, including an application for a permanent or temporary injunction, restraining order, or other order against the person or persons responsible for such pattern or practice or denial of rights, as he deems necessary to insure the full enjoyment of the rights granted by this subchapter.[18]

Like other recent civil rights enactments, the Act creates a judicial remedy that may be invoked by the Attorney General to protect rights of private individuals.[19] One could argue that the Attorney General could bring an action without specific statutory authority. This contention is questionable. In *United States* v. *Republic Steel Corp.*, a 5–4 decision, the Court concluded that the Attorney General could institute a civil action if "the United States had an interest to protect or defend"(492). Since the United States would have no interest, other than as *parens patriae*, and the Act provides adequate remedies for enforcement, the Attorney General probably would not be able to initiate civil actions based on the Civil Rights Act of 1968 without statutory authorization.

Although the Court has not discussed the constitutionality of granting this type of remedy to the Attorney General in detail, the Court has accepted congressional power to permit the Attorney General to bring this type of action.[20] The Court has apparently assumed that the Attorney General has an interest in the enforcement of private rights guaranteed by federal statutes, and that Congress may provide a remedy that elevates the Attorney General's interest to a legally protected right. The instant situation is distinguished from an attempt to obtain an advisory opinion, since both parties have an interest and that interest is adverse.

A more complex question arises when Congress enacts the reme-

dial statute in general terms. These statutes have been enacted primarily as the result of the growth of administrative law. Although numerous examples could be cited of statutes that provide remedies against
administrative action, the most all-encompassing statute is the Administrative Procedure Act of 1946.[21]

> Except so far as (1) statutes preclude judicial review or (2)
> agency action is by law committed to agency discretion—
> (a) Any person suffering legal wrong because of any
> agency action, or adversely affected or aggrieved by such action
> within the meaning of any relevant statute, shall be entitled to
> judicial review thereof. . . .
> (c) Every agency action made reviewable by statute and
> every final agency action for which there is no other adequate
> remedy in any court shall be subject to judicial review.[22]

Except for the limitations noted in the introductory clause, judicial
review is provided for any person who falls into one of the three classes
enumerated in subsection (a). Although the legislative history is ambig-
uous, the real questions are raised by the second and third categories.[23]
By "any person suffering legal wrong," Congress was apparently referring to the traditional concept of protecting a legal right. There can be
little question, however, that the inclusion of those "adversely affected
or aggrieved by such action" is stated in extremely general terms. A
person "aggrieved" may be one who has not suffered a "legal wrong."
Since this language was used prior to the enactment of the APA and
was given an expansive interpretation by the Supreme Court, the language can hardly be attributed to legislative inadvertence. Who is entitled to judicial review under the "adversely affected" provision is the
most difficult question. While persons who claim to have been "aggrieved" must show that their grievance is within the meaning of a
"relevant statute," it is not clear that this phrase modifies or limits those
"adversely affected." If it does, the statute still expands the legal remedy beyond those who can show a legal injury. If it does not, the statute
opens the judicial doors to anyone "adversely affected in fact" without
showing that "any relevant statute" has been violated. In either instance, a remedy is made available that did not exist prior to the passage of the APA and its precursors.

Federal Communications Commission v. *Sanders Bros. Radio Station* is
the case that established the doctrine that Congress may provide a legal
remedy for one who otherwise would not have a legally protected right.
Although *Sanders* was decided prior to the enactment of the APA, the
decision was predicated upon similar language contained in the Federal
Communications Act of 1934. From a procedural perspective, the question was whether the owners of an existing radio station could chal-

lenge the granting of a license to a competitor. The Government argued that on the basis of the common law rule followed in the TVA disputes, a radio station had no legal right to be free from competition. The Communications Act of 1934 declared, however, that an FCC decision could be appealed to the Court of Appeals for the District of Columbia (1) by an applicant for a license or permit, or (2) "by any other person aggrieved or whose interests are adversely affected by any decision of the Commission granting or refusing any such application"(476–77). In upholding Sanders's right to institute the action, Justice Owen J. Roberts offered the following explanation for a unanimous Court:

> The petitioner insists that as economic injury to the respondent was not a proper issue before the Commission it is impossible that sec. 402 (b) was intended to give the respondent standing to appeal, since absence of right implies absence of remedy. This view would deprive subsection (2) of any substantial effect.
>
> Congress had some purpose in enacting sec. 402 (b) (2). It may have been of opinion that one likely to be financially injured by the issue of a license would be the only person having a sufficient interest to bring to the attention of the appellate court errors of law in the action of the Commission in granting the license. It is within the power of Congress to confer such standing to prosecute an appeal.(477)

Unfortunately, the Court did not return to the question of the reciprocal nature of a legal right and a legal remedy. Congress provided a remedy that gave the respondents standing, but the Court did not specify what legal right of their own they were litigating. In fact, the Court appeared to deny that the radio station had any personal right to protect, but permitted Sanders to bring the action to insure that the Commission was acting in the "public convenience, interest, or necessity."

Does *Sanders* and its progeny stand for the principle that one may have a legal remedy without possessing a legal right? The problem and the solution have been cogently described by Professor Kenneth Culp Davis.

> The notion that the complaining station has no "legal right" but that its financial or economic "interest" in avoiding new competition is entitled to legal protection is the sheerest logomachy, for the only practical issue is whether or not the right or interest should be entitled to legal protection. To provide legal protection to what the Court solemnly asserts is not a "right" is merely twisting the usual meaning of words, impairing an established

means of communication, and causing needless confusion and complexity. If the Court gives legal protection to the interest, then denying that the holder of the interest has a "right" is contradictory, if the usual meaning of these terms is followed. The most amusing consequence of this web of unreality lies in the proposition for which the Sanders case now stands—that the complaining station has a remedy without a right!

The cure for this excessive conceptual refinement lies in the plain and practical simplicity of acknowledging that if the "interest" is legally protected, then it deserves to be called a "right." . . . To say that a station "aggrieved" or "adversely affected" has a "right" to prevent illegal action would be consistent with the provision limiting rights created by licenses. This simple solution would satisfy the case or controversy doctrine requirement; it would escape needless confusion about the distinction between rights and interests; it would end the artificiality of pretending that a private party upholding one side of an adversary proceeding may not represent his interest.[24]

Whether or not Davis's arguments are accepted, one must admit that, in suits analogous to *Sanders,* the party commencing the action is permitted to protect his own legal right or a public legal right. In either instance, the enforceable legal right exists solely as a result of a remedial statute enacted by Congress, i.e., since Congress has established a legal remedy, which would not be available except for the remedial statute, it has simultaneously created a legally protected right that may be the basis of a "case" or "controversy."

This does not mean that Congress may create a "case" or "controversy" but rather that Congress does have substantial control over one of the inherent elements of the requirement. If any of the other three elements is absent, e.g., adversity, Congress may not create a "case" or "controversy." Conversely, if the other three elements are present, Congress may provide the missing link in the form of a legal right or legal remedy. In this limited sense, Congress may create a "case" or "controversy." Congressional power is tempered, however, by the judiciary's power to determine the constitutionality of statutes as well as its power to interpret such enactments.

Treaties—Legal Rights

In surveying the potential sources of legal rights that may be the basis of a "case" or "controversy," all sources are obviously not of equal importance. Treaties have not been a major source but are a potential source of a legal right. In *Edye* v. *Robertson* (Head Money Cases) Justice Samuel F. Miller indicated that personal legal rights may be created by a treaty.

> But a treaty may also contain provisions which confer certain rights upon the citizens or subjects of one of the nations residing in the territorial limits of the other, which partake of the nature of municipal law, and which are capable of enforcement as between private parties in the courts of the country. An illustration of this character is found in treaties which regulate the mutual rights of citizens and subjects of the contracting nations in regard to rights of property by descent or inheritance when the individuals concerned are aliens. . . . A treaty, then, is a law of the land as an act of Congress is, whenever its provisions prescribe a rule by which the rights of the private citizen or subject may be determined. And when such rights are of a nature to be enforced in a court of justice, that court resorts to the treaty for a rule of decision for the case before it as it would to a statute.(598–99)

United States v. *Rauschler* is a case in which this principle was applied. Great Britain extradited Rauschler on a murder charge. Rauschler was tried, however, on a minor offense not covered by the treaty. In upholding Rauschler's legal right under the treaty, Justice Miller concluded:

> [I]t is impossible to conceive of the exercise of jurisdiction in such a case for any other purpose than that mentioned in the treaty, and ascertained by the proceedings under which the party is extradited, without an implication of fraud upon the rights of the party extradited, and of bad faith to the country which permitted his extradition.(422)

Executive agreements have also been a source of legal rights, albeit an extremely limited one. In *United States* v. *Belmont* and *United States* v. *Pink*, both based on the Litvinov Agreement of 1933, the Court held that executive agreements could be the source of legal rights. In both instances, however, the Executive Agreement created a legal right enforceable by the United States Government on the basis of an assignment of Soviet assets in this country. To what extent, if any, executive agreements could create rights for private individuals is purely an academic question. While treaties and executive agreements are potential sources of legal rights, the federal courts employ remedies drawn from equity, common law, and/or statutory law in order to enforce these rights.

Other Potential Sources of Legal Rights and Remedies

Since the Constitution, laws passed by Congress in pursuance thereof, and treaties are the supreme law of the land, the federal courts obviously may enforce legal rights derived from these three sources.[25] Are the federal courts limited to enforcing rights derived from these sources? Although they are important sources, the federal judiciary does act to protect legal rights derived from other sources. These are: (1) State Law. Diversity of citizenship cases are predicated on the enforcement of legal rights created by state law. A major proportion of the "cases" and "controversies" decided by the federal district courts are diversity of citizenship cases. Also the Supreme Court is often confronted with the dilemma of an appeal from a state judicial system where a federal question was decided, although the original action would not have been a "case" or "controversy" in a federal court. The Court must either dismiss the appeal, allowing the state decision on the federal question to stand, or ignore the procedural question and rule on the federal question. If the Court selects the latter option, state law has determined the existence of a legal right. (2) Common Law. Although the general rule is that there is no federal common law, the Court has indicated in a few instances that the federal judiciary may enforce legal rights predicated on common law. (3) Equity. Equity is primarily a source of remedies. Since rights and remedies are reciprocal in nature, however, the federal courts may apply an equitable remedy to protect an interest or prevent a loss when no remedy is available at law. A federal court may issue an injunction in a situation where there would be no remedy and thus no right at law.

State Law—Legal Rights and Remedies

No one can deny that federal judicial power may be invoked to protect legal rights and enforce legal remedies created by federal law. One might assume, however, that state law could not be used to determine whether there was a right or remedy that could lead to the exercise of the federal judicial power. In two situations, state law may be the determining factor. These are diversity of citizenship cases and cases appealed to the United States Supreme Court from a state court.

The Constitution, in Article III Section 2, extends the federal judicial power to controversies between citizens of different states, and since the First Congress, Congress has authorized the application of state law in diversity cases.[26] The two famous cases in this area, *Swift* v. *Tyson* and *Erie Railroad Co.* v. *Tompkins,* were concerned primarily with the substantive law to be applied. In 1938 *Erie* overruled the 1842 *Swift* decision by holding that state law, from whatever source derived, including decisions of the state's highest court, should be dispositive of a diversity case. The Court's opinion in *Erie* is broad enough, however, to include procedural as well as substantive law. Justice Louis D. Brandeis held for the Court:

> Except in matters governed by the Federal Constitution or by Acts of Congress, the law to be applied in any case is the law of the State. And whether the law of the State should be declared by its Legislature in a statute or by its highest court in a decision is not a matter of federal concern. There is no federal general common law. Congress has no power to declare substantive rules of common law applicable in a State whether they be local in their nature or "general," be they commercial law or a part of the law of torts.(78)

In diversity of citizenship cases, should the federal courts protect legal rights and apply remedies recognized by state law but not by federal law?

Federal courts do protect legal rights created by state law in diversity actions. Although the Court has not given an authoritative answer concerning remedies, it has indicated that the answer may be in the affirmative.[27] In *Guaranty Trust Co. of New York* v. *York,* the Court considered whether a state statute of limitations barred a diversity action. Justice Felix Frankfurter's opinion suggests that state law is determinative of the existence of a legal right as well as a remedy in diversity actions.

> Since a federal court adjudicating a state-created right solely because of the diversity of citizenship of the parties is for that purpose, in effect only another court of the State, it cannot afford recovery if the right to recover is made unavailable by the State nor can it substantially effect the enforcement of the right as given by the State.(108–9)

The Court has not clearly indicated, therefore, the impact that state remedies may have in diversity actions.

A more perplexing problem arises when an action originates in a state court and is properly appealed to the United States Supreme Court. State courts are not limited to deciding "cases" or "controversies," nor are they limited by federal law concerning what constitutes a legal right or a legal remedy. State constitutions or state laws may provide that state courts may render advisory opinions or provide legal remedies that are not recognized by federal law. (This was the situation when the federal courts refused to recognize the declaratory judgment action.) Yet when the state court acts, it is still bound by the supreme law of the land, so that a federal question may be decided. Thus a state court may interpret the United States Constitution, statutes enacted by Congress, or a treaty and do so in an action that is not recognized as a "case" or "controversy" to which federal judicial power extends. The United States Supreme Court has two options when an action otherwise properly before it has been appealed from a state court, and when the legal right or remedy involved is one not recognized by federal courts. The Court may ignore the procedural question and rule on the substantive issue, or it may dismiss the action as not presenting a "case" or "controversy." (The Court may also adjust its concept of a "case" or "controversy"; see discussion of federalism in Chapter 9 *infra.*)

Doremus v. *Board of Education* is an example of the latter situation. The New Jersey Supreme Court had sustained a State statute that provided for Bible reading in the State's public schools. The United States Supreme Court declined to rule on the action because it lacked "jurisdiction." Of the two original plaintiffs, the Court held the issue had become moot with respect to one litigant because the right alleged as a parent no longer existed since the child had graduated. The other plaintiff's right was predicated on his being a state taxpayer. In dismissing the appeal, Justice Robert H. Jackson indicated that the state could decide federal questions in actions that could not be appealed to the United States Supreme Court.

> We do not undertake to say that a state court may not render an opinion on a federal constitutional question even under such circumstances that can be regarded only as advisory. But, because our own jurisdiction is cast in terms of "case" or "controversy" we cannot accept as the basis for review . . . any procedure which does not constitute such.
>
> The taxpayer's action can meet this test, but only when it is a good-faith pocketbook action. It is apparent that the grievance which is sought to litigate here is not a direct dollars-and-cents injury but is a religious difference.(434)

Since no pecuniary loss was shown as the result of the Bible reading, the taxpayer had no legal interest to protect.[28] The plaintiffs were permitted to bring the action in New Jersey's courts and they had, therefore, an enforceable legal right in the state courts. Despite the Court's inference, the New Jersey courts had not treated the action as an advisory opinion.[29]

Justice William O. Douglas dissented.

> New Jersey can fashion her own rules governing the institution of suits in her courts. If she wants to give these taxpayers the status to sue . . . I see nothing in the Constitution to prevent it. And when the clash of interests is as real and as strong as it is

here, it is odd indeed to hold there is no case or controversy within the meaning of Art. III § 2 of the Constitution.(436)

In an action appealed from a state court to the United States Supreme Court, the Court determines whether the parties possess a legal right. The Court may, therefore, ignore the issue of the existence of a legal right and decide the substantive issue. In 1952 the Court handed down two other decisions that illustrate the Court's ability to disregard the question of legal rights. In *Adler* v. *Board of Education,* decided the same day as *Doremus,* the Court upheld New York's Feinberg Law in an action brought by parents, taxpayers, and teachers (see *Keyishian* v. *Board of Regents,* which struck down the Feinberg Law). For the six-man majority, Justice Sherman Minton completely ignored the question of the plaintiffs' legal rights. Justices Hugo Black and William O. Douglas dissented solely on substantive grounds. In a separate dissenting opinion, Justice Felix Frankfurter was the only member of the Court to question the existence of a federally protected legal right.[30]

Wieman v. *Updegraff* is even more indicative of the Court's discretion. Updegraff brought the action in the Oklahoma state courts to enjoin payment of salaries to the appellants, who were members of the faculty and staff of the Oklahoma Agricultural and Mechanical College, because they had not signed the state's loyalty oath as required by state statute. As Justice Tom C. Clark indicated for the Court, Updegraff brought the action "as a citizen and taxpayer"(185). Updegraff apparently possessed no other right or interest. All eight justices who participated concurred in the opinion striking down the Oklahoma loyalty oath as contrary to the Fourteenth Amendment's due process clause. (Justice Robert H. Jackson did not participate, and Justices Hugo Black and Felix Frankfurter, each joined by Justice William O. Douglas, filed concurring opinions.) Updegraff's legal right was not discussed in either the Court's opinion or in two concurring opinions. He did not possess any pecuniary interest as a taxpayer since there was no indication that, even if the Court had upheld the oath and the appellants had been dismissed, their positions would not be immediately filled. Yet the Court assumed, *sub silentio,* that a bona fide "case" or "controversy" was present.

To the extent that a legal right is a necessary element of a "case" or "controversy," one must assume that a legal right was present in *Wieman.* When one considers the circumstances, however, the Court's preoccupation with the substantive issue may result in a decision in which, under the Court's own previous interpretations, the party may not possess a legal right. The significant fact is that the initial determination of an enforceable legal right has been made by the state judiciary. The United States Supreme Court is then faced with the dilemma of applying the same rules that it has enunciated for the federal judiciary in such circumstances, and possibly dismissing the appeal and allowing the decision of the highest state court to stand, or ignoring the procedural issue and assuming it has been presented with a bona fide "case" or "controversy."

Common Law—Legal Rights and Remedies

According to conventional wisdom there is no federal common law.[31] As a general rule relating to substantive law, this is true.[32] Its validity concerning procedural questions, however, is questionable. In a famous concurring opinion in *Joint Anti-Fascist Refugee Committee* v. *McGrath*, Felix Frankfurter suggested that the federal courts might protect a legal right based on common law.

> A litigant ordinarily has standing to challenge governmental action of a sort that, if taken by a private person, would create a right of action cognizable by the courts. . . . Or standing may be based on an interest created by the Constitution or a statute. . . . But if no comparable common law right exists and no such constitutional or statutory interest has been created, relief is not available judicially.(152)

A series of suits attempting to test the constitutionality of the Tennessee Valley Authority clearly illustrates how the common law may be a potential source of a legal right in the federal courts. *Ashwander* v. *Tennessee Valley Authority* is the first and most famous of these cases. Preferred stockholders of the Alabama Power Company instituted a stockholders' derivative suit and alleged that the Power Company had contracted with TVA to the detriment of the corporation's interests. Such a suit was traditionally an equitable action, and the remedy sought was an injunction. The source of the legal right is not clear.

> In such case it is not necessary for stockholders—when their corporation refuses to take suitable measures for its protection—to show that the managing board or trustees have acted with fraudulent intent or under legal duress. To entitle the complainants to equitable relief, in the absence of an adequate legal remedy, it is enough for them to show the breach of trust or duty involved in the injurious and illegal action. Nor is it necessary to show that the action was *ultra vires* of the corporation. The illegality may be found in the lack of lawful authority on the part of those with whom the corporation is attempting to deal. Thus, the breach of duty may consist in yielding, without appropriate resistance, to governmental demands which

are without warrant of law or are in violation of constitutional restrictions.(319)

Although the Court did not specify the derivation of the legal right involved in *Ashwander,* the right was not predicated on the Constitution or any statute. The two succeeding cases suggest that the legal wrong involved, harm to the stockholders' interest because of the Government's allegedly unlawful action, was predicated on the principles of common law.

In *Alabama Power Co.* v. *Ickes,* the Court affirmed the dismissal of a suit attempting to enjoin the Federal Emergency Administrator of Public Works from making loans and grants to municipalities for the construction of electric systems that would compete with Alabama Power. In rejecting the idea that such competition would violate the power company's legal right, Justice George Sutherland spoke for the Court:

> Unless a different conclusion is required from the mere fact that petitioner will sustain financial loss by reason of the lawful competition which will result from the use by the municipalities of the proposed loans and grants, it is clear that petitioner has no such interest and will sustain no such legal injury as enables it to maintain the present suits. . . . [The Court then pointed out that petitioner had no legal right to protect as a taxpayer that would create a "case" or "controversy."] "An injury, legally speaking, consists of a wrong done to a person, or, in other words, a violation of his right. It is an ancient maxim, that a damage to one, without an injury in this sense (*damnum absque injuria*), does not lay the foundation of an action; because if the act complained of does not violate any of his legal rights, it is obvious that he has no cause to complain. *** Want of right and want of remedy are justly said to be reciprocal. Where therefore there has been a violation of right, the person is entitled to an action." *Parker* v. *Griswold,* 17 Conn. 288, 302, 303, 42 Am. Doc. 739. The converse is equally true, that where, although there is damage, there is no violation of a right, no action can be maintained.
>
> If conspiracy or fraud or malice or coercion were involved, a different case would be presented, but in their absence, plainly enough, the mere consummation of the loans and grants will not constitute an actionable wrong. . . . If its business be curtailed or destroyed by the operations of the municipalities, it will be by lawful competition from which no legal wrong results.
>
> What petitioner anticipates, we emphasize, is damage to

something it does not possess—namely a right to be immune
from lawful municipal competition.(478–80)

The Court ruled that no legal right had been violated, but did so
basically on the ground that no common-law right had been violated.
One should note that the Court's emphasis on lawful competition does
not concern the constitutionality of the federal government's making
the loans and grants to finance the competition but merely the legality
of the competition itself. The petitioner, therefore, could not show a
violation of a legal right.

The Court made the latter point explicit the following year in
Tennessee Electric Power Co. v. *Tennessee Valley Authority.* In this attempt
to challenge TVA's constitutionality, the appellant contended that,
even if it had no legal right to be protected from competition, it could
challenge lawful competition if this competition resulted from the exercise of unconstitutional power. For the Court, Justice Owen J. Roberts
rejected this assertion: "The contention is foreclosed by prior decisions
that the damage consequent on competion, otherwise lawful, is in such
circumstances *damnum absque injuria,* and will not support a cause of
action or a right to sue"(140). Justice Roberts had earlier specified
instances that involved an invasion of a legal right:

> The appellants invoke the doctrine that one threatened
> with direct and special injury by the act of an agent of the
> government which, but for statutory authority for its perfor-
> mance, would be a violation of his legal rights, may challenge
> the validity of the statute in a suit against the agent. The princi-
> ple is without application unless the right invaded is a legal
> right—one of property, one arising out of contract, one pro-
> tected against tortious invasion, or one founded on a statute
> which confers a privilege.(137)

Roberts did not mention the source of the first three rights, but when
one examines them in context, the legal rights concerning property,
contracts, or tortious invasions could be predicated upon the common
law.

In *Ashwander,* the Court held that the stockholders had a legal
right to challenge the corporate board's action. The legal right did not
arise from either a statute or the Constitution. Therefore, one must
conclude that the legal right was predicated on common law or equitable principles. In *Alabama Power* and *Tennessee Electric,* the Court held
that the power companies' legal rights had not been invaded because,
under common law, there was no right to remain free from competition. The logical inference would be that, if a right to remain free from
competition had been recognized under common law, this would be an
acceptable basis on which to predicate a "case" or "controversy."[33]

One should note that there is a distinction between the legal right that gives rise to a "case" or "controversy" and a party's ability to raise a constitutional issue. In *Ashwander,* the plaintiffs were permitted to institute a "case" or "controversy" to protect their rights as stockholders. Once the "case" or "controversy" was before the Court, they were permitted to raise the constitutional issue in order to settle the case. In *Alabama Power* and *Tennessee Electric,* the Court concluded that the issue was the right to remain free from competition, and since no comparable legal right existed under common law, there was no "case" or "controversy" and thus no right to raise the constitutional issue.

The TVA cases indicate that common law may be one source of a legal right. The existence or absence of a legal right was determined by whether or not a legal right existed under common law. Although statutory or constitutional rights have undoubtedly been relied upon more often than rights under common law, the federal courts recognize a common law right as the basis for a "case" or "controversy."

Although *Robinson* v. *Campbell* suggested that common law might also be the basis for providing remedies in the federal courts, there is no evidence that this has been true.[34] The federal courts have relied on equity, however, as a major source for remedies.

Equity—Legal Rights and Remedies

The federal courts' equitable jurisdiction is so elastic that the subject deserves separate treatment (see further discussion of equity in Chapter 6 *infra*). Once Congress has granted the courts jurisdiction, equity provides a major source of remedies for protecting legal rights. When a court invokes equity to prevent irreparable harm to a legal right, the remedy is equitable, but the source of the legal right may be the Constitution, statutes, treaties, state law, or common law. The difficult question is whether equity may also provide the legal right on which a "case" or "controversy" is commenced.

This latter situation is evident when the federal courts use another criterion to determine whether to exercise their equitable jurisdiction: Does the plaintiff have an adequate remedy at law? Technically, the federal courts invoke their equitable jurisdiction only if the answer is in the negative. But what is the situation if the plaintiff does not have any remedy at law? Since rights and remedies are reciprocal, the plaintiff would not possess any legally enforceable right. If the federal courts exercised judicial power in this situation, equity would be the source of both the remedy and the right.

An example of equity providing the remedy and possibly the legal right is in the restraining of unauthorized or illegal action by govern-

mental officials. In *Stark* v. *Wickard,* milk producers sought an injunction to restrain the Secretary of Agriculture from enforcing an order
made under the Agricultural Marketing Agreement Act of 1937. The
Act established no rights for producers, and the order was directed to
the distributors. The lower federal courts had dismissed the suit because it failed to state a claim on which relief could be granted.

The Supreme Court reversed the lower courts' decisions. For the
six-man majority, Justice Stanley Reed examined the question of the
existence of a legal right and emphasized the federal courts' power to
exercise their equitable jurisdiction if a right did exist.

> The district court for the District of Columbia has a gen-
> eral equity jurisdiction authorizing it to hear the suit, but in
> order to recover, the petitioners must go further and show that
> the act of the Secretary amounts to an interference with some
> legal right of theirs. If so, the familiar principle that executive
> officers may be restrained from threatened wrongs in the ordi-
> nary courts in the absence of some exclusive alternative remedy
> will enable the petitioners to maintain their suit; but if the
> complaint does not rest upon a claim of which courts take cog-
> nizance, then it was properly dismissed. The petitioners place
> their reliance upon such rights as may be expressly or impliedly
> created by the Agricultural Marketing Agreement of 1937 and
> the order issued thereunder.(290)

The government contended that the producers had no legally protected right. After pointing out that the order reduced the amount the
producers received for their milk, Reed argued: "To reach the dignity
of a legal right in the strict sense, it must appear from the nature and
character of the legislation that Congress intended to create a statutory
privilege protected by judicial remedies"(306). Reed concluded, however, that the "privilege" could be implied from the statute. "The authority for a judicial examination of the validity of the Secretary's action is found in the existence of courts and the intent of Congress as
deduced from the statutes and precedents as hereafter considered"
(308). The Court held that, although the statute did not provide any
specific remedy for the producers, it did provide that the remedies
specifically provided were to be in addition to any existing remedies,
either at law or in equity. The fact that the producers alleged an actual
financial loss, combined with Congress's implied intent to provide judicial review, created a legal right that could be the basis for invoking the
Court's equitable jurisdiction.

> When ... definite personal rights are created by federal
> statute, similar in kind to those customarily treated in courts of
> law, the silence of Congress as to judicial review is, at any rate

in the absence of an administrative remedy, not to be construed as a denial of authority to the aggrieved person to seek appropriate relief in the federal courts in the exercise of their general jurisdiction.(309)

Although the Court consistently spoke in terms of its general jurisdiction, the action was in equity for an injunction. The producers alleged that a governmental official had exceeded his statutory authority. The producers were not, however, directly protected or given any rights under the statute. The Court did not mention irreparable injury, but suggested that "personal rights" plus the implied intent of Congress were enough to give the producers the right to maintain the action.

Justice Felix Frankfurter dissented on the ground that the real question was whether the producers had a legal right to challenge administrative action carried out under an intricate plan devised by Congress. Since Congress had not provided a legal right for the producers, he argued that the Court should defer to congressional intent.

> Of course the statute concerns the interests of producers, handlers and consumers. But it does not define or create any legal interest for the consumer, and it specifically provides that "No order issued under this title shall be applicable to any producer in his capacity as producer." § 8 C (13) (B).
>
> The statute as an entirety makes it clear that obligations are imposed on handlers alone.(316)

Frankfurter conceded that the producers had an interest, but urged that Congress had not elevated that interest to a legal right. He argued that Congress did provide a remedy for the producers, but strictly an administrative remedy and not a legal remedy. Although Frankfurter argued in terms of remedies, the denial of a legal remedy meant that the party had no legally enforceable right.

The producers did not have any remedy at law and therefore possessed no legal right. The Court did not rely on any equitable right, but on the fact that the producers sought equitable relief in order to find a judicially protected right. Without the existence of the equitable remedy, the producers would not have had any judicially protected right. *Stark* v. *Wickard* does not prove that equity is a source of judicially enforceable rights, but does indicate that the remedy and right are so closely interrelated that, if the Court supplies a remedy, it is tacitly recognizing a judicially enforceable right.

Equity is of primary importance, however, in supplying a remedy to enforce legal rights derived from one of the sources previously discussed. The federal courts' power to invoke equitable remedies is not always based on specific statutes. If Congress has granted the federal courts jurisdiction, and if a legal right is invoked, the courts may supply an equitable remedy in absence of a specific statutory remedy.[35]

Summary—Sources of Legal Rights and Remedies Enforced in Federal Courts

This examination of potential sources of legal rights and remedies that may give life to a "case" or "controversy" has been exhaustive concerning potential sources, although obviously no attempt has been made to be exhaustive concerning each source. Nor has any attempt been made to rank or quantify the sources. The purpose of the present study is to indicate the sources that the federal courts may use to determine the existence of a legal right or a legal remedy. The important point is not the number of cases involved but that the courts may use any of these avenues to find the existence of a legal right or a legal remedy.

The dynamic nature of these sources and consequently the expansion of one of the bases for commencing a "case" or "controversy" is indisputable. New legal rights created by congressional enactments, treaties, and amendments to the United States Constitution as well as by judicial interpretations have greatly expanded the potential sources of legal rights since 1789. Likewise, remedial statutes have increased access to the federal courts, largely as a result of the growth of administrative law.

Congress may establish legal rights and legal remedies but may not create a "case" or "controversy."[36] Congressional action may help to determine whether a "case" or "controversy" exists—i.e., Congress may create a legal right and/or a legal remedy—but, unless the courts find that the other elements are present, there is no "case" or "controversy." In *Sanders,* Congress elevated a preexisting interest into a legally protected interest by providing a legal remedy. If adversity or any other element had been absent, congressional action would not have created a "case" or "controversy." When the other elements are present, however, Congress may supply this one element by either a remedial statute or by creating a new legal right if, of course, it is acting pursuant to its constitutional powers.

Despite the important role that Congress plays in creating legal rights and remedies, the federal courts exercise the primary power of determining the existence of legal rights and remedies. The federal judiciary determines the extent of legal rights from whatever source derived, and if Congress has not explicitly done so, whether or not a legal remedy is available. The federal courts exercise, therefore, great discretion in determining the existence of a legal right, the extent of such right, and whether or not a remedy may be available. Furthermore, once the federal courts have determined that a legal right exists, they may supply the remedy, whether Congress has provided one or not. In the final analysis, the federal courts determine whether a legal right and a legal remedy exist in each specific action, although the courts may have to rely on congressional action to a greater extent in determining the existence of this element of a "case" or "controversy" than in determining any other element.

Judicial power may be invoked only to protect a legal right and only in instances where the court is able to supply a legal remedy. At first blush, this appears to be a tremendous restraint on the activation of the judicial process. On closer examination, one finds that the limitation may be more apparent than real. The federal courts have several sources that they may use in determining the existence of legal rights and remedies. Furthermore, a federal court may emphasize the existence of a legal remedy without explicitly, or even implicitly, mentioning the legal right that gives life to a "case" or "controversy." When the federal judiciary desires to participate in the policy-making process, the necessary existence of a legal right and a legal remedy are not real impediments. When the federal courts desire to remain outside the political arena, the obvious existence of a legal right and legal remedy may prevent the courts from avoiding the issue although the courts may find other elements necessary for a "case" or "controversy" to be absent. If either the right or remedy is not explicit, then the federal courts may use this as a means of avoiding a controversial issue as they did in *Alabama Power* and *Tennessee Electric Power*.

5 The Existence of a Sufficient Interest

Federal courts act only to protect legal rights, but theoretically they do so only to redress or prevent a legal injury. That is, federal judicial power is invoked only when necessary to protect a legal right. This implies that someone has invaded or is about to invade a legal right and therefore commit a legal wrong. Before a "case" or "controversy" exists, one party must invade or threaten to invade another's legal right.

Once a federal court has determined that a legal right exists, basically a question of law, the court must then decide whether the parties before the court are the proper ones to contest the alleged or threatened invasion of the legal right, basically a question of fact. The court must determine whether the parties have the proper interest in the legal right to invoke federal judicial power. (The term "interest" is used here to denote the parties' relationship to the disputed legal right: Does the party possess the requisite relationship to the disputed legal right so that he should be permitted to commence or defend a "case" or "controversy?") More than any other factor, this factor illustrates the distinction between private law actions and public law actions. In a private law action, the plaintiff must be the one whose legal right has been invaded or one who has a fiduciary relationship with him. Likewise, the defendant must be the one who allegedly perpetrated the legal wrong or someone who has a fiduciary relationship with him.

Professor Westel W. Willoughby expressed the traditional position as derived from private law concepts.

> The general rule is that courts will not pass upon the constitutionality of laws or other official acts except in suits duly brought before them, and at the instance of parties whose material interests will be, or have been adversely affected by the enforcement of the laws or the recognition of the validity of the executive or judicial acts which are complained of.[1]

The emphasis on material interest is evidence of the impact that private law has had on public law actions. Professor Edward S. Corwin indicated that adjectives other than "material" were needed to describe the type of interest the Court was requiring in public law actions.

> Equally important as an essential element of a case is the concept of real or substantial interests. Judicial exaction of this

requirement, which is derived from the constitutional limitation of the business of federal courts to cases and controversies, has given rise to a doctrine of judicial restraint confining litigation of official action to cases where the parties assert a direct and immediate interest.[2]

The federal courts have encountered substantial difficulty in determining who has the proper interest to bring a public law action. The Supreme Court has required, for instance, that the interest be real, direct, personal, or substantial. More recently the Court has suggested that a party may bring a "case" or "controversy" to protect the public interest. The Court has not only applied these different tests, but the criteria for each test have not remained constant. Today one may question whether a party must have a direct, personal, or substantial interest to institute a "case" or "controversy," and some commentators have even questioned whether a party needs to have any legal interest (see citations in notes 29 and 33 *infra*). By liberalizing the concept of the necessary interest one must have to institute a "case" or "controversy," the Court has opened the door to more actions involving public policy decisions. Like adversity, the federal courts have almost complete discretion in determining whether the proper parties are before the court. (Congress does play an important role in enacting statutes that provide a remedy for "persons aggrieved" or "adversely affected" by administrative action.) Unlike adversity, the Supreme Court has significantly altered the concept of the interest necessary to institute a "case" or "controversy."

The Court's interpretation of the requisite interest to institute a "case" or "controversy" will be analyzed in this chapter. The Court's use of the terms "direct," "personal," and "substantial" to characterize the type of interest one must have in a legal right will be examined in the first three sections. The Court has not always used these terms consistently and has not always treated them as mutually exclusive. Nevertheless, the terms will be examined separately for analytical purposes. The existence of a judicially enforceable public interest will be examined in the fourth section, while the final section will suggest why "sufficient interest" is the most appropriate of the existing terms.

Substantial Interests

Massachusetts v. *Mellon* is the landmark case concerning substantial interests. The Court decided two actions simultaneously: one was an original action by the State of Massachusetts, and the other was an appeal by an individual litigant. For purposes of clarity, the latter action will be referred to as *Frothingham* v. *Mellon*. Both actions sought to enjoin enforcement of the Maternity Act of 1921. Although other issues were involved, a unanimous Court unequivocally held that neither party had an adequate interest in the litigation. The State's lack of interest will be discussed under direct interest.

Mrs. Frothingham had predicated her action on her interest as a taxpayer, and the lower federal courts had dismissed the action. After claiming that the Act was an unconstitutional infringement of the Tenth Amendment, Mrs. Frothingham contended that the administration of the Act took her property (taxes) in violation of the Fifth Amendment's due process clause. The Supreme Court held that a federal taxpayer qua taxpayer did not have a substantial enough interest to test the Maternity Act's constitutionality. The Court acknowledged that municipal taxpayers were often recognized as having a substantial enough interest to test the legality of municipal expenditures. "The interest of a taxpayer of a municipality in the application of its moneys is direct and immediate and the remedy by injunction to prevent their misuse is not inappropriate"(486). The Court indicated that this was proper because the relationship between a municipal taxpayer and the municipality was analogous, to some extent, to the relationship between a stockholder and a private corporation. The Court held, however, that the analogy could not be extended to a federal taxpayer.

> But the relation of a taxpayer of the United States to the Federal Government is very different. His interest in the moneys of the Treasury—partly realized from taxation and partly from other sources—is shared with millions of others, is comparatively minute and indeterminable, and the effect upon future taxation, of any payment out of the funds, so remote, fluctuating and uncertain, that no basis is afforded for an appeal to the preventive powers of a court of equity.
>
> The administration of any statute, likely to produce additional taxation to be imposed upon a vast number of taxpayers, the extent of whose several liability is indefinite and constantly changing, is essentially a matter of public and not individual concern.(487)

The Court did not completely close the door to federal taxpayers' suits, but indicated that Mrs. Frothingham had not shown a substantial interest. The Court did not specify whether this lack of substantial interest resulted in the absence of a "case" or "controversy" or was the basic reason why the federal courts should not invoke their discretionary equitable jurisdiction. While the Court did refer to the corporate nature of municipalities, it did so only after indicating that the monetary interests in such situations were substantial. What if Mrs. Frothing-ham's tax payments had not been "minute"?[3]

Decisions in state taxpayers' suits suggest that the Court has not relied on the corporate analogy but on the substantial interest test. As indicated, the Court may ignore the question of substantial interest and review a decision appealed from a state court involving a state taxpayer solely on substantive grounds. When the Court has come to grips with the problem, it has held that a state taxpayer may have a substantial interest, but he must establish that fact. In *Doremus* v. *Board of Education,* the Court dismissed the appeal, not because a state taxpayer could not have a sufficient interest to institute a "case" or "controversy" but because the plaintiff had failed to establish that interest. Speaking for the Court, Justice Robert H. Jackson inferred that a state taxpayer might have a substantial interest under the proper circumstances.

> If appellants established the requisite special injury necessary to a taxpayer's case or controversy, it would not matter that their dominant inducement to action was more religious than mercenary. It is not a question of motivation but of possession of the requisite financial interest that is, or is threatened to be, injured by the unconstitutional conduct. We find no such direct and particular financial interest here. If the Act may give rise to a legal case or controversy on some behalf, the appellants cannot obtain a decision from this Court by a feigned issue of taxation.(434–35)

Jackson distinguished *Doremus* from *Everson* v. *Board of Education* by indicating that Everson had shown "a measurable appropriation or disbursement of school-district funds occasioned solely by the activities complained of"(434). In *Doremus,* the Court concluded that the injury to the taxpayer must be "a good faith pocketbook action" or "a direct dollars-and-cents injury"(434). The plaintiff had failed, however, to show any interest as a state taxpayer. Although the Court spoke of a "measurable appropriation" involved in *Everson,* the Court implied in *Doremus* that it is enough if a state taxpayer establishes his interest as a "good faith pocketbook action" without suggesting any quantifiable lim-its—i.e., the Court suggested that showing the activity involves the expenditure of state funds and that the one who is challenging the action contributes taxes to such state funds is enough to establish the requisite interests.

Flast v. *Cohen* can best be viewed in this perspective. *Frothingham* had stressed a federal taxpayer's lack of substantial interest as a ratio-nale for denying the plaintiff the right to bring the action. In *Doremus,* the Court did not stress the plaintiff's lack of a substantial interest but the fact that the suit was not "a good faith pocketbook action." In deciding *Flast,* the Court completely ignored the question of substantial interest and established that in at least one situation, when the congressional power invoked was Article I Section 8's taxing and spending clause and when there was an allegation by a taxpayer that such expenditures violated the First Amendment's establishment clause, a taxpayer had a sufficient interest to institute a "case" or "controversy." The Court did not even imply that the amount of taxes paid was a relevant question.

Speaking for the Court, Chief Justice Earl Warren discussed *Frothingham* and the debate over whether that decision was based solely on the requirements for a "case" or "controversy" or on policy considerations (91–94). The Court held, however, that Mrs. Flast had standing without discussing the issue of a substantial interest. *Frothingham* was distinguished from *Flast* and not overruled, because the claim in the earlier action was predicated on the Fifth Amendment. In *Flast,* the Court explained that "the Due Process Clause of the Fifth Amendment does not protect taxpayers against increases in tax liability, and the taxpayer in *Frothingham* failed to make any additional claim that the harm she alleged resulted from a breach by Congress of the specific constitutional limitations imposed upon an exercise of the taxing and spending power"(105). Warren suggested that Mrs. Frothingham had attempted to assert the State's reserved powers and not a specific limitation imposed on the congressional taxing and spending power. In this respect, the Court concluded:

> We have noted that the Establishment Clause of the First Amendment does specifically limit the taxing and spending power conferred by Art. 1 § 8. Whether the Constitution contains other specific limitations can be determined only in the context of future cases. However, whenever such specific limitations are found, we believe a taxpayer will have a clear stake as a taxpayer in assuring that they are not breached by Congress.(105)

While the Court did not overrule *Frothingham,* the Court did implicitly reject the contention that a federal taxpayer must have a substantial monetary interest in order to institute a "case" or "controversy." The Court's decisions concerning state taxpayers stand for the same principle.[4]

One may question whether the substantial interest test was ever a basic requirement of a "case" or "controversy." The Court's decisions in stockholders' actions indicate that the requirement of substantial interest has been more directly related to determining whether the federal courts should exercise their discretionary equitable jurisdiction. Like *Frothingham,* stockholders' derivative suits are equitable actions in which the federal courts have discretionary jurisdiction based partially on whether irreparable harm is involved. The Court explicitly stated this when it held in *Corbus* v. *Alaska Treadwell Gold Mining Co.* that a stockholder's interest was too minute to result in irreparable harm.

> It appears from the bill that the capital stock of the corporation is divided into 200,000 shares of the par value of $25 each, of which the plaintiff is the owner of 100 shares; that the total annual tax, including fees, amounts to $1,875, which results in a charge upon the plaintiff's interest of less than $1 a year. This would scarcely be a case of "irremediable injury or a total failure of justice." [Quoting from *Hawes* v. *Oakland*, 104 U.S. 450, 460 (1892).](463)

The lack of substantial interest was not related to the existence of a "case" or "controversy" but was a means of determining whether or not the federal courts should invoke their discretionary equitable power.

The federal courts generally determine the adequacy of a stockholder's interest required by the case-or-controversy provision along the lines proffered by Chief Justice Charles Evans Hughes in *Ashwander* v. *Tennessee Valley Authority*.

> While their stock holdings are small, they have a real interest, and there is no question that the suit was brought in good faith. If otherwise entitled, they should not be denied the relief which would be accorded to one who owns more shares.[5](318)

The substantial interest test is further strained by the United States Supreme Court's acceptance of class actions.[6] Since 1938, one who represents a class may institute a case or controversy without consideration of the named plaintiff's actual monetary interest.[7] In *Eisen* v. *Carlisle & Jacquelin*, the Court recognized that Eisen's claim was only for $70 damages, but did not raise any question concerning substantial interest. (The Court did limit the use of class action in *Eisen*, however, by holding that individual notice must be given to all identifiable members of the class.) One may argue that the interests of all the class members are being represented, and therefore there is a substantial interest. One author suggests, however, that the only real party with an interest may be the plaintiff's attorney.[8] No matter how one views the situation, the class action permits an individual who may not meet the traditional substantial interest test to institute a case or controversy.

The demarcation line between what constitutes a substantial interest and what does not is impossible to determine without being completely arbitrary. The Court has never attempted to define or quantify what constitutes a substantial interest. The rule today is that, if any stockholder or taxpayer may bring suit, all in the same situation have sufficient interest, no matter how small their holding or tax bill. The same rule applies to class actions. Since these actions are ordinarily equitable in nature, the federal courts may avoid a decision by holding that irreparable harm will not result if the court fails to act. The court would be refusing to exercise its discretionary jurisdiction, however, and would not be determining whether a "case" or "controversy" is present. In fact, the terminology "substantial interest" is and always has been more directly related to determining the exercise of discretionary equitable jurisdiction than it has to whether a justiciable "case" or "controversy" is before the court.[9] Although *Frothingham* has not been overruled, the requirement of substantial interest as it relates to the "case" or "controversy" provision has fallen by the wayside.

Direct Interest

While the term "substantial interest" denotes the quantity of a party's interest in a disputed legal right, direct interest refers to the party's proximity to the right involved. No problem exists when the party's own right has been directly infringed. When the legal right in dispute is not a specifically protected right of one of the parties, however, a federal court must determine whether that party has a direct enough interest in the action. Justice Felix Frankfurter discussed "directness" in his concurring opinion in *Joint Anti-Fascist Refugee Committee* v. *McGrath.*

> Frequently governmental action directly affects the legal interests of some person, and causes only a consequential detriment to another. Whether the person consequentially harmed can challenge the action is said to depend on the "directness" of the impact of the action on him. . . .
> But it is not always true that only the person immediately affected can challenge the action. . . . The likelihood that the interests of the petitioner will be adequately protected by the person directly affected is a relevant consideration . . . as is, probably, the nature of the relationship involved.(153–54)

Actions in which a state sues as *parens patriae* of its citizens illustrate Justice Frankfurter's point. In *Massachusetts* v. *Mellon,* Massachusetts attempted to invoke the Supreme Court's original jurisdiction to protect its citizens' rights as well as its own reserved powers. In rejecting this as a direct interest, Justice George Sutherland suggested that a state might have an adequate interest in protecting its citizens' rights under some circumstances, but not when the issue involved was the constitutionality of a federal statute.

> It cannot be conceded that a State, as *parens patriae,* may insti-
> tute judicial proceedings to protect citizens of the United States
> from the operation of the statutes thereof. While the State,
> under some circumstances, may sue in that capacity for the
> protection of its citizens . . . it is no part of its duty or power to
> enforce their rights in respect of their relations with the Fed-
> eral Government. In that field it is the United States, and not
> the State, which represents them as *parens patriae,* when such
> representation becomes appropriate.(485–86)

The Court concluded that a state had no direct interest in protecting its
citizens from federal legislation.

The Court has held, however, that one state may sue another state
to protect its citizens. In *Missouri* v. *Illinois,* the Court permitted Missouri to bring an original action to protect its citizens against the drain-
age of large quantities of sewage into the Mississippi River. "But it must
surely be conceded that if the health and comfort of the inhabitants of
a State are threatened, a State is the proper party to represent and
defend them"(241). The Court also held in *Hopkins Federal Savings and
Loan* v. *Cleary* that a state may bring an action against a state-chartered
corporation partially on the grounds of protecting its citizens. "Aside
from the direct interest of the state in the preservation of agencies
established for the common good, there is thus the duty of the *parens
patriae* to keep faith with those who have put their trust in the parental
power"(340). The Court distinguished this situation from *Massachusetts*
v. *Mellon.*

> The ruling was that is was no part of the duty or power of a
> state to enforce the rights of its citizens in respect of their
> relations to the Federal Government. . . . Here, on the con-
> trary, the state becomes a suitor to protect the interests of its
> citizens against the unlawful acts of the corporations created by
> the state itself.(341)

While a state has no interest in protecting its citizens from the Federal
Government, the states' position as *parens patriae* is a direct enough
interest to enable it to protect its citizens' rights in other situations.
(One should note that, in these situations, the state is attempting to
protect the interests of all its citizens. The same situation does not
prevail when the state is attempting to assert a specific citizen's right
possibly to circumvent the Eleventh Amendment. See *New Hampshire* v.
Louisiana.)

The Court has often allowed a litigant to raise a third party's right
once a "case" is properly in existence.[10] This situation is not related to
the necessary interest to commence a "case" or "controversy" but to the
exercise of judicial power once a "case" is properly before the court. In

some instances, however, the Court has not really distinguished between the legal right that is the basis of the "case" or "controversy" and the ability of a party to raise a third person's legal right once the action has been instituted.

Truax v. *Raich* and *National Assoc. for the Advancement of Colored People* v. *Alabama* ex rel. *Patterson* are examples of the latter situation. *Truax* is probably the closest that the Court has come to allowing a party to base a "case" or "controversy" on a third party's legal right, but even in *Truax*, the Court suggested that the original plaintiff had a direct interest.[11] An Arizona law provided that any employer of five or more persons must employ "not less than eighty (80) percent qualified electors or native-born citizens of the United States or some subdivision thereof"(35). An employer who violated this provision was guilty of a misdemeanor. (The only penalty imposed on the employee was for failure to report that he was an alien.) Raich was a native-born Austrian and not a qualified elector. He commenced an equity action against his employer (Truax), Arizona's Attorney General, and a county attorney. A federal district court had issued a temporary restraining order, since it appeared that the county was enforcing the act against Truax so that Raich might be discharged while the action was pending.

The Supreme Court discussed the procedural questions in the context of the defendants' motion to dismiss. The defendants alleged that the suit was barred by the Eleventh Amendment as one against a state, but the Court rejected this argument. The defendants also argued that there were three other reasons why Raich had no right to institute the action. With Justice Charles Evans Hughes speaking for the eight-man majority, the Court answered all three contentions in one long paragraph. One has difficulty, therefore, in determining where the Court was placing its emphasis.

First, to the contention that the suit attempted to enjoin the enforcement of a criminal statute, the Court replied that, while the general rule was that an equity court had no jurisdiction in such instances, there was an exception. Hughes held that a federal court could invoke equitable jurisdiction to enjoin a criminal prosecution to protect property rights from the enforcement of an unconstitutional law. He did not mention, however, that the only person liable to prosecution was the employer.

Second, the Court examined the defendants' contention that Raich had not presented sufficient facts to invoke a court's equity jurisdiction. Hughes urged that "the right to earn a livelihood and to continue in employment unmolested by efforts to enforce void enactments" was a right that a court of equity should enforce when there was no adequate remedy at law (38). The Court relied, therefore, on the employee's right—a right to employment. Hughes indicated, however, that even here the employee had an interest in his employer's right.

> The fact that the employment is at the will of the parties, respectively, does not make it one at the will of others. The employé has manifest interest in the freedom of the employer to exercise his judgment without illegal interference or compulsion, and, by the weight of authority, the unjustified interference of third persons is actionable although the employment is at will.(38)

After establishing that the employee had an enforceable right of his own, the Court held that Raich also had an interest in protecting the employer's right to remain free of illegal interference with the employment contract.

The defendants' third objection was, in part, that "the plaintiff was not entitled to sue for the relief asked"(37). In rejecting this contention, the Court held:

> It sufficiently appears that the discharge of the complainant will be solely for the purpose of meeting the requirements of the act and avoiding threatened prosecution under its provisions. It is, therefore, idle to call the injury indirect or remote.(39)

Since Raich had no adequate remedy at law, the Court decided that the action was one that should be heard by a court of equity. The Court apparently assumed that Raich's interests would not be adequately protected by the person directly affected, his employer.

In *Truax,* the Court did not clearly specify whether Raich had a direct interest or whether he was permitted to bring the action to vindicate his employer's rights. The case is important because it indicates that there may be circumstances when a party may commence a "case" or "controversy" although the basic legal right involved is not one that directly protects or regulates the plaintiff.

Tileston v. *Ullman* is a decision that is the antithesis of *Truax. Tileston* is the first case in the trilogy involving the Connecticut Anti-Contraceptive Law.[12] In a *per curiam* opinion, the Supreme Court dismissed the action on the grounds that a physician had no standing to assert his patients' constitutional rights. The Court did not state that a physician had no interest in his patients' constitutional rights. The Court did emphasize, however, that Dr. Tileston had not asserted any personal interest. "The complaint set out in detail the danger to the lives of appellant's patients in the event that they should bear children, but contained no allegation asserting any claim under the Fourteenth Amendment of infringement of appellant's liberty or his property rights"(45). In holding that the state court proceedings "present no constitutional question which appellant has standing to assert," the Court again emphasized Tileston's lack of any direct interest.

> The sole constitutional attack upon the statutes under the Fourteenth Amendment is confined to their deprivation of life—obviously not appellant's but his patients'. There is no allegation or proof that appellant's life is in danger. His patients are not parties to this proceeding and there is no basis on which we can say that he has standing to secure an adjudication of his patients' constitutional right to life, which they do not assert in their own behalf.(46)

The Court concluded that the only question before it was one concerning the patients. The Court held that it would be improper, at the appellate level, to consider any possible deprivation of Tileston's constitutional rights.

What is the real distinction between *Truax* and *Tileston?* The relationship involved seems to be of little importance. The confidential relationship that exists between a physician and his patient certainly gives the physician as much or more interest in protecting his patients' legal rights than an employee has in protecting his employer's rights. The distinction between the two cases is that Raich was able to show some personal interest in a legal right, while Tileston made no attempt to establish any personal interest. In order to commence a "case" or "controversy" and raise a third person's legal right, therefore, a party must establish a personal interest, no matter how tenuous.[13] Of course, the Court may interpret the interest involved either stringently if it wishes to avoid a decision as in *Tileston* or liberally if it wants to render a decision as in *Truax.*

In *National Assoc. for the Advancement of Colored People* v. *Alabama* ex rel. *Patterson,* a unanimous Court upheld an organization's right to assert its members' constitutional rights as a defense to an action brought by Alabama's Attorney General. The action was instituted in the Alabama courts, seeking an injunction to prevent the NAACP from operating in that State because it had failed to register. While the action was pending, Alabama's Attorney General requested that the State court require the NAACP to furnish the State certain records, including "the names and addresses of all Alabama 'members' and 'agents' of the Association"(453). When the NAACP failed to produce the documents as ordered by the court, the Association was held in civil contempt and fined $10,000. The NAACP then "produced substantially all the data called for by the production order except its membership lists"(454). The fine was then increased to $100,000, and after the Alabama Supreme Court upheld the contempt judgment, the United States Supreme Court granted certiorari.

The United States Supreme Court held that the NAACP could assert the right to freedom of association under the Fourteenth Amendment's due process clause. For a unanimous Court, Justice John Marshall Harlan argued that the NAACP could raise the issue of freedom of association to protect its members' rights.

> The Association both urges that it is constitutionally entitled to resist official inquiry into its membership lists, and that it may assert, on behalf of its members, a right personal to them to be protected from compelled disclosure by the State of their affiliation with the Association as revealed by the membership lists. We think that petitioner argues more appropriately the rights of its members, and that its nexus with them is sufficient to permit that it act as their representative before this Court. In so concluding, we reject respondents' argument that the Association lacks standing to assert here constitutional rights pertaining to the members, who are not of course parties to the litigation.(458–59)

While the issue involved the right to assert a defense, Harlan's opinion indicated that, under proper circumstances, an organization has a direct enough interest in its members' rights to commence a "case" or "controversy." The Court held that the only way the members' rights could be adequately protected was by the organization.

> If petitioner's rank-and-file members are constitutionally entitled to withhold their connection with the Association despite the production order, it is manifest that this right is properly assertable by the Association. To require that it be claimed by the members themselves would result in nullification of the right at the very moment of its assertion. Petitioner is the appropriate party to assert these rights, because it and its members are in every practical sense identical. The Association . . . is but the medium through which its individual members seek to make more effective the expression of their own views.[14](459)

If the members' constitutional rights could be protected only by the organization, the organization could originate a "case" or "controversy" in some circumstances.

The Court has not abolished the requirement of direct interest, but has not always insisted on a direct interest. If a party has any interest in the disputed legal right, a federal court has great discretion in determining whether the interest is direct enough to create a "case" or "controversy." In certain circumstances, a state may institute a "case" or "controversy" to protect the rights of its citizens. An association has an interest in protecting its members' rights, especially when the members would have no adequate remedy. The most difficult situation involves an individual who is attempting to assert the rights of another individual. *Tileston* suggests that the action may not be based solely on the third party's right. *Truax* indicates, however, that if a party establishes any interest of his own, he may predicate a "case" or "controversy" primarily on the rights of a third party.

Personal Interest

The Court has also asserted that a party must possess a personal interest in the legal right before a federal court. Although the Court has not been consistent, it has primarily used this terminology to differentiate an official interest based on the public office one holds, usually a state or local office, and the personal interest one must have to assert a legal right. (The term "personal interest" may also be used to describe a direct interest as well as the antithesis of a public interest.) The Court explicitly stated this requirement in *Marshall* v. *Dye.*

> Among the limitations upon this right [the right of the United States Supreme Court to review the judgment of the highest court of a state] is the principle which requires those who seek to bring in review in this court the judgment of a state court to have a personal, as distinguished from an official interest in the relief sought and in the Federal right alleged to be denied by the judgment of the state court.(257)

The Court followed the personal interest doctrine prior to and subsequent to *Marshall.* [15]

In *Coleman* v. *Miller,* the Court ignored these earlier precedents and permitted Kansas state legislators to appeal a state Supreme Court decision. The legislators alleged that the proposed Child Labor Amendment had not been properly approved by the state senate as the senate journal indicated. Speaking for the Court, Chief Justice Charles Evans Hughes held that the senators had "a plain, direct and adequate interest in maintaining the effectiveness of their votes"(438). Four Justices concurred in the result, but contended that the legislators should not have been permitted to bring the action since they had no "specialized interest of their own to vindicate"(464).

Board of Education v. *Allen* raises further questions about the validity of the dichotomy between official and personal interest. In delivering the Court's opinion, Justice Byron White related some pertinent facts concerning the action.

> Appellant Board of Education of Central School District No. 1 in Rensselaer and Columbia Counties brought suit in the

New York courts against appellee James Allen [New York's
Commissioner of Education]. The complaint alleged that § 701
[of New York State's Education Law] violated both the State
and Federal Constitutions; that if appellants, in reliance on
their interpretation of the Constitution, failed to lend books to
parochial school students within their counties appellee Allen
would remove apellants from office; and that to prevent this,
appellants were complying with the law and submitting to their
constituents a school budget including funds for books to be
lent to parochial school pupils. Appellants therefore sought a
declaration that §701 was invalid, an order barring appellee
Allen from removing appellants from office for failing to comply with it, and another order restraining him from apportion-
ing state funds to school districts for the purchase of textbooks
to be lent to parochial students. After answer, and upon cross-
motions for summary judgment, the trial court held the law
unconstitutional under the First and Fourteenth Amendments
and entered judgment for appellants. . . . The Appellate Division reversed, ordering the complaint dismissed on the ground
that appellant school boards had no standing to attack the validity of a state statute. . . . On appeal, the New York Court of
Appeals concluded by a 4–3 vote that appellant did have standing but by a different 4–3 vote held that §701 was not in violation of either the state or the Federal Constitution.(240–41)

The action involved no personal interest, it was brought in the name of
the Board of Education, and Allen had no personal interest to defend.
Although one New York appellate court had held that the Board of
Education had no standing, and the New York Court of Appeals had
reversed this by only a 4–3 vote, the United States Supreme Court
dismissed the issue in a note.

Appellees do not challenge the standing of appellants to
press their claim in this Court. Appellants have taken an oath
to support the United States Constitution. Believing §701 to be
unconstitutional, they are in the position of having to choose
between violating their oath and taking a step—refusal to comply with §701—that would be likely to bring their expulsion
from office and also a reduction in state funds for their school
districts. There can be no doubt that appellants thus have a
"personal stake in the outcome" of this litigation. *Baker* v. *Carr,*
369 U.S. 186, 204 (1962).(241)

The Court mentioned only the official interest of the Board of Education's members. If taking an oath to uphold the United States Constitution gave them a sufficient interest to challenge a state law that they

believed to be unconstitutional, any local, state, or Federal official should have the same personal stake. A reduction in the school district's funds is not a personal interest. The personal stake involved was no greater than in the earlier actions in which the Court had denied review (see cases cited in note 15 *supra*).

The Court has not rejected the necessity of a personal interest as opposed to an official interest but, as *Allen* indicates, the present application of the requirement is questionable. In *Allen,* the Court's explanation is tantamount to recognizing that official interest is sufficient—especially when the action has originated in a state court and when the highest state court has recognized the interest to be sufficient. The Court may use the requirement of personal versus official interest as a basis for not deciding an issue that it wishes to avoid. On the other hand, the Court could follow *Allen* and permit the issue to be decided on the merits if the Court wanted to decide the issue.

Public Interest

Under traditional legal concepts, one must possess an individual interest to commence a "case" or "controversy." Some recent Supreme Court decisions raise doubts, however, about this concept's relevancy to twentieth-century American constitutional law. May an individual institute a "case" or "controversy" to protect the public interest? This is the reverse of permitting the Attorney General to institute a "case" or "controversy" to protect private rights. In this instance the issue is: May a private individual be given access to the judicial system to protect the public interest or public rights? May a private individual be permitted to perform functions that have historically been assumed to be the sole prerogative of public officials?[16]

Fairchild v. *Hughes* illustrates the traditional concept. The United States Supreme Court dismissed a suit that sought to have the Nineteenth Amendment declared void and to secure an injunction against its enforcement. For a unanimous Court, Justice Louis D. Brandeis indicated that Fairchild lacked the necessary interest in the Nineteenth Amendment's validity.

> Plaintiff has only the right, possessed by every citizen, to require that the government be administered according to law and that the public moneys be not wasted. Obviously this general right does not entitle a private citizen to institute in the federal courts a suit to secure by indirection a determination

whether a statute, if passed, or a constitutional amendment, about to be adopted, will be valid.(129–30)

The Court did recognize that a right existed, although it was not a legally enforceable right. The right belonged to everyone, but an individual citizen did not have a sufficient interest in the legal right to institute a "case" or "controversy."[17]

In 1937 the Court dismissed an original action to require newly appointed Justice Hugo Black "to show cause why he should be permitted to serve as an Associate Justice of the Supreme Court." In a *per curiam* opinion in *Ex parte Levitt,* the Court suggested that the petitioner lacked the requisite interest.

> The motion papers disclosed no interest upon the part of the petitioner other than that of a citizen and a member of the bar of this Court. That is insufficient. It is an established principle that to entitle a private individual to invoke the judicial power to determine the validity of executive or legislative action he must show that he has sustained, or is immediately in danger of sustaining, a direct injury as the result of that action and it is not sufficient that he has merely a general interest common to all members of the public.(634)

In *Frothingham* v. *Mellon,* the Court did not explicitly discuss the public interest, but did make two indirect references to the concept. "The administration of any statute, likely to produce additional taxation to be imposed upon a vast number of taxpayers, the extent of whose several liability is indefinite and constantly changing, is essentially a matter of public and not individual concern"(487). Apparently referring to both Mrs. Frothingham and the state of Massachusetts, the Court later declared:

> The party who invokes the [Court's] power must be able to show not only that the statute is invalid but that he has sustained or is immediately in danger of sustaining some direct injury as the result of its enforcement, and not merely that he suffers in some indefinite way in common with people generally.(488)

The Court has suggested, therefore, that an action involves the public interest when a substantially large portion of the population is affected but no one person may be directly injured, or at least injured more than anyone else. As these cases indicate, prior to 1939 the Court had held that a private individual could not institute a "case" or "controversy" in order to protect the public interest.[18] Since 1939, the Court has explicitly recognized a private individual's right to commence a "case" or "controversy" to protect the public interest. Most of these cases have involved administrative law and have arisen as a result of a statute authorizing a "person aggrieved" or "adversely affected" to bring such action.

In *Federal Communications Commission* v. *Sanders Bros. Radio Station,* the Court held that Sanders had no personal right to protect, but could protect the public interest under a remedial statute. Since the Federal Communications Act gives the FCC power to grant licenses "if public convenience, interest, or necessity will be served"(473), the Court was forced to face the public interest issue. For the Court, Justice Owen J. Roberts discussed the public's interest rather extensively.

> An important element of public interest and convenience affecting the issue of a license is the ability of the licensee to render the best practicable service to the community reached by his broadcasts. . . .
>
> The policy of the Act is clear that no person is to have anything in the nature of a property right as a result of the granting of a license. Licenses are limited to a maximum of three years' duration, may be revoked, and need not be re-newed. Thus the channels presently occupied remain free for a new assignment to another licensee in the interest of the listening public.
>
> Plainly it is not the purpose of the Act to protect a licensee against competition but to protect the public. Congress intended to leave competition in the business of broadcasting where it found it, to permit a licensee who was not interfering electrically with other broadcasters to survive or succumb according to his ability to make his programs attractive to the public.(475)

The Court determined that Congress created a public legal right when it enacted the Federal Communications Act. The public had the right to be served with the "best practicable service" through "programs attractive to the public."

Yet the question remains: If the Act created a public legal right, who has the proper interest to commence a "case" or "controversy" to protect that right? In *Sanders,* an existing station challenged the FCC's granting a license to another station to serve the same area. The Court concluded that the existing station had no personal right to remain free from competition, but was a proper party to protect the public's interest. The Court suggested that the existing station was in a position to show whether the public interest would be served by a new station. Roberts inferred that this was the intent of Congress, which "may have been of opinion that one likely to be financially injured by the issue of a license would be the only person having a sufficient interest to bring to the attention of the appellate court errors of law in the action of the Commission in granting the license"(477).

Two years later, the Court confirmed that *Sanders* was predicated on the concept of protecting the public interest. In *Scripps-Howard Radio Inc. v. Federal Communications Commission,* the FCC had not held a hearing before granting a license to a new station that would be in competition with one owned by Scripps-Howard. In delivering the Court's opinion, Justice Felix Frankfurter explicitly reaffirmed *Sanders.*

> The Communications Act of 1934 did not create new private rights. The purpose of the Act was to protect the public interest in communications. By §402(b)(2) Congress gave the right of appeal to persons "aggrieved or whose interests are adversely affected" by Commission action. 48 Stat. 1064, 1093. But these private litigants have standing only as representatives of the public interest. . . . That a Court is called upon to enforce public rights and not the interest of private property does not diminish its power to protect such rights.(14–15)

Justices William O. Douglas and Frank Murphy argued that the Court was erroneously interpreting *Sanders.* Douglas contended that the existing station in *Sanders* had shown some personal interest, while Scripps-Howard had not.

> But it is said Congress entrusted the vindication of the public interest to private litigants. The Sanders case properly construed merely means that the Court of Appeals had *jurisdiction* of appeals by a "person aggrieved" or by one "whose interests are adversely affected" by the Commission's decision. . . . But that does not mean that an appellant has a cause of action merely because he has a competing station. Unless he can show that his individual interest has been unlawfully invaded, there is merely *damnum absque injuria* and no cause of action on the merits.(20–21)

Douglas suggested that Congress could have created a right to remain free of competition, but that *Sanders* held this had not been done. He argued that no "case" or "controversy" existed because Scripps-Howard had not established any personal interest.[19]

After its initial acceptance of public interest suits in the FCC cases, the Supreme Court had little to say on the subject until late in the 1960s. During this period, the lower federal courts followed and expanded the public interest theory as set forth in *Sanders* and *Scripps-Howard.* For instance, the lower federal courts established and relied on the concept of private attorneys general.[20] According to this theory, a private attorney general is anyone who has been granted standing to protect the public interest or the interests of a very large class.

A summary of the lower federal courts' expansion of the public interest doctrine was offered in a 1966 Court of Appeals decision,

Office of Communication of the United Church of Christ v. *Federal Communications Commission.* (Circuit Judge Warren Burger delivered the court's opinion.)

There is nothing unusual or novel in granting the consuming public standing to challenge administrative actions. In *Associated Industries of New York State, Inc.* v. *Ickes,* 134 F 2d 694 (2d Cir. 1943), vacated as moot, 320 U.S. 707 (1943), coal consumers were found to have standing to review a minimum price order. In *United States* v. *Public Utilities Commission,* 80 U.S. App. D.C. 227, 151 F. 2d 609 (1945), we held that a consumer of electricity was affected by the rates charged and could appeal an order setting them. Similarly in *Bebchick* v. *Public Utilities Commission,* 109 U.S. App. D.C. 298, 287 F. 2d 337 (1961), we had no difficulty in concluding that a public transit rider had standing to appeal a rate increase. A direct economic injury, even if small as to each user, is involved in the rate cases, but standing has also been granted to a passenger to contest the legality of Interstate Commerce Commission rules allowing racial segregation in railroad dining cars. *Henderson* v. *United States,* 339 U.S. 816 (1950). Moreover, in *Reade* v. *Ewing,* 205 F. 2d 630 (2d Cir. 1953), a consumer of oleomargarine was held to have standing to challenge orders affecting the ingredients thereof.(1002)

The court pointed out that these cases were not decided under the Federal Communications Act but under other statutes involving persons "affected" or "aggrieved." With the exception of *Henderson,* the cases cited are all lower federal court decisions. In *Henderson,* the plaintiff had been denied service on a railroad dining car. When the ICC refused to rule that this was a violation of the Interstate Commerce Act, Henderson appealed. The Supreme Court did not mention the consuming public or the public interest but simply referred to Henderson as an "aggrieved party"(823).

In the *Church of Christ* case, the court of appeals held that the listening public had standing to challenge the FCC's renewal of a television license.[21]

The United States Supreme Court adopted many of the developments in the lower federal courts in *Association of Data Processing Service Organizations, Inc.* v. *Camp.* Justice William O. Douglas delivered the Court's opinion and referred approvingly to the concept of private attorneys general.[22] Douglas's opinion is particularly noteworthy because it has been interpreted by some observers as signaling the end of the legal interest test as part of the case-or-controversy requirement (see citations in notes 28–29 *infra*). Data Processing brought the action under the Administrative Procedure Act to challenge a ruling by the Comptroller of the Currency that national banks could make data processing services available to other banks and to bank customers.

Douglas suggested that *Flast* v. *Cohen* indicated that the only constitutionally based requirements of standing were "whether the dispute sought to be adjudicated will be presented in an adversary context and in a form historically viewed as capable of judicial resolution"(151–52). Douglas held that the cases were not really comparable beyond the *Flast* requirement for Article III standing.

> *Flast* was a *taxpayer's* suit. The present is a *competitor's* suit. And while the two have the same Article III starting point, they do not necessarily track one another.
>
> The first question is whether the plaintiff alleges that the challenged action has caused him injury in fact, economic or otherwise. There can be no doubt but that petitioners have satisfied this test.(152)

Douglas argued that the legal interest test was not relevant in determining whether Data Processing could commence a "case" or "controversy."

> The "legal interest" test goes to the merits. The question of standing is different. It concerns, apart from the "case" or "controversy" test, the question whether the interest sought to be protected by the complainant is arguably within the zone of interests to be protected or regulated by the statute or constitutional guarantee in question. Thus the Administrative Procedure Act grants standing to a person "aggrieved by agency action within the meaning of a relevant statute." 5 U.S.C. § 702.(153)

The gist of Douglas's opinion was that once the basic requirements for Article III standing were established, which could be done by showing injury in fact, then Data Processing need only establish that its interests were "arguably within the zone of interests to be protected." In other words, Data Processing did not have to establish that it was commencing the action to protect a legal interest, but only that it had been injured in fact. Douglas emphasized that the question of legal interests was one to be decided solely on the merits.

> Whether anything in the Bank Service Corporation Act or the National Bank Act gives petitioners a "legal interest" which protects them against violations of those Acts, and whether the actions of respondents did in fact violate either of those Acts, are questions which go to the merits and remain to be decided below.(158)

Douglas inferred that Data Processing's position was that of a private attorney general.

Certainly he who is "likely to be financially" injured, *FCC* v. *Sanders Radio Station,* 309 U.S., at 477, may be a reliable private attorney general to litigate the issue of the public interest in the present case.(154)

Douglas also delivered the Court's opinion in a companion case to *Data Processing, Barlow* v. *Collins.* In permitting tenant farmers to challenge regulations promulgated by the Secretary of Agriculture, Douglas followed the criteria established by *Data Processing.*

First, there is no doubt that in the context of this litigation the tenant farmers, petitioners here, have the personal stake and interest that impart the concrete adverseness required by Article III.

Second, the tenant farmers are clearly within the zone of interests protected by the Act.(164)

Justices William J. Brennan and Byron White dissented in both cases. In an opinion written by Brennan, the dissenters expressed the view that the Court's criteria exceeded that needed for standing.

My view is that the inquiry in the Court's first step is the only one which need be made to determine standing. I thought we had discarded the notion of any additional requirement when we discussed standing solely in terms of its constitutional content in *Flast* v. *Cohen,* 392 U.S. 83 (1968). By requiring a second nonconstitutional step, the Court comes very close to perpetuating the discredited requirement that conditioned standing on a showing by the plaintiff that the challenged governmental action invaded one of his legally protected interests.(168)

The Court's most recent discussion of the public interest and private attorneys general is found in *Sierra Club* v. *Morton.* In a 4–3 decision, the Court held that the Sierra Club did not have standing to protect the public interest. More importantly, all seven justices accepted the public interest and private attorneys general concepts. The Sierra Club sought a declaratory judgment and an injunction against the development of a resort area by a private developer in the national forest of the Sierra Nevada Mountains known as the Mineral King Valley. The Club did not allege that any of its members actually used the national forest area and refused to amend its petition to include such allegations. In delivering the Court's opinion, Justice Potter Stewart indicated that such allegations were necessary to establish the Club's standing.

The Club apparently regarded any allegations of individualized injury as superfluous, on the theory that this was a "public" action involving questions as to the use of natural resources, and that the Club's longstanding concern with and expertise in such matters were sufficient to give it standing as a "representative of the public." This theory reflects a misunderstanding of our cases involving so-called "public actions" in the area of administrative law.(736)

Stewart summarized the Court's view of public actions and private attorneys general in the area of administrative law.

> Taken together, *Sanders* and *Scripps-Howard* thus established a dual proposition: the fact of economic injury is what gives a person standing to seek judicial review under the statute, but once review is properly invoked, that person may argue the public interest in support of his claim that the agency has failed to comply with its statutory mandate. It was in the latter sense that the "standing" of the appellant in *Scripps-Howard* existed only as a "representative of the public interest." It is in a similar sense that we have used the phrase "private attorney general" to describe the function performed by persons upon whom Congress has conferred the right to seek judicial review of agency action.(737–38)

Stewart held that the appellant must allege injury in fact as the Court's decisions in *Data Processing* and *Barlow* had indicated. This injury in fact is not the same, however, as the traditional legal injury. As the Court had suggested in *Data Processing* and *Barlow,* the injury in fact test is met "under the Administrative Procedure Act and other statutes authorizing judicial review of federal agency action" when the appellant is able to show that he has been "aggrieved" or "adversely affected." Although Stewart did not use the term "legal interest," he did suggest that solely an "interest in a problem" or even a "special interest" promoted by an organization with "an historic commitment to the cause of protecting" our environment was insufficient to enable a party to seek judicial review. "[T]he party seeking review must have himself suffered an injury"(738). Within these limits, Stewart suggested that the federal judiciary had accepted the explanation of judicial review that Congress had initiated.

> The trend of cases arising under the APA [Administrative Procedure Act] and other statutes authorizing judicial review of federal agency action has been toward recognizing that injuries other than economic harm are sufficient to bring a person within the means of the statutory language, and towards discarding the notion that an injury that is widely shared is *ipso facto* not an injury sufficient to provide the basis for judicial review.(738)

Stewart concluded that the public interest could be protected by one who had a "direct stake in the outcome." The APA should not be interpreted, however, "to authorize judicial review at the behest of organizations or individuals who seek to do no more than vindicate their own value preferences through the judicial process"(740). The three dissenters did not reject Stewart's treatment of protecting the public interest and private attorneys general. They did believe that the Sierra Club should have been granted standing.

The *Sierra Club* case is of special significance because the Court emphasized what is often ignored, i.e., the cases in which the Court has explicitly recognized a right to protect the public interest all arose under statutes that authorized a person "adversely affected" or "aggrieved" to commence a "case" or "controversy." *Sanders* and its progeny are all limited to one area of public law—administrative law. The cases are important and do indicate that in this one very important area, the traditional legal interest test is not applicable when an action is brought under a statute authorizing a person "adversely affected" or "aggrieved" to do so.

Although the Court has not explicitly recognized a right to protect the public interest in other areas, it has implied that such a right does exist in at least two other areas. These areas are actions involving taxpayer's suits and freedom of speech and association. The Court has applied the essential elements of the public action in certain cases involving freedom of expression and association. This situation exists when the Court finds that statutes or other governmental actions are so vague or so broad that they have a "chilling effect" on expression or association.[23] The implication is that the very existence of such a statute, executive order, or other governmental action deters individuals from exercising freedoms guaranteed by the First and Fourteenth Amendments and therefore invades legal rights. An analysis of the cases involved indicates that the Court has not proffered a decisive answer concerning who may commence this type of action.

The cases do indicate, however, that something less than a substantial, direct, or personal interest is required, although the Court has not stated that a mere public interest is sufficient. In *Cramp* v. *Board of Public Instruction*, the Court upheld a public school teacher's right to seek a declaratory judgment and an injunction against the enforcement of a Florida loyalty oath, although he attested that he could truthfully execute the oath. The Court suggested that Cramp was not completely safe from prosecution, since he attacked the statute as constitutionally vague, and others might reasonably interpret the statute differently than he did. With Justice Potter Stewart delivering the opinion, the Court inferred that any employee required to sign such an oath had a sufficient interest to institute judicial action.

The vices inherent in an unconstitutionally vague statute—the

risk of unfair prosecution and the potential deterrence of constitutionally protected conduct—have been repeatedly pointed
out in our decisions. . . . These are dangers to which all who are
compelled to execute an unconstitutionally vague and indefinite oath may be exposed.(283–84)

Although the class included only those required to sign the loyalty
oath, one may ask what the situation would be if the class included all
the public.[24]

Zwickler v. *Koota* is the closest that the Court has come to discussing
the public interest in First Amendment cases. Zwickler had been tried
under a state law prohibiting the distribution of anonymous political
handbills. He was convicted, but the state appellate court reversed his
conviction. Zwickler then brought an original action in the federal
courts for declaratory and injunctive relief. He alleged that the New
York statute involved "was repugnant to the guarantee of free expression secured by the Federal Constitution" and "suffers impermissible
'overbreadth' "(244). Justice William J. Brennan delivered the Court's
opinion and did not indicate that Zwickler had any special interest
except that he had been tried and acquitted under the anonymous
handbill law. Zwickler did allege that he wished to distribute handbills
during the 1966 elections and feared further prosecution, but the
Court rendered its decision after the 1966 elections. (The Court did
use this as a basis for declaring the action moot when it reached the
Court the second time; see *Golden* v. *Zwickler.*) Brennan stated the issue
involved in nonpersonal terms.

[H]is constitutional attack is that the statute, although lacking neither clarity nor precision, is void for "overbreadth," that
is, that it offends the constitutional principle that "a governmental purpose to control or prevent activities constitutionally subject to state regulation may not be achieved by means which
sweep unnecessarily broadly and thereby invade the area of protected freedoms. *NAACP* v. *Alabama*, 377 U.S. 288, 307.(249–50)

Brennan argued that the district court had erroneously applied the
standard to determine whether federal courts should abstain from issuing an injunction against enforcement of a state statute since Zwickler
also sought declaratory relief. While "special circumstances" must be
shown before a federal court should grant injunctive relief against a
state statute, Brennan held that the same stringent test should not be
applied when a declaratory judgment is sought against a state statute
on grounds of overbreadth (253–54). The Court did not discuss Zwickler's right to commence a "case" or "controversy" in public interest
terminology but, quite obviously, the Court did not apply traditional
standards to determine Zwickler's interest.[25]

   The Court has not explicitly recognized the right of an individual to protect the public interest when he alleges that a statute has a chilling effect on freedom of expression or association. Cases such as *Cramp* and *Zwickler* indicate, however, that the Court has not always insisted on the traditional personal, direct, or substantial interest. When an individual may commence a "case" or "controversy" without showing that he has a personal, direct, or substantial interest, the Court has obviously enlarged access to the judicial system. (The Court has often focused on whether an actual justiciable controversy is present rather than on the parties' interest; see discussion of this subject in Chapter 6 *infra.*) If the Court has not yet recognized a right to protect the public interest in cases involving vagueness or overbreadth, one can hardly deny that the Court has been moving in that direction.[26]
   Taxpayers' suits are a third group of cases relating to the public interest. Although the Court has not discussed these cases in terms of protecting the public interest, the only interest that a party must establish is that he is a member of an extremely large class, i.e., taxpayers. The Court is obviously requiring something less than a direct, personal, or substantial interest. The Court has upheld a state taxpayer's right to appeal a state court's decision to the United States Supreme Court as long as the action is a good faith pocketbook action. In *Flast* v. *Cohen*, the Court indicated that, in at least one situation, a federal taxpayer would be permitted to bring a "case" or "controversy" solely as a taxpayer. In *Flast*, the Court did not use the terminology "public interest," but an analogy to the Federal Communications Act cases is not inappropriate. Like Sanders's status as the radio station's owner, Flast's status as a taxpayer was not directly related to the legal right to be decided by the Court. In each instance the plaintiff's status was used to justify his right to bring an action to protect the public interest. In *Sanders*, the Court specifically denied that the existing station had a right to protect itself from competition, but the station was granted standing to protect the public interest. The Supreme Court might have clarified the situation if it had applied the same analogy to *Flast*. Instead, the Court applied a two-pronged test by holding that, when Congress exercised its power to tax and spend for the general welfare, a federal taxpayer had the right to test the constitutionality of such legislation on a legitimate claim that the statute violated the First Amendment's establishment clause. The Court did not discuss, however, any personal right of Flast or any other taxpayer. The Court did discuss a "stake of a taxpayer," but did not indicate that anyone's taxes would be reduced if the taxpayer's suit was successful. The taxpayer fiction was necessary because the establishment clause creates a public

right and not a private right. The Court admitted this, *sub silentio,* when it suggested the second requirement.

> Under this requirement, the taxpayer must show that the challenged enactment exceeds specific constitutional limitations imposed upon the exercise of the congressional taxing and spending power, and not simply that the enactment is generally beyond the powers delegated to Congress.(102)

The real issue was the public's interest in whether Congress had violated a specific constitutional restriction on its powers.

May an individual commence a "case" or "controversy" to protect the public interest although he possesses no traditional legal interest of his own? Where Congress has enacted a statute that provides for judicial review of administrative action by a person "aggrieved" or "adversely affected," the answer is "yes." The Court has indicated that the party must be injured in fact, but the party need not establish that he has suffered a legal injury. The party may then challenge administrative action in order to protect the public interest. In *Flast,* the Court established that a taxpayer may initiate a "case" or "controversy" to protect the public interest under specific circumstances. In cases involving vague or overly broad statutes that allegedly infringe freedom of speech and association, the Court has indicated that a standard less stringent than the traditional one will be applied to determine who may commence a "case" or "controversy."[27]

The Court has not generally accepted the public action outside the area of administrative law. It has, however, accepted the right to protect the public interest in the area of administrative law and has moved in that direction in certain cases involving freedom of speech and association and in taxpayers' suits. The traditional requirement that one must possess a direct, personal, or substantial interest has not been completely discarded, but certainly has been eroded.

Conclusion—The Existence of a Sufficient Interest

The Court has not substantially altered the basic requirements of adversity and the existence of a legal right as they relate to a "case" or "controversy," but it has significantly altered the legal interest test. Today federal courts do not exercise judicial power, theoretically, unless adverse parties are disputing a legal right, but the United States Supreme Court has relaxed the requirements of what interest a party must possess in the disputed legal right before the federal judiciary may act.

The Court and some commentators have even suggested that the existence of a legal interest is not a necessary prerequisite to a "case" or "controversy." In *Association of Data Processing Service Organizations, Inc.* v. *Camp*, the Court indicated that the legal interest test could be decided only when a court determined the issue on the merits and was therefore solely a substantive and not a procedural issue.

In reference to *Data Processing* and its companion case, *Barlow* v. *Collins*, one commentator suggested:

> Thus, the Court rejected the traditional "legally protected interest" test, which required the plaintiff to assert an interest which it was the purpose of a statute, the common law, or the Constitution to protect.[28]

In discussing *Association of Data Processing*, Professor Kenneth Culp Davis asserted that: "[a] huge portion of the former foundation of the law of standing was thus knocked out. The old test of a 'recognized legal interest' was specifically rejected."[29] The commentators have often ignored the limited applicability of the Court's decisions in *Data Processing* and *Barlow*. In each instance, the action was commenced under a statute that granted a remedy to parties who otherwise might be denied access to the judiciary. In other words, the Court concluded that Congress had intended to grant standing to these plaintiffs, and the question of their legal interest was irrelevant.[30] The extent to which those decisions are applicable to actions not brought under the Administrative Procedure Act or a similar statute is a question that the Court has not explicitly answered.

Outside of the area of administrative law, the United States Supreme Court has decided only one case that could suggest the total demise of the legal interest test. In *Flast* v. *Cohen*, the Court adopted the terminology "stake in the outcome."

> [I]n terms of Article III limitations on federal court jurisdiction, the question of standing is related only to whether the dispute sought to be adjudicated will be presented in an adversary context and in a form historically viewed as capable of judicial resolution. It is for that reason that the emphasis in standing problems is on whether the party invoking federal court jurisdiction has "a personal stake in the outcome of the controversy," *Baker* v. *Carr, supra*, at 204 and whether the dispute touches upon "the legal relations of parties having adverse legal interest." *Aetna Life Insurance Co.* v. *Haworth, supra*, at 240–241. A taxpayer may or may not have the requisite personal stake in the outcome, depending upon the circumstances of the particular case. Therefore, we find no absolute bar in Article III to suits by federal taxpayers challenging allegedly unconsti-

tutional federal taxing and spending programs. There remains, however, the problem of determining the circumstances under which a federal taxpayer will be deemed to have the personal stake and interest that imparts the necessary concrete adverseness to such litigation so that standing can be conferred on the taxpayer qua taxpayer consistent with the constitutional limitations of Article III.(101)

The Court did mention interest, but established criteria to determine a taxpayer's standing that did not require the traditional personal legal interest. The Court did not suggest that either the exercise of congressional power to tax and spend for the general welfare or the First Amendment's establishment clause gave the appellants any legal interest in the traditional sense. The two tests did establish the appellants' "stake in the outcome" since they were taxpayers.[31]

In his dissenting opinion, Justice John Marshall Harlan articulated the legal interest issue better than did the Court. Harlan suggested that the case did not involve the taxpayers' personal interest in the traditional sense, i.e., the taxpayers were not contesting a specific tax obligation or attempting to obtain a tax refund. Harlan argued that the appellants were attempting to challenge the expenditure of public funds. He saw a significant difference between the traditional taxpayer's suit and this challenge to public expenditures.

> These differences in the purposes of the cases are reflected in differences in the litigants' interests. An action brought to contest the validity of tax liabilities assessed to the plaintiff is designed to vindicate interests that are personal and proprietary. The wrongs alleged and the relief sought by such a plaintiff are unmistakably private; only secondarily are his interests representative of those of the general population. I take it that the Court, although it does not pause to examine the question, believes that the interests of those who as taxpayers challenge the constitutionality of public expenditures may, at least in certain circumstances, be similar. Yet this assumption is surely mistaken.
>
> The complaint in this case, unlike that in *Frothingham,* contains no allegation that the contested expenditures will in any fashion affect the amount of these taxpayers' own existing or forseeable [sic] tax obligations.(117–19)

In examining the Court's two criteria, Harlan found that neither one indicated the traditional personal interest or even plaintiff's interest in the outcome of the suit. Harlan said the Court was engaging in a semantic sleight of hand by attempting to show that a taxpayer had a personal stake in the outcome of a suit involving expenditures under the general welfare clause that might conceivably violate the First Amendment's establishment clause.[32]

Harlan's dissent was not predicated, however, on constitutional but on policy grounds. He did not suggest that the Court was ignoring Article III's limitations but rather that the Court was attempting to justify the existence of a personal interest or stake in the outcome when none existed. Harlan's solution was that the Court should exercise judicial self-restraint and wait until Congress authorized such suits(130–33).

All nine justices apparently agreed that a taxpayer did not have to establish a personal legal interest to commence a "case" or "controversy" in *Flast*. Commentators have suggested that *Flast* created a new class of "specially harmed" parties, or possibly abolished the legal interest test altogether.[33] Since the *Flast* decision, however, the Court has not indicated whether *Flast* was a mere aberration or the demise of the legal interest test.

In *United States* v. *Richardson,* the Court attempted to limit *Flast* by integrating it with *Frothingham* (see also *Schlesinger* v. *Reservists Committee to Stop the War*). In a 5–4 decision, Chief Justice Warren Burger declared for the majority that a taxpayer could not establish the proper interest under the *Flast* test to challenge the Government's failure to account for Central Intelligence Agency expenditures under Article I Section 9 Clause 7. In analyzing *Flast*, Burger held that the *Flast* test must be applied subject to the *Frothingham* philosophy.

> While the "impenetrable barrier to suits against Act of Congress brought by individuals who can assert only the interest of federal taxpayers," had been slightly lowered, the Court made clear it was reaffirming the principle of *Frothingham* precluding a taxpayer's use of "a federal court as a forum in which to air his generalized grievances about the conduct of government or the allocation of power in the Federal System."(2945)

The Court seemed to indicate that *Flast* was neither a mere aberration nor the demise of the legal interest test, but somewhere in between.

In a concurring opinion in *Richardson,* Justice Lewis F. Powell, Jr. suggested that *Flast* should be treated as an aberration(2948–56). Although he did not advocate the overruling of *Flast*, Powell did argue that the Court should make it clear that the *Flast* rule is applicable only to First Amendment establishment clause cases. Justice William J. Brennan came to a similar conclusion in a dissenting opinion although he would limit the *Flast* test to establishment and free exercise cases(2963).

Whether the federal judiciary has completely interred the legal interest test is beyond this study's scope. One can hardly deny, however, that significant changes have occurred in the application of the legal interest test. In recent years, the Court has permitted parties to institute a "case" or "controversy" without requiring the traditional direct, personal, or substantial interest.

Congressional action has partially accounted for this change by establishing legal remedies for parties whose injury was considered *damnum absque injuria* under common law. Competitors have been permitted to commence "cases" or "controversies" under these statutes, although they had been denied standing in similar situations before the statutes' enactment. In *Hardin* v. *Kentucky Utilities Co.*, the Court summarized the evolution that had taken place.

> This Court has, it is true, repeatedly held that the economic injury which results from lawful competition cannot, in and of itself, confer standing on the injured business to question the legality of any aspect of its competitors' operations. *Railroad Co.* v. *Ellerman*, 105 U.S. 166 (1882); *Alabama Power Co.* v. *Ickes,* 302 U.S. 464 (1938); *Tennessee Power Co.* v. *TVA*, 306 U.S. 118 (1939); *Perkins* v. *Lukens Steel Co.*, 310 U.S. 113 (1940). But competitive injury provided no basis for standing in the above cases simply because the statutory and constitutional requirements that the plaintiff sought to enforce were in no way concerned with protecting against competitive injury. In contrast, it has been the rule, at least since the *Chicago Junction Case,* 264 U.S. 258 (1924), that when the particular statutory provision invoked does reflect a legislative purpose to protect a competitive interest, the injured competitor has standing to require compliance with that provision.(6).

Hardin is particularly significant because the Utilities Company was permitted to contest action by the TVA under a congressional enactment that the Court held was designed to protect private utilities.

Although Congress has played a role in increasing access to the federal judiciary by reducing the personal interest required, the United States Supreme Court has played the greater role in reducing, if not eliminating, the legal interest test. The Court has not only given a liberal interpretation to the "person aggrieved or injured" statutes enacted by Congress, but it has altered its own requirements or ignored them. While the Court at one time seemingly applied the direct, personal, and substantial requirements, today the Court seemingly ignores these requirements. This has been particularly true in instances in which the Court has permitted public officials to contest public laws or in which taxpayers have been permitted to institute a "case" or "controversy."

The Court has been going through the process of adopting rules derived primarily from private law actions to public law actions. Taxpayers' suits, suits by public officials protecting rights of third parties, and actions concerning the public interest were not basic problems in private litigation. As the area of public law has grown and as the role of the federal judiciary in the policy-making process has grown, the federal judiciary has become more of a political battleground. The Court has met this challenge by relaxing some of the more stringent requirements that are applicable in private law actions.

The Court ultimately determines the interest that enables one to commence a "case" or "controversy." Whether a party is permitted to institute a "case" or "controversy" to protect the rights of a third party is primarily within the Court's discretion. Whether the party's interest is direct, personal, or substantial enough is for the Court to determine. Even when Congress has enacted a statute providing a judicial remedy, the Court determines whether the party's interest is within the area Congress intended to protect. The test today would seem to be whether the party has a sufficient interest to commence a "case" or "controversy." Although "sufficient" may be even less specific than the terms previously used, it does denote one significant aspect of the legal interest test. The Court really determines who is the proper party to commence a "case" or "controversy." If the Court determines that a party may bring a "case" or "controversy," the party has a sufficient interest. This is not to suggest that there are no limitations on the Court's power, but as this chapter suggests, the limitations are very flexible. The Court's discretion is much greater in this respect than in the area of adversity and legal rights. When the Court wishes to become an active participant in the political process, it has little difficulty in determining that a party has a sufficient interest.

6 The Existence of an Actual Justiciable Controversy

Adversity concerns the relationship between the parties, and the existence of a sufficient interest concerns the parties' relationship to a disputed legal right. If adverse parties who have a sufficient interest in a disputed legal right are before a federal court, the question remains: when may the federal judiciary act to protect a legal right? (The term "ripeness" is often used to describe this problem, but the term "ripeness" is also used to describe problems that are not directly related to the case-or-controversy provision; see discussion of ripeness in Chapter 8 *infra.*) The Supreme Court stated in *Smith* v. *Adams:* "Whenever the claim or contention of a party takes such a form that the judicial power is capable of action upon it, then it has become a case or controversy"(173). The point in time when, if ever, a controversy becomes an actual justiciable controversy is the subject of this chapter.

Like the existence of a sufficient interest, this criterion of the case-or-controversy provision revolves around a legal right. At times, federal courts determine the presence or absence of both criteria simultaneously. That is, a federal court's decision that a party has a sufficient interest may automatically determine that an actual controversy exists.[1] This is particularly true in actions involving allegations that a statute is void because of vagueness or overbreadth. In other words, a federal court's determination that a statute may possibly infringe on one's freedom of speech or association because it is vague or overly broad may simultaneously determine that a party possesses a sufficient interest to institute a "case" and that an actual justiciable controversy exists. Since the statute may be attacked on its face, an actual justiciable controversy is present even though government officials have not attempted to enforce the statute. The existence of an actual controversy is, nevertheless, analytically separable from the existence of a sufficient interest. A federal court may find that there are adverse parties with sufficient interest in a legal right, but still determine that the time is not yet appropriate to invoke judicial machinery.[2]

When a federal court finds that an actual controversy is not present, two potential situations may exist. First, the court may determine that it is being asked to decide legal rights in an abstract, academic, feigned, or hypothetical situation. "A justiciable controversy is thus distinguished from a difference or dispute of a hypothetical or abstract character; from one that is academic or moot"(*Aetna Life Insurance Co. v. Haworth*, 240).[3] These terms indicate that an actual justiciable controversy does not exist at the time the action is instituted and that an actual justiciable controversy may never be present. In this situation, one can hardly argue that the federal judiciary should act. The federal courts' role in the political process would be unlimited if they could determine hypothetical issues and would amount to acting as the repudiated "Council of Revision." "[N]o court sits to determine question of law *in thesi*. There must be a litigation upon actual transactions between real parties, growing out of a controversy affecting legal or equitable rights as to person or property" (*Marye v. Parsons* 330).

If the only problem were a simple dichotomy between an abstract question and the invasion of a legal right, the federal courts could easily determine when an actual controversy exists. The courts would have some discretion, but the borderline situations'would be few. Once a legal right has been invaded, the court has a justiciable controversy before it. In actions at law, a justiciable controversy is present only when a legal right has actually been invaded. In actions seeking an injunction or a declaratory judgment, however, a federal court may act to prevent an invasion of a legal right or to declare existing legal rights, although a legal injury has not been inflicted in the traditional sense. The second potential situation arises in these latter instances when the federal courts' discretion is not simply to distinguish an abstract issue from a live justiciable controversy but to draw a fine line between an embryonic controversy and one that is appropriate for judicial action. For instance, an actual justiciable controversy's existence may depend on a federal court's determination of the likelihood of a contingent event. If the court perceives the event as likely to occur, an actual justiciable controversy may be present while the court's determination that the contingency is not likely to occur means it has been presented with a hypothetical situation.

This discussion of an actual controversy's existence will be divided into three sections. The first section will cover the types of action in which the federal courts have the greatest discretion in determining whether an actual controversy exists, and therefore the type of action in which the question invariably arises. The second section will cover the types of subject matter where the federal courts, and especially the United States Supreme Court, have experienced the greatest difficulty in determining whether an actual controversy exists. The third section will cover problems relating to federalism, and the determination of an actual justiciable controversy's existence in the federal courts.

Type of Action

The question of an actual controversy's existence invariably arises in particular types of judicial actions. In an action at law, no problem concerning a controversy's justiciability ordinarily arises, since the action is predicated on the invasion of a legal right. If the other prerequisites of a "case" or "controversy" are met, no real question of justiciability is present. In actions for an injunction or declaratory judgment, however, the question of justiciability often arises, since preventive relief is sought. Federal courts may issue an injunction or a declaratory judgment to prevent future injury, and therefore, unlike actions at law, a legal injury may not yet have occurred. Whether an actual controversy exists when the action is commenced depends on the federal court's view of the need for an injunction or a declaratory judgment. Today, litigants often request both an injunction and a declaratory judgment when they seek preventive relief.

Equity

Article III Section 2 extends judicial power to "cases" and "controversies" in law and equity. ("The judicial power shall extend to all cases, in law and equity, arising under this Constitution.") If Congress has granted jurisdiction, the federal judiciary may protect a legal right through its equity jurisdiction unless Congress has specifically limited the courts' jurisdiction. The Court stated in *Porter* v. *Warner Holding Co.:*

> [T]he comprehensiveness of . . . equitable jurisdiction is not to be denied or limited in the absence of a clear and valid legislative command. Unless a statute in so many words or by a necessary and inescapable inference, restricts the court's jurisdiction in equity, the full scope of that jurisdiction is to be recognized and applied. "The great principles of equity, securing complete justice, should not be yielded to light inferences, or doubtful construction."[4](398)

Therefore, by controlling the federal courts' jurisdiction, Congress may specifically limit the exercise of the federal judiciary's equity power. Since 1793, for example, Congress has prohibited federal courts from exercising jurisdiction to stay proceedings in any court of a state.[5] Unless Congress has specifically limited the federal courts' equity power, however, the federal courts may grant equitable relief if they have jurisdiction.

The federal courts' equitable jurisdiction is discretionary. They may exercise their equity power to prevent irreparable harm if no adequate remedy exists at law. But federal courts may also decline to exercise their equity jurisdiction even when a "case" or "controversy" is present:

> It follows that the bill, which amply alleged the facts relied on to show the abridgement by criminal proceedings under the ordinance, sets out a case or controversy which is within the adjudicatory power of the district court.
>
> Notwithstanding the authority of the district court, as a federal court, to hear and dispose of the case, petitioners are entitled to the relief prayed only if they establish a cause of action in equity. Want of equity jurisdiction, while not going to the power of the court to decide the cause, . . . may nevertheless, in the discretion of the court, be objected to on its own motion. (*Douglas* v. *City of Jeannette,* 162)

Since the United States Supreme Court held that irreparable injury did not exist in this case, one may question whether a justiciable controversy was present. The Court did indicate, however, that the federal courts have the discretionary power to determine whether irreparable injury is actually present.

While a federal court may find the absence of irreparable injury when it wishes to avoid a decision, it may likewise find irreparable injury present when it wishes to render a decision. *Pennsylvania* v. *West Virginia* illustrates the latter situation.

> The second question is whether the suits were brought prematurely. They were brought a few days after the West Virginia act went into force. No order under it had been made by the Public Service Commission; nor had it been tested in actual practice. But this does not prove that the suits were premature. Of course they were not so, if it otherwise appeared that the act certainly would operate as the complainant states apprehended it would. One does not have to await the consummation of threatened injury to obtain preventive relief. If the injury is certainly impending, that is enough. (592–93)

The federal courts may act to provide preventive relief through their equity power when "the injury is certainly impending." Obviously, the federal courts determine whether "the injury is certainly impending."

When an injunction is sought, the federal courts determine whether an actual controversy exists by their perception of whether preventive relief is necessary to prevent irreparable harm. The existence of an actual justiciable controversy often depends on a federal court's perception of the likelihood of irreparable injury.

Declaratory Judgments

The federal courts' equity power has existed since the Constitution's adoption, but their power to issue declaratory judgments is a modern innovation. Although prior to 1933 the United States Supreme Court had indicated that a declaratory judgment action was not a "case" or "controversy," the Court held in *Nashville, Chattanooga & St. Louis Railway* v. *Wallace* that the term "declaratory judgment" was merely a label and all the elements of a "case" or "controversy" might be present. Four years later, in *Aetna Life Insurance Co.* v. *Haworth,* the Court upheld the Federal Declaratory Judgment Act of 1935, which states:

> In a case of actual controversy within its jurisdiction, except with respect to Federal taxes, any court of the United States, upon the filing of an appropriate pleading, may declare the rights and other legal relations of any interested party seeking such declaration, whether or not further relief is or could be sought.
>
> Any such declaration shall have the force and effect of a final judgment or decree and shall be reviewable as such.[6]

One of the men primarily responsible for the Federal Declaratory Judgment Act's adoption, Edwin Borchard, described the declaratory judgment in the following terms.

> The action for a declaratory judgment, having its roots in the Middle Ages and flowering to maturity in the English-speaking world of the twentieth century, has not only afforded a simple judicial device for the speedy adjudication of legal differences, but it has enabled innumerable issues to be determined which are not susceptible of adjudication in any other way. The main characteristic of the declaratory judgment, which distinguishes it from other judgments, is the fact that it conclusively declares the pre-existing rights of the litigants without the appendage of any coercive decree.[7]

As Borchard suggests, the declaratory judgment action is directly related to, if not inseparable from, an actual controversy's existence. If a declaratory judgment "conclusively declares the pre-existing rights of the litigants," a court issuing a declaratory judgment does not have to wait until a legal right has been violated, but may declare the parties' rights before any legal injury has been suffered. The declaratory judgment provides "speedy adjudication" of issues that "are not susceptible of adjudication in any other way." A declaratory judgment action is, therefore, a means of judicially determining the parties' legal rights, even though nobody's rights have been infringed and even though the parties might not be entitled to equitable relief. Borchard suggested that the declaratory judgment's most important feature was that it provided preventive relief.

> Perhaps the principal contribution that the declaratory judgment has made to the philosophy of procedure is to make it clear that a controversy as to legal rights is as fully determinable before as it is after one or the other party has acted on his own view of his rights and perhaps irretrievably shattered the *status quo.* [8]

Borchard stressed the discretion that the declaratory judgment action gave the courts in determining whether a real controversy is present or not. "Whether the facts are ripe enough for determination is usually a matter confided to the discretion of the court."[9]

The Federal Declaratory Judgment Act grants federal courts the power to "declare the rights and other relations of any interested party" in "a case of actual controversy within its jurisdiction." In *Aetna Life Insurance Co.* v. *Haworth,* the Court held that this refers "to controversies which are such in the constitutional sense" and that "[t]he word 'actual' is one of emphasis rather than of definition"(240). Yet, one must ask: If the Declaratory Judgment Act refers to "controversies" in the constitutional sense, and if Article III has already extended judicial power to these controversies, what purpose does the Declaratory Judgment Act serve? Does it simply confirm what Article III has already granted? One could argue that, in this respect, the Court has accepted Congress's interpretation of Article III rather than following its own precedents.[10] Even if this argument is not accepted, one must view the Declaratory Judgment Act as increasing access to the federal judiciary, since the courts can decide questions of public policy that they could not or would not have decided prior to the Act's adoption.

One can best explain the Declaratory Judgment Act by saying that Congress supplied a remedy where none existed before.[11] Congress may provide a remedy and thereby create a "case" or "controversy" if the other elements of a "case" or "controversy" are present. Borchard indicated that a primary impact of the Act was to permit issues to be adjudicated earlier than had been possible before its adoption:

> It is an axiom that the Declaratory Judgment Act has not enlarged the jurisdiction of the courts over subject-matter and parties, although it manifestly has opened to prospective defendants—and to plaintiffs at an early state of the controversy—a right to petition for relief not heretofore possessed.[12]

Despite the Court's assertion in *Aetna,* the existence of a justiciable controversy was altered by the Declaratory Judgment Act, since federal judicial power now could come into play earlier than prior to the Act's adoption. By enacting the Declaratory Judgment Act, Congress provided a remedy to a party before any legal injury occurred, and the litigant did not have to establish his right to equitable relief. There may have been a "controversy" in the general sense of the term before the Declaratory Judgment Act's passage—in the sense that the parties disagreed concerning a legal right—but it became a justiciable controversy only after the Act's adoption.

The Federal Declaratory Judgment Act does require an "actual controversy," but the Act's principal author suggested that this term was inserted for tactical purposes. Borchard says that the term "actual controversies" was used to overcome apprehensions that the statute would empower federal courts to render advisory opinions or decide moot cases.[13] Borchard asserted, however, that "actual controversies" as used in the Declaratory Judgment Act did not simpy adopt the term's previous judicial definition.

> The term "actual controversy" clearly covers cases in which executory or coercive relief has been or could have been prayed. But it also covers cases of "antagonistic assertion and denial of right" in which the court merely declares whether the plaintiff's claim is justified or not. Here the court merely stabilizes legal relations.[14]

In fact, Borchard feared that the inclusion of the term "actual controversy" might destroy the Declaratory Judgment Act's very purpose.

> The danger in the words "actual controversy" lies in the fact that courts hostile to this procedural reform may attempt to suggest that a controversy concerning legal rights arising before physical damage is done or a purported right exercised, is not "actual."[15]

As early as 1941 in *Maryland Casualty Co.* v. *Pacific Coal & Oil Co.*, the Court explicitly recognized that the Declaratory Judgment Act blurred the distinction between an abstract question and a justiciable "case" or "controversy."

> The difference between an abstract question and a "controversy" contemplated by the Declaratory Judgment Act is necessarily one of degree, and it would be difficult, if it would be possible, to fashion a precise test for determining in every case whether there is such a controversy. Basically, the question in each case is whether the facts alleged, under all the circumstances, show that there is a substantial controversy, between parties having adverse legal interests, of sufficient immediacy and reality to warrant the issuance of a declaratory judgment. . . . It is immaterial that frequently, in the declaratory judgment suit, the positions of the parties in the conventional suit are reversed; the inquiry is the same in either case. (273)

The declaratory judgment action permits the federal courts to declare the parties' legal rights even though no legal wrong has been committed and no one has suffered legal injury. Adverse parties are before the court and are seeking a declaration concerning a legal right in which they each have a sufficient interest. A federal court is not acting in a hypothetical situation or granting an advisory opinion, since there is an actual controversy concerning legal rights and Congress has provided a remedy. Since Congress has provided a remedy, the parties do not have to wait until a legal wrong is perpetrated but may seek preventive relief.

Is the declaratory judgment simply another means of providing preventive relief that could be provided under the federal courts' equity jurisdiction? If so, the Declaratory Judgment Act would not have changed the concept of a "case" or "controversy." The Act significantly expanded the federal courts' power to provide preventive relief, however, since the prerequisites for the exercise of equity jurisdiction are not necessary to invoke the federal courts' power to issue a declaratory judgment. Although theoretically, the federal courts' equity jurisdiction cannot be invoked if there is an adequate remedy at law, federal courts may provide declaratory relief even if there is an adequate remedy at law. The Act provides that a federal court may declare the rights of parties "whether or not further relief is or could be sought."[16] In upholding the Act, the Court stated in *Aetna Life Insurance Co.* v. *Haworth:* "And as it is not essential to the exercise of the judicial power that an injunction be sought, allegations that irreparable injury is threatened are not required" (241).[17] Obviously, the Declaratory Judgment Act allows the federal courts to provide preventive relief that could not have been provided under the courts' traditional equity jurisdiction.[18] In this sense, the Act did change the concept of an actual justiciable controversy by providing for possible judicial action at an earlier time than would have been proper without the Act.

The declaratory judgment action is similar to an equitable action, since a federal court has discretion on whether to permit its jurisdiction to be invoked. That is, a federal court may concede that a "case" or "controversy" exists, but may still refuse to hear the action. The Act states that a federal court "may declare the rights" of parties. The Court held in *Public Service Commission of Utah* v. *Wycoff Co.* that the Declaratory Judgment Act "is an enabling Act, which confers a discretion on the courts rather than an absolute right upon the litigant" (241).[19] A federal court has discretion, therefore, not only to determine if a "justiciable controversy" is present but also to deny jurisdiction even if a "justiciable controversy" is present.[20] Thus a federal court that wishes to do so may avoid a decision on a controversial issue of public policy even though an "actual controversy" is present. Federal courts frequently do not explain whether they are refusing to adjudicate an issue in a declaratory judgment action because an "actual controversy" is not present or because they are exercising their discretionary power to deny jurisdiction.

Types of Issues

The federal judiciary's involvement in the political process may depend, in each instance, on whether an actual justiciable controversy is before a federal court. When a legal right is obviously invaded or a legal wrong perpetrated, the federal courts may become an active political participant. The federal courts face a more difficult situation, however, when they are asked to provide anticipatory relief.

As governmental activities have increased, judicial actions attempting to attack the exercise of governmental power have likewise increased. When may an individual challenge governmental action that he believes has or will infringe on his legal rights? This problem should be examined from three perspectives. (1) May a federal court decide the legality or constitutionality of a civil statute or other governmental action before it has actually been enforced? (2) May a federal court decide the legality or constitutionality of a criminal statute before prosecution, and may a court therefore enjoin prosecution under the statute? (3) May a federal court decide the legality or constitutionality of administrative action even though an administrative agency has not ordered anyone to do anything or to refrain from doing anything?

Governmental Action That May Have an Impact on Legal Rights before It Is Implemented or Enforced

When governmental action is implemented and enforced, the federal judiciary may properly decide in a "case" or "controversy" whether the action has violated the legal rights of any person who is affected by such action. The federal judiciary is often asked, however, to determine the legality or constitutionality of governmental action before it is implemented or enforced. In such a situation, the party alleges that the statute's existence invades his legal rights. An actual justiciable controversy exists if a federal court determines that the allegations are true so that the federal judiciary may decide a "case" or "controversy" before the statute is implemented or enforced. The United States Supreme

Court has not always been consistent in determining when this situation exists, but the Court has definitely indicated that the mere enactment of a statute, or other governmental action, may create an actual justiciable controversy without any implementation or enforcement.

During the 1920s, the Court decided several cases that illustrate this point. In *Terrace* v. *Thompson,* a real estate owner sought an injunction against the enforcement of a Washington State statute that forbade aliens to hold real estate. Terrace desired to lease his land to a Japanese alien. If such a lease was consummated, the State could claim the real estate in a forfeiture proceeding. Terrace alleged that the statute violated the Fourteenth Amendment's due process and equal protection clauses. In upholding Terrace's right to seek an injunction, the Court pointed out that there was "no remedy at law which is as practical, efficient, or adequate as the remedy in equity"(215). Speaking for the Court, Justice Pierce Butler noted:

> Equity jurisdiction will be exercised to enjoin the threatened enforcement of a state law which contravenes the Federal Constitution whenever it is essential in order effectively to protect property rights and the rights of persons against injuries otherwise irremediable, and in such a case a person who as an officer of the state, is clothed with the duty of enforcing its laws, and who threatens and is about to commence proceedings, either civil or criminal, to enforce such a law against parties affected, may be enjoined from such action by a Federal court of equity. (214)

Justices James McReynolds and Louis D. Brandeis dissented on the basis that the action did not present a justiciable question, but they did not offer any explanation for their conclusion.

In 1925 a unanimous Court upheld the exercise of judicial power to strike down an Oregon law that was not to take effect until more than a year after the Court's decision. By initiative provisions, Oregon adopted a statute that would have required children between the ages of eight and sixteen to attend public schools beginning September 1, 1926. In *Pierce* v. *Society of Sisters,* the Court upheld an injunction against the operation of the Oregon statute and accepted the argument that the statute's mere existence infringed the appellees' legal rights to operate private schools, since parents would probably obey the law.

> The suits were not premature. The injury to appellees was present and very real, not a mere possibility in the remote future. If no relief had been possible prior to the effective date of the act, the injury would have become irreparable. Prevention of impending injury by unlawful action is a well recognized function of courts of equity. (536)

The following year, the Court upheld the exercise of federal equity power in the landmark zoning case, *Euclid* v. *Ambler Realty*. The realty company alleged that the zoning ordinance took their property without due process of law, since the marketable value of their real property had been reduced by being restricted to residential use for which the price was lower than for industrial use. The Village of Euclid had moved for dismissal in the lower court, since appellees had neither requested a building permit nor made application to the zoning board of appeals. Speaking for the Court, Justice George Sutherland emphasized that the suit was not premature, since the existence of the ordinance resulted in an immediate invasion of a property right.

> The effect of the allegations of the bill is that the ordinance of its own force operates greatly to reduce the value of appellee's lands and destroy their marketability for industrial, commercial and residential uses, and the attack is directed, not against any specific provision or provisions, but against the ordinance as an entirety. Assuming the premises, the existence and maintenance of the ordinance in effect constitutes a present invasion of appellee's property rights and a threat to continue it. Under these circumstances, the equitable jurisdiction is clear. (386)

In these three cases, the Court concluded that a law's mere existence affected a party's legal right. The Court considered the statutes' constitutionality on their face because they immediately invaded a legal right. The latter point distinguishes these cases from advisory opinions and puts them within the scope of the case-or-controversy provision. That is, an actual justiciable controversy existed, in each instance, because the Court determined that a law's existence invaded a legal right.

The Court's decisions in *Terrace, Pierce,* and *Euclid* were not aberrations. In *Pennsylvania* v. *West Virginia,* Pennsylvania invoked the Court's original jurisdiction to determine a West Virginia statute's constitutionality before the statute was implemented. The Court stated that "[o]ne does not have to await the consummation of threatened injury to obtain preventive relief. If the injury is certainly impending, that is enough" (593). Yet the injury alleged was much less certain to occur than were the claimed injuries in *Terrace, Pierce,* and *Euclid.* The West Virginia statute provided that interstate shipment of natural gas would be limited if intrastate requirements could not be met. At the time the Court decided the case, Pennsylvania could not show that this situation existed or would ever exist.[21]

Pennsylvania v. *West Virginia* indicates that the Court may find the existence of an actual justiciable controversy not solely because the statute, on its face, infringes a legal right but because the statute plus a contingency that may occur in the future violates a legal right. If the

Court determines that the contingency is certain to happen, an actual justiciable controversy exists at the time the action is brought.

Adler v. *Board of Education* indicates that the Court has accepted the adjudication of a statute prior to enforcement. In *Adler,* the Court upheld New York's Feinberg Law, which provided for the dismissal of public school teachers who advocated the overthrow of the government by force, or who knowingly belonged to any organization that the New York Board of Regents determined advocated the overthrow of the government. In seeking declaratory and injunctive relief, the plaintiffs did not allege that they had violated the Act or that the Board had listed any organization as being subversive. Without discussing the issue of justiciability, the six-man majority held that the statute did not violate the First and Fourteenth Amendments. Of the nine justices participating, Justice Felix Frankfurter was the only justice to raise the issue of justiciability.[22] One should note that *Adler* had an added variable that had not existed in the four previous decisions. Adler's action had been commenced in the New York courts, while the other actions were instituted in federal district courts. With the exception of Frankfurter, the justices apparently accepted the New York courts' determination that an actual justiciable controversy was present.

In *Public Utilities Commission of California* v. *United States,* the Supreme Court upheld the United States government's right to challenge a California statute that gave the California Public Utilities Commission the power to determine whether the United States government could transport federal government property on common carriers in California at reduced rates. Although the Commission had indicated its intention to enforce the Act, the United States had not requested the reduced rates, and the Commission had not taken any action. In striking down the statute on its face, the Court stated:

> Here the statute limits transportation at reduced rates unless the Commission first gives approval. The controversy is present and concrete—whether the United States has the right to obtain transportation service at such rates as it may negotiate or whether it can do so only with state approval.(539)

Two cases involving Chicago city ordinances indicate that the Court will rule on a statute or ordinance before implementation or enforcement, if an important constitutional issue is involved. In *Chicago* v. *Atchison, Topeka & Santa Fe Railroad Co.,* the Court struck down a Chicago ordinance requiring a certificate to operate motor vehicle service between railroad stations, since the service was "an integral part of interstate railroad transportation authorized and subject to regulation under the Interstate Commerce Act"(89). The Court held that the Company did not have to submit to the administrative procedures, since the ordinance was invalid on its face. In *Times Film Corporation* v. *Chicago,* the Court upheld a Chicago ordinance requiring the submission of all motion pictures to the police commissioner in order to obtain a permit for exhibition. The exhibitor requested a permit but refused to submit the motion picture, "Don Juan," to the commissioner. The Court indicated that it was deciding only the narrow question that the exhibitor had raised.

> Admittedly, the challenged section of the ordinance imposes a previous restraint, and the broad justiciable issue is therefore present as to whether the ambit of constitutional protection includes complete and absolute freedom to exhibit, at least once, any and every kind of motion picture. It is that question alone which we decide. (46)

South Carolina v. *Katzenbach* presents an excellent example of the Court's discretion in determining when an actual controversy exists. In an original action in the United States Supreme Court, South Carolina sought an injunction against the enforcement of the Voting Rights Act of 1965. Although the Act had been applied in South Carolina, the State did not allege any specific violation of its rights but rather that the Act was beyond the constitutional powers of Congress. "Because no issues of fact were raised in the complaint, and because of South Carolina's desire to obtain a ruling prior to its primary elections in June 1966, we dispensed with appointment of a special master and expedited our hearing of the case"(307). The Court did not permit South Carolina to attack the entire Act but did indicate that certain provisions of the Act presented an actual justiciable controversy.[23] The closest that the Court came to indicating why an actual justiciable controversy existed was when it stated:

> The objections to the Act which are raised under these provisions may therefore be considered only as additional aspects of the basic question presented by the case: Has Congress exercised its powers under the Fifteenth Amendment in an appropriate manner with relation to the States?(324)

The Court did not explicitly state why an actual justiciable controversy existed, but one can infer that the Court concluded that the mere enactment of the Voting Rights Act of 1965 raised serious constitutional questions about whether Congress had properly exercised its powers under the Fifteenth Amendment or had invaded the states' reserved powers. The Court did not use this terminology and has ordinarily refused to entertain such issues on the basis that they present political questions. One has great difficulty, however, in discerning why an actual justiciable controversy was present on any other basis.

The preceding cases indicate that a statute or other governmental action may be challenged, even though no implementation or enforcement has been commenced, if a federal court determines that the mere existence of the statute or other governmental action invades a legal right. At times the courts may also have to determine whether a contingency is likely to happen if the statute or governmental action would invade a legal right only after the happening of such contingency. In both instances the courts determine whether the governmental action alone invades a legal right and whether the contingency is likely to happen. This is illustrated even more vividly when one examines a few instances where the Court determined that an actual justiciable controversy was not present.

International Longshoremen's & Warehousemen's Union v. *Boyd* indicates the Court's discretion in this area. Although the Immigration and Naturalization Service admitted that it would apply the Immigration and Nationality Act of 1952 to resident aliens who went to work in the Alaskan territory's salmon canneries and had already excluded resident aliens as new immigrants under these circumstances, the Court concluded that an actual justiciable controversy was not present. "Determination of the scope and constitutionality of legislation in advance of its immediate adverse effect in the context of a concrete case involves too remote and too abstract an inquiry for the proper exercise of the judicial function"(224). In a dissenting opinion, Justice Hugo Black argued that the workers were "threatened with irreparable damages"(226).

United Public Workers v. *Mitchell* also indicates the Court's discretion in this area. Federal government employees sought an injunction and a declaratory judgment against Section 9(a) of the Hatch Act, which prohibited any "officer or employee in the executive branch of the Federal Government" from taking "any active part in political management or in political campaigns."[24] Only one of the employees had violated the Act; the others claimed they desired to participate in political management and political campaigns. The Court refused to rule on the Act's constitutionality except as it applied to the one employee who admittedly had violated it. In denying relief to the other employees, the Court stated:

> These appellants seem clearly to seek advisory opinions upon broad claims of rights protected by the First, Fifth, Ninth and Tenth Amendments. . . . Such generality of objection is really an attack on the political expediency of the Hatch Act, not the presentation of legal issues. . . . A hypothetical threat is not enough.(89–90)

Justices William O. Douglas and Hugo Black thought the Act should be construed on its face as it applied to all the employees. In his dissent, Justice Douglas argued that there was an actual justiciable controversy concerning all the employees.

What these appellants propose to do is plain enough. If they do what they propose to do, it is clear that they will be discharged from their positions. . . . But to require these employees first to suffer the hardship of a discharge is not only to make them incur a penalty, it makes inadequate, if not wholly illusory, any legal remedy which they may have. Men who must sacrifice their means of livelihood in order to test their rights to their jobs, must either pursue prolonged and expensive litigation as unemployed persons or pull up their roots.(116–17)

Boyd and *Mitchell* indicate not only the Court's discretionary power in determining the existence of an actual justiciable controversy but also the difficulty one has in attempting to discern any constant criteria for how this discretion will be exercised. The contingency in *Boyd* was more certain to occur than the one involved in *Pennsylvania* v. *West Virginia,* yet the Court found an actual justiciable controversy in the latter and not in the former. The employees in *Mitchell* could refrain from participating in any political activities, but the Court decided *Terrace* v. *Thompson* even though Terrace could have refrained from selling his property to an alien.

The federal courts may decide an issue involving a statute or other governmental action before any implementation or enforcement, but the courts, and ultimately the United States Supreme Court, have great discretion in determining whether the mere existence of a statute or other governmental decision invades legal rights.

The Right to Challenge Criminal Statutes or Criminal Penalties before Prosecution

In a criminal prosecution, a "case" or "controversy" is definitely present. The government contends that the defendant has violated a law, while the defendant may claim that he has not violated the law, that the law is being improperly applied, or that the law is unconstitutional. In this situation, an actual justiciable controversy is before the court. The courts are faced with a more difficult problem, however, when a litigant attempts to challenge a statute or governmental order that carries a criminal penalty, before the government institutes a criminal action. Does an actual justiciable controversy exist in this situation?

Until late in the nineteenth century, the federal courts refrained from deciding such issues unless they arose in a criminal prosecution. Since 1888, the Supreme Court has indicated, however, that a "case" or "controversy" may be present when criminal statutes are challenged before prosecution if special circumstances exist. The Court has never delineated these special circumstances, so that they must be discerned case by case, and the pendulum has swung back and forth several times since 1888. The Court moved from a strict rule against intervention to fairly easy intervention, then back and forth again. Today the Court appears to be moving back toward limited anticipatory action against criminal statutes.

Since most criminal penalties are enforced by the states, the problem of anticipating criminal actions cannot be completely separated from federalism. This section will concentrate, however, on anticipating criminal actions, since the minimum requirements necessary to create an actual justiciable controversy would be applicable to either state or federal criminal actions. One should note, however, that additional factors presented by federalism may cause the Court to conclude that the federal judiciary should not act before the state courts do.

Although In re *Sawyer* concluded that a court of equity should not intervene to prevent the application of criminal penalties, the Court's opinion provided the opening for future anticipatory relief. A federal circuit court had issued an injunction against the elected officials of Lincoln, Nebraska enjoining them from removing a local police judge. Despite the court's order, the city officials forcibly removed the judge from office. The city officials were found in contempt of court and, when they refused to pay the fines, were committed to federal custody. The case reached the United States Supreme Court as an action for a writ of habeas corpus.

The Supreme Court granted the writ on the basis that the circuit court had neither jurisdiction nor the power to issue the injunction. In discussing the federal court's equity jurisdiction, Justice Horace Gray spoke as follows for the Court:

> The office and jurisdiction of a court of equity, unless enlarged by express statute, are limited to the protection of rights of property. It has no jurisdiction over the prosecution, the punishment, or the pardon of crimes or misdemeanors, or over the appointment and removal of public officers.(210)

The Court did not indicate when a federal court could exercise its equity jurisdiction to protect "the rights of property" prior to any prosecution.[25]

The Court's reliance on *Sawyer* is indicated by *Davis & Farnum Manufacturing Co.* v. *Los Angeles.*

> That a court of equity has no general power to enjoin or stay criminal proceedings unless they are instituted by a party to a suit already pending before it, and to try the same right that is in issue there, or to prohibit the invasion of the rights of property by the enforcement of an unconstitutional law, was so

fully considered and settled in an elaborate opinion by Mr.
Justice Gray, in *Re Sawyer,* 124 U.S. 200 . . . that no further
reference to prior authorities is deemed necessary, and we have
little more to do than to consider whether there is anything
exceptional in the case under consideration to take it out of the
general rule.(217)

The Court's first application of the exception suggested in *Sawyer*
occurred in *Dobbins* v. *Los Angeles.* In affirming an injunction against
the enforcement of a local ordinance, a unanimous Court indicated
that a court's equity jurisdiction could be exercised to protect property
rights against the enforcement of an unconstitutional ordinance.

It is also urged by the defendants in error that a court of
equity will not enjoin prosecution of a criminal case; but, as we
have seen, the plaintiff in error in this case had acquired property rights which by the enforcement of the ordinances in question, would be destroyed and rendered worthless. . . .

It is well settled that, where property rights will be destroyed, unlawful interference by criminal proceedings under a
void law or ordinance may be reached and controlled by a
court of equity.(241)

The Court further elaborated on this exception to the general rule
in the landmark case of Ex parte *Young.* Speaking for the eight-man
majority, Justice Rufus W. Peckham outlined a federal court's power
and limitations in this area.

It is further objected (and the objection really forms part
of the contention that the state cannot be sued) that a court of
equity has no jurisdiction to enjoin criminal proceedings by
indictment or otherwise, under the state-law. This, as a general
rule, is true. But there are exceptions. When such indictment
or proceeding is brought to enforce an alleged unconstitutional
statute, which is the subject matter of inquiry in a suit already
pending in a Federal Court, the latter court, having first obtained jurisdiction over the subject matter, has the right in both
civil and criminal cases, to hold and maintain such jurisdiction,
to the exclusion of all other courts, until its duty is fully performed. . . . But the Federal Courts cannot, of course, interfere
in a case where the proceedings were already pending in a state
court. . . .

Where one commences a criminal proceeding who is already party to a suit then pending in a court of equity, if the
criminal proceedings are brought to enforce the same right
that is in issue before the court, the latter may enjoin such
criminal proceedings. . . . [The Court then discussed *Davis &*

Farnum Manufacturing Co. v. *Los Angeles; Dobbins* v. *Los Angeles; Smyth* v. *Ames.*]

These cases show that a court of equity is not always precluded from granting an injunction to stay proceedings in criminal cases, and we have no doubt the principle applies in a case such as the present. Re *Sawyer,* 124 U.S. 200, 211 . . . is not to the contrary.(161–62)

If the federal courts obtain jurisdiction before a state prosecution is commenced, the federal courts may enjoin the state from instituting a criminal action while the original action is pending or permanently if they find that the state statute is a void enactment.

The Court indicated special circumstances must be present before a federal court may invoke its equitable jurisdiction to enjoin a state criminal statute. A United States circuit court had granted a preliminary injunction against the enforcement of a Minnesota statute and administrative procedure that set railway rates. As state attorney general, Young proceeded to enforce the statute despite the injunction, and the circuit court then ordered Young held in federal custody for contempt of court. Peckham held that the federal question directly related to anticipating criminal action was whether the penalties imposed were so onerous that they deprived the railroads of the Fourteenth Amendment's guarantees of due process and equal protection of the laws. The railways alleged that the penalties were so excessive that they faced the dilemma of either having their property confiscated by the statute's enforcement or having their property confiscated as a result of criminal actions, and the Court accepted this argument.

We hold, therefore, that the provisions of the acts relating to the enforcement of the rates . . . by imposing such enormous fines and possible imprisonment as a result of an unsuccessful effort to test the validity of the laws themselves, are unconstitutional on their face, without regard to the question of the insufficiency of those rates.(148)

In traditional equitable terms, the Court determined that the railways did not have an adequate remedy at law. Professor Westel W. Willoughby has suggested that "[t]here is a line of cases which hold that due process of law is denied when such excessive penalties are attached to the violation of statutory or administrative orders as to make it practically impossible for the individual to test their validity by violating them."[26] At what point the penalties become excessive is obviously within the federal courts' discretion and ultimately the United States Supreme Court's discretion.

In *Young,* the Court also suggested that a federal court might determine a criminal statute's constitutionality before any prosecution to prevent a multiplicity of suits.

> It would be an injury to complainant to harass it with a multiplicity of suits or litigation generally in an endeavor to enforce penalties under an unconstitutional enactment, and to prevent it ought to be within the jurisdiction of a court of equity.(190)

The Court further suggested that a prosecutor might ignore a single violation to prevent a test case (193). Both the excessive penalties and a possible multiplicity of suits would meet the traditional equitable requirements that the plaintiff must be faced with irreparable harm.

The Court first applied the exception to Federal action in *Philadelphia Co.* v. *Stimson.* Under statutory authority, the Department of the Army established harbor lines beyond which the plaintiff had no right to occupation. The plaintiff occupied the area beyond the harbor lines, and the Secretary of the Army threatened criminal proceedings. In permitting the Company to bring an anticipatory action, the Court relied on the exception to the general rule that federal courts will not interfere in prospective criminal actions.

> But a distinction obtains when it is found to be essential to the protection of the property rights, as to which the jurisdiction of a court of equity has been invoked, that it should restrain the defendant from instituting criminal actions involving the same legal questions. This is illustrated in the decisions of this court in which officers have been enjoined from bringing criminal proceedings to compel obedience to unconstitutional requirements.(621)

By 1935 the Supreme Court apparently concluded that the lower federal courts were intervening too often in state criminal actions. In *Spielman Motor Sales Co.* v. *Dodge,* the Court reversed a three-judge district court that had accepted jurisdiction in an action to enjoin state criminal prosecution. "To justify such interference there must be exceptional circumstances and a clear showing that an injunction is necessary in order to afford adequate protection of constitutional rights" (95). The Court concluded that the issue could be properly adjudicated in a criminal action and that irreparable harm had not been shown, since the prosecutor had explicitly stated that he would not institute a multiplicity of suits.

Beal v. *Missouri Pacific Railway* further indicates that the Supreme Court concluded that the lower federal courts were enforcing the exception rather than the rule. A federal district court had granted an injunction against enforcement of a Nebraska statute, and the circuit court had affirmed. A unanimous Supreme Court reversed the lower courts and declared:

> [I]nterference with the process of the criminal law in state courts, in whose control they are lodged by the Constitution, and the determination of questions of criminal liability under state law by federal courts of equity can be justified only in most exceptional circumstances, and upon clear showing that an injunction is necessary to prevent irreparable injury. . . . And, in the exercise of the sound discretion, which guides the determination of courts of equity, scrupulous regard must be had for the rightful independence of state governments and a remedy infringing that independence which might otherwise be given should be withheld if sought on slight or inconsequential grounds.(50)

The lower federal courts had held that a multiplicity of actions could result in irreparable injury, but the Supreme Court concluded that the record did not indicate the probability of a multiplicity of suits. The case does illustrate the discretion that the courts exercise in determining the existence of an actual justiciable case under these circumstances. The Supreme Court did not suggest that the federal courts did not possess this discretion but that "exceptional circumstances" should exist before a federal court intervened.

Shields v. *Utah Idaho Central Railway Co.* indicates that the Court's concern in *Spielman* and *Beal* may have been more with deference to state judiciaries than with the existence of an actual justiciable controversy. The Court has never explicitly stated such a distinction, but *Shields* suggests that such a distinction may be relevant. In *Shields*, the railway claimed that it was an interurban railroad, but the Interstate Commerce Commission had found that it was engaged in interstate commerce and therefore subject to the Railway Labor Act. In seeking to avoid compliance with the Act and the Commission's order, the railway sought an injunction against possible prosecution for its failure to comply with a mediation board's order that it notify its employees that labor disputes were governed by the act. The Court upheld the railway's right to bring the action.

> Disobedience is immediately punishable and it is made the duty of the United States Attorney to institute proceedings against violators. Respondent has invoked the equity jurisdiction to restrain such prosecution and the Government does not challenge the propriety of that procedure. Equity jurisdiction may be invoked when it is essential to the protection of the rights asserted, even though the complainant seeks to enjoin the bringing of criminal action.(183)

The Court did not suggest why the railroad would suffer irreparable injury and the only evident distinction among *Shields, Spielman,* and *Beal* is that the two latter actions involved federalism.

While *Spielman* and *Beal*[27] indicated that the Supreme Court was attempting to limit lower federal courts' intervention in anticipating state criminal actions to exceptional circumstances, a new trend became discernible during the 1940s. As litigation involving civil liberties and civil rights increased, the federal courts were asked to enjoin enforcement of criminal statutes that allegedly violated civil liberties or civil rights. *Douglas* v. *City of Jeannette* is particularly relevant, since the Court explicitly found a "case" or "controversy" present, but held that the federal courts should refuse to exercise their discretionary equitable jurisdiction. Douglas and other Jehovah's Witnesses had distributed religious literature and had taken orders for their publications without obtaining a license or paying a fee as required by a city ordinance. The Jehovah's Witnesses sought an injunction against the ordinance's enforcement on the basis of the Civil Rights Act of 1871. The Act provided that anyone acting under the color of state law to deprive anyone of his constitutional rights "shall be liable to the party injured in an action at law, suit in equity, or other proper proceeding for redress."[28]

> Allegations of fact sufficient to show deprivation of the right of free speech under the First Amendment are sufficient to establish deprivation of a constitutional right guaranteed by the Fourteenth, and to state a cause of action under the Civil Rights Act, whenever it appears that the abridgement of the right is effected under the color of a state statute or ordinance. It follows that the bill, which amply alleges the facts relied on to show the abridgement by criminal proceedings under the ordinance, sets out a case or controversy which is within the adjudicatory power of the district court.(162)

The Court found, however, that petitioners had not established facts that necessitated the federal court's invoking their equitable jurisdiction. The Court emphasized that federal courts should not interfere with the enforcement of state criminal actions "on slight or inconsequential grounds"(163). The Court held that the mere allegation that a multiplicity of suits was possible did not establish irreparable injury. After stating that the record established a "case" or "controversy," the Court concluded that the federal courts should exercise their discretion and refrain from intervening in state criminal matters.

While the Court did decide that *Douglas* was not a proper case for federal judicial intervention, the Court also indicated that under the proper circumstances federal courts could enjoin the enforcement of criminal actions to protect civil liberties and civil rights as well as property. The Court suggested, however, that the grounds must not be "slight or inconsequential."

By 1964 the pendulum swung toward granting anticipatory relief in actions involving civil liberties and civil rights. In *Baggett* v. *Bullitt,* the Supreme Court reversed a three-judge district court decision that an action for declaratory and injunctive relief against a Washington loyalty oath did not present an actual justiciable controversy. The Court held that the Washington statutes were vague and overly broad and therefore presented an actual justiciable controversy on their face.

> The State may not require one to choose between subscribing to an unduly vague and broad oath, thereby incurring the likelihood of prosecution, and conscientiously refusing to take the oath with the consequent loss of employment, and perhaps profession, particularly where "the free dissemination of ideas may be the loser."(374)

The Court found that the mere existence of the statutes created an actual justiciable controversy.

In *Dombrowski* v. *Pfister,* the Supreme Court held that an action seeking declaratory and injunctive relief against Louisiana's statutes controlling subversive activities did present an actual justiciable controversy, although the federal district court had ruled against justiciability. The Court emphasized the chilling effects and overly broad language of the statute.

> A criminal prosecution under a statute regulating expression usually involves imponderables and contingencies that themselves may inhibit the full exercise of First Amendment freedoms. . . . When the statutes also have an overbroad sweep, as is here alleged, the hazard of loss or substantial impairment of those precious rights may be critical.(486)

The Court also suggested that the threat of a multiplicity of actions produced a "chilling effect on free expression"(487). The Court concluded that an actual justiciable controversy was present whenever "statutes are justifiably attacked on their face as abridging free expression, or as applied for the purpose of discouraging protected activities"(489–90).

By 1970 the pendulum had swung toward anticipatory relief in actions involving alleged chilling effects, but in 1971 the Court apparently concluded that the pendulum had swung too far. The federal district courts began entertaining actions for declaratory and injunctive relief even after state criminal action had commenced. In the leading case of *Younger* v. *Harris,* a three-judge district court had issued an injunction against the enforcement of the California Criminal Syndicalism Act after the defendant had been indicted. The Supreme Court reversed primarily on the basis of the abstention doctrine. Speaking for the Court, Justice Hugo L. Black argued, however, that the federal court had exceeded its constitutional powers in granting anticipatory relief.

> Procedures for testing the constitutionality of a statute "on its face" in the manner apparently contemplated by *Dombrowski*, and for then enjoining all actions to enforce the statute until the state can obtain court approval for a modified version, are fundamentally at odds with the function of the federal courts in our constitutional plan.(52)

He suggested that the judiciary's function was to decide "concrete disputes," and that the Constitutional Convention had specifically denied the courts the "unlimited power to survey the statute books."

> Ever since the Constitutional Convention rejected a proposal for having members of the Supreme Court render advice concerning pending legislation it has been clear that, even when suits of this kind involve a "case or controversy" sufficient to satisfy the requirements of Article III of the Constitution, the task of analyzing a proposed statute, pinpointing its deficiencies, and requiring correction of these deficiencies before the statute is put into effect, is rarely if ever an appropriate task for the judiciary. The combination of the relative remoteness of the controversy, the impact on the legislative process of the relief sought, and above all the speculative and amorphous nature of the required line-by-line analysis of detailed statutes . . . ordinarily results in a kind of case that is wholly unsatisfactory for deciding constitutional questions, whichever way they might be decided. In light of this fundamental conception of the Framers as to the proper place of the federal courts in the governmental process of passing and enforcing laws, it can seldom be appropriate for these courts to exercise any such power of prior approval or veto over the legislative process.(52–53)

According to Black, a "case" or "controversy" might technically be present, but a federal court should use its discretion to avoid premature decisions and involvement in the political process.

Although Justices Potter Stewart and John Marshall Harlan concurred in the Court's opinion, they filed a separate opinion indicating that the Court's decision concerned only pending state criminal actions where a federal court should intervene only if the irreparable injury is "both great and immediate"(54–56). In four other decisions handed down in 1971, the Supreme Court held that lower federal courts had improperly granted anticipatory relief when criminal actions were actually pending in the state courts.[29]

Boyle v. *Landry* presents further evidence that the Court concluded that the pendulum had swung too far toward anticipatory action by the federal judiciary. Although other issues were involved in the lower federal court, Illinois city and county officials only appealed a lower court's declaration that an intimidation statute was overly broad and the court's injunction against its enforcement. In reversing the lower court, Justice Black indicated for the Court that an actual justiciable controversy did not exist.

> It is obvious that the allegations of the complaint in this case fall far short of showing any irreparable injury from threats or actual prosecution under the intimidation statute or from any other conduct by state or city officials.(80)

Black suggested that it appeared that the original plaintiffs had searched the statute books for statutes that might be susceptible of bad faith enforcement without showing any actual threat of enforcement against them.

Two 1974 cases indicate that while the Court still felt the pendulum had swung too far toward intervention, the federal judiciary is not completely barred from anticipatory actions against state criminal laws. In *O'Shea* v. *Littleton,* the Court held that a "case" or "controversy" did not exist. Littleton and others alleged that Cairo, Illinois judicial officials were discriminating against black defendants. Since they did not allege that they had been or would be charged with violating any state law, Justice Byron White's majority opinion concluded that any injury was "too remote to satisfy the 'case or controversy' requirement"(498).

In *Steffel* v. *Thompson,* however, the Court found the necessary conditions for anticipatory action against a state criminal law (see also *Ellis* v. *Dyson*). In a unanimous decision, Justice William J. Brennan stressed the factual situation in delivering the Court's opinion. Steffel requested equitable and declaratory relief against the Georgia criminal trespass law. Steffel had been warned twice that if he did not cease handbilling at a private shopping center he would be arrested and charged under the Georgia criminal trespass law. On both occasions Steffel left the premises, but on the second occasion a companion remained and was arrested. Brennan held that Steffel's fear of prosecution was not imaginary or speculative. "In these circumstances it is not necessary that petitioner first expose himself to actual arrest or prosecution to be entitled to challenge a statute that he claims deters the exercise of his constitutional rights"(459). *O'Shea* and *Steffel* indicate that the Court's interpretation of the factual situation determines a "case" or "controversy's" existence.

Since 1888, the Court has held that federal courts may grant injunctive relief against criminal statutes. The Court has not established any rigid criteria, however, that help to determine when a federal court may act in such a situation. This means that the federal courts exercise great discretion in this area. Twice in the past forty years the Court has apparently concluded that the lower federal courts were opening the floodgates, and the Court has moved toward a more stringent application of the exception to the general rule.

Administrative Action That May Be Judicially Challenged before Anyone Is Ordered to Do Anything

Administrative law is another area that has generated many actions involving questions about the existence of an actual justiciable issue. Since judicial review of administrative action is primarily a modern development, the federal courts have not been able to rely on precedent. And Congress has complicated the situation by enacting statutes that specifically provide for judicial review of administrative action. Like anticipatory actions against enforcement of criminal laws, federalism may become an issue in this area, but its impact is less significant since the actions have usually involved federal administrative action. Another potential problem relates to the intricacies of administrative law, since the issue may be one in which the administrative decision is not subject to judicial review.[30]

During the 1920s and 1930s the Court adopted a very restrictive approach to intervention in the administrative process. The Court perceived certain administrative actions as not reviewable and construed congressional authorization of review very strictly. The Court emphasized the type of administrative action taken and placed very little, if any, emphasis on the legal rights of the party challenging administrative action. The Court deviated from this general approach during this period only when an action was commenced under the judiciary's general equitable powers, rather than a specific congressional enactment that provided for judicial review of administrative action.

One of the early congressional enactments in this area, the Urgent Deficiencies Act, provided that federal district courts had jurisdiction over any civil action "to enforce, enjoin, set aside, annul or suspend, in whole or in part, any order of the Interstate Commerce Commission."[31] In *United States* v. *Los Angeles & Salt Lake Railroad,* the railroad commenced an action under the Urgent Deficiencies Act to set aside a valuation of its property made by the Interstate Commerce Commission. The railroad alleged that the ICC had exceeded its powers and that the railroad's credit would be impaired by the Commission's action. With eight justices participating, a unanimous Court concluded that the valuation was merely preparation for possible action by the ICC and not an order within the context of the Urgent Deficiencies Act.[32] "There is the fundamental infirmity that the mere existence of error in the final valuation is not a wrong for which Congress provides a remedy under the Urgent Deficiencies Act"(313).

In *United States* v. *Atlanta, Birmingham & Coast Railroad Co.,* the Supreme Court held that an Interstate Commerce Commission finding that the railroad would be limited to showing its investment in road and equipment to a specified amount was not a justiciable order under the Urgent Deficiencies Act. The Court concluded that the findings were "directory as distinguished from mandatory. No case has been found in which matter embodied in a report and not followed by a formal order has been held to be subject to judicial review"(528).

In *Shannahan* v. *United States,* the trustees of the Chicago, South Shore, & South Bend Railroad brought an action to set aside the Interstate Commerce Commission's finding that the carrier was "not a street, interurban, or suburban electric railway" and therefore was not exempt from the Railway Labor Act. Speaking for a unanimous Court, Justice Louis D. Brandeis concluded that the ICC's action was not an order, but the Court's opinion suggested that the determination of what constituted an order was not so simple as the earlier cases had indicated.

> The function of the Commission is limited to the determination of a fact. Its decision is not even in form an order. It "had no characteristic of an order, affirmative or negative." *United States* v. *Illinois Cent. R. Co.,* 244 U.S. 82, 89. . . . The decision neither commands nor directs anything to be done. . . . The determination is thus not enforceable by the Commission, the only action which could ever be taken on it would be by some other body. It is as clearly "negative" as orders by which the Commission refuses to take requested action. . . . As such it is not reviewable under the Urgent Deficiencies Act.(599)

The Court explained its restrictive view of the Urgent Deficiencies Act more explicitly in *Shannahan* than in earlier cases. In response to the allegation that the ICC's determination made the carrier liable to prosecution for willful failure or refusal to comply, the Court replied that "the determination of a status or similar matter is not action subject to review under the Urgent Deficiencies Act even if disregard of the determination may subject the carrier to criminal prosecution"(602). The Court did not deny that a justiciable action might be present, but emphasized that no action existed under the specific Act authorizing judicial review of ICC orders. "Whether the determination of the Commission is reviewable in a district court by some judicial procedure other than that of the Urgent Deficiencies Act we have no occasion to consider"(603).

Shields v. *Utah Idaho Central R.R.* illustrates the relevance of the Court's latter distinction in *Shannahan.* Like *Shannahan, Shields* was an action challenging the ICC's determination that a carrier was subject to the provisions of the Labor Railway Act. In *Shields,* the carrier sought an injunction against possible criminal prosecution and did not rely on the Urgent Deficiencies Act. Speaking for a unanimous Court, Chief Justice Charles Evans Hughes held that *Shannahan* was inapplicable because it applied only to actions brought under the Urgent Deficiencies Act and concluded that an actual justiciable controversy was present in *Shields.*

> The nature of the determination points to the propriety of judicial review. For while the determination is made by the Interstate Commerce Commission for the purposes of the Railway Labor Act and not for further proceedings by the Commission itself, it is none the less a part of a regulatory scheme. It has the effect, if validly made of subjecting the respondent to the requirements of the Railway Labor Act which was enacted to regulate the activities of transportation companies engaged in interstate commerce.(183)

Shields was distinguishable from *Shannahan* since the Federal Mediation Board had ordered the carrier to post the fact that labor disputes were subject to the Railway Labor Act, but the Court did not mention this order until after it had determined that an actual justiciable controversy was present.

By 1939 the Court had developed two doctrines concerning judicial intervention in the administrative process. If the action was commenced under a statute granting the federal courts the power to review administrative action, the Court construed the statute strictly as in *Shannahan* (see also *Federal Power Commission* v. *Metropolitan Edison Co.*). If the action was brought under the federal judiciary's general equitable jurisdiction, the Court placed its emphasis on whether the complaining party could establish the necessary criteria to invoke the courts' equitable jurisdiction as in *Shields* (see also *Utah Fuel Co.* v. *National Bituminous Coal Commission*). In *Rochester Telephone Corp.* v. *United States,* the Court apparently attempted to clarify this situation, as well as its interpretation of what constituted an order.

The Federal Communications Commission determined that Rochester Telephone was subject to FCC orders, while the corporation claimed its business was solely intrastate and therefore not subject to federal regulations. Rochester Telephone challenged the Commission's action under the Urgent Deficiencies Act. In delivering the Court's opinion, Justice Felix Frankfurter discussed judicial review of "negative" administrative orders, although he ultimately rejected the term.[33] Frankfurter classified negative orders, or orders that did not require a party to take any action, in three categories. First, he suggested that "the order sought to be reviewed does not of itself adversely affect complainant but only affects his rights on the contingency of future administrative action"(130). Frankfurter argued that the judiciary should not review this type of administrative action because the action would either be premature or outside the scope of the federal judicial power.

> Plainly the denial of judicial review in these cases does not derive from a regard for the special functions of administrative agencies. Judicial abstention here is merely an application of the traditional criteria for bringing judicial action into play. Partly these have been written into Article 3 of the Constitution, U.S.C.A., by what is implied from the grant of "judicial power" to determine "cases" and "controversies," Art. 3, Sec. 2, U.S. Constitution. Partly they are an aspect of the procedural philosophy pertaining to the federal courts whereby, ever since the first Judiciary Act, Congress has been loathe to authorize review of interim steps in a proceeding.(131)

Second, Frankfurter classified actions that were "instances of statutory regulations which place restrictions upon the free conduct of the complainant"(132). While actions falling in group one do not present an actual justiciable controversy, actions in group two might be justiciable, according to Frankfurter, if they met a threefold test.

> In this type of situation a complainant seeking judicial review under the Urgent Deficiencies Act of adverse action by the Commission must clear three hurdles: (a) "case" or "controversy" under Article 3; (b) the conventional requisites of equity jurisdiction; (c) the specific terms of the statute granting to the district courts jurisdiction in suits challenging "any order" of the Commission.(132)

He ultimately concluded that Rochester Telephone's action fell into this category, and thus the discussion of the other two categories were *obiter dicta*.

> The order of the Communications Commission in this case was therefore reviewable. It was not a mere abstract declaration regarding the status of the Rochester under the Communications Act, nor was it a stage in an incomplete process of administrative adjudication. The contested order determining the status of the Rochester necessarily and immediately carried direction of obedience to previously formulated mandatory orders addressed generally to all carriers amenable to the Commission's authority. Into this class of carriers the order under dispute covered the Rochester, and by that fact, in conjunction with the other orders, made determination of the status of the Rochester a reviewable order of the Commission.(143–44)

The Court's criteria created the possibility that administrative action could be subject to judicial review at a much earlier time than previous cases had indicated. Frankfurter determined the presence of an actual justiciable controversy not by the form of the administrative action but by the impact the action had on the complaining party.

Third, Frankfurter classified suits where "review is sought of action by the Commission which affects the complainant because it does not forbid or compel conduct with reference to him by a third person"(135). Although this situation was not involved in *Rochester,* the Court's analysis again indicates an emphasis on the party's rights rather than on the administrative action's form. Frankfurter used the same threefold criteria suggested in the second group, including the emphasis on equity jurisdiction. (The Court concluded that a previous action, *Proctor & Gamble Co.* v. *United States,* was erroneously decided since all three criteria had been met.) He held that judicial review of administrative action was proper if it would prevent a multiplicity of suits, and the form of the order was again deemphasized. "An order of the Commission dismissing a complaint on the merits and maintaining the status quo is an exercise of administrative function no more and no less, than an order directing some changes in status"(142).

In an opinion concurring in the result in which Justice James C. McReynolds joined, Justice Pierce Butler contended that the order in *Rochester* was really affirmative in nature and that the Court's opinion concerning negative orders was *dicta* (147–48). Nevertheless, the Court's opinion did prove to be a landmark in determining the existence of an actual justiciable controversy when action was appealed from an administrative agency. After *Rochester,* the Court emphasized the impact of the agency's action on the complaining party rather than the order's form.[34]

Columbia Broadcasting System v. *United States* indicates the Court's subsequent emphasis on the party's right rather than the form of the agency's action in determining when administrative action could be reviewed. The Federal Communications Commission promulgated a regulation setting limitations on the type of contract that a station could enter into with a network. In a 5–3 decision, the Court held that an actual justiciable controversy existed in an action for an injunction, although the FCC had not enforced its regulation. Apparently following the three-pronged test suggested in *Rochester,* Chief Justice Harlan Fiske Stone held that a "case" or "controversy" was present since a legal right was involved, the network's right to contract with the stations. According to Stone, irreparable injury could result since the stations might comply with the regulation rather than challenge it.

> The ultimate test of reviewability is not to be found in an over refined technique, but in the need of the review to protect from irreparable injury threatened in the exceptional case by administrative rulings which attach legal consequences to action taken in advance of other hearings and adjudications that may follow, the results of which the regulations purport to control.(425)

Although the Court's opinion indicated that the requirements established in *Rochester* were met in *CBS,* the *Rochester* opinion's author dissented. Justice Frankfurter argued that an actual justiciable question was not present, since the FCC regulation had no immediate consequences. Frankfurter urged that a final administrative determination was not present, and therefore the judiciary should not intervene in the administrative process.

Between 1939 and 1967 the Court did not develop any significantly new criteria to determine when action by an administrative agency became justiciable, but did apply and elaborate the criteria established in *Rochester.*[35] Congress significantly altered the situation, however, by the enactment of the Administrative Procedure Act. While earlier statutes providing for judicial review of administrative action had placed the emphasis on administrative action, the Administrative Procedure Act emphasized the legal rights of the parties as well as the type of agency action.

> Except so far as (1) statutes preclude judicial review or (2) agency action is by law committed to agency direction—
>
> (a) Any person suffering legal wrong because of any agency action, or adversely affected or aggrieved by such action within the meaning of any relevant statute, shall be entitled to judicial review thereof. . . .
>
> (c) Every agency action made reviewable by statute and every final agency action for which there is no other adequate remedy in any court shall be subject to judicial review.[36]

Since the adoption of the APA, the Court has been primarily concerned with the application of the Act in determining whether challenged administrative action presents an actual justiciable controversy.

United States v. *Storer Broadcasting Co.* illustrates the APA's impact on judicial review of administrative action. The Federal Communications Commission issued regulations specifying that one criterion to be used in issuing new licenses would be the number of licenses presently held by a party, its stockholders, officers, or directors. The Storer Broadcasting Company instituted an action as a party aggrieved by a final order of the FCC.[37] The Company alleged that the rules were beyond the statutory authority of the FCC and that they adversely affected the Company. The Company also alleged that it was adversely affected by the rules relating to stockholders since the Company had no control over its stock, which was traded on the open market.

Speaking for the Court, Justice Stanley Reed suggested that the existence of the regulations did not create an actual justiciable controversy under traditional canons of jurisprudence, but that Congress might have granted the Company the right to judicial review under the Administrative Procedure Act. "[R]eview of Commission action is granted any party aggrieved or suffering legal wrong by that action"(197). The Court concluded that the Broadcasting Company was aggrieved under the statute's terms, and therefore an actual justiciable controversy was present.[38]

> The regulations here under consideration presently aggrieve the respondent. The Commission exercised a power of rulemaking which controls broadcasters. The Rules now operate to control the business affairs of Storer. Unless it obtains a modification of this declared administrative policy, Storer cannot enlarge the number of its standard or FM stations. . . . It cannot plan to enlarge the number of its standard or FM stations, and at any moment the purchase of Storer's voting stock by some member of the public could endanger its existing structure. These are grievances presently restricting Storer's operations.(199–200)

Although the Court did not make the distinction, one could assume that, without the statutory authorization, the above occurrences would have been considered mere contingencies, and that an actual justiciable controversy would not be present until one of the contingencies occurred.

Abbott Laboratories v. *Gardner* indicates the evolution of the Court's attitude toward the question of when the judiciary may review administrative action. Under authority delegated to him by the Secretary of Health, Education and Welfare, the Commissioner of Food and Drugs promulgated regulations requiring prescription drug manufacturers to print a name established by the Secretary of Health, Education, and Welfare each time that the manufacturer's proprietary name appeared on a label or in an advertisement. A group of drug manufacturers and the Pharmaceutical Manufacturers Association sought declarative and injunctive relief against the regulation before it had been enforced on the grounds that the Commissioner had exceeded his authority. The district court granted the relief sought, but the court of appeals reversed on the basis that preenforcement review was unauthorized and also that no actual "case" or "controversy" existed. In a 5–3 decision, the United States Supreme Court upheld the right of preenforcement review and concluded that an actual "case" or "controversy" was present.

Justice John Marshall Harlan's majority opinion indicated a major shift had taken place in the Court's perception of preenforcement review. Rather than beginning with the congressional intent to provide preenforcement review, Harlan first considered whether Congress intended to forbid that review.

> The question is phrased in terms of "prohibition" rather than "authorization" because a survey of our cases shows that judicial review of a final agency action by an aggrieved person will not be cut off unless there is persuasive reason to believe that such was the purpose of Congress. . . . Early cases in which this type of judicial review was entertained . . . have been reinforced by the enactment of the Administrative Procedure Act which embodies the basic presumption of judicial review to one "suffering legal wrong because of agency action, or adversely affected or aggrieved by agency action within the meaning of a relevant statute," 5 U.S.C. § 701(a). The Administrative Procedure Act provides specifically not only for review of "[a]gency action made reviewable by statute" but also for review of "final agency action for which there is no other adequate remedy in a court," 5 U.S.C. § 704.(140)

Harlan concluded that the burden was on the government to show that Congress had intended to preclude preenforcement review. The government argued that since the federal Food, Drug and Cosmetic Act specified judicial review of "certain enumerated kinds of regulations," Congress intended to preclude all other judicial review, including the present action, which was not one of the enumerated regulations. Harlan replied that the government's argument was untenable because, if accepted, it would make the Declaratory Judgment Act and the Administrative Procedure Act and similar statutes meaningless. He urged that Congress intended the remedies available under the Declaratory Judgment Act and the Administrative Procedure Act to be in addition to any specific remedies.

> [I]ndeed, a study of the legislative history shows rather conclusively that the specific review provisions were designed to give an additional remedy and not to cut down more traditional channels of review.(142)

He concluded "that nothing in the Food, Drug and Cosmetic Act itself precludes this action"(148).

Harlan then raised the issue of whether the present action presented an actual justiciable controversy in which a federal court should exercise its discretionary jurisdiction.

Without undertaking to survey the intricacies of the ripeness doctrine it is fair to say that its basic rationale is to prevent the courts, through avoidance of premature adjudication, from entangling themselves in abstract disagreements over administrative policies, and also to protect the agencies from judicial interference until an administrative decision has been formalized and its effects felt in a concrete way by the challenging parties. The problem is best seen in a twofold aspect, requiring us to evaluate both the fitness of the issues for judicial decision and the hardship to the parties of withholding court consideration.(148–49)

Harlan concluded that the issue did present an actual justiciable controversy and held that the regulation was final agency action within the meaning of the Administrative Procedure Act. "The cases dealing with judicial review of administrative actions have interpreted the 'finality' element in a pragmatic way"(149). In applying the pragmatic approach of the earlier cases, he concluded:

There is no hint that the regulation is informal . . . or only the ruling of a subordinate official . . . or tentative. It was made effective upon publication, and the Assistant General Counsel for Food and Drugs stated in the District Court that compliance was expected.(151)

Harlan dismissed as a mere technicality the government's contention that the Food and Drug Administration could not directly enforce its regulations but that the Attorney General had to authorize criminal and seizure actions for violations of the statute.

Harlan suggested that what really created an actual justiciable controversy was the impact of the regulations on the drug manufacturers. "This is also a case in which the impact of the regulations upon the petitioners is sufficiently direct and immediate as to render the issue appropriate for judicial review at this state"(152). He held that the drug manufacturers faced the dilemma of either complying with the regulations, which they believed exceeded the power given the FDA by the statute, or risking serious criminal and civil penalties for noncompliance. In either instance, the drug manufacturers faced heavy financial losses, and Harlan urged that the purpose of the Declaratory Judgment Act was to help resolve this type of dilemma.

Where the legal issue presented is fit for judicial resolution, and where a regulation requires an immediate and significant change in the plaintiffs' conduct of their affairs with serious penalties attached to noncompliance, access to the courts under the Administrative Procedure Act and the Declaratory Judgment Act must be permitted, absent a statutory bar or

some other unusual circumstance, neither of which appears
here.(153)

In a dissenting opinion in *Abbott* and a companion case, *Gardner* v.
Toilet Goods Association, Justice Abe Fortas argued that an actual justicia-
ble controversy was not present. Chief Justice Earl Warren and Justice
Tom Clark joined in Fortas's dissenting opinion.

> With all respect, I submit that established principles of ju-
> risprudence, solidly rooted in the constitutional structure of
> our Government, require that the courts should not intervene
> in the administrative process at this stage, under these facts and
> in this gross shotgun fashion. . . . The contrary is dictated by a
> proper regard for the purpose of the regulatory statute and the
> requirements of effective administration; and by regard for the
> salutary rule that courts should pass upon concrete, specific
> questions in a particularized setting rather than upon a general
> controversy divorced from particular facts.(175–76)

Fortas contended that the Court's decision could lead to undue intervention by the federal judiciary in the administrative process.

> I believe that this approach improperly and unwisely gives indi-
> vidual federal district judges a roving commission to halt the
> regulatory process, and to do so on the basis of abstractions and
> generalities instead of concrete fact situations and that it imper-
> missibly broadens the license of the courts to intervene in ad-
> ministrative action by means of a threshold suit for injunction
> rather than by the method provided by statute.(177)

First, Fortas argued that the Court digressed from its traditional
procedure for determining the intent of Congress in granting the
Court jurisdiction. He held that congressional intent should be "faith-
fully searched out by the courts" and that the courts should not assume
jurisdiction merely because Congress did not specifically prohibit it
(184). Fortas concluded that Congress did not intend that the courts
should assume jurisdiction in actions like *Abbott.*

> Congress did not intend that the regulations at issue in this case
> might be challenged in gross, apart from a specific controversy,
> or in the district courts, or by injunction or declaratory judg-
> ment action.(186)

He emphasized that no constitutional issue was involved, but only the
narrow issue of whether the FDA had exceeded its statutory powers by
requiring that the established name of a drug appear every time that
the trade name appeared and not just once.

Second, Fortas argued that the drug manufacturers had adequate
remedies at law and that no actual justiciable controversy existed. Since
the manufacturers could raise their objections to the regulations when

the government seized products for noncompliance, sought an injunction against the manufacturer, or commenced criminal action, Fortas concluded that the manufacturers had adequate remedies and that the courts should not invoke their discretionary jurisdiction. As to the Court's conclusion that an actual justiciable controversy existed because the regulation immediately imposed an undue burden on the drug manufacturers, he suggested that the public interest should require the federal courts to abstain from judicial intervention in this issue. "[T]he public interest in avoiding the delay in implementing Congress' program far outweighs the private interest"(198). According to Fortas, the Court's intervention was not really necessary at this stage, and refusal to intervene would be more in line with the deference that the Court should show Congress and the administrative agencies. He concluded, therefore, that the courts should not judge the regulations in the abstract but should wait for a specific action to develop after the Government began enforcing the regulations.

Significantly, Fortas did not deny that the federal courts had great discretion in determining when agency action presented an actual justiciable controversy. He did differ with the Court concerning congressional intent, the impact of the regulation on the manufacturers, and most importantly, whether the issue was presented in a justiciable manner. Fortas distinguished earlier cases on the basis that the courts were presented with all the factual information needed to render a decision.[39] In *Abbott,* he felt the issue was not adequately illuminated by the factual situation that the courts needed to render a decision. "We should confine ourselves—as our jurisprudence dictates—to actual, specific, particularized cases and controversies, in substance as well as in technical analysis"(200).

Whether the Court's decision in *Abbott* will have the impact in determining the existence of an actual justiciable controversy that some commentators have implied is debatable.[40] In the area of administrative law, *Abbott* does represent the basic criteria applied by the Court in determining whether a challenge to administrative action presents an actual justiciable controversy. The Court has moved from the early position of strictly construing congressional enactments giving the courts jurisdiction to a position of liberal interpretation. In addition to *Abbott,* the Court's position is indicated by several cases wherein the Court permitted preinduction review of Selective Service registrants, although Congress had apparently attempted to prevent such review.[41] Likewise, the Court has moved from determining the existence of an actual justiciable controversy on the basis of the type of order issued to examining an administrative action's impact on the complaining party. The Court's recognition of this change in approach is illustrated by *Port of Boston Marine Terminal Association* v. *Rederiaktiebolaget Trans Atlantic.*

> [I]ts argument that the order lacked finality because it had no independent effect on anyone and resembled an interlocutory court order denying a motion to dismiss a complaint has the hollow ring of another era. Agency orders that have no independent coercive effect are common.... Moreover, the relevant considerations in determining [an administrative action's] finality ... are whether the process of administrative decision-making has reached a state where judicial review will not disrupt the orderly process of adjudication and whether rights or obligations have been determined or legal consequences will flow from the agency action.(70–71)

Significant changes have occurred in the administrative-law area during the past fifty years in determining when an actual justiciable controversy exists.

Federalism and the Existence of an Actual Justiciable Issue—The Abstention Doctrine

The federal courts are often confronted with issues that either have been or could have been adjudicated by the state courts. In the former situation, the United States Supreme Court must determine if a "case" or "controversy" exists and whether the issues have been completely adjudicated in the state courts. Since the state courts have acted, the Supreme Court may assume *sub silentio* that an actual justiciable controversy is present, as it did in *Adler* v. *Board of Education*. The Court may, however, determine that a justiciable controversy is not properly before it even though the state courts have rendered a decision (see *Rescue Army* v. *Municipal Court*). When a case begins in a lower federal court, the court must determine whether an actual justiciable issue is present and whether it should exercise its jurisdiction or defer to the state courts. The United States Supreme Court has developed the abstention doctrine to apply to the latter situation.[42]

Federal district courts may exercise original jurisdiction in diversity of citizenship cases. Congress has granted jurisdiction to three-judge district courts to hear and determine the validity of state laws when they are properly challenged by equitable or declaratory actions.[43] The federal courts may exercise their discretion in such a situation and decline to entertain an action because the parties could obtain adequate relief in the state courts or because the case involves an issue of state law that the state courts have not yet interpreted. If the federal courts are to defer to the state courts in some circumstances, the question arises: What criteria should federal courts use in determining whether to abstain in deference to the state courts? Speaking for the Court in two cases in the 1960s, Justice William J. Brennan delivered two opinions that indicate the Court's difficulty in establishing any definite criteria.

In *Dombrowski* v. *Pfister,* Brennan briefly traced the evolution of federal court intervention and suggested that the abstention doctrine was primarily one of judicial self-restraint.

> In Ex parte *Young,* 209 U.S. 123, the fountainhead of federal injunctions gainst state prosecutions, the Court characterized the power and its proper exercise in broad terms: it would be justified where state officers "* * * threaten and are about to commence proceedings, either of a civil or criminal nature, to enforce against parties affected an unconstitutional act, violating the Federal Constitution* * * *" 209 U.S., at 156. Since that decision, however, considerations of federalism have tempered the exercise of equitable power, for the Court has recognized that federal interference with a State's good-faith administration of its criminal laws is peculiarly inconsistent with our federal framework. It is generally to be assumed that state courts and prosecutors will observe constitutional limitations as expounded by this Court, and that the mere possibility of erroneous initial application of constitutional standards will usually not amount to the irreparable injury necessary to justify a disruption of orderly state proceedings.(483–85)

In *Zwickler* v. *Koota,* Brennan proffered a completely different approach to federal court intervention in actions involving the constitutionality of state laws. After reviewing the history of congressional expansion of the lower federal courts' jurisdiction, Brennan concluded:

> In thus expanding federal judicial power, Congress imposed the duty upon all levels of the federal judiciary to give due respect to a suitor's choice of a federal forum for the hearing and decision of his federal constitutional claims. Plainly, escape from that duty is not permissible merely because state courts also have the solemn responsibility equally with the federal courts, "* * * to guard, enforce, and protect every right granted or secured by the constitution of the United States * * * ." *Robb* v. *Connolly,* 111 U.S. 624, 637. . . . The judge-made doctrine of abstention, first fashioned in 1941 in *Railroad Commission of Texas* v. *Pullman Co.,* 312 U.S. 496, sanctioned such escape only in narrowly limited "special circumstances."(248)

Although the Court sanctioned federal court action in *Dombrowski* and *Zwickler,* the tests articulated by Brennan in each instance are diametrically opposite. In *Dombrowski,* the basic criterion seems to be that the federal courts should abstain unless "special circumstances" are shown, while *Zwickler* suggests that the federal courts should intervene unless "special circumstances" are shown.

If the federal courts exercise a great deal of discretion in determining when to invoke the abstention doctrine, the question still remains: What is the relationship between the abstention doctrine and the existence of a "case" or "controversy"? When the federal courts abstain in favor of state adjudication, are they determining that an actual justiciable controversy does not exist? An analysis of the Court's application of the abstention doctrine indicates that the Court accepts the presence of a "case" or "controversy," but holds that the federal courts possess the discretion to insist that the action first be tried in the state courts.

In the seminal abstention doctrine case, *Railroad Commission of Texas* v. *Pullman Co.,* the Court invoked the doctrine so that the Texas courts could determine whether the Commission had exceeded its powers under Texas law before the federal courts considered a Fourteenth Amendment issue. The Court explicitly stated that it was exercising its discretionary equitable powers to avoid a premature decision. "The resources of equity are equal to an adjustment that will avoid the waste of a tentative decision as well as the friction of a premature constitutional adjudication"(500). The Court could have concluded that an actual justiciable issue could not be presented to the federal courts until the state issue was decided. The Court ordered the district court to retain jurisdiction, however, until the state issue was decided, and since the federal court's jurisdiction only extends to "cases" or "controversies," a "case" or "controversy" must have been present.

The Court explicitly declared in *Douglas* v. *City of Jeannette* that a "case" or "controversy" was present but applied the abstention doctrine. Speaking for the Court, Chief Justice Stone concluded that a "case" or "controversy" was present within the context of the Civil Rights Act of 1871.

> It follows that the bill, which amply alleges the facts relied on to show the abridgement by criminal proceedings under the ordinance, sets out a case or controversy which is within the adjudicatory power of the district court.(162)

After declaring that a "case" or "controversy" was present, Stone held that "a cause in equity was not present."

> Notwithstanding the authority of the district court as a federal court, to hear and dispose of the case, petitioners are

> entitled to the relief prayed only if they establish a cause of
> action in equity. Want of equity jurisdiction, while not going to
> the power of the court to decide the cause . . . may neverthe-
> less, in the discretion of the court, be objected to on its own
> motion. . . . Especially should it do so where its powers are in-
> voked to interfere by injunction with threatened criminal
> prosecutions in a state court.(162)

Stone argued that, since congressional legislation indicated an intent that state courts should try criminal cases involving state laws, the
federal courts should accept jurisdiction only if irreparable injury is
"clear and imminent" and that equitable remedies "should be withheld
if sought on slight or inconsequential grounds"(163). Stone found that
the lower court did not find irreparable harm present and that the
prosecutor's declared intention of instituting further prosecutions did
not amount to irreparable injury. Finally, Stone suggested that the
plaintiffs would have adequate protection of their constitutional rights
in the state courts, and therefore the federal courts should refrain
from exercising their equitable jurisdiction (164). Unlike the *Pullman*
case, the Court did not decide that the lower federal court should
retain jurisdiction since, according to the Court, the "case" or "controversy" could be adequately handled by the state judiciary with the possibility of an appeal to the United States Supreme Court.[44]

A recent decision substantiates the Court's view that a "case" or
"controversy" may be present, but that the abstention doctrine may
require the federal courts to await state judicial action. In *Lake Carriers
Association* v. *MacMullan*, the Association sought a declaratory judgment
against the Michigan Watercraft Pollution Control Act of 1970, but a
three-judge district court held that an actual justiciable controversy was
not present and that the abstention doctrine applied. The Supreme
Court held that an actual justiciable controversy was present, but
affirmed the application of the abstention doctrine. "Appellants now
urge that their complaint does present an 'actual controversy' within
the meaning of the Declaratory Judgment Act, 28 U.S.C. § 2201, that is
ripe for decision. We agree"(506). Speaking for the Court, Justice
Brennan held that the Act placed the Association's members under an
immediate obligation to install sewage storage devices on their vessels
or face heavy penalties. According to Brennan, this issue was a live
controversy and not an attempt to obtain an advisory opinion.

Although the Court rejected most of the grounds on which the
district court applied the abstention doctrine, Brennan affirmed that
one compelling reason for abstention existed.

> The last factor relied on by the District Court—the publica-
> tion of proposed federal standards that might be considered by

Michigan in the interpretation and enforcement of its statute—does, however, point toward considerations that fall within the "special circumstances" permitting abstention. The paradigm case for abstention arises when the challenged state statute is susceptible to a "construction by the state courts that would avoid or modify the [federal] constitutional question." *Harrison* v. *NAACP,* 360 U.S. 167. Compare *Baggett* v. *Bullitt,* 377 U.S. 360. *Zwickler* v. *Koota, supra,* 389 U.S. at 249. . . . That is precisely the circumstance presented here.[45](510–11)

Brennan concluded that an authoritative interpretation of the Michigan Act might modify or even completely avoid the federal questions raised. The Court remanded the case to the three-judge district court "with directions to retain jurisdiction pending institution by appellants of appropriate proceedings in Michigan courts"(513).

Justice Lewis F. Powell filed a dissent in which Chief Justice Warren Burger joined. Although Powell expressed agreement with the "central thrust of the Court's reasoning," he argued that it was not a proper case for abstention. Powell suggested that the federal questions would probably remain the same whatever interpretation the Michigan courts applied to the Act. Furthermore, he suggested that the abstention doctrine should have a limited application:

> We have spoken previously of "the delay and expense to which application of the abstention doctrine inevitably gives rise." *England* v. *Louisiana State Board of Medical Examiners,* 375 U.S. 411, 418. The relegation to state courts of this important litigation, involving major federal issues and affecting every ship operating in Michigan waters, is likely to result in serious delay, substantial expense to the parties (including the State), and a prolonging of the uncertainty which now exists.(516–17)

With the exception of the actions already pending in state courts, the federal courts exercise great discretion in determining whether to apply the abstention doctrine.[46] As *Pullman, Douglas,* and *Lake Carriers* indicate, the federal courts may find that all the elements of a "case" or "controversy" are present, but still invoke the abstention doctrine. In cases like *Douglas,* the federal courts may decide that an issue can best be handled by the state courts with the possibility of appeal to the United States Supreme Court. In cases like *Pullman* and *Lake Carriers,* the federal courts retain jurisdiction until the issue of state law is authoritatively decided by the state courts. Then the federal district court may adjudicate the federal issues, unless the state courts' interpretation of the state law has resolved the federal issues.

When the federal courts refuse to invoke the abstention doctrine, they are determining that an actual justiciable controversy is present and that the federal district court is the proper forum for the adjudication at the time the issue is presented. In the past decade the Court has been particularly reluctant to invoke the abstention doctrine when a state law was challenged on the basis of vagueness or overbreadth.[47]

If the federal courts desire to decide an issue, they may simply ignore the abstention doctrine and decide the case without raising the issues presented by the federal system. Although no evidence exists that the federal courts regularly follow this procedure, a few cases do indicate that the practice is possible.[48]

Summary

In actions at law, the federal courts are presented with a situation in which a party alleges that his legal rights have been invaded, and if the facts alleged are true, there is no question that an actual justiciable controversy is before the court. In equitable actions or actions for a declaratory judgment, the federal courts possess discretionary jurisdiction, and when they determine that they should exercise their discretionary jurisdiction, they simultaneously decide that an actual justiciable controversy is present. The mere fact that the court declines to exercise its discretionary jurisdiction does not prove the absence of an actual justiciable controversy. In declaratory judgment actions, the federal courts have never established any concrete criteria for determining when to exercise their jurisdiction. Since the Declaratory Judgment Act gives the courts complete discretion, they may refuse to decide an actual controversy. In an equitable action, a federal court may determine, for instance, that the plaintiff has an adequate remedy at law or apply the abstention doctrine. In neither instance is the court denying the existence of an actual justiciable controversy: the court is simply refusing to exercise its discretionary jurisdiction.

Although the problem of an actual justiciable controversy's existence arises only in certain types of actions, the federal courts exercise their greatest discretion in determining the existence or absence of a "case" or "controversy" when this question does arise. As indicated above, the federal courts have generally moved toward recognizing the existence of an actual justiciable controversy in public law actions at a point in time earlier than they previously did. Congress has affected this process by the enactment of the Declaratory Judgment Act and the Administrative Procedure Act. The Court has, however, been the major factor in this movement. The movement has not been a steady progression toward recognizing the existence of an actual justiciable controversy at the earliest moment in time, but certainly the general trend has been in that direction.

The movement toward preventive action has been predicated on the idea that this is the best way to protect legal rights. That is, anticipatory judicial action may be the best means of insuring the protection of an individual's legal rights against governmental action. Justice Black, in *Younger* v. *Harris,* and Justice Fortas's dissent, in *Abbott Laboratories* v. *Gardner,* suggested that there is the other side of the coin. When a court is asked to rule on a statute on its face, the court may lack factual data concerning the statute's application that could determine the outcome of the action. If the Supreme Court determines that the pendulum has swung too far toward anticipatory actions, it has the discretion to reverse the trend.

7 Finality

Adversity, a sufficient interest in a legal right, and an actual justiciable controversy relate to the situation that exists when a federal court is asked to decide a dispute. Finality, however, concerns the federal court's ability to resolve the dispute. If adverse parties present a justiciable controversy concerning a legal right in which they each have a sufficient interest, the question still remains whether the federal court has the power to settle the controversy. Unless the court possesses this power, a "case" or "controversy" is not present. (If finality is not present, the court would be issuing an advisory opinion. Finality is also related to the political questions doctrine. See discussion of advisory opinions and political questions in Chapter 8 *infra*.) The court's power to make a decisive output, in the form of a final judgment, must be present before it may accept an input in the form of a "case" or "controversy." All the other elements that activate the judicial power may be present, but if the court can not fulfill the ultimate purpose of a judicial action in the strictest legal sense—that is, decide the disputed issue between the parties—a "case" or "controversy" is not present.

Although finality is an integral part of a "case" or "controversy," the Court often uses the term "finality" in other contexts. Thus the United States Supreme Court will refuse to exercise its appellate jurisdiction unless there is finality below. In this situation the Court is not denying a "case" or "controversy's" existence but is rejecting a premature appeal (see, e.g., *Rescue Army* v. *Municipal Court*). The Court also uses the term "finality" in determining whether administrative action is ripe for judicial review. As discussed in Chapter 6, this problem concerns whether a justiciable controversy exists when the court is requested to act.[1]

The term "finality" as an element of a "case" or "controversy" concerns the court's ability to resolve the issue presented by the adverse parties. The court's judgment must conclusively settle the legal dispute between the parties. One must note, however, that a court's decision is not necessarily final in an absolute sense. For instance, in a successful criminal prosecution, which contains all the necessary elements of a "case" or "controversy," the court's final judgment may be subject to the executive's power to grant reprieves or pardons.

A judicial decision is not necessarily final in a broad political context either. That is, if one examines a judicial decision's political implication rather than its impact on the parties, the decision is seldom final. It may be overruled by a future court, by congressional action, or by a constitutional amendment.[2]

Finality is directly related to a remedy's existence. If a party has a legal remedy, a federal court may render a final judgment predicated on that remedy. For this reason, the Supreme Court has encountered fewer problems concerning finality than any other element of a "case" or "controversy." The Court has encountered difficulty, however, in two situations. First, the Court has held that finality is absent if the executive or legislative branch may directly review a federal court's judgment. Second, the Court has encountered difficulty concerning whether a federal court's judgment must be executed to be final.

Judgments Subject to Executive or Legislative Review

If a federal court's judgments may be reviewed and altered by the executive or legislative branches, the existence of a "case" or "controversy" is usually only one of the problems that arises. Since the judiciary may be participating in executive or legislative functions rather than exercising judicial power, whether the action violates separation of powers is a problem that often arises (see discussion of political questions in Chapter 8 *infra*). Nevertheless, finality is an issue often present in such situations.

The landmark case concerning this issue is actually a compilation of three circuit court opinions. In *Hayburn's Case,* the Attorney General sought a writ of mandamus to require the Circuit Court for the District of Pennsylvania to determine whether Revolutionary War veterans were eligible for pensions as invalids. Before the court handed down a decision, the law providing for circuit court participation was amended, but the court reporter reported the three circuit court opinions in which five of the six Supreme Court Justices had participated. (Justice Thomas Johnson was the only Justice who did not participate in any of the reported decisions.) All three circuit courts unanimously refused to hear claims for pensions, since the Secretary of War had the power to review the courts' decisions.

With Supreme Court Justices James Wilson and John Blair joining in the "decision," the United States Circuit Court for Pennsylvania held that Congress had attempted to assign nonjudicial duties to the courts.[3]

Congress have lately passed an act, to regulate, among other things "the claims to invalid pensioners."

Upon due consideration, we have been unanimously of

opinion that, under this fact, the Circuit Court held for the Pennsylvania district could not proceed:

1st Because the business directed by this act is not of a judicial nature. It forms no part of the power vested by the Constitution in the courts of the United States; the circuit court must, consequently, have proceeded without constitutional authority.

2nd Because, if, upon that business, the court had proceeded, its judgments (for its opinions are its judgments) might under the same act have been revised and controlled by the legislature, and by an officer in the executive department. Such revision and control we deemed radically inconsistent with the independence of that judicial power which is vested in the courts; and, consequently, with that important principle which is so strictly observed by the Constitution of the United States.(411–12)

Justice William Cushing and Chief Justice John Jay participated in the decision of the United States Circuit Court for New York, which also concluded that the assigned duties were not judicial in nature.

[N]either the legislature nor the Executive branches, can constitutionally assign to the judicial any duties, but such as are properly judicial, and to be performed in a judicial manner.

That the duties assigned to the circuit courts, by this act, are not of that description, and that the act itself does not appear to contemplate them, as such; in as much as it subjects the decisions of these courts, made pursuant to those duties, first to the consideration and suspension of the secretary at [sic] war, and then to the revision of the Legislature, whereas by the Constitution neither the secretary of war or any other executive officer, nor even the Legislature, are authorized to sit as a court of errors on the judicial acts or opinions of this court.[4](410)

With Justice James Iredell participating, the United States Circuit Court for North Carolina placed its emphasis on the lack of finality.

[W]hatever doubt may be suggested whether the power in question is properly of a judicial nature, yet inasmuch as the decision of the court is not made final, but may be at least suspended in its operation by the secretary at [sic] war if, he shall have cause to suspect imposition or mistake; this subjects the decision of the court to a mode of revision which we consider to be unwarranted by the Constitution; for, though Congress may certainly establish, in instances not yet provided for courts of appellate jurisdiction, yet such courts must consist of judges appointed in the manner the Constitution requires, and holding their offices by no other tenure than that of their good behavior, by which tenure the office of secretary at [sic] war is not held. And we beg leave to add, with all due deference, that no decision of any court of the United States can under any circumstances, in our opinion, agreeable to the Constitution, be liable to a reversion, or even suspension, by the legislature itself, in whom no judicial power of any kind appears to be vested, but the important one relative to impeachments.(413)

These three circuit court opinions established the principle that finality is absent if a coordinate branch of the government may directly review or revise a judicial decision.[5]

The establishment of the Court of Claims resulted in several cases concerning whether its judgments were final judicial judgments. In *Gordon* v. *United States,* the Supreme Court dismissed an appeal from the Court of Claims for want of jurisdiction.[6] The Supreme Court concluded that, since the Court of Claims was not exercising judicial power, its decisions could not be appealed to the United States Supreme Court.

We think that the authority given to the head of an Executive Department by necessary implication in the 14th section of the amended Court of Claims Act, to revise all the decisions of that court requiring payment of money, denies to it the judicial power from the exercise of which alone appeals can be taken to this court.(562)

The Court did not use the term "finality," but this element was obviously lacking.

The language that the Court objected to in *Gordon* declared "[t]hat no money shall be paid out of the treasury for any claim passed on by the court of claims till after an appropriation therefor shall have been estimated for by the secretary of the treasury."[7] In *United States* v. *Jones,* a unanimous Supreme Court held that this section's repeal removed the only impediment to the Supreme Court's review of Court of Claims' judgments. Again the Supreme Court did not use the term "finality," but the obvious distinction between *Gordon* and *Jones* was that, in the latter, Court of Claims judgments were no longer subject to review by the Secretary of the Treasury.

In re *Sanborn* also involved a Court of Claims judgment, but the Supreme Court followed *Gordon* and not *Jones.* In *Sanborn,* the Interior Department submitted an issue to the Court of Claims. Under the existing law, if a claimant consented, a department could submit an issue to the Court of Claims, which would report its findings to the department. Speaking for the Court, Justice George Shiras held that this was not a final judgment.

Such a finding is not made obligatory on the department to which it is reported—certainly not so in terms, and not so we think by any necessary implication. We regard the function of the Court of Claims, in such a case, as ancillary and advisory only. The finding or conclusion reached by that court is not enforceable by any process or execution issuing from the court, nor is it made by the statute the final and indisputable basis of action either by the department or by Congress.

It is therefore within the scope of the decision in *Gordon* v. *U.S.*(226)

Although other issues were involved, the fact that the decision was not obligatory and could be revised was one of the reasons that the Court held that a "case" or "controversy" was not present.

In *Postum Cereal Co.* v. *California Fig Nut Co.*, the Court indicated that the federal courts in the District of Columbia could perform administrative duties in their capacity as legislative courts, but these actions could not be appealed to the Supreme Court since the decisions lacked finality.

The decision of the court of appeals . . . is not a judicial judgment. It is a mere administrative decision. It is merely an instruction to the Commissioner of Patents by a court which is made part of the machinery of the Patent Office for administrative purposes. In the exercise of such function it does not enter a judgment binding parties in a case as the term "case" is used in the third article of the Constitution.(698–99)

Chicago & Southern Air Lines v. *Waterman Steamship Corp.* indicates how the Court may use lack of finality to avoid a decision. Waterman sought review of a Civil Aeronautics Board order that recommended granting certain foreign air routes to Chicago & Southern. Chicago & Southern and the CAB appealed a circuit court's refusal to dismiss the action. The carrier and the CAB contended that the Board's order was nonreviewable since it already had the President's discretionary approval. Congress had specifically provided, however, for judicial review of CAB orders except those pertaining to foreign air carriers, and both Waterman and Chicago & Southern were domestic air carriers. Speaking for the five-man majority, Justice Robert H. Jackson conceded that Congress had apparently granted the federal courts power to review the order, but he held that the courts should decline to exercise such power. "It may be conceded that a literal reading of [49 U.S.C.] § 1006 subjects this order to reexamination by the courts"(110). But according to Jackson, the Court was not bound by a literal reading of the statute.

This Court long has held that statutes which employ broad terms to confer power of judicial review are not always to be read literally. When Congress has authorized review of "any order" or used other equally inclusive terms, courts have declined the opportunity to magnify their jurisdiction, by self-denying constructions which do not subject to judicial control orders which, from their nature, from the context of the Act, or from the relation of judicial power to the subject-matter, are inappropriate for review.(106)

The Court found the order inappropriate for review, since any judgment would be subject to presidential discretion.[8]

Although the CAB held hearings and issued an order, it could not be published until it was approved and possibly even revised by the President.[9] In this instance the President had revised the order, and the CAB published the order as revised by the President. The Court concluded that if the courts acted either before or after the President, the courts' action would not be final.

The court below considered that after it reviewed the Board's order, its judgment would be submitted to the President, that his power to disapprove would apply after as well as before the court acts, and hence that there would be no chance of a deadlock and no conflict of function. But if the President may completely disregard the judgment of the court, it would be only because it is one the courts were not authorized to render. Judgments, within the powers vested in courts by the Judiciary Article of the Constitution, may not lawfully be revised, overturned, or refused faith and credit by another Department of Government.(113)

Judicial action prior to presidential action would be tantamount to an advisory opinion, while judicial action subsequent to presidential action would be subject to revision by the President.

It has also [in addition to refusing to render advisory opinions] been the firm and unvarying practice of Constitutional Courts to render no judgments not binding and conclusive on the parties and none that are subject to later review or alteration by administrative action.(113–14)

Speaking for the four dissenters—Justices Hugo Black, Stanley Reed, Wiley Rutledge, and William O. Douglas—Douglas suggested that the federal courts could properly review the proceedings before the Civil Aeronautics Board as Congress intended them to. The courts would not be concerned with the President's discretionary powers but with the Board's nondiscretionary procedures. Douglas emphasized congressional intent to ensure that the Board did not deny the parties due process. He did not discuss finality per se, but implied that a judgment would be final as it related to the Board's procedures.

Federal Power Commission v. *Pacific Power & Light Co.* indicates that a fine line may exist between judicial finality and executive or administrative discretion. The FPC denied the power and light company the right to acquire all the assets of another power and light company. Although the FPC had the ultimate discretion to approve or disapprove the transfer, the Supreme Court held that a federal court could render a final judgment concerning questions of law.

> [I]t is urged that review of the Power Commission's order does not present a "Case" or "Controversy," because the court itself cannot lift the prohibition of the statute by granting permission for the transfer, nor order the Commission to grant such permission. . . . In none of the situations in which an action of the Interstate Commerce Commission or of a similar Federal regulatory body comes for scrutiny before a Federal court can judicial action supplant the discretionary authority of a commission. . . . So here it is immaterial that the court itself cannot approve or disapprove the transfer. The court has power to pass judgment upon challenged principles of law insofar as they are relevant to the disposition made by the Commission. . . . In making such a judgment the court does not intrude upon the province of the Commission, while the constitutional requirements of "Case" or "Controversy" are satisfied. For the purpose of judicial finality there is no more reason for assuming that a Commission will disregard the direction of a reviewing court than a lower court will do so.(159–60)

The FPC possessed discretion concerning the transfer, but a federal court could review the procedures used in exercising that discretion, and the law applied. Conceivably the Court could have applied the same principle in *Chicago & Southern Air Lines,* but it emphasized the President's discretion in the latter case rather than the Civil Aeronautics Board's action.

An action even more analogous to *Chicago & Southern Air Lines* is *McGrath* v. *Kristensen.* Kristensen sought a declaratory judgment reversing the Attorney General's determination that he was an alien ineligible for citizenship and thus not eligible for a suspension of his deportation orders. As to the question of Kristensen's eligibility for citizenship, the Court held that this issue was properly before the federal courts since the issue would determine only status and did not involve the Attorney General's discretionary power over the suspension of deportation.

As to the Attorney General's power of suspension, the Government contended that it was nonreviewable, since Congress had to approve any order of suspension for longer than six months, and therefore a court order would not be final concerning the deportation. In rejecting the government's contention, Justice Stanley F. Reed's majority opinion distinguished the present case from *Chicago & Southern Air Lines*.

> The congressional power here is quite distinct from the Presidential power concerning overseas licensing in the *Chicago & Southern* case. The license in question there was ineffective until the President acted. The delay here is effective despite subsequent congressional action. This litigation, whatever its ultimate effect, is aimed only at the delay. The judgment sought in this proceeding would be binding and conclusive on the parties if entered and the question is justiciable.(168)

The issue of legislative or executive revision has not been a major problem facing the judiciary, but if a federal court's judgment is directly reviewable, the judgment is not final.[10] In such a situation, a court would not be exercising judicial power but would be rendering an advisory opinion or participating in the administrative process. If the court is unable to issue a final judgment, a "case" or "controversy" is not present, and therefore judicial power may not be exercised. *Pacific Power & Light* and *Kristensen* indicate, however, that a judgment may be final even though there will be further action by the executive or legislative branches. The line between such indirect revision and the prohibited direct revision is obviously a very fine line. The important point is not whether governmental action takes place subsequent to the court's judgment but whether the court's judgment binds the other branches of government.

Execution of Judgment

The other major issue concerning finality is whether the judgment must be executed. The idea that a judgment must be executed apparently originated in a nonopinion. Chief Justice Roger B. Taney prepared a draft opinion for *Gordon* v. *United States,* but he died before there was any agreement on his opinion. Taney's draft opinion was eventually published and assumed to be the Court's opinion.[11] In his draft opinion, Taney declared that:

> The award of execution is a part, and an essential part of every judgment passed by a court exercising judicial power. It is no judgment, in the legal sense of the term, without it. Without such an award the judgment would be inoperative and nugatory, leaving the aggrieved party without a remedy. It

would be merely an opinion which would remain a dead letter.(702)

Justice William R. Day emphasized the lack of execution as one of the Court's reasons for striking down the jurisdictional statute involved in *Muskrat* v. *United States.* Day suggested that a judgment that could not be executed would be tantamount to an advisory opinion. "In a legal sense the judgment could not be executed, and amounts in fact to no more than an expression of opinion upon the validity of the acts in question"(362). Day did not deny that the Court could issue a final judgment concerning the congressional enactments that had altered the property rights, but he held that the Court's judgment would not be final concerning the property rights involved.[12]

Although the case itself may be considered an aberration, the Court indicated in *Tutun* v. *United States,* which declared that the federal courts' participation in the naturalization process was a "case" or "controversy," that something less than execution of the judgment is required in a "case" or "controversy."

> Whether a proceeding which results in a grant is a judicial one does not depend upon the nature of the thing granted, but upon the nature of the proceeding which Congress has provided for securing the grant. . . . Whenever the law provides a remedy enforceable in the courts according to the regular course of legal procedure, and that remedy is pursued, there arises a case within the meaning of the Constitution, whether the subject of the litigation be property or status. A petition for naturalization is clearly a proceeding of that character.(576–77)

In a naturalization proceeding, the Court did not execute its judgment but merely determined status.

The real issue concerning the necessity of a judgment's execution arose, however, in actions involving the declaratory judgment procedure. Like naturalization, the declaratory judgment enabled the courts to determine status, but the courts did not order anyone to do anything. A declaratory judgment did not require, therefore, that the court execute its judgment.

As previously discussed, the Supreme Court displayed an ambivalent attitude toward the declaratory judgment procedure during the 1920s. In *Liberty Warehouse* v. *Grannis,* the Court emphasized the lack of execution in the declaratory judgment procedure. "[N]o relief of any kind is prayed against him [the Attorney General of Kentucky], by restraining action on his part or otherwise"(73). Speaking for the Court, Justice Edward T. Sanford implied that the absence of execution would result in rendering an advisory opinion.

> [T]he judicial power vested by article 3 of the Consti-

tution . . . extends only to "cases" and "controversies" in which the claims of the litigants are brought before them for determination by such regular procedures as are established for the protection and enforcement of rights, or the prevention, redress or punishment of wrongs; and that their jurisdiction is limited to cases and controversies presented in such form, with adverse litigants, that the judicial power is capable of acting upon them, and pronouncing and carrying into effect a judgment between the parties, and does not extend to the determination of abstract questions or issues framed for the purpose of invoking the advice of the court without real parties or a real case.(74)

Later that same year, however, the Court indicated that execution of judgment was not a requisite of a "case" or "controversy." Speaking for a unanimous Court in *Fidelity National Bank & Trust Co.* v. *Swope*, Justice Harlan F. Stone said:

While ordinarily a case or judicial controversy results in a judgment requiring award of process of execution to carry it into effect, such relief is not an indispensable adjunct to the exercise of the judicial function. Naturalization proceedings . . . suits to determine a matrimonial or other status; suits for instructions to a trustee or for the construction of a will . . . bills of interpleader, so far as the stakeholder is concerned . . . bills to quiet title where the plaintiff rests his claim on adverse possession . . . are familiar examples of judicial proceedings which result in an adjudication of the rights of litigants, although execution is not necessary to carry the judgment into effect, in the sense that no damages are required to be paid or acts to be performed by the parties.(132)

Stone held that a declaratory judgment would bind the parties and would not be subject to collateral attack.[13]

In upholding the declaratory judgment procedure, the Court left no doubt that execution of judgment is not a necessary element of a "case" or "controversy." Again speaking for the Court, Stone relied primarily on his opinion in *Fidelity National Bank,* but added slightly to it in *Nashville, Chattanooga & St. Louis Railway* v. *Wallace.*

While the ordinary course of judicial procedure results in a judgment requiring an award of process or execution to carry it into effect, such relief is not an indispensable adjunct to the exercise of the judicial function. *Fidelity National Bank & Trust Co.* v. *Swope, supra,* 274 U.S. 132. This Court has often exerted its judicial power to adjudicate boundaries between states, although it gave no injunction or other relief beyond the determination of the legal rights which were the subject of the controversy be-

tween the parties . . . and to review judgments of the Court of
Claims, although no process issue against the Government.(263)

In upholding the Federal Declaratory Judgment Act in *Aetna Life
Insurance Co.* v. *Haworth,* Chief Justice Charles Evans Hughes reaffirmed, for a unanimous Court, that execution of judgment was not a
necessary element of a "case" or "controversy."

> Where there is such a concrete case admitting of an immediate
> and definite determination of the legal rights of the parties in
> an adversary proceeding upon the facts alleged, the judicial
> function may be appropriately exercised although the adjudica-
> tion of the rights of the litigants may not require the award of
> process or the payment of damages.(241)

Since the acceptance of the declaratory judgment procedure, execution of judgment has not been an important issue. Cases such as
Muskrat and *Liberty Warehouse* have never been directly overruled, however, and may still be used as precedents if the Court so desires.[14]

In *Powell* v. *McCormack,* the government contended that the issue
of Congressman Adam Clayton Powell's back pay was nonjusticiable,
since the federal courts could not provide coercive relief requiring
officials of the House of Representatives to perform specific acts.
Speaking for the Court, Chief Justice Earl Warren held that coercive
relief is not necessary when a declaratory judgment is sought. "We
need express no opinion about the appropriateness of coercive relief in
this case, for petitioners sought a declaratory judgment"(517).

One should note, however, that in many instances execution of
judgment may be an integral part of a court's judgment. In equitable
actions, the court may execute its judgment and use its power to punish
contempt, if necessary, to insure that its orders are executed. The
Court's acceptance of the declaratory judgment procedure indicates,
however, that such execution is not a necessary prerequisite to a "case"
or "controversy." As Professor Edwin Borchard suggested, it is the
determination of legal rights that is the essence of judicial power. "The
command to perform is only collateral and incidental to the determination that there is a duty to perform. The adjudication, not the command, is the essence of judicial power."[15]

Summary

Finality as a necessary requisite of a "case" or "controversy" may be
viewed from two perspectives, although they are not mutually exclusive.
A federal court's judgment must settle a disputed legal right in an actual
justiciable controversy between adverse parties so that the court's judg-

ment binds the parties and, in legal terms, is *res judicata*.[16] The judgment need not be coercive but may merely declare status or existing legal rights. The judgment is final if the same issue may not be litigated again between the same parties. The judgment itself, however, may be the basis of further judicial action.[17] A lower federal court's judgment is final, although the judgment may be subject to appellate review. If appellate review occurs, the locus of finality moves to the appellate court, but judicial power is still being exercised in a "case" or "controversy."

If the judgment binds the parties, however, then the judgment may not be revised by a coordinate branch of the government. Just as a party does not have a direct appeal from the legislature to the judiciary, a party may not directly appeal a federal court's judgment to either the legislative or executive branch. If such action could be taken, a "case" or "controversy" would not authoritatively conclude the dispute before the court. This second aspect of finality is necessitated by the doctrine of separation of powers. The exercise of judicial power in a "case" or "controversy" must not be subject to direct revision by a coordinate branch of government.

If the court's judgment binds the coordinate branches of the government, this issue then merges with the issue of the judgment's execution. A federal court often relies on the coordinate branches of the government to execute its judgment. Speaking for the Court, Chief Justice William Howard Taft emphasized this aspect in *Old Colony Trust Co.* v. *Commissioner of Internal Revenue.*

> In the first place, it is not necessary, in order to constitute a judicial judgment that there should be both a determination of the rights of the litigants and also power to issue formal execution to carry the judgment into effect, in the way that judgments for money or for the possession of land usually are enforced. A judgment is sometimes regarded as properly enforceable through the executive departments instead of through an award of execution by this Court, where the effect of the judgment is to establish the duty of the department to enforce.(725)

The judicial determination of the parties' rights makes the judgment final, although the judgment may be executed by the executive department.

Finality is a requirement of a "case" or "controversy." The court's output must be final as it relates to the parties before the court and not subject to direct revision by a coordinate branch of government. Within these two broad limitations, the federal courts determine whether their decisions are final. From the perspective of public law, finality is the least important element of the case-or-controversy provision in determining whether the courts will be judicially active or judicially self-restrained.[18]

8 The Case-or-Controversy
Provision and Judicially Created
Doctrines of Justiciability

When the Supreme Court is confronted with a problem concerning justiciability, it does not always examine the issue in "case" or "controversy" terms. Today the Court often turns to judicially created doctrines to determine whether a specific action is justiciable. Two of these doctrines, advisory opinions and mootness, predate the American constitutional system. One, the political questions doctrine, is a direct outgrowth of the American constitutional system. Ripeness and standing, two doctrines that have developed in the twentieth century, should also be examined in relation to the case-or-controversy provision.

Since the doctrines discussed in this chapter have been covered elsewhere, no attempt will be made to discuss them comprehensively or to trace their development.[1] Rather, each doctrine will be examined so that its relationship to the case-or-controversy provision may be analyzed, since most analyses have not attempted to demonstrate this relationship.

Advisory Opinions[2]

Professor Edward S. Corwin suggested that "no portion of Constitutional Law pertaining to the judiciary had evoked such unanimity as the rule that the federal courts will not render advisory opinions."[3] The degree of unanimity depends, however, on how one defines an advisory opinion. The Supreme Court and commentators have established three varieties of advisory opinions. The first is the traditional type in which the legislative or executive branch seeks judicial advice, but makes no pretense that a "case" or "controversy" exists. The second type involves a situation where a federal court is asked to act in an alleged "case" or "controversy," but where the court finds that one or more necessary elements of a "case" or "controversy" is absent. The third type involves a situation where a federal court properly decides a "case" or "controversy," but offers advice that is not necessary to dispose of the action.

The Traditional Advisory Opinion

The traditional advisory opinion does not involve the exercise of judicial power, and no suggestion is made that a "case" or "controversy" is present. In the traditional advisory opinion, the executive or legislative branches request advice from the judiciary.[4] No suggestion is made that adverse parties with a sufficient interest in a legal right are presenting a justiciable controversy in which the judiciary can render a final and binding judgment. Technically, all the necessary elements of a "case" or "controversy" are absent. This was the definition given advisory opinions at the time the Constitution was written.[5]

In 1793 Secretary of State Thomas Jefferson requested an advisory opinion when he submitted twenty-nine questions concerning foreign relations to the Supreme Court. In his accompanying letter Jefferson made no pretense that he was requesting the Court to exercise judicial power. He readily admitted that the questions submitted "are often presented under circumstances which do not give a cognizance of them to the tribunals of the country."[6] He did not request an opinion of the Court but "of such of the judges as could be collected in time for the occasion."[7] Jefferson first raised the question "whether the public may, with propriety, be availed of their advice on these questions?"[8] He further admitted that he was seeking advice on abstract questions and that the Court could "strike out such as any circumstances might, in their opinion, forbid them to pronounce on."[9] Jefferson did not suggest that a "case" or "controversy" was being presented but rather that the executive branch was seeking advice on abstract questions.

The Court's reply to President George Washington emphasized separation of powers, but also indicated that the Court had not been asked to exercise judicial power.

> These [the three departments] being in certain respects checks upon each other, and our being judges of a court of last resort, are considerations which afford strong arguments against the propriety of our extra-judicially deciding the questions alluded to, especially as the power given by the Constitution to the President, of calling on the heads of departments for opinions, seems to have been purposely as well as expressly limited to the executive departments.[10]

Like Jefferson, the Court did not consider the request as a request for the exercise of judicial power. Thus the real question concerning requests for the traditional advisory opinion does not involve the case-or-controversy provision, but whether the federal courts are strictly limited to the exercise of judicial power or whether they may also exercise extrajudicial power. Unanimity does exist that the federal courts will not give the traditional advisory opinion, although there is less unanimity on the question of whether they are constitutionally barred from rendering a traditional advisory opinion.[11]

Although the federal courts created under Article III may not grant advisory opinions, legislative courts may give advisory opinions. The Court said in Ex parte *Bakelite Corp.* that legislative courts "may be clothed with the authority and charged with the duty of giving advisory decisions in proceedings which are not cases or controversies within the meaning of Article 3"(450). In many instances when the Court has held that an advisory opinion was sought, the situation involved an attempted appeal from a legislative court (see, e.g., *Federal Radio Commission* v. *General Electric* and cases cited therein).

When Requisite Elements Are Missing

In a request for a traditional advisory opinion, no allegation is made that a federal court is being presented with a "case" or "controversy." A different situation arises when parties allege that they are presenting the court with a "case" or "controversy," but the court refuses to act on the ground that any decision would be tantamount to an advisory opinion. In this situation the real issue is the court's perception of the factual situation. If the court finds any one of the necessary elements of a "case" or "controversy" absent, it may conclude that it is being asked to render an advisory opinion.

Muskrat v. *United States* indicates the distinction between the traditional advisory opinion and the Court's characterization of an attempt to bring a "case" or "controversy" as tantamount to seeking an advisory opinion. In *Muskrat,* the Government did not bring the action, but a private party brought the action against the Government. Muskrat and others did not seek extrajudicial advice but a final binding judgment. Unlike the traditional advisory opinion, therefore, the action commenced in *Muskrat* had the superficial appearance of a "case" or "controversy." The Court apparently thought that there was enough of an appearance of a "case" or "controversy" that it was necessary to substantiate the absence of each element.

In *Muskrat,* the Court concluded that:

> In a legal sense the judgment could not be executed, and amounts in fact to no more than an expression of opinion upon the validity of the acts in question. . . . If such actions as are here

attempted, to determine the validity of legislation are sustained, the result wll be that this court, instead of keeping within the limits of judicial power and deciding cases or controversies arising between opposing parties, as the Constitution intended it should, will be required to give opinions in the nature of advice concerning legislative action—a function never conferred upon it by the Constitution, and against the exercise of which this court has steadily set its face from the beginning.(362)

A federal court's opinion would be tantamount to an advisory opinion if a "case" or "controversy" is not present (for the exceptions to this statement see text accompanying notes 10–20 in Chapter 1 *supra*).

The Supreme Court has often equated the absence of a final and binding judgment with an attempt to seek an advisory opinion. Professor Corwin suggested that the absence of a final and binding judgment is probably more significant in understanding the federal court's refusal to issue advisory opinions than the famous request during Washington's administration.[12] If a federal court's judgment is not final and binding, the court would be merely offering advice. The presence of finality also necessarily implies that all the other elements of a "case" or "controversy" are present.

The Court's early attitude toward the declaratory judgment procedure indicates the relationship between the lack of finality and the Court's modern-day perception of an advisory opinion.[13] In *Liberty Warehouse* v. *Grannis*, Justice Edward T. Sanford equated an action for a declaratory judgment with merely seeking advice.

[I]t is not open to question that the judicial power vested by Article 3 of the Constitution in this Court and the inferior courts of the United States established by Congress thereunder, extends only to "cases" and "controversies" in which the claims of litigants are brought before them for determination by such regular proceedings as are established for the protection and enforcement of rights, or the prevention, redress, or punishment of wrongs; and that their jurisdiction is limited to cases and controversies presented in such form, with adverse litigants, that the judicial power is capable of acting upon them, and pronouncing and carrying into effect a judgment between the parties, and does not extend to the determination of abstract questions or issues framed for the purpose of invoking the advice of the court without real parties or a real cause.(74)

In upholding the Federal Declaratory Judgment Act in *Aetna Life Insurance Co.* v. *Haworth*, the Court stressed that it was not rendering "an advisory opinion upon a hypothetical basis"(242). The declaratory judgment procedure became an accepted procedure in American constitutional law because the Court's perception changed. Rather than looking at the procedure as merely seeking advice, the Court accepted the view that a declaration of rights without execution of judgment was a final and binding judgment. The important point is that the difference between an action seeking an advisory opinion and one that could be considered a "case" or "controversy" depended solely on the Court's view of the necessary prerequisites of a "case" or "controversy."

The enforcement of Section 5 of the Voting Rights Act of 1965 indicates the fine line between the existence of a "case" or "controversy" and the granting of an advisory opinion.[14] Section 5 required that any amendment to a state or political subdivision's voting laws covered by the Act were to be suspended until the Attorney General of the United States or the District Court for the District of Columbia approved them. In *South Carolina* v. *Katzenbach,* Justice Hugo Black dissented from that portion of the Court's opinion upholding Section 5 and argued that such action was tantamount to rendering an advisory opinion.

> [I]t is hard for me to believe that a justiciable controversy can arise in the constitutional sense from a desire by the United States Government or some of its officials to determine in advance what legislative provisions a State may enact or what constitutional amendments it may adopt. If this dispute between the Federal Government and the States amounts to a case or controversy it is a far cry from the traditional constitutional notion of a case or controversy as a dispute over the meaning of enforceable laws or the manner in which they are applied. . . .
>
> The form of words and the manipulation of presumptions used in § 5 to create the illusion of a case or controversy should not be allowed to cloud the effect of that section. By requiring a state to ask a federal court to approve the validity of a proposed law which has in no way become operative, Congress has asked the State to secure precisely the type of advisory opinion our Constitution forbids.(357–58)

Speaking for the Court, Chief Justice Earl Warren held that the "controversy" was over the suspension.

> Nor has Congress authorized the District Court to issue advisory opinions, in violation of the principles of Article III. . . .
> The Act automatically suspends the operation of voting regulations enacted after November 1, 1964, and furnishes mechanisms for enforcing the suspension. A State or political subdivision wishing to make use of a recent amendment to its voting laws therefore has a concrete and immediate "controversy" with

the Federal Government. . . . An appropriate remedy is a judicial determination that continued suspension of the new rule is unnecessary to vindicate rights guaranteed by the Fifteenth Amendment.(335)

Although Justice Black was alone in his dissent on Section 5, *South Carolina* v. *Katzenbach* indicates the discretion the Court exercises in determining whether a "case" or "controversy" is present or whether it is being asked to render an advisory opinion. Unlike the traditional advisory opinion, federal courts are not asked to act extrajudicially today. They are asked to act in a situation that ordinarily has the appearance of a "case" or "controversy." Only if the federal courts determine that the appearance is not reality will they refuse to act on the basis that an advisory opinion is being requested.

The Court Offers Advice Not Necessary to Decide the Case

A third situation suggested by commentators but not officially recognized by the Court is a case in which the federal courts gratuitously offer advice in an official opinion. A "case" or "controversy" is before the court, and the court is, therefore, properly exercising judicial power. The Court goes further than necessary, however, in disposing of the particular action before it. The seminal work on this topic was by Professor E. F. Albertsworth, who suggested:

> Of course, any negative decision of the Supreme Court, or for that matter any court, performs the indirect function of "advising" with reference to correction of defects of a given law or its complete repeal, as the case may be. But I refer to an entirely different line of development. Through *dicta* in the course of an opinion, or through observations and passing remarks in a proper "case" or "controversy" before the Court, the latter may advise a legislative body, whether the Congress or the several states, how legislation may be corrected in the future.[15]

The important point is that a "case" or "controversy" is before the Court. Although the federal courts will not offer the traditional advisory opinion, they are not reluctant to offer this modern advisory opinion, albeit a "case" or "controversy" is the necessary vehicle for doing so.[16]

There probably is unanimous agreement that the federal courts will not render the traditional advisory opinion when a "case" or "controversy" is obviously not present. In other instances, however, whether a federal court is rendering an advisory opinion may depend on one's perception of a "case" or "controversy." If the federal courts act when any element of a "case" or "controversy" is absent, they technically will be rendering an advisory opinion. This differs from the traditional advisory opinion, since another branch of government may not be requesting advice, and the court claims that it is exercising judicial power so that it may render a final and binding judgment. Also, in deciding a "case" or "controversy," a federal court may give advice that is not essential to the disposition of the action. The latter two situations are obviously closely connected to the existence of a "case" or "controversy," and there is less than unanimous agreement that the federal courts will not render these types of advisory opinions.

Standing

The twentieth-century doctrine of standing is the most widely discussed and debated of the judicially created doctrines of justiciability.[17] Justice Felix Frankfurter's characterization of the problem in *United States* ex. rel. *Chapman* v. *Federal Power Commission* aptly describes the situation.

> We hold that petitioners have standing. Differences of view, however, preclude a single opinion of the Court as to both petitioners. It would not further clarification [sic] of this complicated specialty of federal jurisdiction, the solution of whose problems is in any event more or less determined by the specific circumstances of individual situations, to set out the divergent grounds in support of standing in these cases.(156)

Although there is agreement that standing primarily concerns the parties and not the issues—the two are not always separable—one can find support for almost any position concerning the relationship between standing and the case-or-controversy provision. Some argue that the questions of standing and of the existence of a "case" or "controversy" are completely separate questions.[18] The closest the Court ever came to this position is the *per curiam* opinion in *Tileston* v. *Ullman.*

> Since the appeal must be dismissed on the ground that appellant has no standing to litigate the constitutional question which the record presents, it is unnecessary to consider whether the record shows the existence of a genuine case or controversy essential to the exercise of the jurisdiction of this court.(46)

The prevalent view is, however, that standing is directly related to the case-or-controversy provision.[19] Standing is often equated with the requirement of a "case" or "controversy" that the party have the requisite interest. "It is frequently said that to have standing the plaintiff must be able to demonstrate injury to a legally protected interest."[20]

The Court has indicated that adversity is also included within the rubric of standing. In *Flast* v. *Cohen,* the Court held that:

> [I]n terms of Article III limitations on federal court juris-
> diction, the question of standing is related only to whether the
> dispute sought to be adjudicated will be presented in an adver-
> sary context and in a form historically viewed as capable of
> judicial resolution.(101)

Yet the standing doctrine includes more than the requirements of
adverseness and a sufficient interest. The Court has applied the standing doctrine not only to determine a "case" or "controversy's" existence
but also to determine the extent of the judicial power once a "case" or
"controversy" is before a federal court. The Court enunciated this distinction in *Barrows* v. *Jackson.*

> Ordinarily, one may not claim standing in this court to
> vindicate the constitutional rights of some third party. Refer-
> ence to this rule is made in varied situations. . . . The require-
> ment of standing is often used to describe the constitutional
> limitation on the jurisdiction of this Court to "cases" and "con-
> troversies." . . . Apart from the jurisdictional requirement, this
> Court has developed a complementary rule of self-restraint for
> its own governance (not always clearly distinguished from the
> constitutional limitation) which ordinarily precludes a person
> from challenging the constitutionality of state action by invok-
> ing the rights of others.(255)

The term "standing" is, therefore, also used to determine whether a
party may raise a specific issue in a "case" or "controversy" that is
properly before a federal court.

The confusion over the term "standing" seems to derive from two
major sources. First, commentators explain standing by using "cases"
that were decided before the term "standing" was used. Thus a case
like *Frothingham* v. *Mellon* has been used as a prime example of "lack of
standing," although the Court never used the term "standing" in *Frothingham.* This is not to suggest that *Frothingham* did not involve standing
but rather that the definition of standing has often been supplied by
the commentators rather than by the Court. Second, the Court has only
recently attempted to analyze standing.

The first comprehensive discussion of standing is found in Justice
Felix Frankfurter's concurring opinion in *Joint Anti-Fascist Refugee Committee* v. *McGrath,* decided in 1951.[21]

> Limitation on "the judicial power of the United States" is
> expressed by the requirement that a litigant must have "stand-
> ing to sue" or more comprehensively, that a federal court may
> entertain a controversy only if it is "justiciable."(150)

Although Frankfurter's discussion of standing has been criticized because he seemingly equated standing and justiciability, his analysis of

standing is among the most comprehensive found in the Court's opinions.[22] He explicitly limited his discussion, however, "to suits seeking relief from governmental action"(151).

Frankfurter first suggested that adversity is one element of the standing doctrine.

> The simplest application of the concept of "standing" is to situations in which there is no real controversy between the parties. . . . A petitioner does not have standing to sue unless he is "interested in and affected adversely by the decision" of which he seeks review.(151)

Second, unless a statute has specifically granted standing, the party must be able to answer three questions in the affirmative, according to Frankfurter.

> (a) Will the action challenged at any time substantially affect the "legal" interests of any persons? (b) Does the action challenged affect the petitioner with sufficient "directness"? (c) Is the action challenged sufficiently "final"?(152)

Frankfurter's third point was his most general, but indicated the discretion exercised by the federal courts.

> Whether "justiciability" exists, therefore, has most often turned on evaluating both the appropriateness of the issues for determination by courts and the hardship of denying judicial relief.(156)

Although Frankfurter's discussion seems to merge the problems of ripeness and standing, he specified that standing included adversity and that a party's legal interest must be affected with sufficient directness. Frankfurter addressed himself to "standing to sue" in cases involving governmental action and made a specific exception for instances wherein Congress has expressly provided standing.

In *Baker* v. *Carr,* Justice William J. Brennan offered the next significant discussion of standing.

> A federal court cannot "pronounce any statute, either of a State or of the United States, void, because irreconcilable with the Constitution, except as it is called upon to adjudge the legal rights of the litigants in actual controversies." *Liverpool Steamship Co.* v. *Commissioners of Emigration,* 113 U.S. 33, 39. Have the appellants alleged such a personal stake in the outcome of the controversy as to assure that concrete adverseness which sharpens the presentation of issues upon which the court so largely depends for illumination of difficult constitutional questions? This is the gist of the question of standing. It is, of course, a question of federal law.(204)

Beside emphasizing adverseness, Brennan substituted "a personal stake in the outcome" for the more traditional direct interest in a legal right.

Two recent cases analyzed the doctrine of standing rather extensively. *Flast* v. *Cohen* looked at standing in a situation where the plaintiff was relying on general jurisdictional statutes, while *Association of Data Processing Service Organizations, Inc.* v. *Camp* analyzed standing for a person aggrieved or adversely affected by administrative action.

In delivering the Court's opinion in *Flast,* Chief Justice Earl Warren discussed the relationship between the case-or-controversy provision and the standing doctrine. Warren suggested that, since *Frothingham* v. *Mellon* could be read either as establishing a constitutional bar or as simply a judicially imposed policy of self-restraint, "a fresh examination of the limitations upon standing to sue in a federal court and the application of those limitations to taxpayers' suits" was needed (94). Warren held that standing was an aspect of justiciability and could not be completely separated from other aspects of justiciability. He urged, however, that "[t]he fundamental aspect of standing is that it focuses on the party seeking to get his complaint before a federal court and not on the issues he wishes to have adjudicated"(99). He emphasized the requirement of a proper party.

> A proper party is demanded so that federal courts will not be asked to decide "ill defined controversies over constitutional issues," . . . or a case which is of "a hypothetical or abstract character." . . . So stated the standing requirement is closely related to although more general than, the rule that federal courts will not entertain friendly suits . . . or those which are feigned or collusive in nature.(100)

Warren then summarized the standing doctrine's relationship to the case-or-controversy provision.

> [I]n terms of Article III limitations on federal court jurisdiction, the question of standing is related only to whether the dispute sought to be adjudicated will be presented in an adversary context and in a form historically viewed as capable of judicial resolution. It is for that reason that the emphasis in standing problems is on whether the party invoking federal court jurisdiction has "a personal stake in the outcome of the controversy," . . . and whether the dispute touches upon "the legal relations of parties having adverse legal interests." . . . A taxpayer may or may not have the requisite personal stake in the outcome, depending upon the circumstances of the particular case. Therefore, we find no absolute bar in Article III to suits by federal taxpayers challenging allegedly unconstitutional federal taxing and spending programs.(101)

Warren concluded that standing could not be completely separated from the issue presented for adjudication. The substantive issue must be examined "to determine whether there is a logical nexus between the status asserted and the claim sought to be adjudicated"(102).

Association of Data Processing v. *Camp* involved the question of standing under congressional enactments providing for review of administrative action by a person aggrieved or adversely affected. The Court discussed the relationship between standing and the case-or-controversy provision as well as standing under the Administrative Procedure Act.[23] Speaking for the Court, Justice William O. Douglas indicated that standing was related to the case-or-controversy provision, but inferred it involved more.

> Generalizations about standing to sue are largely worthless as such. One generalization is, however, necessary and that is that the question of standing in the federal courts is to be considered in the framework of Article III which restricts judicial power to "cases" and "controversies."(151)

After quoting from *Flast*, Douglas suggested that, although a taxpayers' suit and a competitor's suit, which was the situation in *Data Processing*, "have the same Article III starting point, they do not necessarily track one another"(152). Douglas did not explain why the two diverged or when, but one must assume the distinction occurs because the competitor's suit is predicated on a congressional enactment that grants competitors standing. (Under common law, a competitor had no standing; see text accompanying note 33 in Chapter 4 *supra*.)

In *Data Processing*, Douglas held that "[t]he first question is whether the plaintiff alleges that the challenged action has caused him injury in fact, economic or otherwise"(152). He indicated that the Court of Appeals had erroneously relied on the legal interest test as announced in cases such as *Tennessee Electric Power Co.* v. *Tennessee Valley Authority.*

> The "legal interest" test goes to the merits. The question of standing is different. It concerns apart from the "case" or "controversy" test, the question whether the interest sought to be protected by the complainant is arguably within the zone of interests to be protected or regulated by the statute or constitutional guarantee in question. Thus the Administrative Procedure Act grants standing to a person "aggrieved by agency action within the meaning of a relevant statute." . . . That interest, at times, may reflect "aesthetic, conservational, and recreational" as well as economic values. . . . A person or a family may have a spiritual stake in First Amendment values sufficient to give him standing to raise issues concerning the Establish-

ment Clause and the Free Exercise Clause. . . . We mention
these noneconomic values to emphasize that standing may stem
from them as well as from economic injury on which petitioner
relied here.(153–54)

Douglas concluded that standing involved questions of Article III jurisdiction and questions of judicial self-restraint. In the latter area, Congress may enlarge the category of those who have standing to protest
administrative action to include those who are injured in fact. To have
standing under such an act, a party injured in fact must show only that
he is "within the class of persons which the statutory provision was
designed to protect," and not the traditional legal injury (155).

The rules established in *Data Processing* were applied to *Barlow* v.
Collins decided the same day.

First, there is no doubt that in the context of this litigation
the tenant farmers, petitioners here, have the personal stake
and interest that impart the concrete adverseness required by
Article III.

Second, the tenant farmers are clearly within the zone of
interest protected by the act.(164)

In an opinion in which Justice Byron White joined, Justice William J.
Brennan concurred in the result of both cases, but dissented concerning the Court's treatment of standing. Brennan characterized the
Court's test as requiring two steps. First, the establishment of injury in
fact, and second, showing that the party is within the zone of interest
that Congress intended to protect. Brennan urged that only the first
step was necesssary to establish standing. He argued that the second
test was too similar to "the discredited requirement that conditioned
standing on a showing by the plaintiff that the challenged governmental action invaded one of his legally protected interests"(168). Brennan
held that the only other question of justiciability was one of reviewability (169).

A comprehensive discussion of standing is found in *Sierra Club* v.
Morton. Like *Data Processing*, *Sierra Club* involved the question of standing under the Administrative Procedure Act. Speaking for the Court,
Justice Potter Stewart emphasized that in such cases "the inquiry as to
standing must begin with a determination of whether the statute in
question authorizes review at the behest of the plaintiff"(732). Stewart
indicated that the injury in fact criterion established in *Data Processing*
was limited to actions under the Administrative Procedure Act.

Early decisions under this statute interpreted the language as
adopting the various formulations of "legal interest" and "legal
wrong" then prevailing as constitutional requirements of standing. But in *Association of Data Process Service Organizations, Inc.* v.

Camp, 397 U.S. 150, and *Barlow* v. *Collins,* 397 U.S. 157, decided the same day, we held more broadly that persons had
standing to obtain judicial review of federal agency action
under § 10 of the APA where they had alleged that the challenged action had caused them "injury in fact," and where the
alleged injury was to an interest "arguably within the zone of
interests to be protected or regulated" by the statutes that the
agencies were claimed to have violated.(733)

Stewart held that injury in fact did not have to be economic and it
could be widely shared. Yet the party seeking judicial review must
actually suffer an injury and be adversely affected by the governmental
action.[24]

In three recent actions the Court has emphasized the requirement
of a personal stake in the outcome where neither a congressional enactment establishing standing nor taxpayer's standing is involved.[25] *Linda
R.S.* v. *Richard D.* involved an action brought by the mother of an
illegitimate child to have a Texas statute declared unconstitutional. She
alleged that a criminal nonsupport statute was discriminatory since it
had been construed to apply only to parents of legitimate children. She
also sought an injunction requiring state district attorneys to apply the
statute to fathers of illegitimate children. In a 5–4 decision, the Court
ruled that Linda R.S. did not have standing to bring the action because
"a private citizen lacks a judicially cognizable interest in the prosecution
or nonprosecution of another"(619).[26] In reaching its conclusion, the
Court emphasized the necessity for a plaintiff to clearly establish a
personal stake in the outcome in the absence of a congressional statute
granting standing.

> Recent decisions by this Court have greatly expanded the
> types of "personal stake[s]" which are capable of conferring
> standing on a potential plaintiff. . . . But as we pointed out only
> last Term, "broadening the categories of injury that may be
> alleged in support of standing is a different matter from aban-
> doning the requirement that the party seeking review must him-
> self have suffered an injury." *Sierra Club* v. *Morton.* . . . Although
> the law of standing has been greatly changed in the last 10 years,
> we have steadfastly adhered to the requirement that, at least in
> the absence of a statute expressly conferring standing, federal
> plaintiffs must allege some threatened or actual injury resulting
> from the putatively illegal action before a federal court may
> assume jurisdiction.(616–17)

The Court seemed to be equating the "personal stake" test with the
traditional personal injury.

In *Schlesinger* v. *Reservists Committee to Stop the War,* the Court denied standing to the Committee to bring a class action on behalf of all United States citizens and taxpayers to challenge the constitutionality of the reserve status of members of Congress under the Incompatibility Clause (Art. I, § 6 cl. 2). In discussing citizen standing, Chief Justice Warren Burger stressed the abstract nature of the Committee's claim. "To permit a complainant who has no concrete injury to require a court to rule on important constitutional issues in the abstract would create the potential for abuse of the judicial process"(2932–33). Burger discussed the necessity of a personal stake, but he did not attempt to delineate what type of personal stake might be necessary to give a citizen standing. In fact, he leaves the impression that it would be impossible for a citizen to have standing (2933–35).[27]

Apparently to answer the dissenting opinions and possibly to clarify the Court's opinion, Justice Potter Stewart specified in a concurring opinion that no one alleged a personal injury.[28] "Standing is not today found wanting because an injury has been suffered by many, but rather because *none* of the respondents has alleged the sort of direct, palpable injury required for standing under Art. III"(2936).

In *Warth* v. *Seldin,* Justice Lewis F. Powell's majority opinion analyzes the constitutional and nonconstitutional elements of standing.

> In its constitutional dimensions, standing imports justiciability; whether the plaintiff has made out a "case or controversy" between himself and the defendant within the meaning of Art. III. This is the threshold question in every federal case, determining the power of the court to entertain the suit. As an aspect of justiciability, the standing question is whether the plaintiff has "alleged such a personal stake in the outcome of the controversy" to warrant *his* invocation of federal court jurisdiction and to justify exercise of the court's remedial powers on his behalf. . . . The Article III judicial power exists only to redress or otherwise to protect against injury to the complaining party, even though the court's judgment may benefit others collaterally. A federal court's jurisdiction therefore can be invoked only when the plaintiff himself has suffered "some threatened or actual injury resulting from the putatively illegal action. . . . " *Linda R.S.* v. *Richard D.,* 410 U.S. 614, 617, 93 S. Ct. 1146, 1148, 35 L. Ed. 2d 536 (1973). . . .
>
> Apart from this minimum constitutional mandate, this Court has recognized other limits on the class of persons who may invoke the courts' decisional and remedial powers. First, the Court has held that when asserted harm is a "generalized grievance" shared in substantially equal measure by all or a large class of citizens, that harm alone normally does not warrant exercise

of jurisdiction. . . . Second, even when the plaintiff has alleged injury sufficient to meet the "case or controversy" requirement this Court has held that the plaintiff generally must assert his own legal rights and interests, and cannot rest his claim to relief on the legal rights or interests of third parties. . . . Without such limitations—closely related to Article III concerns but essentially matters of judicial self-governance—the courts would be called upon to decide abstract questions of wide public significance even though other governmental institutions may be more competent to address the questions and even though judicial intervention may be unnecessary to protect individual rights.(2205–6)

Since Powell relies on *Linda R.S.* v. *Richard D.* to a great extent and *Schlesinger* v. *Reservists Committee to Stop the War* to a lesser extent, one may conclude that Powell's explication of standing indicates the direction that the Court is currently moving. In actions involving neither Section 10 of the Administrative Procedure Act nor *Flast*-type taxpayer actions, the Court currently seems to be emphasizing the necessity of establishing the traditional private law type of personal injury in order to gain standing. As Powell indicates in *Warth,* if anything less than a direct personal injury that may be directly remedied by judicial action is present, the Court may deny standing as a prudential limitation on the exercise of judicial powers. The Court did deny standing in *Warth.* [29]

Unfortunately, Powell does not really indicate a clear line of demarcation between the constitutional and nonconstitutional elements of standing. One could logically conclude, however, that when Congress has not specifically granted standing and the plaintiff is unable to meet the traditional private law personal injury criterion, then the question of standing becomes one to be decided on the basis of the Court's self-imposed discretionary prudential limitations. Powell suggested no real criteria that were to be used in the latter instance, however.

Although the Court has offered several extensive explanations of standing, the term still remains a complicated specialty of federal jurisdiction. In attempting to discern the relationship between standing and the case-or-controversy provision, the first problem is to analyze the different ways the generic term "standing" is used. If the analysis is limited to the issue of proper parties, one may make two useful distinctions. First, standing is used to determine whether a party is the proper party to initiate a "case" or "controversy." Second, standing is used to determine whether a party may raise a particular issue in a "case" or "controversy" that is properly before a federal court.

When standing is used to denote standing to sue or be sued (the terminology "standing to sue" is used hereinafter to include "standing to be sued"), the term includes the traditional questions concerning the appropriateness of the parties before the court. Today a party must have the necessary stake in the outcome so that the dispute will be presented in an adversary manner. When a federal court accepts jurisdiction over a "case" or "controversy," the court is either implicitly or explicitly recognizing the standing of the party to sue.

Standing is also used, however, to determine whether the parties to a "case" or "controversy" properly before a federal court may raise certain issues. In this situation the problem is not a threshold question but the extent of judicial power once it has been properly invoked in a "case" or "controversy." Thus, whether a plaintiff may raise a third party's legal rights in a case that is properly before a federal court concerns the extent of the judicial power. Although the argument has been made that a party may initiate a "case" or "controversy" on the basis of a third person's legal rights, a close analysis indicates that the Court has usually found some basis for the party initiating a "case" or "controversy" in his own right and then has permitted a party to raise the rights of a third party. The issue usually arises, however, not concerning the plaintiff's but the defendant's right to raise the right of a third party (see, e.g., *Barrows* v. *Jackson* and *Mancusi* v. *DeForte*). In either event, the issue does not concern the exisence of a "case" or "controversy." It is one means of expanding the judicial power, however, once it has been properly invoked (see, e.g., *Singleton* v. *Wulff*).

Even when standing is limited to standing to sue, the present situation is far from clear. The Court now uses the criteria of adverseness and stake in the outcome to determine whether a party has standing to sue (see e.g., *Sierra Club* v. *Morton; Association of Data Processing Service Organizations, Inc.* v. *Camp; Flast* v. *Cohen;* and *Baker* v. *Carr*). The Court has not established any general rule, however, for determining the second criteria. Thus the test used to determine whether a party has a stake in the outcome varies. One test is applied in actions instituted under the Administrative Procedure Act, a second test seems to be limited to a federal taxpayers' suit challenging congressional enactments under the taxing and spending power as violative of the First Amendment's establishment clause and an unarticulated third test applies to all other public law actions.

In actions initiated under the Administrative Procedure Act, the present rule is that a party has standing to sue if he has been injured in fact and such injury is within the zone that Congress intended to protect. The Court has explicitly rejected the traditional legal interest test in actions under the Administrative Procedure Act although, as has been suggested, one who is granted standing can be assumed to have a legally protected interest. In these cases, one who establishes injury in fact and is within the zone of interest that Congress intended to protect meets the stake in the outcome test.

Although *Flast* v. *Cohen* has been followed concerning the general tests of adverseness and stake in the outcome, the Court has not applied the specific criteria used in *Flast* to establish the stake in the outcome to any other situation. At the present time, the *Flast* decision is limited to taxpayers attacking congressional exercise of the taxing and spending power in alleged violation of the First Amendment's establishment clause. The Court did indicate there might be other specific limitations on congressional exercise of the taxing and spending power that would give a taxpayer the necessary stake in the outcome, but to date no Supreme Court decision has expanded the *Flast* holding. (See *United States* v. *Richardson* and *Schlesinger* v. *Reservists Committee to Stop the War*. In both actions, the Court found that the *Flast* test was not met.) The Court did not specify whether it was establishing a new legal interest in *Flast,* such as a taxpayer's legal interest in seeing that tax revenue was not being spent in violation of a specific constitutional prohibition on congressional power, or whether it was rejecting the traditional legal interest test.

The tests for determining the necessary stake in the outcome are fairly clear in cases arising under the Administrative Procedure Act or in taxpayer's actions falling within the *Flast* doctrine. The important question remains concerning public law actions that do not fall into either of these categories. In *Baker* v. *Carr,* the Court applied the stake in the outcome test and determined that appellants met this test, since they were asserting an "interest of their own, and of those similarly situated"(207). The appellants' "right to a vote free of arbitrary impairment by state action has been judicially recognized as a right secured by the Constitution"(208), and therefore they had an interest protected by the Fourteenth Amendment.

The Court has not clarified the relationship between the legal interest test and the stake in the outcome test in other public law actions. The Court did move, at least temporarily, toward liberalizing the legal interest test. In *Sierra Club* v. *Morton,* Justice Potter Stewart suggested that the constitutional requirements had changed.

> Early decisions under the statute [the Administrative Procedure Act] interpreted the language as adopting the various formulations of "legal interest" and "legal wrong" then prevailing as constitutional requirements of standing.(733)

In a note, Stewart added that "[t]he theory of a 'legal interest' is expressed in its extreme form in *Alabama Power Co.* v. *Ickes,* 302 U.S. 464, 479–481"(733). Stewart clearly indicated that the test concerning legal interest had been liberalized, but not abandoned.

The Court's acceptance of the class action clearly indicates the legal interest test's erosion.[30] A party need show only that he is a member of the class affected and that he will adequately represent the class to establish standing, but the party need not establish a personal legal interest. Possibly an extreme example, but one that indicates the legal interest test's erosion in class actions, is *Dunn* v. *Blumstein.* Blumstein brought an action in July 1970 challenging the Tennessee durational residence requirement of one year in the State and three months in the county. The Supreme Court decided the case on March 21, 1972. Concerning the question of standing, Justice Marshall held for the Court in a note:

> Although appellee now can vote, the problem to voters posed by the Tennessee residency requirements is "capable of repetition, yet evading review." . . . In this case . . . the laws in question remain on the books, and Blumstein has standing to challenge them as a member of the class of people affected by the presently written statute.(333)

Blumstein was held to have standing and presumably a stake in the outcome as the representative of a class to which he no longer belonged. A similar erosion of the legal interest test has occurred in actions recognizing the right of a party, whether the United States Attorney General or a private attorney general, to represent the public interest.

Three cases decided during the period of 1973 to 1975 appear to indicate movement in the opposite direction, however (see text accompanying notes 25–29 *supra*). Although it may be too early to make any valid conclusions, the Court appears to be moving back toward what Justice Potter Stewart characterized as the legal interest test in its extreme form, at least in actions that do not arise under the Administrative Procedure Act.

The standing doctrine increases the federal courts' discretion in determining whether to exercise the judicial power.[31] As the Court has merged the constitutional and policy considerations, it has further increased judicial discretion. Thus, by applying the stake in the outcome criteria, a federal court may ignore the traditional prerequisite of a "case" or "controversy"—an injury to a legally protected interest. The latter situation has resulted in some commentators' suggesting that injury to a legally protected interest is no longer a prerequisite to the existence of a "case" or "controversy."[32] Since the Court has placed its emphasis on standing, one cannot tell whether it has rejected the legal interest test in all instances or only in those cases involving a challenge to administrative action under the Administrative Procedure Act and the *Flast* doctrine. Perhaps the Court has simply redefined a legally protected interest.

Ripeness

Like standing, the term "ripeness" is a twentieth-century innovation.[33] Also like standing, the commentators have used cases to define and describe ripeness, although the Court itself did not use ripeness terminology in its opinion.[34] Unlike standing, the Court has not offered any extensive explanation of ripeness or its relationship to the case-or-controversy provision. The Court has often applied ripeness, but has not explained its derivation or application.

Although one could assume that ripeness is equivalent to the case-or-controversy requirement of an actual justiciable controversy, the Supreme Court has inferred that ripeness concerns not only the existence of a "case" or "controversy" but also policy considerations concerning, for instance, the exercise of the federal courts' discretionary power over jurisdiction in equitable actions and actions for a declaratory judgment. In other words, the federal courts may dismiss an action for lack of ripeness not because an actual justiciable controversy is absent but because the court wishes to avoid a decision. Justice John Marshall Harlan suggested that this was the situation in *Poe* v. *Ullman* (see discussion of *Poe* in text accompanying notes 21–25 in Chapter 3 *supra*). His dissent in that action is one of the few attempts to define or characterize what is meant by ripeness.[35]

> I do not think these appeals may be dismissed for want of "ripeness" as that concept has been understood in its "varied applications." There is no lack of "ripeness" in the sense that is exemplified by cased such as *Stearns* v. *Wood,* 236 U.S. 75; *Electric Bond & Share Co.* v. *Securities & Exch. Com.,* 303 U.S. 419; *United Public Workers* v. *Mitchell,* 330 U.S. 75; *International Longshoremen's & Warehousemen's Union* v. *Boyd,* 347 U.S. 222; and perhaps again *Parker* v. *Los Angeles County,* 338 U.S. 327, *supra.* In all of those cases the lack of ripeness inhered in the fact that the need for some further procedure, some further contingency of application or interpretation, whether judicial, administrative or executive, or some further clarification of the intentions of the claimant, served to make remote the issue which was sought to be presented to the Court.(527–28)

Although he did not use "case" or "controversy" terminology, Harlan equated earlier ripeness cases with the requirement of an actual justiciable controversy. Harlan argued that this was not the situation in *Poe* since "there is no circumstance besides that of detection or prosecution to make remote the particular controversy"(528). Harlan's argument can only lead to the conclusion that the lack of prosecution was a reason for not exercising the Court's discretionary jurisdiction over a declaratory judgment action and not a finding that a "case" or "controversy" did not exist.

In delivering the Court's opinion in *Abbott Laboratories* v. *Gardner,* Harlan offered another explanation of ripeness.

> The injunctive and declaratory judgment remedies are discretionary, and courts traditionally have been reluctant to apply them to administrative determinations unless these arise in the context of a controversy "ripe" for judicial resolution. Without undertaking to survey the intricacies of the ripeness doctrine it is fair to say that its basic rationale is to prevent the courts, through avoidance of premature adjudication, from entangling themselves in abstract disagreements over administrative policies, and also to protect the agencies from judicial interference until an administrative decision has been formalized and its effects felt in a concrete way by the challenging parties. The problem is best seen in a twofold aspect, requiring us to evaluate both the fitness of the issues for judicial decision and the hardship to parties of withholding court consideration.(148–49)

Although *Abbott* was limited to judicial review of administrative actions, Harlan emphasized the relationship between the federal courts' discretionary jurisdiction and the ripeness doctrine, but did not mention the case-or-controversy provision. The "fitness of the issue for judicial decision" could be equivalent to the existence of an actual justiciable controversy, although Harlan did not use the latter terminology. "[T]he hardship to the parties of withholding court consideration" indicates a policy consideration and not any criteria used to determine the existence of a "case" or "controversy." Harlan's treatment of ripeness indicates that it is a combination of constitutional requirements of an actual justiciable controversy combined with broader policy considerations.

Significantly, Harlan did not cite any previous case for his explanation of the ripeness doctrine in *Abbott* but cited two commentators, Kenneth Culp Davis and Louis L. Jaffe. Although both are primarily concerned with administrative law, their treatment of the ripeness doctrine is helpful, since the Court has cited it as authority. Davis states:

> The basic principle of ripeness is easy to state: Judicial machinery should be conserved for problems which are real and present or imminent, not squandered on problems which are abstract or hypothetical or remote.[36]

Davis finds the relationship between ripeness and the case-or-controversy provision present but insignificant.

> Some of the opinions indulge in the pretense that the responsibility for solution of the ripeness problem is that of the Fathers of the Constitution and not that of the courts. The

reality is obvious, however, that the words of the Constitution permit a solution at either extreme or at any point between the extremes. The only relevant words in the Constitution are those of Article III, which require a "case" or "controversy." These words are in truth a little like "due process of law" in that their content has to be determined by courts on the basis of understanding of particular problems in particular cases.[37]

Jaffe limits his discussion to review of administrative action, but suggests that the ripeness doctrine is not really definable.

The requirement of "ripeness" as a condition for judicial review is not so much a definable doctrine as a compendious *portmanteau*, a group of related doctrines arising in diverse but analogically similar situations.[38]

Jaffe also suggests that the ripeness doctrine may vary according to the type of action before a federal court.

The requirement that there be a "controversy" is applicable to the exercise of the judicial function. But the criteria for determining the existence of a controversy are flexible; the judgments are thus ones of degree and balance. . . . This flexibility . . . permits courts to insist on the ripeness requirement to a greater degree in constitutional than in other cases.[39]

Two recent opinions fail to clarify the relationship between ripeness and the case-or-controversy provision. In *Blanchette* v. *Connecticut General Insurance Corp.*, the Court categorized ripeness as related to both the case-or-controversy provision and the Court's discretionary jurisdiction.

All of the parties now urge that the "conveyance taking" issues are ripe for adjudication. However, because issues of ripeness involve, at least in part, the existence of a live "Case or Controversy," we cannot rely upon concessions of the parties and must determine whether the issues are ripe for decision in the "Case or Controversy" sense. Further, to the extent that questions of ripeness involve the exercise of judicial restraint from unnecessary decision of constitutional issues, the Court must determine whether to exercise that restraint and cannot be bound by the wishes of the parties.(356)

In *Buckley* v. *Valeo*, however, the Court apparently rejected this dual nature of ripeness. "[I]n this case appellants claim is of impending future rulings and determinations by the Commission. But this is a question of ripeness, rather than lack of case or controversy under Art. III . . . "(618). Although there were other issues present so that a "case" or "controversy" was before the Court, the Court does indicate that ripeness does not involve the case-or-controversy provision.

Despite the impossibility of defining ripeness, several general statements may be made concerning its application. First, ripeness cannot be separated from standing as indicated by the cases involving vagueness or overbreadth. Second, in administrative law actions, ripeness also merges with the question of finality of the agency's action. If the administrative agency's action is not final, a federal court may determine that the issue is not ripe for judicial review and, therefore, a "case" or "controversy" is not present. Lack of finality in a lower court, however, does not indicate the absence of a "case" or "controversy."[40] When the United States Supreme Court remands a case to a lower court for further proceedings, it is recognizing the existence of a case, since it is sending the case back to the lower court for further proceedings.

The Supreme Court has also used ripeness to describe the situation when additional issues are raised in a "case" or "controversy" properly before the Court. In *Communist Party of the United States* v. *Subversive Activities Control Board,* the Court upheld an order of the Subversive Activities Control Board that the Communist Party register as a Communist-action organization under section 7 of the Subversive Activities Control Act. The Court held, however, that the requirement of the Act that individual members of the party must register if the party failed to register was not ripe for adjudication. Speaking for the Court, Justice Felix Frankfurter held that "[e]ven when some of the provisions of a comprehensive legislative enactment are ripe for adjudication, portions of the enactment not immediately involved are not thereby thrown open for a judicial determination of constitutionality"(71). Since a case was admittedly before the Court, this use of ripeness is not a threshold question but concerns the extent of judicial power once it is properly invoked.[41] As Frankfurter admitted, the Court's unwillingness to consider certain issues in a case properly before it is partially a discretionary policy of judicial self-restraint.[42]

The Court's lack of explication concerning the meaning and content of ripeness make any conclusions difficult and tentative. As Kenneth Culp Davis has admitted, conclusions concerning ripeness are primarily those of observers and not the Court.

> The extreme deficiencies in the Supreme Court's ripeness law . . . have probably been largely corrected during the 1960s. Yet the Court has made no announcement to that effect, and the correction can be discerned only by looking at all the ripeness law in perspective.[43]

Davis asserted that the "most important development during the 1958–70 period is a negative one," in that the ripeness doctrine was not applied in the strict sense that it had been in cases such as *United Public Workers* v. *Mitchell.*[44]

In attempting to relate ripeness to the case-or-controversy provision, one can come to two fairly definite conclusions. When a federal court finds an action ripe for judicial determination, the court determines, explicitly or implicitly, that there is an actual justiciable controversy before the court. On the other hand, when a federal court finds that an action is not ripe for judicial determination, this does not necessarily indicate the absence of a "case" or "controversy." Since questions of ripeness invariably arise in actions seeking an injunction or a declaratory judgment, the federal courts' jurisdiction is discretionary. In Harlan's words in *Abbott,* the court will "evaluate both the fitness of the issues for judicial decision and the hardship to the parties of withholding court consideration"(149). A federal court may, therefore, find the issues fit for adjudication, but exercise judicial self-restraint and not exercise its discretionary jurisdiction if the latter action will not result in a hardship to the parties.

The latter situation may be described as one where the "case" or "controversy" is ripe for judicial action but the federal court, or more probably the United States Supreme Court, concludes that the broader issue is not politically ripe.[45] This permits the federal courts to avoid, at least temporarily, a controversial political issue by invoking the ripeness doctrine. In cases such as *Poe* v. *Ullman,* the Court may use the ripeness doctrine to avoid a decision without clearly explaining whether a case does not exist or whether the Court is refusing to exercise its discretionary jurisdiction.

Moot Cases

The doctrine that courts do not decide moot cases is derived from the common law and predates the American Constitutional System.[46] The terminology "moot cases" or "mootness" has been used to cover almost any aspect of nonjusticiability, as an often-quoted federal district court opinion reveals.

> [A] moot case is one which seeks to get a judgment on a pretended controversy, when in reality there is none, or a decision in advance about a right before it has been actually asserted and contested, or a judgment upon some matter which, when rendered, for any reason, cannot have any practical effect upon a then existing controversy. (Ex parte *Steele,* 701)

The generic term "moot cases" could therefore include advisory opinions, lack of standing, or lack of ripeness. In the early years of its history, the Court dismissed cases as moot without any reference to the case-or-controversy provision.[47]

During the twentieth century, the United States Supreme Court has discussed mootness in terms of the case-or-controversy provision. The Court has adapted mootness to the American constitutional system to indicate that "a case is moot if after once being suitable for adjudication subsequent events remove the need for adjudication."[48] When the issue of mootness arises today, the assumption is that a "case" or "controversy" existed at one time, but that some intervening variable has now made the action nonjusticiable.

A recent Supreme Court opinion indicated that mootness is related to the case-or-controversy provision, although the Court failed to define mootness. In a *per curiam* opinion in *North Carolina* v. *Rice,* the Court refused to reach the substantive issue.

> [T]he threshold issue of mootness was improperly disposed of by the Court of Appeals. Although neither party has urged that this case is moot, resolution of the question is essential if federal courts are to function within their constitutional sphere of authority. Early in its history, this Court held that it had no power to issue advisory opinions . . . and it has frequently repeated that federal courts are without power to decide questions which cannot affect the rights of litigants in the case before them. . . . To be cognizable in a federal court, a suit "must be definite and concrete, touching the legal relations of parties having adverse legal interests. * * * It must be a real and substantial controversy admitting of specific relief through a decree of a conclusive character, as distinguished from an opinion advising what the law would be upon a hypothetical state of facts." *Aetna Life Ins. Co.* v. *Haworth,* 300 U.S. 227, 240–241 (1937). However, "[m]oot questions require no answer." *Missouri, Kansas & Texas Railway Co.* v. *Ferris,* 179 U.S. 602, 606 (1900). Mootness is a jurisdictional question because the Court "is not empowered to decide moot questions or abstract propositions," *United States* v. *Alaska Steamship Co.,* 253 U.S. 113, 116 (1920); our impotence "to review moot cases derives from the requirement of Article III of the Constitution under which the exercise of judicial power depends upon the existence of a case or controversy." *Liner* v. *Lafco, Inc.,* 375 U.S. 301, 306 n. 3 (1964). . . . Even in cases arising in the state courts, the question of mootness is a federal one which a federal court must resolve before it assumes jurisdiction.(245–46)

In *Powell* v. *McCormack,* the Court held that "a case is moot when the issues presented are no longer 'live' or the parties lack a legally cognizable interest in the outcome"(496). Although it made no reference to Article III, the Court adopted this concept of mootness in *United States* v. *Alaska Steamship Co.* "Where by an act of the parties, or a subsequent law, the existing controversy has come to an end, the case becomes moot and should be treated accordingly"(116). Charles Alan Wright has suggested that: "It is easy to understand, for example, why moot cases are held to be beyond the judicial power. There is no case or controversy once the matter has been resolved."[49]

Although few would dispute Wright's general statement, the Court has carved out some important exceptions to what constitutes a moot case. The Court has eased the traditional standards of mootness when there is reasonable expectation that allegedly illegal conduct will be repeated, although it has ceased, and also when there is the possibility of evasion of review if the mootness doctrine were invoked. The Court enunciated the first exception in *United States* v. *W. T. Grant Co.* The Government brought a civil action alleging a violation of the Clayton Act's prohibition against interlocking directorates. Before judgment in the district court, the alleged violation ceased and the district judge granted a summary judgment for the defendants. The Supreme Court held that the action had not become moot by the cessation of alleged illegal conduct. (The Court did affirm the lower court's refusal to grant injunctive relief.) Speaking for the Court, Justice Tom C. Clark outlined the federal courts' discretion in determining mootness in such instances.

> Both sides agree to the abstract proposition that voluntary cessation of allegedly illegal conduct does not deprive the tribunal of power to hear and determine the case i.e. does not make the case moot. . . . A controversy remains to be settled in such circumstances . . . e.g., a dispute over the legality of the challenged practices. . . . The defendant is free to return to his old ways. This, together with a public interest in having the legality of the practices settled, militates against a mootness conclusion. . . . For to say that the case has become moot means that the defendant is entitled to a dismissal as a matter of right. . . . The courts have rightly refused to grant defendants such a powerful weapon against public law enforcement.(632)

Although Clark did not explicitly discuss Article III, he did indicate that a "controversy may remain to be settled." Clark emphasized the "public interest" and "public law enforcement" as outweighing the defendant's right to invoke traditional standards of mootness.

Clark explained the federal courts' discretion in determining whether a live controversy still existed.

> The case may nevertheless be moot if the defendant can demonstrate that "there is no reasonable expectation that the

wrong will be repeated." The burden is a heavy one. Here the defendants told the court that the interlocks no longer existed and disclaimed any intention to revive them. Such a profession does not suffice to make a case moot.(633)

Although Clark did not indicate what would suffice to make the case moot, the federal courts obviously have discretion to determine whether the heavy burden has been met.[50] The *Grant* case indicates that the federal courts will not readily relinquish the exercise of judicial power once it has been properly invoked simply because the defendant has ceased his allegedly illegal acts if the "public interest" and "public law" questions are involved. The federal court may determine that a "case" or "controversy" continues to exist.[51]

In two recent cases involving the electoral process, the Court held that the cases were not moot even though the specific election involved had been held. In *Moore* v. *Ogilvie,* Illinois refused to place a "new Party's" presidential electors on the 1968 ballot since the nominating petitions did not include at least 200 names from each of 50 counties as required by state law. Although the United States Supreme Court did not hear the case until March 27, 1969, the Court held that the case was not moot. Speaking for the Court, Justice William O. Douglas argued that the holding of the 1968 election did not moot the case.

> But while the 1968 election is over, the burden . . . placed on the nomination of candidates for statewide offices remains and controls future elections, as long as Illinois maintains her present system as she has done since 1935. The problem is therefore "capable of repetition, yet evading review." *Southern Pacific Terminal Co.* v. *Interstate Commerce Commission,* 219 U.S. 498, 515. The need for resolution thus reflects a continuing controversy in the federal-state area where our "one man, one vote" decisions have thrust.(816)

Justice Potter Stewart could not accept the majority's interpretation of the mootness issue.

> [T]he case is moot. The appellants brought this action merely as prospective candidates for the office of Electors of President and Vice-President of the United States from the State of Illinois to be voted on at the general election to be held on November 5, 1968. But the 1968 election is now history, and no relief relating to its outcome is sought. In the absence of any assertion that the appellants intend to participate as candidates in any future Illinois election, the Court's reference to cases involving "continuing controversies" between the parties is wide of the mark. . . . There simply remains no judicially cognizable dispute in this case.(819)

Although one could assume that the appellants in *Moore* might likely be affected by the Illinois statute in the future, the same could not be said in *Dunn* v. *Blumstein.* Blumstein moved to Tennessee on June 12, 1970 and attempted to register to vote on July 1, 1970. He was not able to register because he did not meet the Tennessee durational residence requirements of one year in the state and three months in the county. By the time his case reached the United States Supreme Court, Blumstein met the durational residence requirements, but the Court dismissed the mootness question in a note relying on *Moore.* "Although appellee now can vote, the problem to voters posed by the Tennessee residency requirement is 'capable of repetition, yet evading review' "(333). The significant distinction between the two cases is that Blumstein was very unlikely to be the one affected in the future by Tennessee's durational residence requirement.[52]

The best explanation of the Court's action in cases "capable of repetition, yet evading review" is found in Justice Thurgood Marshall's dissenting opinion in *Hall* v. *Beals.* (The majority relied primarily on the fact that the durational residency statute being challenged had been amended and not on the fact that the election had been held or that the appellants met the residence requirements.)

> [This case] involves one of those problems, "capable of repetition, yet evading review," which call for relaxation of traditional concepts of mootness so that appellate review of important constitutional decisions not be permanently frustrated. . . .
>
> Indeed one of the unfortunate consequences of a rigid view of mootness in cases such as this is that the state and lower federal courts may well be left as the courts of last resort for challenges to relatively short state residency requirements.(51)

In *Sibron* v. *New York,* the Court emphasized that mootness should not be strictly applied when it might cut off review of state criminal convictions for minor offenses. Sibron's sentence had been completed before any appeal could be made. Although the Court did not use the terminology "capable of repetition, yet evading review," the Court stressed the possibility that unconstitutional conduct might be repeated if mootness was strictly applied.

> Many deep and abiding constitutional problems are encountered primarily at a level of "low visibility" in the criminal process—in the context of prosecutions for "minor" offenses which carry short sentences. We do not believe that the Constitution contemplates that people deprived of constitutional rights at this level should be left utterly remediless and defenseless against repetitions of unconstitutional conduct.(52–53)

In the abortion cases *Roe* v. *Wade* and *Doe* v. *Bolton,* the Court concluded that actions relating to pregnancy were a prime example of actions "capable of repetition, yet evading review."

> The usual rule in federal cases is that an actual controversy must exist at stages of appellate or certiorari review, and not simply at the date the action is initiated. . . .
>
> But when, as here, pregnancy is a significant fact in the litigation, the normal 266-day gestation period is so short that the pregnancy will come to term before the usual appellate process is complete. If that termination makes a case moot, pregnancy litigation seldom will survive much beyond the trial stage, and appellate review will be effectively denied. Our law should not be that rigid. . . . Pregnancy provides a classic justification for a conclusion of nonmootness. It truly could be "capable of repetition, yet evading review." *Southern Pacific Terminal Co.* v. *ICC*, 219 U.S. 498 (1911).(125)

In a recent *per curiam* opinion in *Weinstein* v. *Bradford*, the Court clarified, albeit slightly, the application of the "capable of repetition, yet evading review" doctrine.

> *Sosna* decided that in the absence of a class action, the "capable of repetition, yet evading review" doctrine was limited to the situation where two elements combined: (1) the challenged action was in its duration too short to be fully litigated prior to its cessation or expiration, and (2) there was a reasonable expectation that the same complaining party would be subjected to the same action again.(349)

The Court's first criterion would appear to be easily applied. If the challenged action ceased or expired prior to review by the United States Supreme Court, the first criterion would be met. The second criterion is the more difficult one to apply. *Weinstein* involved the procedures used in North Carolina for considering and granting parole. Since Bradford had been completely released from supervision, the Court concluded that "there is no demonstrated probability that respondent will again be among that number" who seek a parole (349). In the absence of a class action, the Court will apparently require that the complaining party demonstrate the probability that he will be affected again.

The Court's discretion concerning mootness is increased by the modern innovation of the class action. Speaking for the Court, Justice William H. Rehnquist clearly specified in *Sosna* v. *Iowa* that the class action altered the situation concerning mootness.[53]

> [A]ppellant brought this suit as a class action and sought to litigate the constitutionality of the durational residency requirement [to obtain a divorce] in a representative capacity. When

the District Court certified the propriety of the class action, the class of unnamed persons described in the certification acquired a legal status separate from the interests asserted by appellants. We are of the view that this factor significantly affects the mootness determination.(557)

The Court may find that the specific original controversy is moot—in *Sosna* the plaintiff was divorced when the action reached the United States Supreme Court—but conclude that a live controversy continues to exist between the plaintiff's class and the defendant. "Although the controversy is no longer alive as to appellant Sosna, it remains very much alive for the class of persons she has been certified to represent"(558). Rehnquist emphasized, however, that this is an exception to be applied only where status was bound to change after the lapse of time.[54]

> We note, however, that the same exigency that justified this doctrine serves to identify its limits. In cases in which the alleged harm would not dissipate during the normal time required for resolution of the controversy, the general principles of Art. III jurisdiction require that the plaintiff's personal stake in the litigation continue throughout the entirety of the litigation.(558–59)

The Court appeared to indicate that the presence of a class action would have prevented mootness in *DeFunis* v. *Odegaard*. In holding the action moot, the Court emphasized that DeFunis was in his last term of law school and that no live controversy remained concerning his admission to law school. "A determination by this Court of the legal issues tendered by the parties is no longer necessary to compel that result, and could not serve to prevent it. DeFunis did not cast his suit as a class action, and the only remedy he requested was an injunction commanding his admission to the Law School"(1706). The Court did not say that a class action would have saved *DeFunis* from mootness, but *Sosna* would seem to imply that it might have.[55]

While the preceding cases hardly prove "that the Court is moving, rather rapidly, toward a complete abolition of the mootness doctrine,"[56] the Court has undeniably relaxed standards of justiciability when a party has voluntarily ceased allegedly illegal conduct but may resume it, and even more particularly where governmental action is "capable of repetition, yet evading review." From the perspective of the case-or-controversy provision, a case such as *Dunn* v. *Blumstein* indicates that a federal court may hold that a case is not moot, even though the initial prerequisites of a "case" or "controversy" are not present. If Blumstein had commenced his action after he met the durational residency requirements, one could hardly argue that a "case" or "controversy" would have been present.

The Court has virtually abolished the mootness doctrine, however, in the area of review of criminal convictions. In *St. Pierre* v.
United States, the Court held "that the case is moot because, after
petitioner's service of his sentence and its expiration, there was no
longer a subject matter on which the judgment of this Court could
operate"(42). Since *St. Pierre* was decided in 1943, the Court has
adopted the doctrine of collateral consequences, and the exception
has virtually eaten up the rule. The Court's most comprehensive and
enlightening discussion of the collateral consequences doctrine is
found in *Sibron* v. *New York.* Sibron was convicted of the unlawful
possession of heroin and sentenced to a six-month term. With time
off for good behavior, Sibron was released from custody before any
appeal of his original conviction was heard. In holding that the action
was not moot, the Court relied on both the fact that Sibron's appeal
could not have reached the Court before the expiration of his sentence and on collateral consequences. Speaking for the Court, Chief
Justice Earl Warren distinguished *St. Pierre* but left little breath of life
in the rule established by that case. Warren noted first that the Court
in *St. Pierre* had suggested an exception to the general rule of mootness after release from custody if the appeal could not have reached
the Supreme Court before his release (51). He then turned to a second exception noted in *St. Pierre.*

> The second exception recognized in *St. Pierre* permits adju-
> dication of the merits of a criminal case where "under either
> state or federal law further penalties or disabilities can be im-
> posed * * * as a result of the judgment which has * * * been
> satisfied." 319 U.S., at 43. Subsequent cases have expanded this
> exception to the point where it may realistically be said that
> inroads have been made upon the principle itself.(53–54)

Warren discussed cases that had not been held moot (*Fiswick* v. *United
States, United States* v. *Morgan,* and *Pollard* v. *United States*), although a
prisoner had completed his sentence at the time the appeal was heard.
In discussing *Pollard* v. *United States,* Warren concluded that: [57]

> The Court thus acknowledged the obvious fact of life that most
> criminal convictions do in fact entail adverse collateral legal
> consequences. The mere "possibility" that this will be the case is
> enough to preserve a criminal from ending "ignominiously in
> the limbo of mootness."(55)

Warren concluded that a criminal appeal would be assumed to be a live
controversy even though the prisoner had served his sentence, unless
there is no possibility that collateral consequences will result from the
conviction.[58]

Warren not only offered policy reasons for the adoption of the collateral consequence doctrine but also argued that it was within the confines of the Constitution.[59]

> None of the concededly imperative policies behind the constitutional rule against entertaining moot controversies would be served by a dismissal in this case. There is nothing abstract, feigned, or hypothetical about Sibron's appeal. Nor is there any suggestion that either Sibron or the State has been wanting in diligence or fervor in the litigation. We have before us a fully developed record of testimony about contested historical facts, which reflects the "impact of actuality" to a far greater degree than many controversies accepted for adjudication as a matter of course under the Federal Declaratory Judgment Act, 28 U.S.C. § 2201.(57)

As Warren infers, all the prerequisites to a "case" or "controversy" remain, and the Court is in essence recognizing that the potential collateral consequences keep the appeal alive even after the sentence has been served. There are adverse parties with a sufficient interest in a disputed legal right presented in an actual justiciable controversy, and the Court, or any other court, may give a final judgment.

As in other areas of justiciability, the Supreme Court has liberalized its application of the mootness doctrine. The preceding cases indicate that when an important question of public law is present and the public interest is involved, the federal courts may relax the traditional requirements of the case-or-controversy provision in determining if an action is moot.[60] Just as the federal courts have discretion in determining whether a "case" or "controversy" exists in the first instance, federal courts have discretion in determining whether a "case" or "controversy" has ceased to exist because of mootness.

Political Questions

Of all the judicially created doctrines concerning justiciability the political questions doctrine is the most nebulous.[61] The Supreme Court has neither offered a definition nor attempted to explain the relationship between political questions and the case-or-controversy provision. The dilemma arises in part from the terminology itself. The term "political question" seems to indicate that issues can be divided into a neat dichotomy of political questions and judicial questions. Justice William J. Brennan indicated the futility of such a distinction in *Baker* v. *Carr*.[62]

> Of course the mere fact that the suit seeks protection of a political right does not mean it presents a political question.

Such an objection "is little more than a play upon words." *Nixon v. Herndon,* 273 U.S. 536, 540.(209)

Prior to the Court's elaboration on political questions in *Baker,* Professor John P. Frank described the nebulous nature of political questions.

> The term "political question" is applied to a species of the genus "non-justiciable" questions. It is, measured by any of the normal responsibilities of a phrase of definition, one of the least satisfactory terms known to the law. The origin, scope, and purpose of the concept have eluded all attempts at precise statement.[63]

Even after the Court elaborated on political questions in *Baker,* the best definition that the eminent constitutional scholar Edward S. Corwin could offer was:

> [A] political question may be defined as a question relating to the possession of political power, of sovereignty, of government, the determination of which is vested in Congress and the President whose decisions are conclusive upon the courts.[64]

As Corwin's ensuing discussion shows, he offers a broad framework within which to classify political questions, rather than actually defining the term.[65]

"Political question" is not a definable term but is a category that includes all issues that are nonjusticiable because the Supreme Court determines that the Constitution grants complete power over the issue to either the executive or legislative branch.[66] As long as the coordinate branches do not exceed their discretionary powers, the issue is not susceptible to judicial scrutiny. In *Marbury* v. *Madison,* Chief Justice John Marshall held that acts "for the performance of which entire confidence is placed by our Constitution in the supreme executive" are an exception to the general rule that, where there is an injury, a legal remedy exists (164). Marshall pointed out that these included discretionary acts of the President and/or his agents, but not their ministerial acts. In *Chicago & Southern Air Lines* v. *Waterman,* the Court explained judicial absention in such an instance in terms of judicial power.

> [I]f the President may completely disregard the judgment of the court, it would be only because it is one the courts were not authorized to render. Judgments, within the powers vested in courts by the judiciary Article of the Constitution, may not lawfully be revised, overturned or refused faith and credit by another Department of Government.(113)

In *Coleman* v. *Miller,* the Court stressed that if either the executive or legislative branch could make a final determination, the issue was within the political questions doctrine.

In determining whether a question falls within that category, the appropriateness under our system of government of attributing finality to the action of the political departments and also the lack of satisfactory criteria for a judicial determination are dominant considerations.(454–55)

In *Luther* v. *Borden,* Chief Justice Roger B. Taney held that a political question was beyond the judicial power, and therefore the federal courts had no jurisdiction.

Much of the argument on the part of the plaintiff turned upon political rights and political questions, upon which the court has been urged to express an opinion. We decline doing so. The high power has been conferred on this court of passing judgment upon the acts of the State sovereignties, and of the legislative and executive branches of the federal government, and of determining whether they are beyond the limits of power marked out for them respectively by the Constitution of the United States. This tribunal, therefore, should be the last to overstep the boundaries which limit its own jurisdiction. And while it should always be ready to meet any question confided to it by the Constitution, it is equally its duty not to pass beyond its appropriate sphere of action, and to take care not to involve itself in discussions which properly belong to other forums. (46–47)

Justice Brennan offered the most elaborate explanation of this relationship between political questions and separation of powers in *Baker* v. *Carr.* First, Brennan indicated that the political questions doctrine was related solely to separation of powers and not federalism.

[I]t is the relationship between the judiciary and the coordinate branches of the Federal Government, and not the federal judiciary's relationship to the States, which give rise to the "political questions."(210)

Second, he said that what is a political question must be determined case by case. "Much confusion results from the capacity of the 'political question' label to obscure the need for case-by-case inquiry"(210–11). Finally, after reviewing some of the cases involving political questions, Brennan set down some broad guidelines that help to determine if a political question is before a federal court.

It is apparent that several formulations which vary slightly according to the settings in which the questions arise may describe a political question, although each has one or more elements which identify it as essentially a function of the separation of powers. Prominent on the surface of any case held to involve a political question is found a textually demonstrable constitutional commitment of the issue to a coordinate political department; or a lack of judicially discoverable and manageable standards for resolving it; or the impossibility of deciding without an initial policy determination of a kind clearly for nonjudicial discretion; or the impossibility of a court's undertaking independent resolution without expressing lack of the respect due coordinate branches of government; or an unusual need for unquestioning adherence to a political decision already made; or the potentiality of embarrassment from multifarious pronouncements by various departments on one question.(217) Brennan's first criterion is self-explanatory, although the courts obviously determine whether there is "a textually demonstrable constitutional commitment of the issue to a coordinate political department." The other criteria are apparently to be used when there is no "textually demonstrable constitutional commitment." That is, the federal courts may find that a political question exists if any one of these criteria is present. Yet each of these criteria is imprecise and difficult to apply. As Justice Felix Frankfurter argued in his dissenting opinion, and as history has indicated, one could question whether there are "judicially discoverable and manageable standards" for resolving the reapportionment controversy (267–70). One could readily catalogue cases that violate the other criteria, but the important point is that the criteria give the federal courts great discretion and, outside of the broad limitation of separation of powers, leave the political questions doctrine as enigmatic as ever.[67]

While the Supreme Court has partially clarified the political questions doctrine's relationship to separation of powers, it has not clarified its relationship to the case-or-controversy provision.[68] One could readily conclude that, if an action involves a political question, no judicial remedy is available, since the federal courts cannot render a final and binding judgment, and thus there is no actual justiciable controversy. Yet the Court seems to have purposely avoided any such description of a political question. In both *Baker* v. *Carr* and *Powell* v. *McCormack,* the Court held that the existence of a "case" or "controversy" was a jurisdictional question. In both cases, however, the Court held that "[o]ur conclusion . . . that this case presents no non-justiciable 'political question' settles the only possible doubt that it is a case or controversy"(198). In each instance, however, the Court avoided showing any direct relationship between a political question and a "case" or "controversy."[69]

A closer examination of *Baker* and *Powell* indicates that the Court examines the Constitution to determine if a political question is present only after establishing that a "case" or "controversy" is present in all other respects. That is, a justiciable "case" or "controversy" appears to be present unless separation of powers makes it nonjusticiable. In *Baker,* although the Court stated that the only possible doubt concerning the existence of a justiciable case was the presence of a political question, the Court apparently deemed it necessary to show that the appellants had standing before discussing the political question issue (see text accompanying note 38 *supra*). After establishing jurisdiction, the Court disposed of the standing question before moving to the question of justiciability (198–208). The Court established, therefore, that it had jurisdiction and that a "case" or "controversy" appeared to be present before they reached the political questions doctrine.

The situation was even clearer in *Powell.* Under the heading "justiciability" Warren stated:

> Two determinations must be made in this regard. First, we must decide whether the claim presented and the relief sought are of the type which admit of judicial resolution. Second, we must determine whether the structure of the Federal Government renders the issue presented a "political question"—that is, a question which is not justiciable in federal court because of the separation of powers provided by the Constitution.(516–17)

Before reaching the political questions doctrine, the Court concluded "that in terms of the general criteria of justiciability, this case is justiciable"(518).

Baker and *Powell* both substantiate that a federal court theoretically determines if a "case" or "controversy" exists in every respect before turning to the political questions doctrine. Once the Court reaches the political questions issue, the Court must interpret the Constitution. Brennan explicitly stated this fact in *Baker*.

> Deciding whether a matter has in any measure been committed by the Constitution to another branch of government, or whether the action of that branch exceeds whatever authority has been committed, is itself a delicate exercise in constitutional interpretation, and is a responsibility of this Court as ultimate interpreter of the Constitution.(211)

Thus the political questions doctrine is unique among the doctrines of justiciability. The issue of a political question is not reached unless all the elements of a "case" or "controversy" appear to be present. The question then becomes, has the Constitution allocated the power to decide the issue to a coordinate branch of the federal government? To determine this question of justiciability, the federal courts must examine the pertinent constitutional provision. If the court holds that the issue is one to be determined by another branch, then the exercise of judicial power is foreclosed unless the coordinate branch exceeds its constitutional power. If the coordinate branch is properly exercising its power, a justiciable "case" or "controversy" is not present, since the federal court is not able to render a final and binding judgment.

Summary

All the judicially created doctrines of justiciability are related to the case-or-controversy provision. They range on a spectrum from a traditional advisory opinion where all the elements of a "case" or "controversy" are absent to a political question where all the elements of a "case" or "controversy" appear to be present, but the action is not justiciable because of the separation of powers doctrine. With the exception of the traditional advisory opinion, the Court has liberalized the application of all these doctrines during the past generation.

From the perspective of the case-or-controversy provision, the most important factor concerning all the judicially created doctrines of justiciability, with the exception of advisory opinions, is that they permit the federal courts to combine policy considerations with the Article III requirements. That is, in applying the standing, ripeness, mootness, and political questions doctrines, the federal courts, and most importantly the Supreme Court, may ignore or deemphasize the case-or-controversy provision. Thus, in determining whether an action is justiciable, these doctrines provide the federal courts with added discretion. As previous chapters have indicated, the federal courts have exercised great discretion in determining whether a "case" or "controversy" exists. The judicially created doctrines increase this discretion. Although in recent years this discretion has been used to increase judicial activism, the Supreme Court could use the same doctrines to increase judicial self-restraint.

9 Summary and Conclusion

Summary: The Case-or-Controversy Provision

According to Article III, the federal courts exercise judicial power primarily in a "case" or "controversy," but unfortunately, these terms are elusive and imprecise. This study has attempted to examine the meaning and application of these significant terms. The case-or-controversy provision's evolution can best be examined within the framework of the two basic functions that federal courts perform. Federal courts not only settle disputes between litigants but also establish public policy.[1] The first function is performed in every "case" or "controversy," while the policy-making function is involved in only some "cases" or "controversies." For analytical purposes, a private law action will refer to a "case" or "controversy" in which a federal court is performing the primary, or only, function of settling a dispute. A public law action will refer to a "case" or "controversy" in which a federal court is not only settling a dispute between the parties but is also establishing public policy, since its action affects the political system and not merely the parties before the court.[2] That is, the distinction is based on the function that the federal courts are performing and not on the parties. As the federal courts have become more involved in the policy-making function, the United States Supreme Court has adjusted the traditional "case" or "controversy" requirements that were established for performing the function of settling disputes. The distinction between a private law action and a public law action may not be completely precise, but the distinction does facilitate an exploration of the case-or-controversy provision.

The Case-or-Controversy Provision in General

Neither the Constitution nor the Constitutional Convention's debates shed any significant light on the case-or-controversy provision. Justice Felix Frankfurter's assumption that the framers intended the judicial power to be limited to what was then considered a legal action on this side of the Atlantic and in the courts of Westminster seems logically sound. The closest the framers came to discussing the provision was when they indicated that judicial power would be limited to "cases of a judiciary nature."[3] They apparently concluded, therefore, that the case-or-controversy provision was self-explanatory.

For almost a century, the United States Supreme Court had little need to elaborate on the case-or-controversy provision. The Court did reject a request for an advisory opinion and did reject a patently collusive suit. Otherwise, the Court discussed the case-or-controversy provision only when its jurisdiction was questioned. After *Marbury* v. *Madison*, the Court undoubtedly played an important political role. Yet, during the first three quarters of the nineteenth century, no one seriously questioned that the Court's political role was merely the result of deciding bona fide "cases" or "controversies."

After 1880 the Court examined the case-or-controversy provision more closely. Not surprisingly, this occurred simultaneously with an increase in the exercise of governmental power and with a corresponding increase in the use of the judiciary as a political battleground. In 1911 the Court rendered its first complete elaboration of the provision in *Muskrat* v. *United States.* Subsequent to *Muskrat*, the Court was confronted with a new procedure known as the declaratory judgment. Since this procedure primarily determined status, the Court first rejected it as tantamount to an advisory opinion. In 1933, however, the Court accepted the declaratory judgment procedure and held that execution of judgment was not a necessary prerequisite to a "case" or "controversy." In *Aetna Life Insurance Co.* v. *Haworth,* the Court upheld the Federal Declaratory Judgment Act. Since the *Aetna* decision in 1937, the Court has seldom elaborated on the case-or-controversy provision. Rather, the Court has turned to judicially created doctrines such as ripeness and standing to determine justiciability.

Commentators have ordinarily catalogued the prerequisites for a "case" or "controversy" without examining the elements in detail. Thus, on the basis of *Muskrat,* it is often stated that a "case" or "controversy" includes (1) adverse parties (2) who have an interest in a disputed legal right (or are attempting to prevent a legal wrong) (3) and who present the court with an actual justiciable controversy (4) in which the court can present a final and binding judgment.

The Constitution's framers would probably have little difficulty accepting these as four prerequisites for "cases of a judiciary nature." The four elements are as applicable to a traditional private law action as they are to public law actions. Simply cataloguing the terms does not prove, however, that the prerequisites are applied similarly in both actions. Did a written Constitution that established federalism and separation of powers alter the traditional concept of a "case" or "controversy"? Did the power of judicial review create a climate in which there would be attempts to alter the traditional concept? These questions can be answered only by examining the Court's application of each element of a "case" or "controversy" as well as the judicially created doctrines of justiciability.

Adversity

The Supreme Court has consistently insisted that adversity is a prerequisite to a "case" or "controversy" and has not explicitly altered this element. The Court has conceded, however, that adversity is a relative matter. A legal action may be amicable, but the parties must not be in collusion. That is, a friendly suit is adverse as long as both parties do not desire the same outcome. The Court has conceded that potential adversity is sufficient in naturalization proceedings, but has not otherwise lessened its insistence on actual adversity.

Public law influence has been evident in two specific instances. The Court has held that the United States Government may be both plaintiff and defendant in a "case." Also the Court has accepted the test case in public law actions. In both instances, however, the Court has held that adversity is present.

Most importantly, adversity is the element over which the federal courts have the least control in public law actions. That is, adversity is a factual question, and if the parties appear to be adverse, a federal court may unknowingly decide a collusive case. In other words, the parties may easily evade this requirement of a "case" or "controversy."

Adversity is as important in deciding a public law action as in deciding a private law action. A federal court should not participate in the "authoritative allocation of values" unless at least two conflicting views are present.[4] Although it is true that a federal court may be presented with necessary factual data by *amicus curiae* and intervenors, the initial input should come in the form of an adversary action. Moreover, adversity is a relative and tenuous requirement that is not really a serious roadblock to the federal courts' policy-making function. A test case is an accepted concept in American constitutional law as long as the parties are in disagreement to some extent and one party does not completely control the litigation.

Sources of a Legal Right and Remedy

Like adversity, the existence of a legal right or the attempt to prevent a legal wrong remains central to a "case" or "controversy." In both private and public law actions, the federal courts exist primarily to protect legal rights or prevent legal wrongs. Federal courts do not exist to decide abstract, hypothetical, or academic questions. There is a dispute over who possesses the necessary interest to commence a "case" or "controversy," but no one has suggested that federal courts exist for a purpose other than determining legal rights. The issue here is the existence of legal rights and remedies, which are usually assumed to be reciprocal.

Although they are not equally important, the sources of legal rights and remedies include the United States Constitution, congressional enactments, treaties, state law, common law, and equity. As governmental power has increased, Congress has created new legal rights and remedies that have increased the number of public law actions. Even without any fundamental change in the case-or-controversy concept, the increase in governmental powers was bound to increase the federal courts' involvement in the political process. Judicial activity has been increased in private law actions as well as public law actions, but one could logically hypothesize that the increase has been much greater in the public law arena.

The Court has changed its perception of what constitutes a legal right in public law actions. As late as 1938, the Court was still defining a legal right in private law terms as "one of property, one arising out of contract, one protected against tortious invasion, or one founded on a statute which confers a privilege."[5] The Court did not even mention the United States Constitution as a source of legal rights! Since 1938 the Court has not only emphasized constitutional rights such as civil liberties and civil rights but has also recognized the federal courts' power to protect "aesthetic, conservational, and recreational" interests. In public law actions, the Court has moved away from the legal right concept as one primarily concerned with the protection of property or economic rights.

Finally, the legal right that gives rise to a "case" or "controversy" may not be the only issue the federal court determines. Thus there can be no absolute distinction between public law and private law actions. *Aetna Life Insurance Co.* v. *Haworth* was essentially a private law action between an insurance company and a policy holder. In disposing of this private issue, the Court determined that the Federal Declaratory Judgment Act was constitutional, a very important issue of public law but one that had nothing to do with the rights on which the original action was based.

Existence of a Sufficient Interest

The Court has encountered its greatest difficulties in determining who may commence a public law action and has made its most significant changes concerning this issue. In this area the rules of private law actions have been least adaptable to public law actions. In a private law action, an individual is attempting to protect his personal rights, and therefore the federal courts are not ordinarily presented with any problem of the plaintiff's interest in the disputed legal right. In a public law action, however, the federal courts are often confronted with a difficult problem concerning the party's interest in the disputed legal right. In applying private law criteria to public law actions, the Court has refused parties the right to commence a "case" or "controversy" because a matter was one "of public and not individual concern."[6] Or because "[p]laintiff has only the right, possessed by every citizen, to require that the government be administered according to law and that the public moneys be not wasted."[7] These decisions indicated that a party to a public law action must establish the same legal injury as a party in a private law action. The Court has struggled with requirements such as direct interest, personal interest, and substantial interest in attempting to determine who may commence a "case" or "controversy." All these doctrines have been inadequate in public law actions.

In *Flast* v. *Cohen,* the late Justice John Marshall Harlan stated the problem most cogently in his dissenting opinion. Although Harlan disagreed with the Court's conclusion that the taxpayer had "standing," he did not deny the Court's constitutional power to reach this conclusion. He vehemently disagreed, however, with the Court's attempt to apply the traditional "legal injury" concept in this situation. After pointing out that this was not an action to prevent the collection of a tax or to recover a tax already paid, in which instance a personal interest would be present, Harlan discussed the public action:

> The interests he represents, and the rights he espouses, are, as they are in all public actions, those held in common by all citizens. To describe those rights and interests as personal, and to intimate that they are in some unspecified fashion to be differentiated from those of the general public, reduces constitutional standing to a word game played by secret rules.(128–29)

Later Harlan succinctly stated that "the issue is simply whether an *additional* category of plaintiffs, heretofore excluded from those courts [the federal courts] are to be permitted to maintain suits"(133).

The Court's answer has been a rather resounding "yes," not just concerning *Flast*-type taxpayer's actions but in other public law actions as well. The broadest category includes actions commenced under the Administrative Procedure Act in which Congress has given remedies to persons aggrieved or adversely affected by administrative action.[8] The Court has also accepted an expanded role for the United States Attorney General to protect private interests as well as the concept of "private attorneys general" to protect the public interest. The liberalized use of the class action is another instance in which the Court has implicitly distinguished public actions. The Court's recent adoption of the "stake in the outcome" test has further liberalized the type of interest a party must possess to institute a "case" or "controversy" in a public law action.

The proverbial floodgates have not been opened, but the federal courts no longer require that a party in a public law action establish the same interest as a party in purely private litigation. The Court no longer takes the basic attitude that everyone may be injured but no single individual may be injured enough to invoke judicial machinery to determine if governmental action is illegal or unconstitutional. Of course, the Court may contract this requirement in the future.

The Existence of an Actual Justiciable Controversy

A federal court must be presented with an actual justiciable controversy to exercise judicial power in a "case" or "controversy." In actions at law, this requirement ordinarily presents no problem since there must be an allegation that a specific law has been violated before an actual justiciable controversy exists. In actions in equity or for a declaratory judgment, however, the federal courts are often confronted with problems concerning whether an actual justiciable controversy exists. The federal courts are being asked to provide preventive relief before a legal injury has occurred. Besides determining whether a "case" or "controversy" exists, the federal courts' jurisdiction is discretionary, so that they may refuse to exercise their jurisdiction even if a "case" or "controversy" is present. A federal court may refuse to act, therefore, without clearly distinguishing whether it is refusing to exercise its discretionary jurisdiction or whether it has determined that a "case" or "controversy" is not present.

The Court has not established any general criteria to determine how this discretion should be exercised. Although there has been some liberalization, particularly in the areas of preventive action against administrative action and against criminal statutes before they are enforced, only in the former has the trend been fairly consistent. In fact, recent decisions seem to indicate that the Court has concluded that preventive action may have been too liberal in permitting attacks on criminal laws before they are enforced.

The latter situation is complicated by federalism, since most preventive actions against criminal laws involve state criminal laws. The Court has developed the abstention doctrine, which basically asserts that a federal court should not provide preventive relief in a challenge to a state statute even when it has jurisdiction, if adequate state judicial relief is available or the state courts have not yet interpreted an important state law issue.

In exercising preventive justice, the Court encounters problems in public law actions that are not relevant in private law actions. Unlike the sufficient interest test, these problems have often resulted in more stringent requirements in public law actions than in private law actions. The abstention doctrine is one prime example. Because of federalism, a federal court may stay its hand even though it has jurisdiction and has been presented with a "case" or "controversy." The federal courts may also consider separation of powers as a criterion for declining to exercise its discretionary jurisdiction. The Court has not been explicit, however, in this latter instance.

The Declaratory Judgment Act's passage has allowed the federal courts to act at an earlier point in time. This has undoubtedly accounted for some increased exercise of judicial power in "cases" or "controversies," but the consensus seems to be that it has not increased judicial power to the extent that its advocates had hoped. The exceptions have been primarily in First Amendment actions when a statute has been attacked as vague or overly broad.

Finality

For a "case" or "controversy" to exist, a federal court must be able to render a final and binding judgment. The Court has encountered difficulty concerning two aspects of finality: (1) review by a coordinate branch of government, and (2) the necessity for execution of judgment.

If a federal court's judgment is directly reviewable or reversible by a coordinate branch of government, a "case" or "controversy" does not exist. In essence, a federal court's action in such a situation would be tantamount to an advisory opinion. The coordinate branches may eventually change the impact of the federal courts' decision, but they may not directly alter the judgment.

The necessity of a judgment's execution was one of the major problems concerning the adoption of the declaratory judgment procedure. Since a declaratory judgment declares status, the Court first rejected this procedure, in part because there was no execution of the judgment. With the acceptance of the declaratory judgment procedure, the federal courts may render a final and binding judgment without the judgment's execution.

The concept of finality is much more important in a private law action than in a public law action. In the former, finality determines the rights of the parties and is *res judicata*. In public law actions, finality may be important if the political system readily accepts the federal court's judgment. But, unlike the loser in a private law action, the deprived litigant in a public law action may turn to some other forum to gain his ends. Finality is an important aspect of the case-or-controversy provision but the least important from a public law perspective.

Judicially Created Doctrines of Justiciability

In recent years, the Court has often discussed justiciability in terms other than the case-or-controversy provision. All the judicially created doctrines of justiciability are, however, related to the case-or-controversy provision. Technically, they must be since a federal court may exercise judicial power only in a "case" or "controversy."

Advisory Opinions. Actually, there are several types of advisory opinions. The traditional type involves a request from a legislature or executive for the judiciary's advice without any pretense that a "case" or "controversy" exists. This does not involve judicial power but a request for extrajudicial power. Early in the Washington administration, the Court determined that it would not render this type of extrajudicial advice.

The court has also used the term "advisory opinion" to characterize any situation in which the parties claimed a "case" or "controversy" existed but in which the Court found some element lacking. If a "case" or "controversy" is not actually present, any federal court action would, in effect, be rendering an advisory opinion. The Court has often equated a federal court's inability to render a final and binding judgment as tantamount to a request for an advisory opinion.

Once a "case" or "controversy" is properly before a federal court, a form of advisory opinion may be rendered. That is, simply by explaining why a statute is unconstitutional or in *obiter dicta,* a federal court may give what is tantamount to an advisory opinion.

Standing. "Standing" is a shorthand term relating to who may institute a public law action. Standing includes both adversity and the interest a party must possess. This doctrine has greatly increased the Supreme Court's discretion in permitting access to the federal courts. By concentrating on standing, the Court has been able to substitute such tests as "stake in the outcome" and "injury in fact" for the traditional legal interest test. Standing is also used to indicate whether a party already before a federal court in a "case" or "controversy" may raise a specific issue.

Ripeness. The Supreme Court has combined the traditional "case" or "controversy" requirement of an actual justiciable controversy with the federal courts' discretionary power over jurisdiction in equitable actions and actions for a declaratory judgment in the term "ripeness." The

Court often applies ripeness but seldom explains it. When the Court concludes that an action is ripe, it is saying that the federal courts' discretionary jurisdiction should be exercised and that a "case" or "controversy" exists. When the Court concludes that an action is not ripe, it seldom explains whether the lack of ripeness is a refusal to exercise discretionary jurisdiction or because a "case" or "controversy" is not present.

Mootness. The term "mootness" indicates that a "case" or "controversy" was before a federal court at one time but subsequently one or more elements of a "case" or "controversy" has ceased to exist. Thus, technically, judicial power can no longer be exercised. Recently, the Supreme Court has developed two significant exceptions to this doctrine. First, if an action is "capable of repetition, yet evading review," and especially if the public interest is involved, the Court has held that judicial power may still be exercised even though the action is technically moot. Second, the Court has adopted the collateral consequences doctrine, which holds essentially that a person who has served a criminal sentence may still commence a "case" or "controversy" attacking his original conviction if he is subject to any collateral consequences such as disfranchisement. All the elements of a "case" or "controversy" are present in this situation, but actions "capable of repetition, yet evading review" are technically moot. The Court has applied this latter exception primarily in public law actions where the public interest is involved.

Political Questions Doctrine. The political questions doctrine is a direct result of constitutional separation of powers. When the Court applies the political questions doctrine, it is indicating that a federal court could exercise judicial power except for the fact that the Constitution, explicitly or implicitly, has allocated the power to decide the issue to the legislative or executive branch. That is, the Court does not apply the political questions doctrine unless a "case" or "controversy" is apparently present, but separation of powers has withdrawn its disposition from the judicial power.

The Evolution of the Case-or-Controversy Provision

Like other constitutional provisions, the case-or-controversy provision has been adapted to make the Constitution a truly living document. Even as great an exponent of judicial self-restraint as Felix Frankfurter readily admitted that the case-or-controversy provision had to be adapted to the increasingly complex public law actions coming before the federal courts. In *Coleman* v. *Miller,* after stressing the traditional private law origin of the case-or-controversy provision, Frankfurter continued:

> As abstractions these generalities represent common ground among judges. Since, however, considerations governing the exercise of judicial power are not mechanical criteria but derive from conceptions regarding the distribution of the governmental powers in their manifold, changing guises, differences in the application of canons of jurisdiction have arisen from the beginning of the Court's history. Conscious or unconscious leanings toward the serviceability of the judicial process in the adjustment of public controversies clothed in the form of private litigations eventually affect decisions.(461)

Although he advocated self-restraint, Frankfurter admitted that the case-or-controversy provision was not a static concept and involved the problem of adjusting "private litigation" to settle "public controversies."

The Court has made the greatest adjustment in the area now called "standing," i.e., who may commence a "case" or "controversy." Although actual adversity, or at least its appearance, is still required, the Court has moved toward the concept that one need only establish a sufficient interest, as determined by the Court, in a public law action. In suits attacking administrative action, "injury in fact" seems to meet the Administrative Procedure Act's requirements that one who is adversely affected or aggrieved by administrative action has standing in a judicial proceeding. Under congressional enactments, the Court permits the United States Attorney General to protect constitutional or statutory rights of private citizens. The Court has also accepted the proposition that an individual may act as a "private attorney general" to protect the public interest. A class action may be instituted by one individual in behalf of everyone in the class. Finally, the Court has adopted the term "stake in the outcome" to determine who is a proper party to a "case" or "controversy."

These developments do not mean that anyone has standing to protect the public interest. The Supreme Court has recognized, however, that public law actions do not require the same type of direct, personal, or substantial interest that must be present in private litigation.

With congressional assistance, the second most significant change has occurred in the timing of when judicial power may be activated. Federal courts have traditionally possessed discretion in determining whether preventive relief was necessary in equitable actions so that irreparable harm could be avoided. With the enactment and acceptance of the Federal Declaratory Judgment Act, however, the federal courts were given almost unlimited discretion concerning when an action was justiciable. Since the federal courts were able to determine status, they could perform this function without the party's showing that irreparable harm would result if the court failed to act. The Supreme Court has combined these ideas into the doctrine of ripeness, but has given little guidance to the lower federal courts on how this discretion should be exercised. The Court has been reluctant to permit the widespread use of the declaratory judgment procedure in public law actions since, for instance, legislative enactments must be considered on their face. That is, the federal courts may not have sufficient data to act. In administrative law actions the tendency has been toward permitting earlier review, but there is no clear-cut trend in other public law cases.

The Court has also adapted the mootness doctrine to public law actions. In situations where the government may engage in illegal or unconstitutional activity, the Court has held that a "moot case" may be heard if the action is "capable of repetition, yet evading review." Although the same standard may be applied in private law actions, the Court has stressed the public interest as the primary reason for this exception.

Other factors also indicate that the Court has given a liberalized view to the public law action. The Court has accepted the class action as a means of settling public law disputes. Recently, the Court has significantly narrowed the political questions doctrine. The Court has also found an indirect way of rendering advisory opinions through *obiter dicta*. Although the recognition of the test case is not a modern development, it does differentiate the public law action from the private law action.

The Supreme Court has never admitted that there is a distinction between the prerequisites to a public law action and a private law action. Historically, the Court has taken the requirements for the latter and attempted to apply them to the former. As this study has suggested, the Court has not been completely successful in this endeavor. The Court has established doctrines such as standing and ripeness so that it could apply different standards without admitting that it was doing so.

Important Variables and the Case-or-Controversy Provision

Separation of Powers

As executive and legislative power has expanded, judicial power has also expanded. The terms "case" or "controversy" determine, in part, the power balance between the judiciary and the other branches of the federal government. Despite the common usage of the term "co-equal," the three branches never have been nor probably ever will be equal, as the political realities of the 1970s indicate. The federal courts, and ultimately the Supreme Court, are able in many instances to define not only the constitutional power of the other two branches but also their own power if jurisdiction exists.

Yet the judiciary possesses neither the purse nor the sword and must consider expansion of its power in this perspective. The Court has created the political questions doctrine basically for this purpose, i.e., to prevent direct confrontations with the other branches in which the judiciary was bound to be the loser. Even beyond the area of political questions, the Court has often exercised judicial self-restraint when separation of powers was involved. For instance, the Court was very slow to assume review over action by administrative agencies. Separation of powers is central to the political questions doctrine, but the Court undoubtedly considers the ramifications of separation of powers, at least subconsciously, in deciding other questions of justiciability. Andrew Jackson's famous statement, even if apocryphal, is a constant warning to the Court that it might be best to avoid a direct confrontation with the executive or legislative branches.[9]

Legislative Power and the Existence of a "Case" or "Controversy"

Another significant but distinct aspect of separation of powers is the control, if any, that Congress may exercise over the existence of a "case" or "controversy" and thus judicial power. There is no question that Congress controls the lower federal courts' complete jurisdiction and the Supreme Court's appellate jurisdiction. Congress cannot directly control judicial power, however, since the Constitution grants this power to the federal courts.[10]

> [T]here is a clear distinction between a grant of jurisdiction and an attempt to determine the manner in which the jurisdiction which is granted shall be exercised by the courts to which it is given. To do the latter is, in effect, to exercise the judicial power. This, Congress cannot constitutionally do.[11]

Jurisdiction determines the federal courts' power over certain parties or subject matter within constitutional and statutory limitations. Despite the Court's attempt to characterize the case-or-controversy provision as an aspect of jurisdiction in *Baker* v. *Carr* and *Powell* v. *McCormack*, the case-or-controversy provision is an aspect of judicial power and can be determined only by the federal courts and ultimately the United

States Supreme Court. Congress may not, therefore, alter the concept of a "case" or "controversy" under its power to control jurisdiction.

Muskrat v. *United States* is the prime example that Congress may not create a "case" or "controversy." Yet this does not mean that Congress may not control any element of a "case" or "controversy." Since the Constitution does not define a "case" or "controversy", the United States Supreme Court as the Constitution's sovereign definer determines the elements of a "case" or "controversy." Once the Court has made this determination, a different question arises concerning legislative powers over a case or controversy. Although Congress may not create a "case" or "controversy," Congress may possess power over specific elements that the Court has included within a "case" or "controversy."

Congress may not create adversity but may create legal rights under its delegated and implied powers. Furthermore, Congress may provide judicial remedies for federal legal rights under its implied powers. The primary example is the Federal Declaratory Judgment Act. The Court treated this as a "jurisdictional" statute, although it did not increase the federal courts' jurisdiction but opened the existing jurisdiction to a larger number of parties. This was explicitly stated by the Declaratory Judgment Act's author, Edwin Borchard.

> It is an axiom that the Declaratory Judgment Act has not enlarged the jurisdiction of the courts over subject-matter and parties, although it manifestly has opened to prospective defendants—and to plaintiffs at an early state of the controversy—a right to petition for relief not heretofore possessed. In that sense, it has decidedly extended the power of courts to grant relief in cases otherwise within their jurisdiction to pass upon.[12]

The Administrative Procedure Act also enlarged the class of potential litigants by granting legal remedies to persons aggrieved or adversely affected by administrative action, but did not enlarge the federal courts' jurisdiction.

The distinction between jurisdiction and remedy is a relevant one. Jurisdiction concerns the federal courts' right to exercise judicial power over certain parties and subject matter. Remedy concerns an individual's right to invoke the federal courts' jurisdiction. Congressional power to create remedies gives Congress substantial power to determine who may invoke the judicial power in a "case" or "controversy." The Supreme Court determines whether Congress has exceeded its power, but as the case-or-controversy provision has evolved, Congress has significantly helped to expand the concept.

Congress has had an impact on each "case" or "controversy" element except adversity.[13] As indicated, Congress has created legal rights and remedies. The Administrative Procedure Act has been used to determine who has a sufficient interest to commence a "case" or "controversy." The Declaratory Judgment Act has been used to determine whether an actual justiciable controversy exists and to determine that finality did not necessarily involve the execution of judgment.

Congress does not determine what constitutes a "case" or "controversy"; the United States Supreme Court does. But within the confines established by the Constitution and the Supreme Court, Congress plays an important role in determining who may commence a "case" or "controversy" and when. The Court can always circumscribe congressional power but, with the exception of *Muskrat,* the Court has accepted congressional expansions of the judicial power.

Federalism

A political system with a dual system of courts is bound to encounter some stresses and strains. The states determine what constitutes judicial power in a state judicial system, but the state courts are bound by the supreme law of the land. If a federal question is involved, the action may ultimately reach the United States Supreme Court. The lower federal courts exercise diversity of citizenship jurisdiction and apply state law rather than federal law in these actions. Congress has also granted three-judge district courts jurisdiction to determine the validity of state laws in equitable and declaratory judgment actions. Thus encounters may occur between the dual system of courts at both the original and appellate jurisdictional levels.

At the level of original jurisdiction, two significant issues arise concerning federal judicial power. In diversity of citizenship cases, the federal courts apply state law, and therefore the sources of a "case" or "controversy" are expanded. Although there is no question that federal courts enforce legal rights created by any form of state law, it is not clear what impact state-created remedies have in diversity cases. Undoubtedly, the federal court could not render an advisory opinion in a diversity action, but as the declaratory judgment's evolution indicates, questions may arise concerning state remedial procedures that are unknown and untested in federal courts.

The United States Supreme Court created the abstention doctrine to avoid some friction between the federal and state courts. The abstention doctrine permits a lower federal court to refrain from exercising its jurisdiction in a legitimate "case" or "controversy" if adequate relief is available in the state courts or if the state courts have not adequately determined an important issue of state law. The federal courts may use the abstention doctrine to avoid undue friction in the federal system, even though they possess jurisdiction and a "case" or "controversy" is present. The Supreme Court has not established any consistent criteria, however, to guide the lower federal courts in making this decision.

From the perspective of the case-or-controversy provision, the most significant problem occurs when an action is properly appealed from a state judicial system to the United States Supreme Court although some element that the Court has determined to be a prerequisite to a "case" or "controversy" is absent. Since Article III does not limit the state judicial systems, a state court may decide a federal question in an action that the federal courts do not recognize as a "case" or "controversy." The Supreme Court has three options. The Court may dismiss the action as not presenting a "case" or "controversy" and permit the state court's decision to stand. Second, the Court may ignore the procedural question and decide the substantive issue. Third, the Court may adjust its concept of a "case" or "controversy" to include the state procedure. This is essentially what occurred during the 1920s and early 1930s when the Court eventually accepted the declaratory judgment procedure as being within the purview of the case-or-controversy provision.

Problems concerning the exercise of judicial power are presented by our federal system. Like the area of substantive law, the Court has not found these as perplexing or as insurmountable as the problems created by separation of powers. This is best illustrated by the Court's pronouncement that the political questions doctrine applies only to separation of powers and not to federalism.

The Court's Concentration on Substantive Issues

Although one cannot completely separate procedural and substantive questions of law, the United States Supreme Court has concentrated primarily on substantive law, i.e., the Court's output in the form of the determination of legal rights, rather than on procedural aspects, i.e., the input of a "case" or "controversy." One major consequence is that the terms "case" or "controversy" remain nebulous and imprecise, as does the entire area of justiciability.

More importantly, however, the Court has seldom explicitly overruled prior decisions concerning procedural questions. Thus *Muskrat* v. *United States* still stands as *stare decisis* even though commentators with such diverse views on judicial power as Alexander Bickel and Kenneth Culp Davis have suggested that the Federal Declaratory Judgment Act has made the opinion obsolete.[14] The significant fact is that the Court has never reexamined the *Muskrat* decision in light of further developments. Justiciability criteria have changed tremendously since 1911, but *Muskrat* continues to be cited as the Court's most significant pronouncement on the case-or-controversy provision.

One other problem exists concerning the distinction between procedure and substance. In recent cases, especially those involving administrative law, the Court has suggested that the legal interest test concerns the merits. The Court's terminology is unfortunate and accentuates the difficulty in attempting to separate procedural and substantive problems. Of course, the legal interest test goes to the merits in determining whether a plaintiff may ultimately prevail, but the Court could hardly mean to infer that one who has no legal interest may commence a "case" or "controversy." In *Association of Data Processing Service Organizations, Inc.* v. *Camp*, the Court did not reject the legal interest test but redefined it in terms of statutory standing. That is, Congress granted a remedy, and therefore the Association had a sufficient legal interest to institute a "case" or "controversy", albeit not the traditional legal interest.

The Court is capable of finding occasions to expound on substantive matters, and it should be able to do so on procedural matters. This is not to suggest that the Court should or can develop a simplistic definition of a "case" or "controversy." The Court could, however, establish clearer criteria for standing and ripeness, for instance, and reexamine the *Muskrat* opinion in light of procedural developments since 1911.

Conclusion: The Case-or-Controversy Provision and the Role of the Federal Judiciary in the American Political System

According to Chief Justice John Marshall, the federal judiciary's role in the American political system sounded quite mechanistic albeit significant. "The judiciary cannot, as the legislature may, avoid a measure because it approaches the confines of the Constitution. With whatever doubts, with whatever difficulties, a case may be attended, we must decide it if it be brought before us."[15] The federal courts might play an important political role but only in performing their function of deciding a case.

Today Marshall's statement sounds naive. First, he assumed that the definition of a case was self-explanatory, but this is not necessarily true in public law actions. Moreover, he was referring to actions at law,

since the federal courts' discretionary equitable power was still relatively unimportant and declaratory judgments were unknown. Finally,
Marshall probably did not foresee that parties would attempt to gain
access to the judiciary primarily because an issue did approach the
confines of the Constitution.

Just as the Court's perception of interstate commerce and due
process has changed, the Court's perception of a "case" or "controversy" has changed. The Court has adapted the rigid rules of private
law actions to public law actions. Yet legal rules still control inputs into
the federal judicial system. The Court has not abandoned the legal
rules but has adapted them. In doing so, however, the Court has increased the federal courts' discretion in determining whether an action
is justiciable.

The federal courts' role in the American political system is, therefore, not so mechanistic as Marshall said. The federal courts, and ultimately the Supreme Court, determine what constitutes a "case" or
"controversy." The federal courts exercise discretionary jurisdiction in
equitable actions and actions for a declaratory judgment. Furthermore,
the federal courts exercise discretion in applying doctrines, such as
standing, ripeness, mootness, political questions, and abstention.

As the impact of the federal courts' output on the political system
has increased, input activity has increased. Organizations such as the
Environmental Defense Fund, Public Citizens, Inc., and Common
Cause attempt to gain access to the judicial system for primarily political purposes. As the courts' role in the political system has increased, it
is hardly surprising that inputs have increased. The question then becomes how the Court should view the federal judiciary's role in terms
of the case-or-controversy provision.[16]

The terms "judicial activism" and "judicial self-restraint" are ordinarily applied to the federal courts' output, i.e., are the courts defer-
ring to the popularly elected branches, or are they actively participating
in the political process by judicial legislation? The terms are also applicable, however, to the Supreme Court's treatment of the case-or-controversy provision. Although he was talking of substance and not
procedure, Justice Harlan F. Stone's famous remark is applicable to
both. "[W]hile unconstitutional exercise of power by the executive and
legislative branches of the government is subject to judicial restraint,
the only check upon our own exercise of power is our own sense of
self-restraint."[17] From a constitutional perspective, once the federal
courts have been granted jurisdiction, the only restraint on their judicial power is the federal courts themselves and, most importantly, the
United States Supreme Court.

Yet there is a significant distinction between applying the terms "judicial activism" and "judicial self-restraint" to substance and procedure. Judicial self-restraint in the procedural area has a different impact on the political system than does self-restraint in the substantive area. When the federal courts foreclose or make judicial scrutiny of legislative and executive action very difficult or impossible, the courts eliminate one of the checks in the American political system. One scholar has cogently pointed out that judicial inaction has the effect of legitimizing the other branches' actions.[18] As Stone indicated, it is assumed that executive and legislative action (as well as state action) are "subject to judicial restraint." This is true only if the courthouse doors are open.

Unfortunately, there are no "neutral principles" of justiciability.[19] Beyond those actions at law that the federal courts must accept, the federal courts' dual role as a legal and political institution must be considered. That is, in determining whether to act, a federal court must not only find the minimum essentials of a "case" or "controversy" present, but it must also consider whether there are political reasons for judicial self-restraint.

From the legal perspective, procedural self-restraint in public law actions means that the federal courts must be presented with the factual data by adverse parties who have a sufficient interest in the action. The federal courts are judicial bodies and are making final and binding judgments even when acting as policy makers. The standards may be less stringent than in the traditional private law action, but the court cannot ignore that it is a court of law settling a dispute.

There are also political reasons for procedural self-restraint. The federal courts are subject to legislative control over their jurisdiction. Although this factor may be more apparent than real today, a complete lack of procedural self-restraint might well bring about a congressional reduction in the federal courts' jurisdiction. Other, less direct threats may cause the federal courts to limit the case-or-controversy concept. Increase in the inputs in the form of "cases" or "controversies" would lead to an increase in the output of public policy decisions. This could lead to friction not only with Congress but with the President as well. That is, judicial self-restraint in the form of a limited perception of the case-or-controversy provision does help to lessen the friction between the judiciary and its two coordinate branches of government. Furthermore, an increase in judicial power through a broadening of the case-or-controversy provision might further undermine the "cult of the robe" and decrease public acceptance of the judicial power's legitimacy. By any standard, the judiciary is the least democratic of the three coordinate branches. In a political system in which the idea of democracy has become firmly entrenched, any perceptible increase in the federal courts' power might eventually lead to a reduction of their influence in the political system.

There are valid arguments, however, for judicial activism in the procedural area. In this instance, the arguments are primarily political and not legal. From the legal perspective, the problem with procedural activism is that the courts may not be presented with enough factual data if they act precipitously. A court that considers a statute's constitutionality before it has been enforced may not know what actual impact the statute may have. The Court has condoned judicial action, however, before a statute's enforcement to protect both property rights and civil rights (see Chapter 6). Procedural activism can remain within the "case" or "controversy" context only if it is admitted that special circumstances exist when a statute is construed on its face. The concept of a "case" or "controversy" may be stretched in special circumstances but not in all instances. The same may be said for standing and ripeness. There may be special circumstances when the federal courts should stretch the case-or-controversy provision to its outer limits. But this is not the same as opening the judicial doors to all comers under all circumstances.

The political arguments for procedural activism are much more persuasive. To the extent that the American political system is a government of laws and not of men, the federal courts must play a fairly active role. What is a strict construction of the case-or-controversy provision? Is it one that applies private law principles to a written instrument that theoretically limits governmental power? Or is it one that interprets the case-or-controversy provision in such a manner that the supreme law of the land embodied in a Lockean contract may be enforced? Should the federal courts permit individual rights to be infringed or governmental power to be abused because of eighteenth-century legal principles that lawyers have assumed are adopted in the United States Constitution? One does not have to concede that the federal courts are acting as a Council of Revision in order to conclude that procedural activism may be proper in certain circumstances.

The only answer to the dilemma is that the federal courts, and ultimately the United States Supreme Court, must balance their dual roles.[20] The federal courts, especially the United States Supreme Court, are political as well as legal institutions. Like other political actors, the federal courts must retain some discretion concerning their involvement in the policy making process. The Supreme Court's discretionary jurisdiction in writs of certiorari is an example. Just as Congress or the President may make a decision not to act, the federal courts should have the same discretion in certain instances. When a federal court is presented with a "case" or "controversy" that is obviously a public law action, the court should have discretion to balance the minimum requirements of a "case" or "controversy" against the public interest. If the public interest requires judicial action, then the federal court should require only the bare minimum essentials of a "case" or "controversy."

This is not an argument for judicial supremacy or unlimited judicial power. The judiciary can and must remain outside of the political arena in certain instances. The judiciary is a coordinate political branch of the government, however, and does not properly fulfill that role when it uses technical private law standards to avoid determining whether governmental power has been abused. The case-or-controversy provision must be examined in a political as well as a legal framework.

Notes

Chapter 1

1. 1 A. DE TOCQUEVILLE, DEMOCRACY IN AMERICA 290 (1945). One should note that de Tocqueville used "political question" in the generic sense concerning conflict over public power and not in the limited sense eventually adopted by the United States Supreme Court.

2. Ibid., 107. De Tocqueville did not believe, however, that this was normally an insurmountable barrier: "In truth, few laws can escape the searching analysis of the judicial power for any length of time, for there are few that are not prejudicial to some private interest or other, and none that may not be brought before a court of justice by the choice of parties or by the necessity of the case." Ibid., 106.

3. 1 B. SCHWARTZ, A COMMENTARY ON THE CONSTITUTION OF THE UNITED STATES 422 (1963).

4. E.S. CORWIN, THE CONSTITUTION OF THE UNITED STATES: ANALYSIS AND INTERPRETATION 598 (1964).

5. J. Davis, *Present Day Problems*, 9 A.B.A.J. 557 (1923).

6. See, e.g., R.H. JACKSON, THE SUPREME COURT IN THE AMERICAN SYSTEM OF GOVERNMENT, Ch. 3 (1955); G. SCHUBERT, JUDICIAL POLICY-MAKING (rev. ed. 1974); M. SHAPIRO, LAW AND POLITICS IN THE SUPREME COURT (1964).

7. The distinction between private law and public law is not always clear: "Law is frequently divided into two grand divisions, public and private law, which follows the Roman method of analysis and is used on the European continent. However, the terms *public* and *private* do not always distinguish between concrete types of American law, and there is much to be gained in clarity by using the single term law and to distinguish the various categories of law which are blended into the total legal system. As Professor Friedrich has noted, the distinction between public and private law is 'not really part of the American legal system and thought. In its place we find the distinction between constitutional and other (ordinary) law. The same tendency has appeared in those European countries—be it monarchical, be it democratic—which have been turning toward genuine constitutionalism. In England even this distinction has never been really accepted; no separation of constitutional and other law is admitted. All law is seen as simply one body for the creation of which the popularly elected parliament is responsible.' " R. YOUNG, AMERICAN LAW AND POLITICS: THE CREATION OF PUBLIC ORDER 157 (1967). See also L.H. Levinson, *Toward Principles of Public Law*, 19 J. PUB. LAW 327–69 (1970). Public law will be used herein to include "cases" or "controversies" involving constitutional, administrative, or criminal law. Public law is also used to include international law, which is beyond the scope of this study. The most important distinction is the impact that the decision has. Although no simple dichotomy exists, the real distinction is that private law decides rights between individual litigants, while public law establishes public policy. Obviously, a single case may serve both purposes.

8. J.A. SIGLER, AN INTRODUCTION TO THE LEGAL SYSTEM 17 (1968).

9. For discussions of judicial activism and judicial self-restraint, see H.J. ABRAHAM, THE JUDICIAL PROCESS 353–80 (3d ed. 1975); W.F. MURPHY and C.H. PRITCHETT, COURTS, JUDGES, AND POLITICS, Ch. 17 (2d ed. 1974); J.P. Roche, *Judicial Self-Restraint*, 49 AM. POL. SCI. REV. 762–72 (1955); G. SCHUBERT, JUDICIAL POLICY-MAKING 209–12 (rev. ed. 1974); J.S. Wright, *The Role of the Supreme Court in a Democratic Society—Judicial Activism or Restraint?*, 54 CORNELL L. REV. 1–28 (1968). "[I]t is the burden of my thesis to show that judicial deference is as relevant to procedural as to substantive decisions." L. Jaffe, *Judicial Review of Procedural Decisions and the Philco Cases*, 39 GEO. L. J. 664 (1962). See also Justice Harlan F. Stone's dissent in *United States* v. *Butler* (78–79).

10. Judicial power is used here solely in the constitutional sense. That is, although Congress is granted the legislative power, it does possess "judicial power" in the impeachment process. Since this study concerns the judicial power exercised in a "case" or "controversy," no attempt will be made to discuss "judicial power" or "quasi-judicial power" exercised by other branches of government.

One should also note that judicial power is sometimes used in a nonconstitutional sense to indicate the actual influence the federal courts, and especially the United States Supreme Court, are able to exercise in the American political system. See W.F. MURPHY and C.H. PRITCHETT, COURTS, JUDGES, AND POLITICS 28 (2d ed. 1974).

11. R.H. JACKSON, THE SUPREME COURT IN THE AMERICAN SYSTEM OF GOVERNMENT 11 (1962).

12. F. Frankfurter and J.M. Landis, *The Business of the Supreme Court of the United States—A Study in the Federal Judicial System*, 38 HARV. L. REV. 1006 (1925).

13. T.M. COOLEY, A TREATISE ON THE CONSTITUTIONAL LIMITATIONS 397 (1868).

14. See U.S. CONST. amend. XI, which limits this jurisdiction. One should note that the framers of the Eleventh Amendment did not use the terms "case" or "controversy": "The judicial power of the United States shall not be construed to extend to any suit in law or equity, commenced or prosecuted against one of the United States by Citizens of another State, or by citizens or subjects of any Foreign State."

15. For a comprehensive discussion of the limited jurisdiction of the federal courts, see C.A. WRIGHT, LAW OF THE FEDERAL COURTS 15–26 (2d ed. 1970). See also *Cohens* v. *Virginia*.

16. On the Supreme Court's original jurisdiction, see *Kentucky* v. *Dennison* (98). On the Supreme Court's appellate jurisdiction, see *Daniels* v. *Railroad Co.* (254). On the lower federal courts' jurisdiction, see *Kline* v. *Burke Construction Co.*, (234). For a comprehensive discussion of these types of jurisdiction, see 1 B. SCHWARTZ, A COMMENTARY ON THE CONSTITUTION OF THE UNITED STATES 252–59, 365–81 (1963).

17. The phrase is Charles Alan Wright's. See WRIGHT, HANDBOOK OF THE LAW OF FEDERAL COURTS 50–53 (2d ed. 1970).

18. A federal court may exercise the important power of constitutional review in determining jurisdictional questions.

19. C.H. PRITCHETT, THE AMERICAN CONSTITUTION 141 (2d ed. 1968).

20. Corwin says: "Except for the original jurisdiction of the Supreme Court, which flows directly from the Constitution, two prerequisites to jurisdic-

tion must be present. First, the Constitution must have given the courts the capacity to receive it, second an act of Congress must have conferred it." E.S. CORWIN, THE CONSTITUTION OF THE UNITED STATES OF AMERICA: ANALYSIS AND INTERPRETATION 564 (1964).

21. For a comprehensive discussion of legislative courts, see WRIGHT, HANDBOOK OF THE LAW OF FEDERAL COURTS 26–34 (2d ed. 1970).

22. E.g., "As it is plain that the court of customs appeals is a legislative and not a constitutional court, there is no need for now inquiring whether the proceeding . . . is a case or controversy within the meaning of Sec. 2 of Art. 3 of the Constitution, for this section applies only to constitutional courts." Ex parte *Bakelite Corp.* (460). However, see text discussion of *Glidden* v. *Zdanok* that follows.

23. Wright suggests that the district courts for Puerto Rico, Guam, the Virgin Islands, and the Canal Zone are the only remaining legislative courts, and that the federal courts in the District of Columbia may be both constitutional and legislative courts. WRIGHT, HANDBOOK OF THE LAW OF FEDERAL COURTS 34 (2d ed. 1970).

24. The right of intervention is excluded since a "case" or "controversy" exists. On intervention, see WRIGHT, HANDBOOK OF THE LAW OF FEDERAL COURTS 327–32 (2d ed. 1970).

25. THE FEDERALIST No. 78, at 504. See also Felix Frankfurter's dissent in *Baker* v. *Carr* (267).

26. See W.F. MURPHY, ELEMENTS OF JUDICIAL STRATEGY (1964).

27. W.F. MURPHY and J. TANENHAUS, THE STUDY OF PUBLIC LAW 5 (1972).

28. The secondary material is essentially from legal sources since relevant political science sources are virtually nonexistent.

Chapter 2

1. "The Constitution was written to be understood by the voters; its words and phrases were used in their normal and ordinary as distinguished from their technical meaning; where the intention is clear there is no room for construction and no excuse for interpolation or addition." *United States* v. *Sprague* (731–32).

2. U.S. CONST. art. III, § 2 provides: "the Supreme Court shall have Appellate jurisdiction, both as to law and to fact, with such exceptions, and under such regulations as the Congress shall make." Art. I, § 8 grants Congress power "to constitute tribunals inferior to the Supreme Court." See note 16 in Chapter 1 *supra*.

3. The term "judicial power" was substituted for "jurisdiction" in Art. III, § 2 on August 27, 1787. See text accompanying note 25 *infra*.

4. 5 J. ELLIOT, DEBATES ON THE ADOPTION OF THE FEDERAL CONSTITUTION 128 (1901).

5. Ibid., 188 (quotation marks in the original).

6. 1 M. FARRAND, RECORDS OF THE FEDERAL CONVENTION OF 1787 238 (1911).

7. "It is to be noted, however, that as Madison wrote later: 'By questions

involving the National peace and harmony, no one can suppose more was meant than might be *specified* by the Convention, as proper to be referred to the judiciary either by the Constitution or the Constitutional authority of the legislature. . . . That the Convention understood the entire Resolutions of Mr. Randolph to be a mere sketch in which omitted details were to be supplied and the general terms and phrases to be reduced to their proper details is demonstrated by the use made of them in the Convention. . . . Candour discovers no ground for the charge that the Resolutions contemplated a Government materially different from, or more National than, that in which they terminated. . . . The plan expressly aimed at a specification, and, of course, a limitation of the powers.' " C. WARREN, THE MAKING OF THE CONSTITUTION 331 (1929). Warren cites as his source WRITINGS OF JAMES MADISON (Hunt's ed.), IX, Madison to John Tyler, 1833.

8. 5 J. ELLIOT, DEBATES ON THE ADOPTION OF THE FEDERAL CONSTITUTION 332 (1901).

9. Ibid., 376. The sixteenth resolution read: "*Resolved,* That the jurisdiction of the national judiciary shall extend to cases arising under the laws passed by the general legislature, and to such other questions as involve the national peace and harmony."

10. 5 J. ELLIOT, DEBATES ON THE ADOPTION OF THE FEDERAL CONSTITUTION 131 (1901).

11. Ibid.

12. Ibid., 190.

13. DOCUMENTARY HISTORY OF THE CONSTITUTION OF THE UNITED STATES 325 (1894). This proposal does not appear in Madison's Notes.

14. In both Madison's Notes and the Journal, the resolution on the judiciary was number five, while the proposal for resolution of disputes between the United States and individual states was number nine in the Journal.

15. 2 FARRAND, THE RECORDS OF THE FEDERAL CONVENTION OF 1787 146–47 (1911). The material in brackets was added by Rutledge. For evidence supporting the authenticity of the document, see W. MEIGS, THE GROWTH OF THE CONSTITUTION IN THE FEDERAL CONVENTION OF 1787 317–24 (1900). The original document is reproduced in Meigs preceding p. 317.

16. 2 FARRAND, THE RECORDS OF THE FEDERAL CONVENTION OF 1787 172 (1911). *Cf.* MEIGS, THE GROWTH OF THE CONSTITUTION IN THE FEDERAL CONVENTION OF 1787 324 (1900).

17. 5 ELLIOT, DEBATES ON THE ADOPTION OF THE FEDERAL CONSTITUTION 380 (1901).

18. Randolph's original proposal referred to "cases in which foreigners, or citizens of other states, applying to such jurisdiction may be interested." Ibid., 128.

19. Ibid., 379. A similar provision was contained in THE ARTICLES OF CONFEDERATION: "The United States, in Congress assembled, shall also be the last on appeal in all disputes and differences now subsisting, or that hereafter may arise between two or more states concerning boundary, jurisdiction or any other cause whatever." In providing for special courts, the Articles used the term "controversy." It also provided that Congress should resolve "[a]ll controversies concerning the private right of soil, claimed under different grants of two or more states." ART. OF CONFED. art. IX.

20. 5 ELLIOT, DEBATES ON THE ADOPTION OF THE FEDERAL CONSTITUTION 445–46 (1901).

21. Ibid., 462. The Committee inserted the Pinckney proposal after the first mention of controversies so that it read: " . . . controversies between the United States and an individual state, or the United States and an individual person."

22. Ibid., 481.

23. Ibid., 482. This replaced the phrase cited in text accompanying note 10 *supra.*

24. Ibid., 483.

25. Ibid.

26. Ibid., 507.

27. Ibid., 528–29.

28. Ibid., 471.

29. Ibid., 563.

30. Ibid., 128.

31. Ibid., 151–55.

32. Ibid., 164–66, 344–49.

33. "Both by what they said and by what they implied, the framers of the Judiciary Article gave merely the outlines of what was to them the familiar operation of the English judicial system and its manifestations on this side of the ocean before the Union. Judicial power could come into play only on matters that were the traditional concern of the courts at Westminster." *Coleman* v. *Miller* (460) (concurring opinion). See also *Joint Anti-Fascist Refugee Committee* v. *McGrath* (150) (concurring opinion), and *United Steel Workers* v. *United States* (59) (concurring opinion).

34. "The historical relations of the English judges to the Crown and to the House of Lords explain the practice by which English judges gave opinions upon legal questions extrajudicially, that is to say, otherwise than as judgments. . . . By 1770[,] this power was well recognized." F. Frankfurter, *Advisory Opinions,* 1 ENCYCLOPAEDIA OF THE SOCIAL SCIENCES 475–76 (1930). See discussion of advisory opinions in Chapter 8 *infra.*

35. Notes, *Cases Moot on Appeal: A Limit on the Judicial Power,* U. PA. L. REV. 722 (1955).

36. The opinions were delivered *seriatim.*

37. Apparently Marshall's *dictum* in *Marbury* caused some public discussion of justiciability. This discussion concerned Marshall's contention that federal courts could issue a writ of mandamus to executive officers when the duty to be performed was merely ministerial. The contemporary objections were predicated more on this point than on the power of constitutional review. See 1 C. WARREN, THE SUPREME COURT IN UNITED STATES HISTORY 243–55 (1932).

38. "The judicial power of the U.S. is therefore vested in the courts, and can only be exercised by them in cases and controversies enumerated, and in petitions for writs of habeas corpus. In no other proceedings can that power be invoked, and it is not competent for Congress to require its exercise in any other way" (255).

39. "By these terms [cases and controversies] are intended the claims or controversies of litigants brought before the courts for adjudication by regular proceedings established for the protection or enforcement of rights or the prevention, redress or punishment of wrongs. Whenever the claim or contention of a party takes such a form that the judicial power is capable of acting upon it, then it has become a case or controversy." *Smith* v. *Adams* (173).

40. See 3 K.C. DAVIS, ADMINISTRATIVE LAW TREATISE 119–24 (1958).

41. *Cf.* E.S. CORWIN, THE CONSTITUTION OF THE UNITED STATES OF AMERICA: ANALYSIS AND INTERPRETATION 599 (1964).

42. The action was brought as a diversity of citizenship action based on a Kentucky declaratory judgment statute. There was no Federal Declaratory Judgment Act at the time.

43. 48 Stat. 955 (1935), 28 U.S.C. § 400 (1940 ed.). [Currently 28 U.S.C. § 2201 (1970).] See discussion of declaratory judgments in Chapter 6 *infra.*

44. See C.A. WRIGHT, LAW OF THE FEDERAL COURTS 35 (2d ed. 1970) and Comments, *Threat of Enforcement—Prerequisite of a Justiciable Controversy,* COL. L. REV. 108–9 (1962).

45. Marshall's statement is quoted here to show that the federal judiciary may have to decide a "case" or "controversy." The Supreme Court's jurisdiction is primarily discretionary today as a result of the writ of *certiorari.* See 28 U.S.C. § 1254–58 and SUP. CT. R. 19 (1970).

46. THE FEDERALIST Nos. 80–83, 515–55 (Modern Library edition, n.d.).

47. Ibid., 516.

48. Ibid.

49. Ibid., 520.

50. Ibid.

51. J. STORY, A FAMILIAR EXPOSITION OF THE CONSTITUTION OF THE UNITED STATES 189–90 (1840). The identical quotation is found in: J. STORY, COMMENTARIES ON THE CONSTITUTION OF THE UNITED STATES 451–52 (5th ed. 1891).

52. S.F. MILLER, LECTURES ON THE CONSTITUTION OF THE UNITED STATES 312–13 (1891).

53. Ibid., 316.

54. Ibid., 317. Miller did not explain why admiralty was an exception.

55. Note, *What Constitutes a Case or Controversy within the Meaning of Article III of the Constitution,* 41 HARV. L. REV. 232–33 (1927).

56. Ibid., 233–35.

57. E. Borchard, *Justiciability,* 4 U. CHI. L. REV. 4 (1936).

58. R.H. JACKSON, THE SUPREME COURT IN THE AMERICAN SYSTEM OF GOVERNMENT 11–12 (1955).

59. 1 B. SCHWARTZ, A COMMENTARY ON THE CONSTITUTION OF THE UNITED STATES 422 (1963).

60. L. JAFFE, JUDICIAL CONTROL OF ADMINISTRATIVE ACTION 99 (1965).

61. C.H. PRITCHETT, THE AMERICAN CONSTITUTION 116 (2d ed. 1968).

62. E.S. CORWIN, THE CONSTITUTION OF THE UNITED STATES: ANALYSIS AND INTERPRETATION 599 (1964).

63. "The typical common law adjudication presupposes three conditions: first, parties in such a relation to each other and to the relevant facts that they seek opposing results; second, a controversy so developed that its effects and ramifications can be presented to the court against a specific factual matrix such that intelligent decision can be rendered; and third, that whatever answer is given to a more abstract question of law, it will be part of an adjudication concerning a specific injury or substantial danger of injury to one of the parties." Notes, *Judicial Determinations in Nonadversary Proceedings,* 72 HARV. L. REV. 724 (1959).

64. Commentators basically have not gone beyond the act of repeating the Court's criteria, as the discussion in this chapter illustrates. One well-known scholar, C. Herman Pritchett, has suggested exploration beyond this point is

not needed. After listing his four criteria (text accompanying note 61 *supra*), he has stated: "These conditions are so well understood that they customarily raise no difficulties." C.H. PRITCHETT, THE AMERICAN CONSTITUTION 116 (2d ed. 1968). See also PRITCHETT, THE AMERICAN CONSTITUTIONAL SYSTEM 67 (4th ed. 1976).

    65. See *Willing* v. *Chicago Auditorium Assoc.* (289).

Chapter 3

    1. Notes, *What Constitutes a Case or Controversy within the Meaning of Article III of the Constitution,* 41 HARV L. REV. 233 (1927).

    2. See Notes, *Judicial Determinations in Nonadversary Proceedings,* 71 HARV. L. REV. 724 (1959).

    3. "1. The Court will not pass upon the constitutionality of legislation in a friendly, non-adversary proceeding, declining because to decide such questions 'is legitimate only in the last resort, and as a necessity in the determination of real, earnest and vital controversy between individuals. It never was thought that by means of a friendly suit, a party beaten in the legislature could transfer to the courts an inquiry as to the constitutionality of the legislative act.' *Chicago & G.T.R. Co.* v. *Wellman.*" *Ashwander* v. *Tennessee Valley Authority* (346) (concurring opinion).

    4. Notes, *Judicial Determination in Nonadversary Proceedings,* 71 HARV. L. REV. 724 (1959).

    5. A.S. Miller and W. Scheflin, *The Power of the Supreme Court in the Age of the Positive State: A Preliminary Excursus—Part Two: On the Need for Adaptation to Changing Reality,* 1967 DUKE L. REV. 538 (1967).

    6. See Notes, *Judicial Determinations in Nonadversary Proceedings,* 71 HARV. L. REV. 735 (1959); S. Krislov, *The Amicus Curiae Brief: From Friendship to Advocacy,* 72 YALE L. J. 697–721 (1965); and A.S. Miller and W. Scheflin, *The Power of the Supreme Court in the Age of the Positive State: A Preliminary Excursus—Part Two: On the Need for Adaptation to Changing Reality,* 1967 DUKE L. REV. 538–41 (1967).

    7. The term "test case" is also often used to describe a case that an interest group or the Department of Justice has selected to appeal to the United States Supreme Court. Several cases may have been commenced, but the interest group or the Department of Justice selects the one that will best serve their respective purposes on appeal. In this context, the term "test case" is not directly related to the existence of a "case" or "controversy."

    8. Some authorities have equated a test case with lack of adversity. *Cf.* R.K. CARR, THE SUPREME COURT AND JUDICIAL REVIEW (1942). "A collusive suit or test case will supposedly be rejected." Ibid., 185. On at least one occasion, however, the Court has specifically recognized an individual's right to create a test case. In *Evers* v. *Dwyer,* the Supreme Court reversed a three-judge district court's decision that had dismissed an action concerning segregated seating on local buses in Memphis, Tennessee on the ground that the plaintiff did not regularly ride the bus and had boarded it in this one instance only for the purpose of instituting litigation. After finding the other necessary elements of a "case" or "controversy" present, the Court concluded in a *per curiam* opinion:

"That the appellant may have boarded this particular bus for the purpose of instituting this litigation is not significant" (204).

See also *Beal* v. *Missouri Pacific R.R. Corp.*, wherein the Supreme Court reversed with instructions to dismiss a bill in equity seeking an injunction against a multiplicity of state criminal actions. In part, the decision was based on the state attorney general's promise to "cause a single test suit to be instituted in the state courts for some one alleged violation of the act by respondent, so conducted as to cause a minimum of financial expense to respondent" (48). This was held to show that no irreparable injury would result.

9. Unfortunately, these terms are often used loosely and interchangeably by the Court and by commentators. *Cf.* Notes, *Judicial Determinations in Nonadversary Proceedings*, 71 HARV. L. REV. 733 (1959): "A friendly suit is a variety of test case in which the substantial interests of the ostensible adverse parties are the same." And, in a footnote: "[C]ollusion is not used because of its pejorative connotations." It is suggested here, however, that collusive suits are much more descriptive of a nonadversary action than friendly suits, primarily because of the pejorative connotation of the former term.

10. See also *Goosby* v. *Osser*. The Court unanimously held that adversity continued to exist between Philadelphia County prisoners awaiting trial and Philadelphia officials, even though the Commonwealth of Pennsylvania, also a named defendant, agreed with the prisoners that the Pennsylvania Election Code had been improperly used to deny the plaintiffs the right to vote. Since the Philadelphia officials were not bound by the Commonwealth's decision, the Court concluded that adversity still existed between the plaintiffs and the Philadelphia officials.

11. *Chamberlain* v. *Cleveland* and *American Wood Paper Co.* v. *Heft.* In both instances, the Court relied on lack of adversity and did not discuss the cases in terms of mootness. A similar decision was rendered in *South Spring Hill Gold Mining Co.* v. *Amador Medean Gold Mining Co.*, wherein both companies came under control of the same persons after the original judgment.

12. See E.S. CORWIN, THE CONSTITUTION OF THE UNITED STATES: ANALYSIS AND INTERPRETATION 601 (1964), and W.F. MURPHY, ELEMENTS OF JUDICIAL STRATEGY 29 n. 47 (1964).

13. This stipulation was necessary in order to meet the monetary requirements for diversity jurisdiction. The fact that the stipulation was fictitious, however, also raises the question of possible collusion. See 1 C. WARREN, THE SUPREME COURT IN UNITED STATES HISTORY 147–48 (rev. ed. 1932).

14. See ibid., 393–95.

15. See 2 C. WARREN, THE SUPREME COURT IN UNITED STATES HISTORY 279–82 (rev. ed. 1932). Another famous case in which there was evidence of collusion is *Buck* v. *Bell*. See W. Berns, *Buck v. Bell: Due Process of Law*, 6 WESTERN POLITICAL QUARTERLY 765–66 (1953).

16. E. BORCHARD, DECLARATORY JUDGMENTS 32–33 (1941).

17. In the original decision, Chief Justice Melville W. Fuller argued that equity courts have jurisdiction over stockholders' suits and that no contention was made that there was an adequate remedy at law, "and so far as it was within the power of the government to do so, the question of jurisdiction, for the purpose of the case was explicitly waived on the argument." 157 U.S. 429, 553–54 (1895). The points about an adequate remedy at law and jurisdiction are questionable. If an adequate remedy exists at law, it is within the court's discretion to dismiss the equitable action, whether the point is raised by the parties or

not. The same is even more true of jurisdiction—no party is able to grant a federal court jurisdiction by waiving the issue. Fuller concluded that there was a justiciable dispute between the stockholder and the company. In dissents, Justices Edward D. White and John Marshall Harlan argued that the action should not be maintainable because the corporation was precluded by law from restraining the collection of a tax, and the stockholders should not be permitted to do indirectly what the corporation could not do directly. The second decision focused completely on the substantive issues.

18. In stating the facts of the case, Justice George Sutherland indicated the lack of adversity: "The board considered the demand, determined that, while it believed the act to be unconstitutional and economically unsound and that it would adversely affect the business of the company if accepted, nevertheless it should accept the code provided for by the act because the penalty in the form of a 15 percent tax on its gross sales would be seriously injurious and might result in bankruptcy" (286–87). Sutherland then dismissed the question of the right of the stockholders to bring such actions in one short paragraph, relying on *Ashwander* v. *Tennessee Valley Authority*. In a dissenting opinion for himself, Louis D. Brandeis, and Harlan F. Stone, Benjamin Cardozo did not discuss the question of justiciability or the right of stockholders to bring such an action.

19. An exception is *Corbus* v. *Alaska Treadwell Gold Mining Co.*, wherein the Court upheld the dismissal of a stockholder suit as collusive. In doing so, the Court said: "Evidently the plaintiff patterned his proceeding upon *Pollock* v. *Farmers' Loan & T. Co.*, 157 U.S. 429 (1895). But that case does not determine to what extent a court of equity will permit a stockholder to maintain a suit nominally against the corporation but really for its benefit" (459). The Federal Rules of Civil Procedure specifically provide for shareholders' suits. Rule 23.1 provides for derivative actions by shareholders and provides in part that the complaint must allege "that the action is not a collusive one to confer jurisdiction on a court of the United States which it would not otherwise have." Although the rule was promulgated apparently to prevent collusion concerning diversity of citizenship, *Corbus* v. *Alaska Treadwell Gold Mining Co.* (459–62), it is broad enough to indicate that judicial power should not be exercised if the court is aware of collusion.

20. In at least one instance, the Court has rather explicitly recognized that the adversity is possibly more formal than real in such stockholder actions. In *Cotting* v. *Godard*, although there was no opinion of the Court because of substantive reasons, the Court recognized that the adversity was at best formal: "There is no force in the suggestion that the officers of the corporation agreed with the stockholders as to the unconstitutionality of the statute and that therefore the suit is a collusive one . . . the fact [is] that the officers were refusing to protect the interests of the stockholders, not wantonly, it is true, but from prudential reasons." 183 U.S. 70, 113 (1900). (Justice David Brewer announced the Court's judgment.)

21. *Cf.* "The ability to find adversity in narrow crevices of casual disagreement is well illustrated by *Carter* v. *Carter Coal Co.*, where the President of the company brought suit against the company and its officials, among whom was Carter's father who was Vice President of the Company." E.S. CORWIN, THE CONSTITUTION OF THE UNITED STATES: ANALYSIS AND INTERPRETATION 601 (1964).

22. The Court decided a similar action in 1956 without discussing adversity. *United States* v. *Interstate Commerce Commission*. See also *United States* ex rel.

Chapman v. *Federal Power Commission,* wherein the Secretary of the Interior was one of the plaintiffs and the Federal Power Commission was one of the defendants. The question of adversity was not discussed. *Cf. Kendall* [Postmaster General] v. *United States* ex rel. *Stokes.*

23. Tregea, a resident and taxpayer, intervened and filed an answer. *Cf.* similar results in *City of Lampasas* v. *Bell; Braxton County Court* v. *West Virginia; Stewart* v. *Kansas City.*

24. The legal doctrine of estoppel means that one is precluded from commencing an action or pleading a particular defense because of his own past action: "A man's own act or acceptance stops or closes his mouth to plead the truth." H.C. BLACK, BLACK'S LAW DICTIONARY 648 (4th rev. ed. 1968).

25. The Court did ask the question, however. "Thus, in terms of Article III limitations on federal court jurisdiction, the question of standing is related only to whether the dispute sought to be adjudicated will be presented in an adversary context and in a form historically viewed as capable of judicial resolution." 392 U.S. 83 101 (1968).

26. This point is discussed in *The Supreme Court, 1967 Term,* 82 HARV. L. REV. 228–29 (1968).

27. 3 K.C. DAVIS, ADMINISTRATIVE LAW TREATISE 117 (1958).

28. Ibid., 118.

29. As another example to prove his points, Davis cites the fact that the courts of the District of Columbia and the territories exercise jurisdiction over probate matters, which often involve no adverse parties. Despite Davis's suggestion that the requirement of adversity applies to legislative courts as well as Article III courts, the evidence is to the contrary. The fact that these courts, in their capacity as legislative courts, perform functions in nonadversary proceedings proves nothing as far as Article III's case-or-controversy provision is concerned.

30. See R.G. Singer, *Justiciability and Recent Supreme Court Cases,* 21 ALA. L. REV. 281–82 (1969).

Chapter 4

1. Congress has provided for the original jurisdiction of the Supreme Court in 28 U.S.C. § 1251 (1970). The Supreme Court could, however, decide a "case" or "controversy" within its original jurisdiction without this congressional authorization. See C.A. WRIGHT, LAW OF THE FEDERAL COURTS 499 (2d ed. 1970).

2. Judiciary Act of 1789 § 14, 1 Stat. 58; in Ex parte *Bollman,* after quoting Art. 1, § 9, Chief Justice John Marshall said of § 14 of the Judiciary Act of 1789: "Acting under the immediate influence of this injunction, they [Congress] must have felt, with peculiar force, the obligation of providing efficient means by which this great constitutional privilege should receive life and activity; for if the means be not in existence, the privilege itself would be lost, although no law for its suspension should be enacted. Under the impression of this obligation, they give to all the courts the power of awarding writs of habeas corpus.

"It has been said that this is a generic term, and includes every species of that writ." (95)

3. 28 U.S.C. § 2241 (c) (4) (1970).

4. 28 U.S.C. § 2241 (c) (3) (1970) provides: "The writ of habeas corpus shall not extend to a prisoner unless—(3) He is in custody in violation of the Constitution or laws or treaties of the United States."

5. 28 U.S.C. § 2241 (a) (1970) grants all federal courts jurisdiction. "Writs of habeas corpus may be granted by the Supreme Court, any justice thereof, the district courts and any circuit judge within their respective jurisdictions. The order of a circuit judge shall be entered in the records of the district court of the district wherein the restraint complained of is had."

6. The pertinent section is 28 U.S.C. § 2241 (a–c) (1970).

(a) [See note 5 *supra.*]

(b) The Supreme Court, any justice thereof, and any circuit judge may decline to entertain an application for a writ of habeas corpus and may transfer the application for hearing and determination to the district court having jurisdiction to entertain it.

(c) The writ of habeas corpus shall not extend to a prisoner unless—

(1) He is in custody under or by color of the authority of the United States or is committed for trial before some court thereof: or

(2) He is in custody for an act done or omitted in pursuance of an Act of Congress, or an order, process, judgment or decree of a court or judge of the United States; or

(3) He is in custody in violation of the Constitution or laws or treaties of the United States; or

(4) He, being a citizen of a foreign state and domiciled therein is in custody for an act done or omitted under any alleged right, title, authority, privilege, protection, or exemption claimed under the commission, order or sanction of any foreign state, or under color thereof, the validity and effect of which depend upon the law of nations; or

(5) It is necessary to bring him into court to testify or for trial.

7. See *Wiley* v. *Sinkler; Swafford* v. *Templeton.* In recent cases, the courts have usually relied on the Fourteenth Amendment's equal protection clause, but have indicated the existence of the right under Art. 1, § 2. See *Gray* v. *Sanders; Wesberry* v. *Sanders; Harper* v. *Virginia State Board of Elections.*

8. *Cf. The Supreme Court, 1967 Term,* 82 HARV. L. REV. 230–31 (1968).

9. C.A. WRIGHT, LAW OF THE FEDERAL COURTS 38 (1st ed. 1963).

10. 3 K.C. DAVIS, ADMINISTRATIVE LAW TREATISE 222 (1958). See text accompanying note 24 *infra.*

11. See, e.g., *Dred Scott* v. *Sandford* and *Marbury* v. *Madison.*

12. 42 U.S.C. §§ 3601–19 (1970).

13. The pertinent provisions are found in 42 U.S.C. §§ 3603, 3604, and 3607 (1970).

14. Ibid., § 3610 (d).

15. Ibid., § 3612.

16. Ibid., § 3617. In *Curtis* v. *Loether,* the Court specifically recognized the legal rights created by this section. Although the Court's opinion was concerned primarily with the right to a jury trial under the Seventh Amendment, the Court accepted without question the creation of legal rights under this section (195).

17. Ibid., § 1982.

18. 42 U.S.C. § 3613 (1970).

19. *Cf.* provisions of Civil Rights Act of 1964: 42 U.S.C. §2000b (1970) (concerning public facilities), 42 U.S.C. §2000c–6 (1970) (concerning public education) and 42 U.S.C. §2000e–6 (1970) (concerning fair employment practices). Similar provisions based on the Voting Rights Act of 1965 are 42 U.S.C. § 1973a (1970), 42 U.S.C. § 1973h (b) (1970), and 42 U.S.C. § 1973 j(d) (1970).

20. In *United States* v. *Raines* (27) the Court upheld the Attorney General's standing to protect private rights under the Civil Rights Act of 1957 without discussing the federal government's legal right. This was followed in *United States* v. *Mississippi* (136); *South Carolina* v. *Katzenbach* (307); *Katzenbach* v. *Morgan* (657).

21. See 3 K.C. DAVIS, ADMINISTRATIVE LAW TREATISE 214–15 (1958).

22. 60 Stat. 243 (1946). (Currently in slightly revised form in 5 U.S.C. §§ 701, 702, and 704.)

23. See 3 K.C. DAVIS, ADMINISTRATIVE LAW TREATISE 211–13 (1958).

24. 3 K.C. DAVIS, ADMINISTRATIVE LAW TREATISE 222 (1958).

25. "This Constitution, and the Laws of the United States which shall be made in Pursuance thereof; and all Treaties made, or which shall be made, under the Authority of the United States, shall be the supreme Law of the Land; and the Judges in every State be bound thereby, any Thing in the Constitution or Laws of any State to the Contrary notwithstanding." U.S. CONST. art. VI.

26. Section 34 of the Judiciary Act of 1789, 1 Stat. 92, which is now 28 U.S.C. § 1652 (1970). The current statute reads: "The laws of the several states, except where the Constitution or treaties of the United States or Acts of Congress otherwise require or provide, shall be regarded as rules of decisions in civil actions in the courts of the United States, in cases where they apply."

27. See C.A. WRIGHT, LAW OF THE FEDERAL COURTS 241–47 (2d ed. 1970).

28. The Court did not use the term "legal interest" but spoke of "direct and particular financial interest" (435).

29. The plaintiffs sought a declaratory judgment.

30. Frankfurter discussed the problem in terms of standing and suggested that the taxpayers, parents, and teachers who brought the action did not have standing to sue (501–4).

31. *Cf.* "The general principle may be stated that there is no federal common law—that, in other words, the law which the Federal courts apply consists wholly and exclusively of the Federal Constitution, treaties, the statutes of Congress, and the laws common and statutory of the several States of the Union." 2 W.W. WILLOUGHBY, THE CONSTITUTIONAL LAW OF THE UNITED STATES 1306 (2d ed. 1929). See *contra*, "It is clear that where the Constitution, or a valid Act of Congress, provides a rule of decision, it must be applied by a federal court—and perhaps even by a state court—in cases where there is current jurisdiction. Beyond that very little is clear. Whether state law or federal law controls on matters not covered by the Constitution or an Act of Congress is a very complicated question, which yields to no simple answer in terms of the parties to the suit, the basis of jurisdiction, or the source of the right to be enforced. Whenever the federal court is free to decide for itself the rule to be applied, and there are many such situations, it is applying or making, 'federal common law.' " C.A. WRIGHT, LAW OF THE FEDERAL COURTS 247 (2d ed. 1970).

32. *Cf. Wheaton* v. *Peters*, "It is clear that there can be no common law of the United States" (658).

33. *Cf.* A. BICKEL, THE LEAST DANGEROUS BRANCH (1962). After discussing *Tennessee Electric Power Co.* v. *Tennessee Valley Authority,* Professor Bickel stated: "And the question whether the Constitution protects them against some forms of competition cannot be assumed away. It was held in *Pierce* v. *Society of Sisters* to protect a parochial school against a certain kind of public school competition. It was held in *Joint Anti-Fascist Refugee Committee* v. *McGrath* to protect an unincorporated association from being arbitrarily listed by the Attorney General of the United States as a Communist front organization and thus damaged in its ability to recruit members and otherwise operate effectively." Ibid., 120.

34. "The court therefore think [sic], that to effectuate the purpose of the legislature, the remedies in the courts of the United States are to be, at common law or in equity not according to the practice of state courts, but according to the principles of common law and equity, as distinguished and defined in that country from which we derive our knowledge of these principles" (222–23). (Justice Thomas Todd delivered the Court's opinion.) See L. Jaffe, *Standing to Secure Judicial Review: Private Actions,* 75 HARV. L. REV. 258–61 (1961) for a discussion of common law remedies.

35. See discussion of *Bell* v. *Hood supra* and *Jones* v. *Mayer Co. supra.* The Court may, of course, refuse to provide a remedy. See, e.g., *National Railroad Passenger Corp.* v. *National Association of Railroad Passengers; Securities Investors Protection Corp.* v. *Barbour;* and *Cort* v. *Ash.*

36. *Cf.* "[I]t is in my opinion extremely difficult to contend that the general law of remedies, by allowing a suit to test constitutionality, can make a case. This, in my judgment, is no more nor less than the advisory opinion situation." A. BICKEL, THE LEAST DANGEROUS BRANCH 120 (1962). With all due respect, it seems that Professor Bickel confuses the supplying of one missing element with the creation of a "case" or "controversy" out of whole cloth.

Chapter 5

1. 1 W.W. WILLOUGHBY, THE CONSTITUTIONAL LAW OF THE UNITED STATES 19 (2d ed. 1929).

2. E.S. CORWIN, THE CONSTITUTION OF THE UNITED STATES OF AMERICA: ANALYSIS AND INTERPRETATION 602 (1964).

3. *Cf.* "The Court's major idea that a municipal taxpayer has a larger and more direct stake in a municipal expenditure than a federal taxpayer has in a federal expenditure may have been sound in 1923 but is now contrary to the facts. General Motors in a recent year paid well over a billion dollars in federal taxes. This means that General Motors has about a two per cent stake in every federal expenditure. When the federal government undertakes a program involving expenditure of ten billion dollars, the General Motors portion is about two hundred million dollars—hardly a minute sum in an absolute sense. Even if General Motors or some other corporation has more than a two per cent share in the expenditures of some municipality, its stake cannot possibly reach such an amount as two hundred million dollars." 3 K.C. DAVIS, ADMINISTRATIVE LAW TREATISE 244 (1958).

4. After stating that a taxpayer would be a proper party only concerning expenditures under the taxing and spending clause, Chief Justice Warren stated: "It will not be sufficient to allege an incidental expenditure of tax funds in the administration of an essentially regulatory statute. This requirement is consistent with the limitation imposed upon state taxpayer standing in federal courts in *Doremus* v. *Board of Education,* 342 U.S. 429 (1952)" (102). In a note in his dissent, Justice John Marshall Harlan discussed the problem of different rules being applied to state and federal taxpayers, but urged that the majority's opinion would hardly make them identical in the future (132 n. 22).

5. In a concurring opinion, Justice Louis D. Brandeis indicated that the plaintiffs owned one three hundred and fortieth of the preferred stock. Ibid., 342.

6. For a general discussion of class actions, see C.A. WRIGHT, HANDBOOK OF THE LAW OF FEDERAL COURTS 306–17 (2d ed. 1970). Wright suggests that stockholders' derivative actions and taxpayers' suits are merely specific types of class actions. Ibid., 309.

7. FED. R. CIV. P. 23.

8. K.W. Dam, *Class Action Notice: Who Needs It?* in 1974 THE SUPREME COURT REVIEW 121 (ed. Philip B. Kurland, 1975).

9. In fact, the idea that a substantial interest is a prerequisite to a "case" or "controversy" is possibly more the result of commentators' interpretations of what the Court said in *Frothingham* than what the Court actually said. See E.S. CORWIN, THE CONSTITUTION OF THE UNITED STATES: ANALYSIS AND INTERPRETATION 602–7 (1964). Corwin titled one of his subsections on "cases" and "controversies" as "Substantial Interest," apparently predicated on *Frothingham,* but proceeded to discuss real, direct, and personal interests as well as substantial interests.

10. E.g., *Buchanan* v. *Warley* and *Barrows* v. *Jackson.*

11. *Cf. Pierce* v. *Society of Sisters.* The Court decided the case partially on the Fourteenth Amendment rights of parents, although no parent was a party. The Court did not discuss direct interest.

12. The subsequent cases were: *Poe* v. *Ullman* and *Griswold* v. *Connecticut. Cf. Eisenstadt* v. *Baird:* "We address at the outset appellant's contention that Baird does not have standing to assert the rights of unmarried persons denied access to contraceptives because he was neither an authorized distributor under §21A nor a single person unable to obtain contraceptives. There can be no question, of course, that Baird has sufficient interest in challenging the statute's validity to satisfy the 'case or controversy' requirement of Article III of the Constitution. . . . And so here the relationship between Baird and those whose rights he seeks to assert is not simply that between a distributor and potential distributees, but that between an advocate of the rights of persons to obtain contraceptives and those desirous of doing so. The very point of Baird's giving away the vaginal foam was to challenge the Massachusetts statute that limited access to contraceptives.

"In any event, more important than the nature of the relationship between the litigant and those whose rights he seeks to assert is the impact of the litigation on the third-party interests" (1033–34).

13. *Cf.* R. A. Sedler, *Standing to Assert Constitutional Jus Tertii in the Supreme Court,* 71 YALE L. J. 627 (1962). Sedler suggests there are four factors that the Court uses in determining a person's standing to assert the rights of others: (1) the interest of the party before the Court, (2) the nature of the right asserted,

(3) the relationship between the party before the Court and the third party whose right he is asserting, and (4) the likelihood that the third parties will have a chance to assert their own rights.

14. The Court did suggest that the NAACP might have a legal interest itself. "The reasonable likelihood that the Association itself through diminished financial support and membership may be adversely affected if production is compelled is a further factor pointing towards our holding that petitioner has standing to complain of the production order on behalf of its members" (459–60).

15. See *Stewart* v. *Kansas City*, 239 U.S. 14, 16 (1915); *Braxton County Court* v. *West Virginia*, 208 U.S. 192, 197 (1907); *Smith* v. *Indiana*, 191 U.S. 138, 149 (1903).

16. *Cf.* L. Jaffe, *Standing to Secure Judicial Review: Private Actions*, 75 HARV. L. REV. 258–61 (1961). Jaffe suggests that English common law may have permitted an individual to protect the public interest.

17. *Cf. Leser* v. *Garnett*. The Court permitted an attack on the Nineteenth Amendment because the laws of Maryland authorized such a suit by a qualified voter and the action originated in the Maryland courts.

18. *Cf. Smiley* v. *Holm* and *Koenig* v. *Flynn*. Without discussing the interest involved, the Court decided challenges to redistricting plans brought by a "citizen, elector and taxpayer" and by "citizens and voters," respectively.

19. See also *Federal Communications Commission* v. *National Broadcasting Co. (KOA)*. The Court upheld the right of a station to commence a "case" or "controversy" on the basis of electrical interference. "Here KOA, while not alleging economic injury, does allege that its license ought not to be modified because such action would cause electrical interference which would be detrimental to the public interest" (247). Justices Felix Frankfurter and William O. Douglas wrote vigorous dissents.

20. The private attorneys general concept was announced in *Associated Industries* v. *Ickes*. For a three-judge court of appeals, Judge Jerome Frank argued: "[W]e believe that the usual 'standing to sue' cases can be reconciled with the *Sanders* and *Scripps-Howard* cases, as follows: While Congress can constitutionally authorize no one, in the absence of an actual justiciable controversy, to bring a suit for the judicial determination either of the constitutionality of a statute or the scope of powers conferred by a statute upon government officers, it can constitutionally authorize one of its own officials, such as the Attorney-General, to bring a proceeding to prevent another official from acting in violation of his statutory powers; for then an actual controversy exists, and the Attorney-General can properly be vested with authority, in such a controversy, to vindicate the interest of the public or the government. Instead of designating the Attorney-General, or some other public officer, to bring such proceedings Congress can constitutionally enact a statute conferring on any non-official person, or on a designated group of non-official persons, authority to bring a suit to prevent action by an officer in violation of his statutory powers; for then in like manner, there is an actual controversy, and there is nothing prohibiting Congress from empowering any person, official or not, to institute a proceeding involving such a controversy, even if the sole purpose is to vindicate the public interest. Such persons so authorized, are, so to speak private Attorney Generals [sic]" (704).

21. "Thus we are brought around by analogy to the Supreme Court's reasoning in *Sanders*: unless the listeners—the broadcast consumers—can be

heard, there may be no one to bring programming deficiencies or offensive over-commercialization to the attention of the Commission in an effective manner. By process of elimination those 'consumers' willing to shoulder the burdensome and costly processes of intervention in a Commission proceeding are likely to be the only ones 'having a sufficient interest' to challenge a renewal application." 359 F. 2d 994, 1004–5 (1966). "The matter now before us is one in which an alleged conduct adverse to the public interest rests primarily on claims of racial discrimination, some elements of religious discrimination, oppressive over-commercialization by advertising announcements, and violation of the Fairness Doctrine. Future cases may involve other areas of conduct and programming adverse to the public interest, at this point we can only emphasize that intervention on behalf of the public is not allowed to press private interests but only to vindicate the broad public interest relating to a licensee's performance of the public trust inherent in every license." Ibid., 1006.

22. The concept of private attorneys general was discussed with approval by Douglas in his concurring opinion in *Flast* v. *Cohen* (109, 111) and was also discussed with approval by Justice John Marshall Harlan in his dissent (119–20). The Court did not rely on the concept or even discuss it.

23. See discussion of these doctrines in Note, *The Void-for-Vagueness in the Supreme Court*, 106 U. PA. L. REV. 67–116 (1960) and *The First Amendment Overbreadth Doctrine*, 83 HARV. L. REV. 844–927 (1970).

24. See also *Dombrowski* v. *Pfister*. Although the action involved an attempt to enjoin a pending state criminal action, the Court indicated that the traditional interest test was not applicable in actions attacking overly broad statutes. "Because of the sensitive nature of constitutionally protected expression, we have not required that all of those subject to overbroad regulations risk prosecution to test their rights. For free expression—of transcendent value to all society, and not merely to those exercising their rights—might be the loser. . . . For example, we have consistently allowed attacks on overly broad statutes with no requirement that the person making the attack demonstrate that his own conduct could not be regulated by a statute drawn with the requisite narrow specificity. *Thornhill* v. *State of Alabama*, 310 U.S. 88, 97–8; *NAACP* v. *Button*, *supra*, 371 U.S., at 432–33, *cf. Apthecker* v. *Secretary of State*, 378 U.S. 500; *United States* v. *Raines*, 362 U.S. 17, 21–2. We have fashioned this exception to the usual rules governing standing . . . because of the . . . danger of tolerating, in the area of First Amendment freedoms, the existence of a penal statute susceptible of sweeping and improper applications. *NAACP* v. *Button*, *supra* 371 U.S., at 433" (486–87). For a discussion of class actions see C.A. WRIGHT LAW OF THE FEDERAL COURTS 306–17 (2d ed. 1970).

25. Although the Court later held the action moot it did not overrule its decision in *Zwickler* v. *Koota*.

26. See *contra*, *Laird* v. *Tatum*. In a 5–4 decision, the Court took a much narrower view of a party's right to bring a "case" or "controversy" without showing any direct injury. See also *Broadrick* v. *Oklahoma*, *Bigelow* v. *Virginia*, and *Young* v. *American Mini Theatres, Inc.*, for more recent discussions of overbreadth and vagueness.

27. *Buckley* v. *Valeo* involved all three of the areas discussed above, i.e., administrative law, freedom of speech and, although not taxpayers, the broad class of all those eligible to vote for the President of the United States. Congress provided in the 1974 Amendment to the Federal Election Campaign Act of 1971 that: "(a) The Commission [Federal Election Commission], the national

committee of any political party, or any individual eligible to vote in any election for the office of President of the United States may institute such actions in the appropriate district court of the United States including actions for declaratory judgment, as may be appropriate to construe the constitutionality of any provision of this Act" 2 U.S.C. § 437h. In its *per curiam* opinion, the Court appeared to accept this provision, but unfortunately, it did so in rather vague terms. "It is clear that Congress, in enacting 2 U.S.C. § 437h, intended to provide judicial review to the extent permitted by Art. III. In our view, the complaint in this case demonstrates that at least some of the appellants have a sufficient "personal stake" in a determination of the constitutional validity of each of the challenged provisions" (631). The Court did not specify the "personal stake" possessed by any of the appellants or whether any of the appellants' "personal stake" was that of one eligible to vote for the President of the United States.

28. *The Supreme Court, 1969 Term*, 84 HARV. L. REV. 179 (1970).

29. K.C. DAVIS, ADMINISTRATIVE LAW TREATISE 706 (Supp. 1970).

30. The Court emphasized this point in *Sierra Club* v. *Morton*. "Early decisions under this statute [the Administrative Procedure Act] interpreted the language as adopting the various formulations of 'legal interest' and 'legal wrong' then prevailing as constitutional requirements of standing. But, in *Association of Data Processing Service Organizations, Inc.* v. *Camp*, 397 U.S. 150 (1970) and *Barlow* v. *Collins*, 397 U.S. 159 (1970) decided on the same day, we held more broadly that persons had standing to obtain judicial review of federal agency action under § 10 of the APA where they had alleged that the challenged action had caused them 'injury in fact,' and where the alleged injury was to an interest 'arguably within the zone of interests to be protected or regulated' by the statutes that the agencies were claimed to have violated" (733).

31. The Court first suggested the "stake in the outcome" test in *Baker* v. *Carr*. "Have the appellants alleged such a personal stake in the outcome of the controversy as to assure that concrete adverseness which sharpens the presentation of issues upon which the court so largely depends for illumination of difficult constitutional questions? This is the gist of the question of standing. It is, of course, a question of federal law" (204). In *Baker*, the Court held that the plaintiffs were attempting to protect their personal legal interests. "These appellants seek relief in order to protect or vindicate an interest of their own, and of those similarly situated. . . . They are asserting 'a plain, direct and adequate interest in maintaining the effectiveness of their votes,' *Coleman* v. *Miller*, 307 U.S. at 438, not merely a claim of 'the right, possessed by every citizen, to require that the Government be administered according to law. . . .' *Fairchild* v. *Hughes*, 258 U.S. 126, 129; compare *Leser* v. *Garnett*, 258 U.S. 130" (207–8). Although the Court used the "stake in the outcome" terminology in *Flast*, it obviously did not apply the test the same way the Court had in *Baker*.

32. "The interests he [the taxpayer] represents, and the rights he espouses are, as they are in all public actions, those held in common by all citizens. To describe those rights and interests as personal, and to intimate that they are in some unspecified fashion to be differentiated from those of the general public, reduces constitutional standing to a word game played by secret rules.

"Apparently the Court, having successfully circumnavigated the issue, had merely returned to the proposition from which it began. A litigant, it seems, will have standing if he is 'deemed' to have the requisite interest, and 'if you . . . have standing, then you can be confident you are' suitably interested. Brown,

Quis Costodiet Ipsos Custodes?—The School Prayer Cases, 1963 Sup. Ct. Rev. 1, 22" (128–30).

33. *The Supreme Court, 1967 Term*, 82 HARV. L. REV. 228–30 (1968); R. Singer, *Justiciability and Recent Supreme Court Cases*, 21 ALA. L. REV. 274–79 (1969).

Chapter 6

1. The terms "real controversy" and "actual controversy" are adopted here because these are the terms the United States Supreme Court uses. Although the term "controversy" is an integral part of the clause being studied, "actual controversy" is used here to indicate that the issue in dispute is at a stage where the judicial process may be brought into play.

2. A federal court may determine, of course, that a legal right has actually been invaded but that the proper parties are not before the court, or as Chief Justice John Marshall suggested, a legal right may have been invaded, but no party may be able to bring a "case" or "controversy." *Cohens* v. *Virginia*.

3. "The courts deal with concrete legal issues presented in actual cases not abstractions." *United States* v. *Appalachian Electric Power Co.* (423). "A declaration on rights as they stand must be sought, not on rights which may arise in the future . . . and there must be an actual controversy over an issue, not a desire for an abstract declaration of the law." In re *Summers* (566). "The province of the courts is to decide real controversies, not to discuss abstract propositions" *Stearns* v. *Woods* (78).

See *New Hampshire* v. *Louisiana* for an example of a feigned issue. "The evident purpose of the [11th] amendment, so promptly proposed and finally adopted, was to prohibit all suits against a state by or for citizens of other states, or aliens, without the consent of the state to be sued, and, in our opinion, one state cannot create a controversy with another state within the meaning of that term as used in the judicial clauses of the constitution, by assuming the prosecution of debts owing by the other state to its citizens. Such being the case, we are satisfied that we are prohibited, both by the letter and the spirit of the constitution, from entertaining these suits, and the bill in each of them is consequently dismissed" (91).

A collusive suit would also fall into this category. If the parties desire the same result or if one party controls both sides of the litigation, an actual controversy is not present.

4. See also *Mitchell* v. *Robert De Mario Jewelry Inc.* (291–92).

5. "A court of the United States may not grant an injunction to stay proceedings in a state court except as expressly authorized by Act of Congress, or where necessary in aid of its jurisdiction, or to protect or effectuate its judgments." 28 U.S.C. § 2283 (1970).

6. 28 U.S.C. § 2201 (1970).

7. E. BORCHARD, DECLARATORY JUDGMENTS xiii (2d ed. 1941).

8. Ibid., 58.

9. Ibid., 61. "The defendant's acts must be sufficiently definite and final to constitute a genuine threat to the plaintiff's peace of mind or pecuniary interests. When that time has come is not always easy to state." Ibid., 62.

"Whether the facts are or are not sufficiently ripe for judicial decision often requires an intelligent appreciation of the need and propriety of relief. Experience with the declaratory judgment has indicated to the courts a wide range of usefulness in determining controversies at a stage when coercive remedies are either impossible or unnecessary." Ibid., 68.

10. One should note that, in *Aetna Life Insurance Co.* v. *Haworth*, both the federal district court and the majority of the court of appeals held that a justiciable controversy was not present. The lower courts relied on previous decisions of the United States Supreme Court. See 11 F. Supp. 1016 (1935) and 84 F. 2d 695 (1936).

11. *Cf.* "The Declaratory Judgment Act is not a grant of jurisdiction to the federal courts. It merely makes available an additional remedy in cases of which they have jurisdiction by virtue of diversity and the prerequisite amount in controversy, or because of a federal question." C.A. WRIGHT, LAW OF THE FEDERAL COURTS 449 (2d ed. 1970).

12. E. BORCHARD, DECLARATORY JUDGMENTS 233 (2d ed. 1941).

13. Ibid., 46.

14. Ibid., 42.

15. Ibid., 41.

16. See also FED. R. CIV. P. 57: "The existence of another adequate remedy does not preclude a judgment for declaratory relief in cases where it is appropriate."

17. See also *Steffel* v. *Thompson*. The Court held that a declaratory judgment action could be maintained even if there was no basis for equitable relief.

18. A debate exists concerning the actual nature of the declaratory judgment action. See, e.g., C.A. WRIGHT, LAW OF THE FEDERAL COURTS (2d ed. 1970): "Although it is sometimes said that an action for a declaratory judgment is 'equitable in nature,' other cases have spoken of an action for a declaratory judgment as 'essentially legal.' The truth is that 'a declaratory judgment action is a statutory creation and by its nature is neither fish nor fowl, neither legal nor equitable.'" Ibid., 449–50.

19. "The declaratory judgment procedure may be resorted to only in the sound discretion of the Court and where the interests of justice will be advanced and an adequate and effective judgment may be rendered." *Alabama State Federation of Labor* v. *McAdory* (462). "Declaratory judgment is a remedy committed to judicial discretion." *Mechling Barge Lines* v. *United States* (331).

20. See, e.g., Justice William O. Douglas's concurring opinion in *Public Affairs Associates, Inc.* v. *Rickover:* "It is conceded that the Declaratory Judgment Act is an authorization, not a command—a conclusion as well settled as is the proposition that the jurisdiction of federal courts is confined to 'cases' or 'controversies.' . . . The requirements of a 'case' or 'controversy' and the propriety of the use of the declaratory judgment are at times closely enmeshed. In resolving those issues the Court has on the whole been niggardly in the exercise of its authority" (114).

21. *Cf.* Justice James McReynolds's dissent: 'It seems to me quite clear that the record presents no justiciable controversy, certainly none within the original jurisdiction of this court. If the pipelines hereafter fail to comply with their contracts, of course, they may be proceeded against in a proper forum, but to say that they probably will fail because of the statute and then to demand that the law-making power be enjoined is not to set up a real controversy cognizable in any court" (603–4).

22. "We are asked to adjudicate claims against its constitutionality before the scheme has been put into operation. . . . I think we should adhere to the teaching of this Court's history to avoid constitutional adjudications on merely abstract or speculative issues and to base them on the concreteness afforded by an actual, present, defined controversy, appropriate for judicial judgment, between adversaries immediately affected by it. In accordance with the settled limits upon our jurisdiction I would dismiss this appeal" (497–98).

23. "No person has yet been subjected to, or even threatened with, the criminal sanctions which these sections [§§ 11 & 12 (a)–(c)] of the Act authorize" (317).

24. 5 U.S.C. § 7324 (1970).

25. Justice Stephen J. Field concurred in the judgment of the Court and stated: "In many cases, proceedings criminal in their character, taken by individuals or organized bodies of men, tending, if carried out, to despoil one of his property or other rights, may be enjoined by a court of equity" (222).

26. W.W. WILLOUGHBY, THE CONSTITUTIONAL LAW OF THE UNITED STATES 729–30 (2d ed. 1929).

27. *Cf. Parker* v. *Brown.* The Court upheld anticipatory action concerning a California statute that attempted to control the marketing of raisins. The Court stated: "The majority of the Court is also of opinion that the suit is within the equity jurisdiction of the court since the complaint alleges and the evidence shows threatened irreparable injury to respondent's business and threatened prosecution by reason of his having marketed his crop under the protection of the district court's decree" (349–50).

28. 8 U.S.C. § 43 [Now 42 U.S.C. § 1983 (1970)].

29. *Samuels* v. *Mackell; Byrne* v. *Karalexis; Dyson* v. *Stein; Perry* v. *Ledesma.*

30. See discussion on nonreviewable orders in 3 K.C. DAVIS, ADMINISTRATIVE LAW TREATISE 187–241 (1958).

31. 38 *Stat.* 219 (1913).

32. Speaking for the Court, Justice Louis D. Brandeis concluded: "The so-called order here complained of is one which does not command the carrier to do, or to refrain from doing anything; which does not grant or withhold any authority, privilege or license; which does not extend or abridge any power or facility; which does not subject the carrier to any liability, civil or criminal; which does not change the carrier's existing or future status or condition; which does not determine any right or obligation. This so-called order is merely the formal record of conclusions reached after a study of data collected in the course of extensive research conducted by the Commission through its employees. It is the exercise solely of the function of investigation. Moreover the investigation made was not a step in a pending proceeding in which an order of the character of those held to be judicially reviewable could be entered later. It was merely preparation for possible action in some proceeding which may be instituted in the future" (309–10).

33. "Subsequent cases have made it abundantly clear that 'negative order' and 'affirmative order' are not appropriate terms of art. Thus, the court has had occasion to find that while an order was 'negative in form' it was 'affirmative in substance.' 'Negative' has really been an obfuscating adjective in that it implied a search for a distinction—non-action as against action—which does not involve the real considerations on which rest, as we have seen, the reviewability of Commission orders within the framework of its discretionary authority and within the general criteria of justiciability" (140–41).

34. *Cf.* "*Rochester* made clear that an order was ripe though it did nothing more than classify or establish a status when the effect of the declaration of status was to make applicable forthwith a corpus of statutes and regulations." L. JAFFE, JUDICIAL CONTROL OF ADMINISTRATIVE ACTION 401 (1965).

35. See, e.g., *Frozen Food Express* v. *United States; United States* v. *Storer Broadcasting Co.; Federal Communications Commission* v. *American Broadcasting Co., Inc.; Federal Power Commission* v. *Hope Natural Gas.*

36. 60 *Stat.* 243 (1946) [Now 5 U.S.C. §§ 701, 702 & 704 (1970)].

37. Storer had been denied a license on the basis of the new rules, but the action was not predicated on that specific denial (197).

38. The Court offered the following explanation of a legal wrong in a note: "Legal wrong as a ground for standing to appeal, was introduced by the Administrative Procedure Act, § 10(a). 60 Stat. 243. In explanation the reports of the Senate, No. 752, 79th Cong. 1st Sess. 26, and the House, No. 1980, 79th Cong., 2d. Sess. 42 define 'legal wrong': 'The phrase "legal wrong" means such a wrong as is specified in section 10(e). It means that something more than mere adverse personal effect must be shown in order to prevail—that is, that the adverse effect must be an illegal effect' " (197 n.6).

39. E.g., *Columbia Broadcasting System* v. *United States; United States* v. *Storer Broadcasting Co.; Frozen Food Express* v. *United States.*

40. See e.g., "The opinion of the Court in *Abbott,* by Mr. Justice Harlan, is likely to have a dominant and durable effect upon the law of ripeness." K.C. DAVIS, ADMINISTRATIVE LAW TREATISE 671 (Supp. 1970). See also: "I think, these cases [*Gardner* v. *Toilet Goods Ass'n* and *Abbott Laboratories* v. *Gardner*] may well be the first harbinger of the day when declaratory judgment, pre-enforcement actions will be allowed against all regulations or statutes which prescribe criminal penalties." R. Singer, *Justiciability and Recent Supreme Court Cases,* 21 ALA. L. REV. 254 (1969).

41. See *Oestereich* v. *Selective Service System Local Board No. 11* and *Breen* v. *Selective Service Local Board No. 16,* but *cf. Fein* v. *Selective Service Local Board No. 7.*

42. For a general discussion of the abstention doctrine see M.A. Field, *Abstention in Constitutional Cases: The Scope of the Pullman Abstention Doctrine,* 122 U. PA. L. REV. 1071 (1974).

43. 28 U.S.C. § 2281 (1970).

44. *Cf. American Federation of Labor* v. *Watson.* The Court applied the *Douglas* test and found the threat of irreparable injury present. The Court still applied the abstention doctrine, but ordered the district court to retain jurisdiction until the state issue was resolved.

45. See also the Court's summary of the abstention doctrine in *Colorado River Water Conservation District* v. *United States* 96 S. Ct. 1236, 1244–46 (1976).

46. See *Dombrowski* v. *Pfister* (484 n. 2) and *Younger* v. *Harris;* but *cf. Mitchum* v. *Foster.* For more recent applications of this doctrine, see also *American Trial Lawyers Association, New Jersey Branch* v. *New Jersey Supreme Court; Harris County Commissioners Court* v. *Moore; Kugler* v. *Helfant; Hicks* v. *Miranda;* and *Doran* v. *Salem Inn Inc.*

47. E.g., *Zwickler* v. *Koota; Keyishian* v. *Board of Regents; Dombrowski* v. *Pfister; Baggett* v. *Bullitt. Cf. Cameron* v. *Johnson,* and *Boyle* v. *Landry.*

48. See *Law Students Civil Rights Research Council* v. *Wadmond* and *Parker* v. *Brown.*

Chapter 7

1. See Chapter 6 *supra.* See also Justice Felix Frankfurter's concurring opinion in *Joint Anti-Fascist Committee* v. *McGrath* (154–56).

2. See G. SCHUBERT, CONSTITUTIONAL POLITICS 256–60 (1960).

3. The Pennsylvania and North Carolina "decisions" were letters sent to President George Washington, and therefore were tantamount to advisory opinions. See C. WARREN, THE SUPREME COURT IN UNITED STATES HISTORY 77–79 (rev. ed. 1932).

4. The Circuit Court in New York did suggest that the Act could be interpreted to mean that Congress intended to appoint the judges as commissioners and that the judges could accept or reject such extrajudicial appointments. See *United States* v. *Ferreira* (49–51). Chief Justice Roger B. Taney relied on *Hayburn's Case* in holding that a territorial court could exercise nonjudicial functions since it was a legislative court. Decisions of a territorial court in such instances could not be appealed to the United States Supreme Court.

6. A draft opinion written by Chief Justice Taney is found in 117 U.S. 697 (1886).

7. 12 *Stat.* 765 (1863). Quoted in *United States* v. *Jones* (478).

8. *Cf.* L. JAFFE, JUDICIAL CONTROL OF ADMINISTRATIVE ACTION 101–2 (1965).

9. "Thus, Presidential control is not limited to a negative but is a positive and detailed control over the Board's decisions, unparalleled in the history of American administrative bodies" (109).

10. See *Glidden* v. *Zdanok* (582). The issue of "extra-judicial revisory authority incompatible with the limitations upon judicial power this Court has drawn from Article III" is discussed. The Court concluded that this issue could be determined sometime in the future since it was not dispositive of the case.

11. The opinion of the Court is found in 69 U.S. (2 Wall.) 561 (1864). Chief Justice Chase delivered the actual opinion after Taney's death. Taney's draft opinion is published in the Appendix of volume 117 of the *United States Supreme Court Reports.* 117 U.S. 697 (1886). The following explanation precedes Taney's draft opinion, which was published some twenty-two years after the case was decided and after Taney's death. "This cause was submitted on the 18th December, 1863. On the 4th of April, 1864, the court ordered it to be argued on the second day of the following December Term. Mr. Chief Justice Taney had prepared an opinion expressing his views upon the question of jurisdiction. This he placed in the hands of the clerk on vacation, to be delivered to the judges on their reassembling in December. Before the judges met he died. The clerk complied with his request. It is the recollection of the surviving members of the court, that this paper was carefully considered by the members of the court in reaching the conclusion reported in 2 Wall. 561; and that it was proposed to make it the basis of the opinion, which, it appears by the report of the case, was to be subsequently prepared. The paper was not restored to the custody of the clerk, nor was the proposed opinion ever prepared. At the suggestion of the surviving members of the court, the reporter made efforts to find the missing paper, and, having succeeded in doing so, now prints it with their assent. Irrespective of its intrinsic value, it has an interest for the court and the bar, as being the last judicial paper from the pen of [Mr. Chief Justice Taney]" (697).

12. "It is therefore evident that there is neither more nor less in this procedure than an attempt to provide for a judicial determination, final in this court, of the constitutional validity of an Act of Congress. . . . Such judgment will not conclude private parties when actual litigation brings to the court the question of the constitutionality of such legislation" (361, 362).

13. *Cf. Willing* v. *Chicago Auditorium.* The Court held that "a final judgment might be given" in a declaratory judgment action, but that the action before it did not present an actual justiciable controversy (289).

14. See 3 K.C. DAVIS, ADMINISTRATIVE LAW TREATISE 119–24 (1958).

15. E. BORCHARD, DECLARATORY JUDGMENTS 12 (2d ed. 1941).

16. "Res judicata. A matter adjudged; a thing judicially acted upon or decided; a thing or matter settled by judgment. . . . Rule that final judgment or decree on merits by court of competent jurisdiction is conclusive of rights of parties or their privies in all later suits on points and matters determined in former suit." H.C. BLACK, BLACK'S LAW DICTIONARY 1470 (4th rev. ed. 1968).

17. "A court may grant declaratory relief even though it chooses not to issue an injunction or mandamus. . . . A declaratory judgment can then be used as a predicate to further relief, including an injunction." *Powell* v. *McCormack,* 395 U.S. 486, 499 (1969).

18. This statement must be tempered by the extent to which the political question doctrine is considered as directly related to the case-or-controversy provision. See Chapter 8. *Cf.* "[T]he finality or lack of it in judicial judgments is the least important and perhaps the least rigidly maintained element in the concept of 'case or controversy.' " A. BICKEL, THE LEAST DANGEROUS BRANCH 117 (1962).

Chapter 8

1. Selected sources are listed under each doctrine. See notes 2, 17, 33, 46, and 61 *infra.*

2. For general discussion of advisory opinions, see E.F. Albertsworth, *Advisory Functions in Federal Supreme Court,* 23 GEO. L. J. 643 (1935); E. BORCHARD, DECLARATORY JUDGMENTS 71–80 (2d ed. 1941); Comments, *The Advisory Opinion and the United States Supreme Court,* 5 FORDHAM L. REV. 94 (1936); E.S. CORWIN, THE CONSTITUTION OF THE UNITED STATES OF AMERICA: ANALYSIS AND INTERPRETATION 616–17 (1964); F. Frankfurter, *Advisory Opinions* in 1 ENCYCLOPAEDIA OF THE SOCIAL SCIENCES 475–78 (1930); F. Frankfurter, *A Note on Advisory Opinions,* 37 HARV. L. REV. 1002 (1924); M.O. Hudson, *Advisory Opinions of National and Inter-National Courts,* 37 HARV. L. REV. 970 (1924); Notes, *The Case for an Advisory Function in the Federal Judiciary,* 50 GEO. L. J. 785 (1962); C.A. WRIGHT, LAW OF THE FEDERAL COURTS 36–38 (2d ed. 1970).

3. E.S. CORWIN, THE CONSTITUTION OF THE UNITED STATES OF AMERICA: ANALYSIS AND INTERPRETATION 616 (1964).

4. An advisory opinion has been defined as: "A formal opinion by a judge or judges or a court or a law officer upon a question of law submitted by a legislative body or a governmental official, but not actually presented in a concrete case at law." H.C. BLACK, BLACK'S LAW DICTIONARY 75 (4th rev. ed. 1968).

5. At the Constitutional Convention, Charles Pinckney made the following proposal: "Each branch of the Legislature, as well as the Supreme Executive, shall have authority to require the opinions of the Supreme Judicial Court upon important questions of law and upon solemn occasions." 5 J. ELLIOT, DEBATES ON THE ADOPTION OF THE FEDERAL CONSTITUTION 445 (1901). Pinckney's proposal was submitted to the Committee to Detail but was never reported out. See also Comments, *The Advisory Opinion and the United States Supreme Court,* 5 FORDHAM L. REV. 96 (1936); and F. Frankfurter, 1 ENCYCLOPAEDIA OF THE SOCIAL SCIENCES 475–76 (1930).

6. 1 C. WARREN, THE SUPREME COURT IN UNITED STATES HISTORY 108 (1932).

7. Ibid., 109.

8. Ibid.

9. Ibid.

10. Ibid., 110–11.

11. Professor James Bradley Thayer suggested that if the Court had not been presented with difficult questions concerning foreign affairs, a different precedent might have been established. J.B. THAYER, LEGAL ESSAYS 54 (1908). In fact, the Court did give an advisory opinion to President Washington in 1790, although it concerned the establishment of the lower federal courts and the propriety of the Supreme Court justices' also sitting on the lower federal courts. See 1 J. STORY, COMMENTARIES ON THE CONSTITUTION OF THE UNITED STATES 401–4 n. 1 (5th ed. 1891). Professor Charles Warren suggested that in 1793 there was no unanimity on the issue of the Court's power to issue the traditional advisory opinion. 1 C. WARREN, THE SUPREME COURT IN UNITED STATES HISTORY 109 (1932).

Apparently, the Court did render an advisory opinion at the request of President James Monroe. See 1 C. WARREN, THE SUPREME COURT IN UNITED STATES HISTORY 596–97 (1932). See also Notes, *The Case for an Advisory Function in the Federal Judiciary,* 50 GEO. L. J. 809 (1962). See discussions of extrajudicial functions performed by individual justices in W.F. MURPHY, ELEMENTS OF JUDICIAL STRATEGY 123–75 (1964). See also discussion of attempts to propose constitutional amendments that would have permitted the United States Supreme Court to render advisory opinions. Comments, *The Advisory Opinion and the United States Supreme Court,* 5 FORDHAM L. REV. 94 (1936).

12. "Even in the absence of this early precedent [i.e., the Washington Administration's request] the rule that constitutional courts will render no advisory opinions would have logically emerged from the rule subsequently developed, that constitutional courts can only decide cases and controversies in which an essential element is a final and binding judgment on the parties." E.S. CORWIN, THE CONSTITUTION OF THE UNITED STATES OF AMERICA: ANALYSIS AND INTERPRETATION 617 (1964).

13. For a discussion of the relationship between advisory opinions and declaratory judgments, see E. BORCHARD, DECLARATORY JUDGMENTS 71–80 (2d ed. 1941).

14. 42 U.S.C. § 1973c (1970).

15. E.F. Albertsworth, *Advisory Functions in Federal Supreme Court,* 23 GEO. L. J. 643 (1935).

16. Since a "case" or "controversy" is present, this type of advisory opinion is beyond the scope of this study. From the perspective of judicial power, the Supreme Court or any federal court may do by indirection what it may not do

directly. Two examples should suffice. In *School District of Abbington Township* v. *Schemp,* the Supreme Court suggested that courses in comparative religion or history of religion were not a violation of the First Amendment's establishment clause (225). In *Irvine* v. *California,* the Court suggested that the police officials may have violated a law and ordered the record and a copy of the opinion sent to the Attorney General (137–38). In neither instance was the advice necessary to dispose of the case before the Court.

17. For a general discussion of standing see A. BICKEL, THE LEAST DANGEROUS BRANCH 113–27 (1962); R. Berger, *Standing to Sue in Public Actions: Is It a Constitutional Requirement?,* 98 YALE L. J. 816 (1969); E.S. CORWIN, THE CONSTITUTION OF THE UNITED STATES OF AMERICA: ANALYSIS AND INTERPRETATION 602–7 (1964); 3 K.C. DAVIS, ADMINISTRATIVE LAW TREATISE 208–94 (1958); K.C. DAVIS, ADMINISTRATIVE LAW TREATISE 702–87 (Supp. 1970); L. Jaffe, *The Citizen as Litigant in Public Actions: The Non-Hohfeldian or Ideological Plaintiff,* 116 U. PENN. L. REV. 1033 (1968); L. Jaffe, JUDICIAL CONTROL OF ADMINISTRATIVE ACTION 459–545 (1965); T.P. Lewis, *Constitutional Rights and the Misuse of "Standing,"* 14 STAN. L. REV. 433 (1962); K.E. Scott, *Standing in the Supreme Court—A Functional Analysis,* 86 HARV. L. REV. 645 (1973); R.A. Sedler, *Standing to Assert Constitutional Jus Tertii in the Supreme Court,* 71 YALE L. J. 599 (1962); R.A. Sedler, *Standing, Justiciability, and All That: A Behavioral Analysis,* 25 VAND. L. REV. 479 (1972); 1 B. SCHWARTZ, A COMMENTARY ON THE CONSTITUTION OF THE UNITED STATES 438–62 (1963); *Standing to Assert Constitutional Jus Tertii,* 88 HARV. L. REV. 423 (1974); *Standing to Sue for Members of Congress,* 83 YALE L. J. 1665 (1974); C.A. WRIGHT, LAW OF THE FEDERAL COURTS 39–45 (2d ed. 1970). Although no exhaustive search has been made to pinpoint the origin of the use of the term, "standing" was mentioned by the Court as early as 1929. "We are of opinion that appellants have no standing, in their own right, to make this attack." *Alexander Sprunt & Son* v. *United States* (254). The Court did not use the term "standing" in *Frothingham* v. *Mellon,* the case that eventually came to be the prime example of this requirement.

18. E.g., "I personally submit, however, that the two are things entirely different, that standing to sue does not involve the question of whether a case or controversy exists within the purview of section 2 of article III." Senator Sam J. Ervin (D.-N.C.). *Hearings on S. 2097* before the Subcomm. on Constitutional Rights of the Senate Comm. on the Judiciary, 89th Cong., 2nd Sess., Pt. 1, at 97 (1966).

19. E.g., "The standing doctrine is a judicial corollary of the constitutional requirement that the litigant must present a case or controversy." Note, *The Supreme Court and Standing to Sue,* 34 N.Y.U. L. REV. 141 (1959).

20. C.A. WRIGHT, LAW OF THE FEDERAL COURTS 38 (1st ed. 1963). *Cf.* "The question of standing is, if anything, even more difficult. . . . The issue is whether the person bringing the suit should be allowed to do so." R. Singer, *Justiciability and Recent Supreme Court Cases,* 21 ALA. L. REV. 244 (1969). See also E.S. CORWIN, THE CONSTITUTION OF THE UNITED STATES OF AMERICA: ANALYSIS AND INTERPRETATION 602 (1964). In discussing the case-or-controversy provision, Corwin places "standing to sue" under the heading "substantial interest."

21. There was no opinion of the Court. In announcing the judgment of the Court, Justice Harold Burton held that: "[T]he standing of the petitioners to bring these suits is clear. The touchstone to justiciability is injury to a legally

protected right and the right of a bona fide charitable organization to carry on its work, free from defamatory statements of the kind discussed, is such a right" (140–41).

22. E.g., "Is Justice Burton's statement that 'the touchstone to justiciability is injury to a legally protected right' circular as Justice Frankfurter suggests? If so, does Justice Frankfurter improve the situation, or advance toward an acceptable analysis by postulating an equivalence between 'standing' and 'justiciability.' " H.M. HART and H. WECHSLER, THE FEDERAL COURTS AND THE FEDERAL SYSTEM 166 (1953).

23. 5 U.S.C. §§ 701–6 (1970).

24. In *Sierra Club*, the Court held that the Club had not alleged or proven an injury. The Club had shown only a "special interest" and this was not enough (739–40). *Cf. United States* v. *Students Challenging Regulatory Agency Procedures* (SCRAP) where the Court held that injury to group members was properly pleaded.

25. One of the cases, *Schlesinger* v. *Reservists Committee to Stop the War*, did involve taxpayer standing as a secondary issue (2935–36). See also *Simon* v. *Eastern Kentucky Welfare Rights Organization* where the Court followed *Sierra Club* on organizational standing but appeared to limit standing for individual members under the APA.

26. Speaking for the Court, Justice Thurgood Marshall continued: "Appellant does have an interest in the support of her child. But given the special status of criminal prosecutions in our system, we hold that appellant has made an insufficient showing of a direct nexus between the vindication of her interest and the enforcement of the State's criminal laws" (619). In a dissenting opinion in which Justice William O. Douglas joined, Justice Byron White argued that the plaintiff had shown a sufficient personal stake in the outcome: "The Court states that the actual coercive effect of those sanctions on Richard D. or others 'can, at best, be termed only speculative.' This is a very odd statement. I had always thought our civilization has assumed that the threat of penal sanctions had something more than a 'speculative' effect on a person's conduct" (621). Justice Harry Blackmun dissented on other grounds and would not have reached the standing issue. Justice William J. Brennan agreed with Blackmun (622).

27. Concerning their status as taxpayers, the Court held the Committee failed to meet the test established in *Flast* (2935–36).

28. In a dissenting opinion, Justice William O. Douglas argued that plaintiffs had standing both as citizens and taxpayers. Concerning citizens, Douglas declared that "[t]he interest of citizens in guarantees written in the Constitution seems obvious. Who other than citizens have a better right to have the Incompatibility Clause enforced? It is their interests that the Incompatibility Clause was designed to protect" (2938). Justice Thurgood Marshall would have granted standing on the basis of protection of freedom of expression (2939–40).

29. *Warth* was a 5–4 decision. Justices William O. Douglas and William J. Brennan each wrote dissenting opinions. Neither Douglas nor Brennan attempted to refute or refine Powell's general discussion of standing, however. They both argued that the Court had improperly applied the doctrine. Douglas suggested that "[s]tanding has become a barrier to access to the federal courts, just as 'the political question,' was in earlier decades" (2215). Speaking for Byron White and Thurgood Marshall, Brennan came to a similar conclusion,

albeit with different emphasis. "While the Court gives lip-service to the principle, oft-repeated in recent years, that 'standing in no way depends on the merits of the plaintiff's contention that particular conduct is illegal,' . . . in fact the opinion which tosses out of court almost every conceivable kind of plaintiff who could be injured by the activity claimed to be unconstitutional, can be explained only by an indefensible hostility to the claim on the merits" (2216).

30. For a discussion of class actions see C.A. WRIGHT, LAW OF THE FEDERAL COURTS 306–17 (2d ed. 1970).

31. E.g., "[T]he federal courts have invented a law of standing that is too complex for the federal courts to apply consistently." 3 K.C. DAVIS, ADMINISTRATIVE LAW TREATISE 291–92 (1958).

32. See K.C. DAVIS, ADMINISTRATIVE LAW TREATISE 728–30 (Supp. 1970) and R.G. Singer, *Justiciability and Recent Supreme Court Cases*, 21 ALA. L. REV. 274–86 (1969).

33. For a general discussion of ripeness see 3 K.C. DAVIS, ADMINISTRATIVE LAW TREATISE 116–207 (1958); K.C. DAVIS, ADMINISTRATIVE LAW TREATISE 670–701 (Supp. 1970); A. BICKEL, THE LEAST DANGEROUS BRANCH 123–56 (1962); L. JAFFE, JUDICIAL CONTROL OF ADMINISTRATIVE ACTION 395–423 (1965); R.G. Singer, *Justiciability and Recent Supreme Court Cases*, 21 ALA. L. REV. 240–43, 247–58 (1969). Edwin Borchard suggests that term originated in a Pennsylvania Supreme Court decision of 1925. "The Pennsylvania Supreme Court in an exhaustive opinion which has been followed extensively, laid down the rule that the court must be 'satisfied that an actual controversy, or the ripening seeds of one, exists between parties, all of whom are *sui juris* and before the Court, and that the declaration sought will be a practical help in ending the controversy.' " E. BORCHARD, DECLARATORY JUDGMENTS 57 (1941). Borchard is quoting *Kariher's Petition* (No. 1), 284 Pa. 455, 471; 131 Atl. 265, 271 (1925).

34. See, e.g., *United Public Workers* v. *Mitchell.* The case undoubtedly involved ripeness, but no member of the Court used that term.

35. Justice Felix Frankfurter delivered the plurality opinion in *Poe* but did not attempt to delineate the issue of ripeness, although he found the issue nonjusticiable because of the lack of ripeness. Frankfurter merged the various doctrines of justiciability. "The various doctrines of 'standing,' 'ripeness,' and 'mootness' . . . are but several manifestations . . . of the primary conception that federal judicial power is to be exercised to strike down legislation, whether state or federal, only at the instance of one who is himself immediately harmed, or immediately threatened with harm, by the challenged action" (503–4).

36. 3 K.C. DAVIS, ADMINISTRATIVE LAW TREATISE 116 (1958).

37. Ibid., 127. Davis concludes: "The reasons for and against any particular solution of the problem of ripeness should be based upon all the understanding that can be mustered, including especially twentieth-century understanding. Nothing in the Constitution prevents the courts from adopting any solution of the problem of ripeness that such understanding may produce." Ibid., 128.

38. L. JAFFE, JUDICIAL CONTROL OF ADMINISTRATIVE ACTION 395 (1965).

39. Ibid., 397. Jaffe takes the position that the federal courts should exercise great discretion in determining ripeness. "*[R]ipeness should not be determined by a formula but by a reasoned balancing of certain typical and relevant factors for and against the assumption of jurisdiction.*" Ibid., 396.

40. See *contra*, 3 K.C. DAVIS, ADMINISTRATIVE LAW TREATISE 128–31

(1958). Davis's use of ripeness to indicate lack of finality below does not jibe with his own definition of ripeness. See text accompanying note 36 *supra*. When the Supreme Court remands a case for further proceeding below, the Court is hardly holding that the issue is abstract.

41. Frankfurter invoked the doctrine of separability. "The decision in *Electric Bond & Share* controls the present case. This Act, like the one involved there, has a section directing that if any of its provisions, or any of its applications, is held invalid, the remaining provisions and other possible applications shall not be affected. . . . This being so, our consideration of any other provision than those of section 7, requiring Communist action organizations to register and file a registration statement, could in no way affect our decision in the present case" (77–78). But *cf. Carter* v. *Carter Coal Co.*

42. "No rule of practice of this Court is better settled than 'never to anticipate a question of constitutional law in advance of the necessity of deciding it.' *Liverpool, New York & Philadelphia Steamship Co.* v. *Commissioner of Emigration*, 113 U.S. 33, 39. . . . In part this principle is based upon the realization that, by the very nature of the judicial process, courts can most wisely determine issues precisely defined by the confining circumstances of particular situations. . . . In part it represents a conception of the role of the judiciary in a government premised upon a separation of powers, a role which precludes interference by courts with legislative and executive functions which have not yet proceeded so far as to affect individual interests adversely" (71–72).

43. K.C. DAVIS, ADMINISTRATIVE LAW TREATISE 670 (Supp. 1970).

44. Ibid.

45. See A. BICKEL, THE LEAST DANGEROUS BRANCH 123–56 (1962).

46. For a general discussion of moot cases, see Comments, *Disposition of Moot Cases by the United States Supreme Court*, 23 U. CHI. L. REV. 77 (1955); E.S. CORWIN, THE CONSTITUTION OF THE UNITED STATES OF AMERICA: ANALYSIS AND INTERPRETATION 608–10 (1964); S.A. Diamond, *Federal Jurisdiction to Decide Moot Cases*, 94 U. PA. L. REV. 125 (1946); D.B. Kates, Jr. and W.T. Barker, *Mootness in Judicial Proceedings: Toward a Coherent Theory*, 62 CALIF. L. REV. 1385 (1974); Notes, *Cases Moot on Appeal: A Limit on the Judicial Power*, 103 U. PA. L. REV. 772 (1955); Notes, *The Mootness Doctrine in the Supreme Court*, 88 HARV. L. REV. 373 (1974); Notes, *Mootness on Appeal in the Supreme Court*, 83 HARV. L. REV. 1672 (1970); R.G. Singer, *Justiciability and Recent Supreme Court Cases*, 21 ALA. L. REV. 243–44, 258–68 (1969); C.A. WRIGHT, LAW OF THE FEDERAL COURTS 35–36 (2d ed. 1970). "Common law courts have long recognized the strict requirement that permits only cases presenting justiciable controversies to be decided. This is a jurisdictional limitation. If the parties are not adverse, if the controversy is hypothetical, or if the judgment of the court for some other reasons cannot operate to grant actual relief, the case is moot and the court is without power to render a decision." S.A. Diamond, *Federal Jurisdiction to Decide Moot Cases*, 94 U. PA. L. REV. 125 (1946).

47. *Cf.* "The inclusion of mootness in article III theory is a relatively recent development. . . . Early Supreme Court opinions treated mootness as a common law limitation on any court's duty, rather than power, to decide cases." Note, *Mootness on Appeal in the Supreme Court*, 83 HARV. L. REV. 1673–74 n. 12 (1970).

48. R.G. Singer, *Justiciability and Recent Supreme Court Cases*, 21 ALA. L. REV. 243 (1969). Although an action may become moot before it is commenced, this discussion is limited to mootness after an action is actually filed. That is, a

"case" or "controversy" exists at the time the legal action is filed, but subsequent events may moot the case.

49. C.A. WRIGHT, LAW OF THE FEDERAL COURTS 35–36 (2d ed. 1970).

50. The Court's discretion in determining whether there is reasonable expectation that the wrong will be repeated is clearly indicated in several recent cases. *Cf. Super Tire Engineering Co.* v. *McCorkle* and *Allee* v. *Medrano,* where the Court held there was a reasonable expectation that the wrong would be repeated, with *Securities and Exchange Commission* v. *Medical Committee for Human Rights* and *Preiser* v. *Newkirk,* where the Court held there was no reasonable expectation that the wrong would be repeated.

51. See also *Gray* v. *Sanders;* "Moreover, we think the case is not moot by reason of the fact that the Democratic Committee voted to hold the 1962 primary on a popular vote basis. But for the injunction issued below, the 1962 Act remains in force; and if the complaint were dismissed it would govern future elections. In addition, the voluntary abandonment of a practice does not relieve a court of adjudicating its legality, particularly when the practice is deeply rooted and long standing. For if the case were dismissed as moot appellants would be 'free to return to . . . [their] old ways' " (375).

52. See also *Nebraska Press Association* v. *Stuart* (2976).

53. See also *Richardson* v. *Ramirez.* The Court does not clearly indicate whether it held that *Richardson* was not moot because it was a class action or because an intervenor who became a defendant by order of the California Supreme Court still had a live controversy (2662–64).

54. In a note, Rehnquist emphasized the practical side of the determination: "A blanket rule under which a class action challenge to a short durational residency requirement would be dismissed upon the intervening mootness of the named representative's dispute would permit a significant class of federal claims to remain unredressed for want of a spokesman who would retain a personal adversary position throughout the course of the litigation. Such a consideration would not itself justify any relaxation of the provision of Art. III which limits our jurisdiction to 'cases and controversies,' but it is a factor supporting the result we reach if consistent with Art. III" (558 n.9).

55. *Cf. Franks* v. *Bowman Transportation Co.* (1258–60) involving both a class action and an issue capable of repetition yet evading review. The Court's discretion is further increased in determining whether or not there is a proper class action. See *Board of School Commissioners* v. *Jacobs,* where the Court held that there had been inadequate compliance with the Federal Rules of Civil Procedures (850). When an action originates in a state court, the Court has even greater discretion. See *Richardson* v. *Ramirez.* Since the state courts are not bound by the Federal Rules of Civil Procedures, the record may not clearly indicate whether the state courts treated a case as a class action. The majority in *Richardson* held that the case was a class action, while the dissenters argued that it was not (2663, 2675–76). The Court may also simply remand a case and permit the lower court to make the determination on mootness. See *Indiana Employment Security Division* v. *Burney.* Finally, the Court may determine that under special circumstances the certification of the class action may even take place after the named plaintiff ceases to be a member of the class. *Gerstein* v. *Pugh.*

56. R.G. Singer, *Justiciability and Recent Supreme Court Cases,* 21 ALA. L. REV. 262 (1969).

57. In *North Carolina* v. *Rice,* the Court listed these potential collateral consequences: (1) disenfranchisement, (2) loss of right to hold federal or state

office, (3) disqualification from certain professions, (4) impeachment of testimony when testifying as a witness, (5) disqualification from service on a jury, and (6) liability to divorce (247 n. 1).

58. "*St. Pierre* v. *United States, supra,* must be read in light of later cases to mean that a criminal case is moot only if it is shown that there is no possibility that any collateral legal consequences will be imposed on the basis of the challenged conviction" (57–58).

59. "It is always preferable to litigate a matter when it is directly and principally in dispute, rather than in a proceeding where it is collateral to the central controversy. Moreover, litigation is better conducted when the dispute is fresh and additional facts may, if necessary, be taken without a substantial risk that witnesses will die or memories fade. And it is far better to eliminate the source of a potential legal disability than to require the citizen to suffer the possibly unjustified consequences of the disability itself for an indefinite period of time before he can secure adjudication of the State's right to impose it on the basis of some past action" (56–57).

60. See *Wirtz* v. *Local 153, Glass Bottle Blowers Ass'n.* The Court held that an action by the Secretary of Labor to invalidate a union election and hold a Government supervised election did not become moot although an intervening unsupervised election had been held. " . . . Congress emphatically asserted a vital public interest in assuring free and democratic union elections that transcends the narrow interest of the complaining union member" (475).

61. For a general discussion of political questions, see R.J. Bean, Jr., *The Supreme Court and the Political Question: Affirmation or Abdication?*, 71 W. VA. L. REV. 97 (1969); E.S. CORWIN, THE CONSTITUTION OF THE UNITED STATES OF AMERICA: ANALYSIS AND INTERPRETATION 611–16 (1964); M. Finkelstein, *Judicial Self Limitation*, 37 HARV. L. REV. 338 (1924); J. Frank, *Political Questions*, in E. CAHN (ed.), SUPREME COURT AND SUPREME LAW 36–47 (1968); 1 B. SCHWARTZ, A COMMENTARY ON THE CONSTITUTION OF THE UNITED STATES 462–70 (1963); M.F. Weston, *Political Questions*, 38 HARV. L. REV. 296 (1925); C.A. WRIGHT, LAW OF THE FEDERAL COURTS 45–48 (2d ed. 1970).

62. But *cf.* "[I]n order to entitle the party to the remedy a case must be presented appropriate for the exercise of judicial power, the rights in danger as we have seen, must be rights of person or property not merely political rights, which do not belong to the jurisdiction of a court, either in law or equity." *Georgia* v. *Stanton* (75). Also *cf. Massachusetts* v. *Mellon,* with *South Carolina* v. *Katzenbach.*

63. J. Frank, *Political Questions* in E. CAHN (ed.), SUPREME COURT AND COURT LAW 36 (1968).

64. E.S. CORWIN, THE CONSTITUTION OF THE UNITED STATES OF AMERICA: ANALYSIS AND INTERPRETATION 612 (1964).

65. Corwin continues: "The more common classifications of cases involving political questions are: (1) those which raise the issue of what proof is required that a statute has been enacted, or a constitutional amendment ratified; (2) questions arising out of the conduct of foreign relations; (3) the termination of wars, or rebellions; the questions of what constitutes a republican form of government, and the right of a State to protection against invasion or domestic violence; questions arising out of political actions of States in determining the mode of choosing presidential electors, and reapportionment of districts for congressional representation; and suits brought by States to test their political and so-called sovereign rights." Ibid., 612–13.

66. No attempt will be made to catalogue political questions. See *Baker* v. *Carr* (208–37).

67. Brennan's criteria on policy consideration were also arguably violated by *Baker* itself. See Frankfurter's dissent (267–70). The Court's decisions in *Youngstown Sheet & Tube* v. *Sawyer* and *Powell* v. *McCormack* could be viewed as showing lack of respect for coordinate branches. Any time the Court exercises its ultimate power of declaring a law passed by Congress unconstitutional, it overrules a political decision already made. The only way the Court could avoid "multifarious pronouncements" would be to never overrule the executive and legislative branches and clear all decisions with these branches before they are made. The point is that Brennan's criteria, beyond the first, are so broad that they permit unlimited discretion.

68. See also *Gilligan* v. *Morgan* and *United States* v. *Nixon*. Although the Court did not rely specifically on the political question doctrine, *O'Brien* v. *Brown* may be an exception. See R. Brooke Jackson, *The Political Question Doctrine: Where Does It Stand After Powell v. McCormack, O'Brien v. Brown and Gilligan v. Morgan?*, 44 U. COLO. L. REV. 477 (1973).

69. In *Powell*, the Court stated that "our determination that this cause presents no nonjusticiable 'political question' disposes of respondents' contentions that this cause is not a 'case' or 'controversy' " (513).

Chapter 9

1. See H.J. SPAETH, AN INTRODUCTION TO SUPREME COURT DECISION MAKING 1–7 (rev. ed. 1972). Spaeth lists a third function—the administration of criminal laws. See also S. GOLDMAN and T.P. JAHNIGE, THE FEDERAL COURTS AS A POLITICAL SYSTEM 34–43, 189–200 (1971). M. Shapiro says: "It is therefore impossible to speak in the abstract of the power or function of the Supreme Court. The Supreme Court, like other agencies, has different powers and different functions depending upon who wants it to do what, when, and in conjunction with or opposition to what other agencies or political forces. If a final answer can ever be offered to the question, What is the role of the Supreme Court? it will be achieved by correlating various powers and functions in specific areas, rather than by a general examination of the nature of the Court." LAW AND POLITICS IN THE SUPREME COURT 2 (1964).

2. See L. Jaffe, *Standing to Secure Judicial Review: Public Actions*, 74 HARV. L. REV. 1265–1314 (1961).

3. 5 J. ELLIOT, DEBATES ON THE ADOPTION OF THE FEDERAL CONSTITUTION 483 (1901). See discussion in text accompanying note 24 in Chapter 2 *supra*.

4. See D. EASTON, A FRAMEWORK FOR POLITICAL ANALYSIS 96–97 (1965).

5. *Tennessee Electric Power Co.* v. *Tennessee Valley Authority* (137).

6. *Frothingham* v. *Mellon* (487).

7. *Fairchild* v. *Hughes* (129–30).

8. 5 U.S.C. §§ 701–2 (1970).

9. " 'Well, John Marshall has made his decision, now let him enforce it,' was the President's commentary on the decision [*Cherokee Nation* v. *Georgia*, 30

U.S. (5 Pet.) 1 (1831)] according to the recollection of a Massachusetts Congressman." 1 C. WARREN, THE SUPREME COURT IN UNITED STATES HISTORY 759 (1932).

10. *Cf.* Ex parte *McCardle.* A unanimous Supreme Court decided that, after Congress restricted the Court's jurisdiction, the Court could not exercise judicial power in an action that was already before the Court. Although the decision has never been overruled, many authorities question its validity. See 1 B. SCHWARTZ, A COMMENTARY ON THE CONSTITUTION OF THE UNITED STATES 375–80 (1963) and C.A. WRIGHT, LAW OF FEDERAL COURTS 22–23 (2d ed. 1970).

11. 1 W.W. WILLOUGHBY, THE CONSTITUTIONAL LAW OF THE UNITED STATES 41 (2d ed. 1929).

12. E. BORCHARD, DECLARATORY JUDGMENTS 233 (1941).

13. In one instance, Congress did direct the Attorney General to institute a test case. See 42 U.S.C. § 1973h (a–b) (1970). The Attorney General was directed to institute a test case on the poll tax, but the Court decided the issue before the Attorney General acted. See *Harper* v. *Virginia Board of Elections.*

14. See *Hearings on H.R. 1198 and S. 3 Before Subcomm. No. 3 of the House Comm. on the Judiciary,* 90th Cong. 2nd Sess., ser. 19, at 117 (1968); See 3 K.C. DAVIS, ADMINISTRATIVE LAW TREATISE 119–24 (1958).

15. *Cohens* v. *Virginia.* (404).

16. See H.P. Monaghan, *Constitutional Adjudication: The Who and When,* 82 YALE L. J. 1363 (1973) for a slightly different answer than the one presented here.

17. *United States* v. *Butler* (78–79) (dissenting opinion).

18. G. Gunther, *The Subtle Vices of the "Passive Virtues"—A Comment on Principle and Expediency in Judical Review,* 64 COLUM. L. REV. 7 (1964).

19. See A. BICKEL, THE LEAST DANGEROUS BRANCH 69–71 (1962).

20. See generally A. BICKEL, THE LEAST DANGEROUS BRANCH (1962); E. Cahn, *Law in the Consumer Perspective,* 112 U. PA. L. REV. 1 (1963); T.A. Cowan, *Group Interests,* 44 VA. L. REV. 331 (1958); G. Gunther, *The Subtle Vices of the "Passive Virtues"—A Comment on Principle and Expediency in Judicial Review,* 64 COLUM. L. REV. 1 (1964); A.S. Miller, *Toward a Concept of Constitutional Duty,* THE SUPREME COURT REVIEW 199 (1968); R.G. Singer, *Justiciability and Recent Supreme Court Cases,* 21 ALA. L. REV. 229 (1969).

Bibliography

General and Special Works

Abraham, Henry J. *The Judicial Process*. 3d ed. New York: Oxford University Press, 1975.

Bickel, Alexander M. *The Least Dangerous Branch: The Supreme Court at the Bar of Politics*. New York: Bobbs-Merrill, 1962.

Black, Henry Campbell. *Black's Law Dictionary*. 4th ed. rev. St. Paul: West Publishing Co., 1968.

Borchard, Edwin. *Declaratory Judgments*. 2d ed. Cleveland: Banks-Baldwin Law Publishing Co., 1941.

Bunn, Charles W. *A Brief Survey of the Jurisdiction and Practice of the Courts of the United States*. 5th ed. St. Paul: West Publishing Co., 1949.

Cahn, Edmond, ed. *Supreme Court and Supreme Law*. New York: Greenwood Press, 1968.

Carr, Robert K. *The Supreme Court and Judicial Review*. New York: Rinehart, 1942.

Cooley, Thomas M. *A Treatise on the Constitutional Limitations which Rest upon the Legislative Power of the States of the American Union*. Boston: Little, Brown, 1868.

Corwin, Edward S. *Court over Constitution*. New York: Peter Smith, 1950.

Cox, Archibald. *The Warren Court: Constitutional Decision as an Instrument of Reform*. Cambridge: Harvard University Press, 1968.

Davis, Kenneth Culp. *Administrative Law Treatise*. 4 vols. St. Paul: West Publishing Co., 1958. *1970 Supplement*. St. Paul: West Publishing Co., 1971.

de Tocqueville, Alexis. *Democracy in America*. Vol. 1. New York: Vintage Books, 1945.

Dietze, Gottfried, ed. *Essays on the American Constitution*. Englewood Cliffs, N. J.: Prentice-Hall, 1964.

Dumbauld, Edward. *The Constitution of the United States*. Norman: University of Oklahoma Press, 1964.

Easton, David. *A Framework for Political Analysis*. Englewood Cliffs, N. J.: Prentice-Hall, 1965.

Elliot, Jonathan. *Debates on the Adoption of the Federal Constitution*. Vol. V. Philadelphia: Lippincott, 1901.

Farrand, Max. *The Records of the Federal Convention of 1787*. 4 vols. New Haven: Yale University Press, 1911.

The Federalist: A Commentary on the Constitution of the United States. New York: The Modern Library, n.d.

Frankfurter, Felix and Landis, James M. *The Business of the Supreme Court: A Study in the Federal Judicial System*. New York: Macmillan, 1928.

Goldman, Sheldon and Jahnige, Thomas P. *The Federal Courts as a Political System*. New York: Harper and Row, 1971.

Haines, Charles Grove. *The American Doctrine of Judicial Supremacy*. New York: Russell and Russell, 1959.

Harris, Robert. *The Judicial Power of the United States*. Baton Rouge: Louisiana State University Press, 1940.

Hart, Henry M., Jr., and Wechsler, Herbert. *The Federal Courts and the Federal System.* Brooklyn: Foundation Press, 1953.

Hughes, Charles Evans. *The Supreme Court of the United States.* New York: Columbia University Press, 1928.

Jackson, Robert H. *The Struggle for Judicial Supremacy.* New York: Knopf, 1941.

————. *The Supreme Court in the American System of Government.* Cambridge: Harvard University Press, 1955.

Jaffe, Louis L. *Judicial Control of Administrative Action.* Boston: Little, Brown, 1965.

McCloskey, Robert G. *The American Supreme Court.* Chicago: University of Chicago Press, 1960.

Meigs, William M. *The Growth of the Constitution in the Federal Convention of 1787.* Philadelphia: Lippincott, 1900.

Miller, Samuel Freeman. *Lectures on the Constitution of the United States.* New York: Banks and Bros., Law Publishers, 1891.

Murphy, Walter F. *Elements of Judicial Strategy.* Chicago: University of Chicago Press, 1964.

———— and Pritchett, C. Herman. *Courts, Judges, and Politics: An Introduction to the Judicial Process.* 2d ed. New York: Random House, 1974.

———— and Tanenhaus, Joseph. *The Study of Public Law.* New York: Random House, 1972.

Prescott, Arthur Taylor. *Drafting the Federal Constitution.* Baton Rouge: Louisiana State University Press, 1941.

Pritchett, C. Herman. *The American Constitution.* 2d ed. New York: McGraw-Hill, 1968.

Schmidhauser, John R., ed. *Constitutional Law in the Political Process.* Chicago: Rand McNally, 1963.

Schubert, Glendon. *Constitutional Politics.* New York: Holt, Rinehart and Winston, 1960.

————. *Judicial Policy-Making.* Rev. ed. Glenview, Ill.: Scott, Foresman, 1974.

Schwartz, Bernard. *American Constitutional Law.* Cambridge, England: Cambridge University Press, 1955.

————. *A Commentary on the Constitution of the United States.* 2 vols. New York: Macmillan, 1963.

Shapiro, Martin. *Law and Politics in the Supreme Court.* New York: Free Press, 1964.

Sigler, Jay A. *An Introduction to the Legal System.* Homewood, Ill.: Dorsey Press, 1968.

Spaeth, Harold J. *An Introduction to Supreme Court Decision Making.* Rev. ed. San Francisco: Chandler, 1972.

Story, Joseph. *Commentaries on the Constitution of the United States.* 3 vols. Boston: Little, Brown, 1891.

————. *A Familiar Exposition of the Constitution of the United States.* Boston: Wm. Crosby and H.P. Nichols, 1840.

Thayer, James Bradley. *Legal Essays.* Boston: Boston Book Co., 1908.

Towle, Nathaniel C. *History and Analysis of the Constitution of the United States.* 3d ed. Boston: Little, Brown, 1871.

Warren, Charles. *The Making of the Constitution.* Boston: Little, Brown, 1929.

————. *The Supreme Court in United States History.* 2 vols. Rev. ed. Boston: Little, Brown, 1932.

Willoughby, Westel Woodbury. *The Constitutional Law of the United States.* 3 vols. 2d ed. New York: Baker, Voorhis and Co., 1929.

Wright, Charles Alan. *Handbook of the Law of Federal Courts.* 1st ed. St. Paul: West Publishing Co., 1963; 2d ed., 1970.

Young, Roland. *American Law and Politics: The Creation of Public Order.* New York: Harper and Row, 1967.

Selected Articles

Albertsworth, E. F. "Advisory Functions in Federal Supreme Court." 23 *Georgetown Law Journal* 643 (May 1935).

Bean, Ralph J., Jr. "The Supreme Court and the Political Question: Affirmation or Abdication?" 71 *West Virginia Law Review* 97 (Feb. 1969).

Berger, Raoul. "Intervention by Public Agencies in Private Litigation in the Federal Courts." 50 *Yale Law Journal* 65 (Nov. 1940).

———. "Standing to Sue in Public Actions: Is It a Constitutional Requirement?" 78 *Yale Law Journal* 816 (April 1969).

Berns, Walter. "*Buck* v. *Bell*: Due Process of Law." 6 *Western Political Quarterly* 762 (Dec. 1953).

Birkby, Robert H. and Murphy, Walter F. "Interest Group Conflict in the Judicial Arena: The First Amendment and Group Access to the Courts." 42 *Texas Law Review* 1018 (Dec. 1964).

Bittker, Boris I. "The Case of the Fictitious Taxpayer: The Federal Taxpayer's Suit Twenty Years After *Flast* v. *Cohen*." 36 *University of Chicago Law Review* 364 (Winter 1969).

Borchard, Edwin. "Justiciability." 4 *University of Chicago Law Review* 1 (Dec. 1936).

———. "The Next Step Beyond Equity—The Declaratory Action." 13 *University of Chicago Law Review* 145 (Feb. 1946).

Cahn, Edmond. "Law in the Consumer Perspective." 112 *University of Pennsylvania Law Review* 1 (Nov. 1963).

Cowan, Thomas A. "Group Interests." 44 *Virginia Law Review* 331 (April 1958).

Dam, Kenneth W. "Class Action Notice: Who Needs It?" 1975 *The Supreme Court Review* 97 (1975).

Davis, John W. "Present Day Problems." 9 *American Bar Association Journal* 553 (Sept. 1923).

Davis, Kenneth Culp. "The Case of the Real Taxpayer: A Reply to Professor Bittker." 36 *University of Chicago Law Review* 375 (Winter 1969).

———. "Judicial Control of Administrative Action: A Review." 66 *Columbia Law Review* 635 (April, 1966).

———. "The Liberalized Law of Standing." 37 *University of Chicago Law Review* 450 (1970).

Diamond, Sidney A. "Federal Jurisdiction to Decide Moot Cases." 94 *University of Pennsylvania Law Review* 125 (Jan. 1946).

Fahy, Charles. "Judicial Review of Executive Action." 50 *Georgetown Law Journal* 709 (Summer 1962).

Field, Martha. "Abstention in Constitutional Cases: The Scope of the Pullman Abstention Doctrine." 122 *University of Pennsylvania Law Review* 1071 (May 1974).

Finkelstein, Maurice. "Further Notes on Judicial Self-Limitation." 39 *Harvard Law Review* 221 (Dec. 1925).

———. "Judicial Self-Limitation." 37 *Harvard Law Review* 338 (Jan. 1924).

Frankfurter, Felix. "Advisory Opinions." 1 *Encyclopaedia of the Social Sciences* 475 (1930).

———. "A Note on Advisory Opinions." 37 *Harvard Law Review* 1002 (June 1924).

——— and Landis, James M. "The Business of the Supreme Court of the United States—A Study in the Federal Judicial System—Part I The Period Prior to the Civil War." 38 *Harvard Law Review* 1005 (June 1925).

Freund, Paul A. "The Supreme Court, 1973 Term Forward: On Presidential Privilege." 88 *Harvard Law Review* 13 (Nov. 1974).

Giessel, Henry P. "The Federal Declaratory Judgment Act in Public Law Cases." 28 *Texas Law Review* 709 (Sept. 1950).

Goldman, Sheldon and Jahnige, Thomas P. "Systems Analysis and Judicial Systems: Potentials and Limitations." 3 *Polity* 334 (Spring 1971).

Gunther, Gerald. "The Subtle Vices of the 'Passive Virtues'—A Comment on Principle and Expediency in Judicial Review." 64 *Columbia Law Review* 1 (Jan. 1964).

Henkin, Louis. "Viet-nam in the Courts of the United States: 'Political Questions.' " 63 *American Journal of International Law* 284 (April 1969).

Heyman, Ira Michael. "Federal Remedies for Voteless Negroes." 48 *California Law Review* 190 (May 1960).

Howard, J. Woodford, Jr. "Adjudication Considered as a Process of Conflict Resolution: A Variation on Separation of Powers." 18 *Journal of Public Law* 339 (1969).

Hudson, Manley O. "Advisory Opinions of National and International Courts." 37 *Harvard Law Review* 970 (June 1924).

Jackson, R. Brooke. "The Political Question Doctrine: Where Does it Stand After *Powell* v. *McCormack*, *O'Brien* v. *Brown* and *Gilligan* v. *Morgan?*" 44 *University of Colorado Law Review* 477 (May 1973).

Jaffe, Louis L. "The Citizen as Litigant in Public Actions: The Non-Hohfeldian or Ideological Plaintiff." 116 *University of Pennsylvania Law Review* 1033 (April 1968).

———. "Judicial Review of Procedural Decisions and the Philco Cases." 39 *Georgetown Law Review* 661 (Spring 1962).

———. "Standing to Secure Judicial Review: Private Actions." 75 *Harvard Law Review* 255 (Dec. 1961).

———. "Standing to Secure Judicial Review: Public Actions." 74 *Harvard Law Review* 1265 (May 1961).

Kates, Don B., Jr. and Barker, William T. "Mootness in Judicial Proceedings: Toward a Coherent Theory." 62 *California Law Review* 1385 (Dec. 1974).

Kramer, Robert. "The Place and Function of Judicial Review in the Administrative Process." 28 *Fordham Law Review* 1 (Spring 1959).

Krislov, Samuel. "The Amicus Curiae Brief: From Friendship to Advocacy." 72 *Yale Law Journal* 694 (March 1963).

Levinson, L. Harold. "Toward Principles of Public Law." 19 *Journal of Public Law* 327 (1970).

Lewis, Thomas P. "Constitutional Rights and the Misuse of 'Standing.' " 14 *Stanford Law Review* 433 (May 1962).

Miller, Arthur Selwyn. "Toward a Concept of Constitutional Duty." 1968 *The Supreme Court Review* 199 (1968).

―――― and Scheflin, Alan W. "The Power of the Supreme Court in the Age of the Positive State: A Preliminary Excursus—Part One: On Candor and the Court, or, Why Bamboozle the Natives?" 1967 *Duke Law Journal* 273 (1967).

――――. "The Power of the Supreme Court in the Age of the Positive State: A Preliminary Excursus—Part Two: On the Need for Adaptation of Changing Reality." 1967 *Duke Law Journal* 522 (1967).

Monoghan, Henry P. "Constitutional Adjudication: The Who and When." 82 *Yale Law Journal* 1363 (June 1973).

Pasvogel, Glenn. "Constitutional Law—Declaratory Judgments—Relaxation of Requirements?" 19 *De Paul Law Review* 171 (Autumn 1969).

Roche, John P. "Judicial Self-Restraint." 49 *American Political Science Review* 762 (Sept. 1955).

Rosenblum, Victor G. "Justiciability and Justice: Elements of Restraint and Indifference." 15 *Catholic University of America Law Review* 141 (May 1966).

Schoonover, Paul D. "Standing to Intervene in Administrative Agency Proceedings." 24 *Southwestern Law Journal* 873 (Dec. 1970).

Scott, Kenneth E. "Standing in the Supreme Court—A Functional Analysis." 86 *Harvard Law Review* 645 (Feb. 1973).

Sedler, Robert Allen. "Standing to Assert Constitutional Jus Tertii in the Supreme Court." 71 *Yale Law Journal* 599 (March 1962).

――――. "Standing, Justiciability, and All That: A Behavioral Analysis." 25 *Vanderbilt Law Review* 479 (April 1972).

Singer, Richard G. "Justiciability and Recent Supreme Court Cases." 21 *Alabama Law Review* 229 (Spring 1969).

Todd, Alton C. "Standing to Sue by the Victim of Racial Discrimination." 24 *Southwestern Law Journal* 557 (August 1970).

Tucker, Edwin W. "The Metamorphosis of the Standing to Sue Doctrine." 17 *New York Law Forum* 911 (Spring 1972).

Weston, Melville Fuller. "Political Questions." 38 *Harvard Law Review* 296 (Jan. 1925).

White, Welsh S. and Greenspan, Robert S. "Standing to Object to Search and Seizure." 118 *University of Pennsylvania Law Review* 333 (Jan. 1970).

Winick, Bruce J. "Direct Judicial Review of the Actions of the Selective Service System." 69 *Michigan Law Review* 55 (Nov. 1970).

Wright, J. Skelly "The Role of the Supreme Court in a Democratic Society—Judicial Activism or Restraint?" 54 *Cornell Law Review* 1 (Nov. 1968).

Selected Notes and Comments

"The Advisory Opinion and the United States Supreme Court." 5 *Fordham Law Review* 94 (Jan. 1936).

"Anticipatory Attacks on Selective Service Classification." 117 *University of Pennsylvania Law Review* 899 (April 1969).

"The Case for an Advisory Function in the Federal Judiciary." 50 *Georgetown Law Journal* 785 (Summer 1962).

"Cases Moot on Appeal: A Limit on the Judicial Power." 103 *University of Pennsylvania Law Review* 772 (April 1955).

"Church of Christ: Standing and the Evidentiary Hearing." 55 *Georgetown Law Journal* 264 (Nov. 1966).

"The CIA's Secret Funding and the Constitution." 84 *Yale Law Journal* 608 (Jan. 1975).

"Disposition of Moot Cases by the United States Supreme Court." 23 *University of Chicago Law Review* 77 (Autumn 1955).

"The Erosion of the Standing Impediment in Challenges by Disappointed Bidders of Federal Government Contract Awards." 39 *Fordham Law Review* 103 (Oct. 1970).

"Exceptions to the Prohibition Against Considering Moot Questions." 17 *De Paul Law Review* 590 (Summer 1968).

"The Federal Declaratory Judgments Act in Public Law Cases." 28 *Texas Law Review* 709 (Jan. 1950).

"The First Amendment Overbreadth Doctrine." 83 *Harvard Law Review* 844 (Feb. 1970).

"Judicial Determinations in Nonadversary Proceedings." 72 *Harvard Law Review* 723 (Feb. 1959).

"The Mootness Doctrine in the Supreme Court." 88 *Harvard Law Review* 373 (Dec. 1974).

"Mootness on Appeal in the Supreme Court." 83 *Harvard Law Review* 1672 (May 1970).

"The Non-Justiciable Controversy." 48 *Virginia Law Review* 922 (June 1962).

"Private Attorneys-General: Group Action in the Fight for Civil Liberties." 58 *Yale Law Journal* 574 (March 1949).

"Recent Developments in the Doctrine of Abstention." 1965 *Duke Law Journal* 102 (Winter 1965).

"Standing Again." 84 *Harvard Law Review* 633 (Jan. 1971).

"Standing to Assert Constitutional Jus Tertii." 88 *Harvard Law Review* 423 (Jan. 1974).

"Standing to Object to an Unreasonable Search and Seizure." 34 *University of Chicago Law Review* 342 (Winter 1967).

"Standing to Sue: A Commentary on Injury in Fact." 22 *Case Western Reserve Law Review* 256 (Jan. 1971).

"Standing to Sue for Members of Congress." 83 *Yale Law Journal* 1665 (July 1974).

"The Supreme Court, 1967 Term." 82 *Harvard Law Review* 95 (Nov. 1968).

"The Supreme Court, 1969 Term." 84 *Harvard Law Review* 32 (Nov. 1970).

"The Supreme Court and the Credentials Challenge Cases: Ask a Political Question, You Get a Political Answer." 62 *California Law Review* 1344 (July 1974).

"The Supreme Court and Standing to Sue." 34 *New York University Law Review* 141 (Jan. 1959).

"Threat of Enforcement—Prerequisite of a Justiciable Controversy." 62 *Columbia Law Review* 106 (Jan. 1962).

"The Void-for-Vagueness Doctrine in the Supreme Court." 109 *University of Pennsylvania Law Review* 67 (Nov. 1960).

"What Constitutes a Case or Controversy Within the Meaning of Article III of the Constitution." 41 *Harvard Law Review* 232 (Dec. 1927).

Selected Documentary Materials

Corwin, Edward S. *The Constitution of the United States of America: Analysis and Interpretation.* Sen. Doc. 39, 88th Cong., 1st sess. Washington: U.S. Government Printing Office, 1964.

Documentary History of the Constitution of the United States. Washington: Department of State, 1894.

Hearings on H.R. 1198 and S. 3, to provide effective procedures for the enforcement of the establishment and free exercise clauses of the First Amendment to the Constitution. H.R. Committee on the Judiciary, 90th Cong., 2d sess. Washington: U.S. Government Printing Office, 1968.

Hearings on S. 2097, a bill to provide for judicial review of the constitutionality of grants or loans under certain acts. 89th Cong., 2d sess. Washington: U.S. Government Printing Office, 1966.

Table of Cases

Name Index

Subject Index